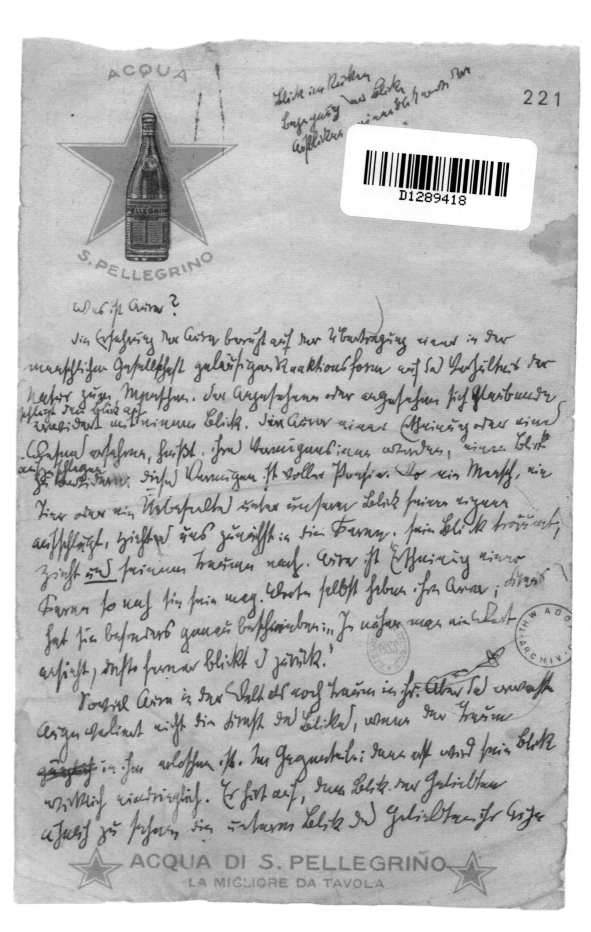

ACQUA

S. PELLEGRINO

Was ist Aura?

Die Erfahrung der Aura beruht auf der Übertragung einer in der menschlichen Gesellschaft geläufigen Reaktionsform auf das Verhältnis der Natur zum Menschen. Der Angesehene oder angesehen sich Glaubende [...] den Blick auf. Die Aura einer Erscheinung oder eines Wesens erfahren, heißt [...]

ACQUA DI S. PELLEGRINO

LA MIGLIORE DA TAVOLA

In Memoriam
Siobhán Marie Kilfeather
9 August 1957–7 April 2007

Editors
Seamus Deane
Breandán Mac Suibhne

Assitants to the Editors
Ciarán Deane
Jessica Dougherty McMichael

Copy
Hilary Bell

Design
Red Dog Design Consultants
www.reddog.ie

Fonts
Headlines — Gill Sans 21/23
Body Copy Essays/Review Essays — Sabon 9/12
Body Copy Reviews — Gills Sans 9/12

Paper Stock
McNaughton's Challenger Offset

Field Day Review is published annually by
Field Day Publications in association with
the Keough-Naughton Institute for Irish
Studies at the University of Notre Dame.

ISSN 1649-6507
ISBN 978-0-946755-33-2

Field Day Review
Keough-Naughton Institute for Irish Studies
86 St. Stephen's Green
Dublin 2
Ireland

fieldday@nd.edu

Roger M Schlossier
2011

FIELD DAY REVIEW
2007

Walter Benjamin
The Construction of Hell

Seamus Deane

Blood and Iron. Bismarck's famous phrase for his policy of making Germany into the dominant European state has an eerie echo in Benjamin's work on the very different cultural domination of Europe by Paris in the nineteenth century.[1]

1   Blood and Iron, 'durch Eisen und Blut'. The phrase occurs in a speech of 1862, 'not by speeches and the will of the majority are the great questions of the time decided … but by blood and iron'. The references to and quotations from Benjamin are drawn for the most part from the following translations and editions: Walter Benjamin, *The Arcades Project*, trans. Howard Eiland and Kevin McLaughlin (Cambridge, Mass., and London, 1999), hereafter cited in text (in parentheses) and in footnotes in the format: A, followed by page number, Section or Convolute letter (upper case) and subsection letters (lower case) and numerals. Walter Benjamin, *Selected Writings*, 4 vols. (Cambridge, Mass., and London, 1996–2003), hereafter SW; *Volume 1: 1913–1926* (1996), ed. Marcus Bullock and Michael W. Jennings; *Volume 2: 1927–1934* (1999), trans. Rodney Livingstone et al., ed. Michael W. Jennings, Howard Eiland and Gary Smith; *Volume 3: 1935–1938* (2002); *Volume 4: 1938–1940* (2003), trans. Edmund Jephcott et al., ed. Howard Eiland and Michael W. Jennings.

In Paris there was blood enough on the streets in the sequence of revolutions from 1848 to 1851, through 1870 to 1871, with the Franco-Prussian War and the slaughter of the Parisian workers during the Commune. Increasingly, the buildings were of iron too, the first man-made, progressively adaptable, building material. The early railway stations and bridges, and the railroad tracks so often associated in the nineteenth century with 'the unmistakable dream world that attaches to them' (A 156, F3, 4), revealed what the engineer and the proletarian builders first experienced, 'what was new and decisive about these structures, the feeling of space' (A 156, F3, 5). This itself is a figure for the new intellectual vista that opens; 'just as the magnificent vistas of the city provided by the new construction in iron … for a long time were reserved exclusively for the workers and engineers, so too the philosopher here to garner fresh perspectives must be immune to vertigo — an independent and, if need be, solitary worker' (A 459, N1a, 1). It was iron that supported the great windows and domes of the arcades and created the lines of gas-lit iron lamps, the petrified trees of the urban savannah (A 422.3, 5). The use of iron girders allowed construction on such a large scale that, by the 1860s, the traditional competition within a building between the horizontal and the vertical took on a new rhythm. In Parisian apartment buildings,

for instance, the *porte-fenêtre* opens on to a balcony of fretted iron work which creates a continuous horizontal strip that echoes the horizontal of the street, and clarifies especially the verticals at the corners and the intersections, to produce an impression of restrained mass and weight that still bespeaks the power and satisfaction of the bourgeoisie. 'The institutions of the bourgeoisie's worldly and spiritual dominance were to find their apotheosis within the framework of the boulevards' (*Exposé of 1935*, A 11). Above all, there was the 'incomparable' Eiffel Tower, the huge naked iron pylon that declared itself as pure structure, engineering and architecture combined, the concept of the Modern with no archaic ornamentation, a skeleton that is also a body, an enormous weight that inhabits the air.[2] The Tower was later to become a radio mast, which is fitting enough; but at first it was sheer exhibit, image as Image, not designed for anything as limiting as a use. Built as the archway to the Exposition Universelle, the exhibition that marked the centenary of the French Revolution, and built too so that it could be demolished within twenty years as per contract, it remained a monument to the New, divorced from those traditions of France (especially its Catholicism) that the Sacré-Coeur, solid and white, an assembly of stylistic forms and not a formula, soon after was designed to embody in a symbolic challenge across the skyline of Paris, each

Lead image: Adolf Hitler at the Eiffel Tower, Paris, with his generals, the sculptor Arno Breker (on his right) and architect Albert Speer (on his left), 25 June 1940. Photograph: Harwood/ Keystone/Hulton Archive/ Getty Images.

Left: Walter Benjamin in the Bibliothèque Nationale, Paris, 1936. Photograph: Gisèle Freund, courtesy of Elisabeth Pérolini.

offering a view, not just of Paris, but of modernity itself. The Eiffel Tower presides over the new Paris of Baron Haussmann, with its wheeling boulevards that segmented the city into coherent units and swept away the huddles of housing and the menace of crowds that used to infest it; this Paris was meant to be, as Versailles had once been, an embodiment of rationality and of power. In the course of its completion, there were great upheavals — of people being transferred, of streets and houses being torn up, of the mess and noise of a building site that so much of central Paris had to become before it was fully Haussmannized. Benjamin's essay, 'Exposé of 1835', which opens *The Arcades Project*, identifies the political aim of the rebuilding of Paris, from the introduction of wooden paving under Louis-Philippe in the 1830s, to Haussmann's programme — 'to secure the city against civil war' (*Exposé of 1939*, A 23). But, 'The burning of Paris is the worthy conclusion to Haussmann's work of destruction' (*Exposé of 1935*, A 13); the Commune, the First World War and Fascism were the three catastrophes through which the nineteenth century and its capital, Paris, fell into ruin.

'Most of the Paris arcades are built in the fifteen years following 1822 … They are the forerunners of department stores' (*Exposé of 1939*, A 15). Eiffel built the first great department store, Au Bon Marché, combining cast iron with gaslighting, in 1850. Throughout the century, Paris remained famous for its arcades and department stores, for the appeal of the astonishing mountains of commodities, for which being new and up-to-date became an inescapable and banal fate. The new technology, that combined iron and glass (especially after Paxton's Crystal Palace in London, in 1851) bore within it the imagery of the new functionalism that was eventually to become manifest in the skyscraper, and from the outset rehearsed the dialectical opposition of the fixity and opacity of one material (iron) against the fragility and almost utopian transparency of the other (glass), was an immense achievement in engineering and architectural rationality. Yet the arcades were not sites of rationality, but of the market, crammed with products that swiftly became junk, sifted by collectors for the objects in which they saw, or believed they saw, that time (a year, a decade, a reign)

2 'The Ring of Saturn or Some Remarks on Iron Construction', *The Arcades Project*, 887

Passage Choiseul, Paris, *c.* 1910; an example of an arcade. Photograph: LL/ Roger Viollet/Getty Images.

had been most successfully or memorably(!) trapped. The collector had a counterpart/ opposite in the mass-market consumer; and the consumer had discovered in the arcade a new vocation — shopping. Both collecting and shopping separated the item bought from use; the point was to have it, not to use it. Most representative of all those who were attracted by this new world of building, investment, financial corruption, political domination and pleasure, was the gambler; 'Gambling converts time into a narcotic', '[Paul] Lafargue explains gambling as an imitation in miniature of the mysteries of economic fluctuation' (*Exposé of 1935*, A 12). Fraud and speculation on a massive scale attended upon the building of Haussmann's Paris. And the working class, decimated in the Commune, belatedly discovered that the illusory pact of the century with the bourgeoisie had finally been exposed. In part this pact had been paraded as philanthropy, the middle classes anxiously alleviating the plight of the poor; in the end it was exposed in massacre. So there was iron in the new Paris and there also was blood. This was the composite gift

of Haussmann and Louis Napoleon, 'the careerist serving the usurper' (A 913), but it was by no means all.

The endless emergence of this new city from the old is one of the recurrent themes in the *Arcades* and a companion to it is the quest for the moment within that process when the new Paris decisively arrives, when the cityscape is illuminated in a flash and the accumulations of history, that had seemed so happenstance, have their inner structure suddenly revealed — if only for that instant, if only in a glimpse. In one sense, we can envisage this as a moment in a continuum between, let us say, the apparent mess of a building site and the finished work, but that only reaches part of Benjamin's elusive thought, which is usually dialectic in form. Afflicted by the spectacular disintegrations of daily, metropolitan life (with Paris always its chief exemplar), and seeking some means by which its 'shock', as he called it, could be captured and overcome simultaneously in one action, Benjamin turned to the practices of art rather than of politics and found in surrealist theory and paintings and in the montage of Eisensteins's films how the 'passagework' between arbitrary detail and significance could be negotiated. This particular dialectical enterprise, predicated on the notions of intense fracture of experience and a countervailing order to be discovered or asserted within it, found its most enduring aesthetic response in the practice and principles of montage. 'This work has to develop to the highest degree the art of citing without quotation marks. Its theory is intimately related to that of montage' (A 458, N1, 10). Adopted in ever greater variations in all the arts (although it seemed film was its natural home), it became so characteristic of European modernist literary works by the mid-1920s that it was, by the time of Joyce's death, almost routine; but it gained a second wind from about 1945, when Joyce, one of whose true fascinations was 'his attraction for Americans',[3] became the iconic modernist (largely because he wrote in a species of English); montage and modernism were thereafter domesticated into the critical commentary of the Free World (but still rejected since the 1930s by doctrinal Communist realism), while Kafka, the great modernist novelist for Benjamin and Adorno, faded in comparison (largely because he wrote in German and had the misfortune to have had Max Brod as his biographer and lead interpreter).[4]

Looking

It is not easy to know what it is that provides the great illumination Benjamin seeks, although, indirectly, he offers various analogies. The flash is like that of an early camera apparatus in which an image is suddenly captured that might reveal a previously unnoticed pattern. Or it is like the flash of inspiration by which the great detective exposes the design that the blind accumulation of evidence by Plod the Policeman never would. In such an exposure, the overall structure is manifest in

every detail. It is the glimpse that matters; the gaze is not so much contemplative, as unseeing, even regressive. Indeed the gaze is of three kinds: the stupefied kind that Benjamin associated with the entranced mass audience of the cinema; the rapturous gaze of the devotee, or *cinéphile*, the specialist, the person who is in effect addicted and for whom rapture is an intensely private pleasure, even a prison, and not a shared joy. These first two kinds combine to form the third. When, for example, photographic stills are replaced by moving images, we experience the to-and-fro of a transition in which a reversal can suddenly take place. In this combined relationship, the third kind of gaze, the mass audience plays a critical role.[5]

Before traditional forms of art, such as a painting, the gaze is individual; it has a concentrated and contemplative element that is invited by the stillness of the painting, by its containment within a frame, by its repertoire of consecrated gestures. There is a literal sense in which a painting is 'timeless'. Unlike the photograph, it does not have the 'temporal factor' as part of its technology; a photograph needs exposure time. Iron construction reorganizes space, the camera reorganizes time, especially important as these categories had been assumed to be unchanging and because, on that account, they could achieve an 'auratic' quality. This famous 'aura' of the work of art dissolved in the rhythms of mass production and in the liquidation of those 'timeless' dimensions in which the sense of the sacred had traditionally nestled.[6] One of Baudelaire's prose poems, 'Perte d'auréole', ('Loss of halo' or 'Loss of aura'), 'spotlights the threat to the aura posed by the experience of shock' (A 375, J84a, 5). By contrast, photography and film — although other arts would come to imitate and rival these — required a different sensibility. The medium and its technology (which is itself integral to the medium, not an add-on) provides in a series of frames a series of little shocks, intolerable to the smooth traditional gaze.

3 Brian Nolan (aka Flann O'Brien), 'A Bash in the Tunnel', in John Ryan, ed., *A Bash in the Tunnel* (Brighton and London, 1970), 20

4 See Benjamin's 'Review of Brod's *Franz Kafka*', SW 3.317–21, and 'Letter to Gershom Scholem on Franz Kafka', 3.322–29. There is a radio review of Kafka, 'Franz Kafka: *Beim Bau der Chinesischen mauer*', SW, 2.494–500; and the famous essay 'Franz Kafka', 2.794–820, also included in Walter Benjamin, *Illuminations*, trans. Harry Zohn, ed. Hannah Arendt (London, 1973), 111–40, along with the review of Brod, 141–48. In his 'Curriculum Vitae (III)' of 1928, SW, 2.78, Benjamin writes: 'In addition, I have been planning a book on the three great metaphysical writers of our day: Franz Kafka, James Joyce, and Marcel Proust.'

5 André Breton's *Manifeste du surréalisme* (Paris, 1924) was cited by Benjamin in footnote 39 of his famous essay, 'The Work of Art in the Age of Reproducibility' (3rd version), on this phenomenon: 'Shortly before film turned the viewing of images into a collective activity, image viewing by the individual, through the stereoscopes … was briefly intensified.' See SW, 4.280.

6 A 343, J64a, 1: 'Mass production is the principal economic cause — and class warfare the principal social cause — of the decline of aura.'

7   On Chaplin, see 'Chaplin', 'Chaplin in Retrospect' and 'Hitler's Diminished Masculinity', *SW*, 1.199–200, 222–24, 792–93.

8   Cited in Emilie Bickerton, 'Adieu to *Cahiers*: Life Cycle of a Cinema Journal', *New Left Review*, 42 (2006), 69–98, 80

9   Georg Christoph Lichtenberg (1742–99), first great German aphorist; Benjamin's own *One-Way Street* (1928), *SW*, 1.444–88, or 'On the Concept of History (better known in English under the title 'Theses on the Philosophy of History' since it was published in *Illuminations*, 255–66), *SW*, 4. 389–400 or Adorno's *Minima Moralia: Reflections from Damaged Life* (1951; trans. 1974) would be notable examples of works composed of aphorisms.

10 Susan Sontag, 'Introduction', in Walter Benjamin, *One-Way Street and Other Writings*, trans. Edmund Jephcott and Kingsley Shorter (London, 1997), 24

11 'Karl Kraus', *SW*, 2.434

12 'Karl Kraus', *SW*, 2.448; 'And in Offenbach's operettas the bourgeois trinity of the true, the beautiful, and the good is brought together, freshly rehearsed and with musical accompaniment, in its star turn on the trapeze of idiocy.'

Thus, the new medium seems to be instantly amenable to the watching mass audience, even though the camera reveals much that the eye had never seen before. However new, it is familiar; the rhythm of the medium is fluent and yet arrives in sudden, separable images. It has a continuity founded on interruption. The mass audience is at home with this new form of looking. It cannot gaze at a film as an élite audience gazes at a traditional painting; for in response to the new medium, the gaze of the mass audience is a sequence of abrupt, lightning-fast adjustments to unreeling images that achieve an apparently natural movement. (This account would also allow for an analysis of the function of the musical track in film, in the history of which accompaniment is replaced by background music until gradually the music is fully incorporated into the predominantly visual medium as an interpretation, enhancement and even as a form of coercion.) In this third gaze we witness a historical dialectic between individual and collective, between a steady, unified gaze and a gaze constituted of a series of glimpses. In slow motion, the gaze would be seen to be a series of glimpses, but that is the point. The speed of looking has altered. Thus, the mass audience is avant-garde when it comes to looking at Charlie Chaplin and regressive when looking at Picasso; it recognizes the rapid, jerky movements of Chaplin as a revelation of something that was always there; it is a form of analysis in which hilarity is provoked by recognition.[7] Picasso, on the other hand, mounts an assault on seeing; because the general appeal of recognizability (realism) of the photo or film is missing, this looks merely like outrageous eccentricity. Later, in 1965, Jacques Rivette, director of *Paris Belongs to Us*, introduced a similar account of the 'pure gaze' of the submissive cinema audience which may owe something to Benjamin, but which certainly retains within it that Benjaminian heritage shared by so many — the recognition that in a mass society there is an intimate connection between the stupefaction of the audience, starkly silhouetted in the darkness before the blaze of the screen, and individual addiction, however diverse its forms.[8] This connection perhaps derives from 'the two aspects of shock — its technological function in the mechanism and its sterilizing function in the experience' (A 692, Y 11, 2).

For Benjamin, this kind of looking and of presentation, founded on interruption or intermittence, has literary approximations — the series of aphorisms (as, for instance, in Lichtenberg, or in modern instances, Karl Kraus, Benjamin himself, Adorno), epigrams, paradoxes, any writing that, like his own, stops and starts and yet is fluent, turns on itself.[9] It evokes his own favoured imageries of the maze, labyrinth, arcade, vortex, web, network of streets, trail of clues, of indecision suddenly mastered by decisiveness, but just for a moment. Susan Sontag said it best: 'His style of thinking and writing, incorrectly called aphoristic, might better be called freeze-frame baroque'.[10] This vertiginous writing never allows its gaze to leave its ubiquitous contemporary enemy, 'the empty phrase. Which is the linguistic expression of the despotism with which, in journalism, topicality sets up its dominion over things.'[11] New social conditions, not just new technology, produce new forms of public communication and the consequence can be chillingly regressive. Journalism, radio and film, like operetta in music (Offenbach is the target here), blend new technologies with old clichés in a peculiarly nauseating soda pop for which the millions thirst. A sugar-laden commodity becomes the water of life. 'Just as prattle seals the enslavement of language with stupidity, so operetta transfigures stupidity through music.'[12] Chatter and triviality are not side-effects of these forms of mass production; they are its goal. Therefore, the condensed, compacted forms of the aphorism, epigram or philosophical parable enter into a constant battle with this new commodity of vacuity, an emptiness to which they may often surrender in their effort to overcome it.

'Narcotic of the Century'

As we can see from his own (controlled) experiments with hashish, Benjamin also wanted to distinguish within addiction itself, both the possibility of enslavement and that of exploration — in this latter instance, making the addiction an adventure into forbidden areas to gain an otherwise inaccessible insight (a long-standing inquiry in the nineteenth century, but underdeveloped in its political implications until Benjamin).[13] But Benjamin was suspicious of the linkages between religious ecstasies and drugs which helped drag surrealism into the regressions of spiritualism.

> But the true, creative overcoming of religious illumination certainly does not lie in narcotics. It resides in a *profane illumination*, a materialistic, anthropological inspiration, to which hashish, opium, or whatever else can give an introductory lesson. (But a dangerous one; and the religious lesson is stricter.)[14]

But while punctual revelations provided by chemicals are not revolutions, they may be understood as allegories of revolution or of utopia. And they are more than that; they reveal a structure the waking consciousness almost entirely ignores:

> The appearances of superposition, of overlap, which come with hashish may be grasped through the concept of similitude. When we say that one face is similar to another, we mean that certain features of this second face appear to us in the first, without the latter's ceasing to be what it has been ... The category of similarity, which for the waking consciousness has only minimal relevance, attains unlimited relevance in the world of hashish. There, we may say, everything is face ... Under these conditions, even a sentence ... puts on a face, and this face resembles that of the sentence standing opposed to it.

In this way every truth points manifestly to its opposite, and this state of affairs explains the existence of doubt. Truth becomes something living; it lives solely in the rhythm by which statement and counterstatement displace each other in order to think each other. (A 418, M1a, 1)

He understood the images in Baudelaire's work that related to hashish as having a similar function — to intensify 'the historical hallucination of sameness which had taken root with the commodity economy'.[15] It is out of that sameness, of the kind that Daumier represented in his lithographs, where everyone had the same recognizable face of greed or meanness, that the possibility of reversal arises. It reaches such a rate of intoxicated hallucination that its sameness becomes semblance — that again is to say that in the poem or in the lithograph we see emerge the historical character of the condition, not simply a repeated grimace. Therefore, sameness is the one face repeated over and over; semblance occurs when those repeated faces merge into the face of a class or type that has become historically important; and the expression on that face — say, an expression of greed — is also taken to be typical. This is the kind of relationship that Lukács had been seeking to establish in the novel, identifying the process whereby the individual becomes generic, all the more difficult in a period in which uniformity has become a social, political and economic value.[16] From sameness to semblance is the distance travelled in Daumier and in Baudelaire; but as the speed necessary to cover that distance increases, so we can begin to recognize that atomized personal experience does in fact have as its other 'face', historical, collective experience. This tempo of recognition marks the characteristic prelude to what Benjamin called 'dialectics at a standstill', the Messiah-like revelation, so hoped-for, so often predicted by the most earnest and unremitting interpreters. At this speed, the present begins to warp; the old image

13 See the collection of Benjamin's notes on drug-taking and its possibilities for understanding modernity in Walter Benjamin, *On Hashish*, ed. Howard Eiland, Introduction by Marcus Boon (Cambridge, Mass., and London, 2006).
14 'Surrealism' in *SW*, 2.209
15 *SW*, 4.208
16 Georg Lukács, *The Theory of the Novel*, first published in Berlin in 1920, trans. Anna Bostock (London, 1971), particularly chapters 3 and 4

Charles Baudelaire (1821–67), self-portrait drawn by the poet and critic, while under the influence of hashish. Photograph: Time Life Pictures/Mansell/Time Life Pictures/Getty Images.

it has been bearing begins to distort and dissolve. This is the image of preordained progress or development — really a dogma masquerading as a discovery. This is what Benjamin calls the 'now' ('*Nu*'); a new image begins to form within it and finally fills it so that it bursts open in a flash:

> It is not that what is past casts its light on what is present, or what is present its light on what is past; rather, image is that wherein what has been comes together in a flash with the now to form a constellation. In other words: image is dialectics at a standstill. For while the relation of the present to the past is purely temporal, the relation of what-has-been to the now is dialectical; not temporal in nature but figural <*bildlich*>. Only dialectical images are genuinely historical — that is, not archaic — images. (A 463, N3. 1)[17]

A constellation, then, is a previously unrecognized structure or network of relations that was always there, like the unconscious, and appears to us, like it, in articulated images, laden with the weight of the past and yet haloed in the light of discovery and recognition. So it is very far from exhibiting any arrow line, or advancing pattern of stadial evolutionary progress, like the Marxist philosophy of history Benjamin wants to replace with this messianic version of the breakthrough, the arrival which is always in preparation as the event which has already happened but is belatedly recognized. Its traces are there to be read but the full image will emulsify suddenly, giving the shock, not of fracture but of completion, its dialectical opposite. It is no surprise, therefore, to find that Benjamin's chief animus is against historicism, the inverse of Marxism, as he understood both. He derided historicism's ambition to show things as they really were and, along with it, he derides too the concept of 'timeless truth', which seems at first to contrast with historicism but actually

provides its monotonous undertone. A 'fortified position of historicism is evident in the idea that history is something which can be narrated. In a materialist investigation, the epic moment will always be blown apart in the process of construction.'[18] This is the discursive form of the visual contrast between the gaze and the flash or glimpse. Instead of that continuous sequence of conventional historicist prose, which is in its very form bound up with the assumption of a smooth, unravelling and wholly explicable sequence, *The Arcades Project* deploys paratactic combinations of quotations, dissolving the univocal authority of the narrator and of the narrative into abrupt, discordant combinations. From the juxtapositions emerge otherwise hidden constellations. Benjamin is the Detective:

> A remark by Ernst Bloch apropos of *The Arcades Project*: 'History displays its Scotland Yard badge.' It was in the context of a conversation in which I was describing how this work — comparable, in method, to the process of splitting the atom — liberates the enormous energies of history that are bound up in the 'once upon a time' of classical historiography. The history that showed things 'as they really were' was the strongest narcotic of the century. (A 463, N3. 4)[19]

For him the present always stands in need of recovery. To effect this, a new kind of experiment must be undertaken, as most notably it had already been, he believed, by those great writers who began to rebuild or even build for the first time the internal structures of consciousness, memory and therefore of history — Baudelaire, Proust, perhaps Freud.

Without such recovery, there is no present; there is only the plastic past of the old Soviet joke — we can't predict the future but we can always change the past. That is what can be done when the present is without

17 Cf. A 456, N1, 1; 'In the fields with which we are concerned, knowledge comes only in lightning flashes. The text is the long roll of thunder that follows.'

18 'Paralipomena to "On the Concept of History"', in *SW*, 4.406

19 See A 442, M13a, 2: 'Performed in the figure of the flâneur is that of the detective ... It suited him very well to see his indolence presented as a plausible front, behind which, in reality, hides the riveted attention of an observer who will not let the unsuspecting observer out of his sight.'

the dimension of the 'now', and lies instead under the spell of the 'new'. It is repeatedly made to march in lockstep with that version of the past — 'civilization', 'progress', 'development', the key terms in a satanic lexicon. From this came the phantasmagoric world of the First World War, the arena in which nineteenth-century technology reached its zenith. Like a dark enchantment, it passed over Europe and changed everything — except property relations. That is the concentration, the obsession, within modern technological capitalism, that everything should change so that everything would stay the same.

Although the marriage of a messianic theology and Marxism in Benjamin is not at all a happy one, it is memorable for the fortunes of both. Certainly it scandalized Benjamin's contrasting friends and mentors, the Talmudic scholar Gershom Scholem and the stalwart of the Frankfurt Institute, Adorno. For the first, Marxism, for the second, Judaism, was a farrago of unenlightened nonsense Benjamin would have done well to abandon. Perhaps he had too much of both ever to be enough of one for either of them.

A Cast of Characters

Benjamin's work has an ensemble of 'characters', whisper versions of the predators who stalk Balzac's novels, although never so vulpine, but just as much products and expressions of Paris. They are all swamped in leisure, an intense version of it, closer to a nervous apathy than relaxation, although Benjamin repeatedly seeks to distinguish leisure from idleness, to which he devotes a whole Convolute in *The Arcades Project*:

> In feudal society, the leisure of the poet is a recognized privilege. It is only in bourgeois society that the poet becomes an idler. Idleness seeks to avoid any sort of tie to the idler's line of work, and ultimately to the labor process in general. That distinguishes it from leisure. (A 802–03, m2a, 5, m3, 1)

Perhaps these figures are better understood as gradations of an idea that increasingly achieves realization as it is pursued.

He picks his way fastidiously from the aristocratic figure of the connoisseur, via that of the collector to the finally pathological figure of the addict (including the gambler and the counterfeiter), allowing us to glimpse how aristocratic leisure is increasingly converted in this progression into a hunger that time can never satisfy, for the gaze and the longing become more and more consuming, manic, until the addict becomes his addiction. This is one of the typical mutations from pre-modern to modern, from a state in which a carefully nurtured and educated individual taste becomes an increasingly generic mass social condition.

The connoisseur is chronologically the first; he still retains his leisure and his refinement as a class privilege. He yields to the collector, who brings with him the smell of mass production, of the arcades, of the sound of a bell tinkling in a dimly lit antique shop, of a taste that is in the process of exchanging the exquisite example for the nostalgic emblem, although the tempo of the quest perceptibly quickens as the idea of a complete understanding of the world is surrendered to the idea of a complete acquisition of a range of the objects that the world produces.

> One need only study with due exactitude the physiognomy of the homes of great collectors. Then one would have a key to the nineteenth-century interior. Just as in the former case the objects gradually take possession of the residence, so in the latter it is a piece of furniture that would retrieve and assemble the stylistic traces of the centuries. (A 218, I3, 2)

Collections have an intimate relation to interiors, as well as to interiority (or 'inwardness'); where they are amassed is usually called their 'home', although the items in themselves have of course no home. But the christening of a place as a home for objects indicates a sickness. Home is an interiority (a condition) that is only available as exteriority (a place). Benjamin quotes Kierkegaard on this in Convolute I ('The Interior, The Trace'): '"The art would be to be able to feel homesick, even though one is at home. Expertness in the use of illusion is required for this." … This is the formula for the interior' (A 218, I3, 5).

After the rather dingy collector comes the dandy, who collects the various 'selves' that make up his 'self', and who shines in his plumage against the dark uniforms of the male respectable classes and of the dirtier, but equally uniform, masses. He is at once an anachronism, the mimic aristocrat of an earlier era, and an avant-garde figure of shock, violating sexual convention and shrilly mocking the solemnities and sobrieties of the respectable. In him the prospect of complete aesthetic autonomy as a political and social project briefly threatens. Subjectivity was never so well dressed, but clearly, in his view of the matter, either it or mass society would have to go. (And of course, it went.) In his clothes, he makes his home; he carries his home on his back. In the composite figure of the dandy, the connoisseur returns to make a style of disdain and satiety; to be bored is a form of distinction. 'Boredom—as index to participation in the sleep of the collective. Is this the reason it seems distinguished, so that the dandy makes a show of it?' (A 108, D3, 7) And in the amalgam, the collector too reappears, with his habits of accumulation, trying to separate the value of a thing from its function. But this intervention neither stops nor slows the pace of remorseless production and consumption; those who regard themselves as doing that by their modified or different variations on consumption, merely demonstrate that to be so eager to be in

advance of their time is to be dominated by the wish to escape from its realities.

These figures have very sharp profiles in Benjamin's work, although there are others in lesser roles in the cast for his *vie de bohème*, less distinct, but cousinly. All of them shared the conviction that they were members of a group, a cell, an élite cohort, that had separated from the middle classes and had a silent contract with the masses — usually to redeem them from their misery but more usually to rouse them from their supposed slumber. With these subordinate groupings, leisure is in shorter supply, although it did flourish well enough in those of them who were unemployed. They would most often be conspirators (anarchists especially), poets, émigrés, or journalists, sometimes all four; their avocations might be occasional or full-time. Certainly, they had to face more frontally the problems of economic survival than their grander counterparts; but in them the relationship between work (a futile, demeaning activity) and leisure (furtive, nocturnal, adventurous, the time/place of 'real' life) was corrosive, typically presenting itself in an ostensibly subversive 'radicalism' and embittered personality. (Benjamin came to consider *The Communist Manifesto* as their dismissal notice from history.[20]) They stood in relation to the real revolutionary as once the alchemist did to the new scientist. These groups thought of themselves as avant-garde; but they were living in a deluded state because, like the dandy, they thought that their egoism was revolutionary, politically and intellectually superior to the role of the collective in modern life. All forms of liberal individualism, even these exotic versions, were unconscious of the collective oblivion which they helped to create. But that — the collective itself — is a central problem, perhaps one that Benjamin never got past. The life of the peacock individual could be seen as primarily a form of display, and in its 'decadence' could be understood as dominated by addiction, including the

20 In Part III, 3, 'Critical-Utopian Socialism and Communism'; Marx's *Manifesto of the Communist Party,* first published in London in 1848, has generally been known since 1872 as *The Communist Manifesto.*

21 See, for a contemporary instance of this attempt to reconfigure the crowd theory of the nineteenth century and the Marxist proletariat, Michael Hardt and Antonio Negri's formulation of the idea of 'multitude' in *Empire* (Cambridge, Mass., and London, 2000), 60–66, 71–75.

22 Benjamin translated part of Aragon's book into German; it seemed to him to be a precursor of his own work on the arcades.

addiction to shocking the respectable classes. But how were the deluded masses of people, entrapped in the idiocy of modern urban life, ever to become the political subject of history, Marx's proletariat, Benjamin's own 'collective'?[21] What *could* work on them if the shock treatment of the surrealists, by far the most politically formidable of these groups, did not? The surrealists were, in their practice, revolutionary, but the masses turned away from experimental art to kitsch. A passage in Convolute K addresses this:

> Socialism would never have entered the world if its proponents had sought only to excite the enthusiasm of the working classes for a better order of things. What made for the power and authority of the movement was that Marx understood how to interest the workers in a social order which would both benefit them and appear to them as just. It is exactly the same with art. At no point in time, no matter how utopian, will anyone win the masses over to a higher art; they can be won over only by one nearer to them. And the difficulty consists precisely in finding a form for art as such that, with the best conscience in the world, one could hold that it *is* a higher art. This will never happen with most of what is propagated by the avant-garde of the bourgeoisie … The masses positively require from the work of art (which, for them, has its place in the circle of consumer items) something that is warming. Here the flame that is most readily kindled is that of hatred. Its heat, however, burns or sears without providing the 'heart's ease' which qualifies art for consumption. Kitsch, on the other hand, is nothing more than art with a 100 per cent, absolute and instantaneous availability for consumption. Precisely within the consecrated forms of expression, therefore, kitsch and art stand irreconcilably opposed. But for developing, living forms, what matters

is … that they take 'kitsch' dialectically up into themselves, and hence bring themselves near to the masses while yet surmounting the kitsch. Today, perhaps, film alone is equal to this task — or, at any rate, more ready for it than any other form. (A 395, K3a.1)

The first home for kitsch was the arcade, recognized as such by the surrealists, who indulged it as a liberation from the pompous and academic notions of art and propriety that were to them deadly and outdated. And it was Louis Aragon's *Paysan de Paris* that inspired the *The Arcades Project*, so much so that Benjamin could barely breathe when reading it for the first time.[22] The surrealists discovered the arcades; Benjamin politicized them, saw in them the isthmus, the passageway, which connected the external life of the street to the internal life of consciousness, in which the milling crowd could be seen as the collective in its living quarters:

> Streets are the dwelling place of the collective. The collective is an eternally wakeful, eternally agitated being that — in the space between the building fronts — lives experiences, understands, and invents as much as individuals do within the privacy of their own four walls … the arcade was the drawing room. More than anywhere else, the street reveals itself in the arcade as the furnished and familiar interior of the masses. (A 879, d°, 1)

Phantasmagoria

However, within this strange living space, interior and exterior at once, amidst both the collective and the bourgeoisie — although Benjamin seems to indicate that it was more shocking for the latter, since it was more conscious of the (richly deserved) erosion of its traditional power — an epidemic had begun. In his bitter rejection of the middle class, whose son he was, Benjamin reserved a particular bile for the privileged and benighted inhabitants of Vienna; it was no surprise to him that this was Freud's city, although its sickness was general all over Europe. (Vienna's dialectical opposite is Naples, the 'porous' city in which public and private consciousness, architecture as the maze of activity rather than the labyrinth of doom, the ruin as living space, evoke from Benjamin one of his rare lyric accounts of utopia, of the city of psychic and social health.[23]) In Vienna, one of the symptoms and sources of the presiding sickness was the feuilleton and its great diagnostician was Karl Kraus, towards whom Benjamin had an ambivalent jealous–admiring attitude. The epidemic disease caused the loss of experience, replaced it with a kind of instantaneity, and found its ripest victim in the private individual, attacking him through the 'nerves': 'How much renunciation and how much irony lie in the curious struggle for the "nerves", the last root fibres of the Viennese to which Kraus could still find Mother Earth adhering.'[24] However, the traces of Mother Earth became ever fainter as the epidemic intensified; the 'reduced human being of our days' was forced to 'seek sanctuary in the temple of living things in that most withered form: the form of a private individual'.[25] Privacy became privation and with that, the separation between the experience human beings had amassed over time and the slash of the instant sensation, unbridgeable:

> On the feuilleton. It was a matter of injecting experience — as it were, intravenously — with the poison of sensation; that is to say, highlighting within ordinary experience the character of immediate experience. To this end, the experience of the big-city dweller presented itself. The feuilletonist turns this to account. He renders the city strange to its inhabitants. He is thus one of the first technicians called up by the heightened need for immediate experiences. (A 803, m3a, 2)

This sharpened, shallowed experience readily atrophied within conditions of mass production; the very form of knowledge and its traditional transmission systems changed:

> Just as the industrial labor process separates off from handicraft, so the form of communication corresponding to this labor process — information — separates off from the form of communication corresponding to the artisanal process of labor, which is storytelling … This connection must be kept in mind if one is to form an idea of the explosive force contained within information. This force is liberated in sensation. With the sensation, whatever still resembles wisdom, oral tradition, or the epic side of truth is razed to the ground. (A 804, m3a, 5)

'Literature submits to montage in the feuilleton.' (*Exposé of 1935*, A 13) The soundbite, the subeditor's heading, the cliché (even when mangled, as it often is), these are the moulds of journalistic banality, attempting always to stimulate for a moment the audience which the very process of newspaper production and the industrial rate of writing finally subdue into listless acceptance. The journalist is someone with nothing to say and the mass-produced skills with which to say it, over and over. Even in a Kraus, the bias of journalism as a genre towards cheapness is hard to resist; even he converts wisdom into opinion in his pursuit of the condensed phrase that, in conditions of mass production, becomes the empty phrase, released of its density so that it can be absorbed by the popular audience, while the writer strives to leave the signature of his subjectivity, of 'the famous journalist', upon his shrunken work. Kraus, though, in his opposition to the First World War and to the pharisaic nature of bourgeois respectability, did expose a vital passagework in modern history:

> Kraus lived in a world in which the most shameful act was still the *faux pas*; he

23 'Naples', *SW*, 1.414–21
24 'Karl Kraus', *SW*, 2.438
25 'Karl Kraus', *SW*, 2.438

26 'Karl Kraus', *SW*, 2.436
27 *SW*, 3.32–49. See also 'Exchange with Theodor W. Adorno on the Essay "Paris, the Capital of the Nineteenth Century"', 50–67, and *SW*, 4.3–92. See also, in the same volume, the 'Exchange with Theodor W. Adorno on "The Paris of the Second Empire in Baudelaire"', 99–113.
28 Balzac, *Old Goriot* (1834), trans. Marion Ayton Crawford (London, 1951), 74–77.

distinguishes between the degrees of the monstrous, and does so precisely because his criterion is never that of bourgeois respectability, which once above the threshold of trivial misdemeanour becomes so quickly short of breath that it can form no conception of villainy on a world-historical scale.[26]

So Kraus (not to mention Marx) is a reminder that a dialectic reversal can take place, that journalism's displacement of literature can be countered in and by philosophy, that instant opinion *can* cross over into truth; perhaps, though, Benjamin regarded himself (rather than Kraus) as the writer whose work would enact that reversal. He had done his successful best to sabotage his academic career but then his other unsuccessful career as freelance intellectual was itself sabotaged by political circumstances. Still, it was the great intellectual demand he made of himself that was central to his failure, however brilliantly he responded to it in his first and only complete work published in his lifetime, the dense, seminal *Origins of German Tragedy* (1928), then in his famous individual essays and in the breathtaking accomplishments of *One-Way Street* (also 1928) and the unfinished, unfinishable and deliberate ruin of *The Arcades Project*. The demand was this: to become the creator of a work but not its author, to abandon an isolating subjectivity for immersion in the collectivity, to be one voice in a choir, one of the quoted in a composite mass of quotation from which a narrative or narratives had been released. Parataxis is not a rhetorical device here; it is now a principle of form. These constellated narratives did not take the shape of antique myths or epics; nor were they whimsically eccentric 'modern' self-communings. Both those elements would be glimpsable within them but they would not be their moulding forces. It is evident that, for example, the great essays 'Paris, the Capital of the Nineteenth Century' and 'The Paris of the Second Empire in Baudelaire',

written in 1935 and 1938 respectively, both unpublished in Benjamin's lifetime, are integrated into *The Arcades Project*, but that their form has been exploded and their content now glitters like shrapnel in the body of the larger work, reflecting in and off the commentaries of scores of other writers, in kaleidoscopic patterns the essays could not otherwise create.[27] Thus *The Arcades Project* is now recognizably a work of the same generation as *Finnegans Wake*, except that it is even more nakedly a construction, free of the traditional padding of the basic mythic narrative in which Joyce embedded his repeated, interlacing structure. Like the iron furniture which people used to cover in wood or plush, in order to hide its starkness and stifle its functional candour, *The Arcades Project* rises out of the nineteenth century as its most complete ruin, the weight and debauchery of the whole era melted down to the startling dinosaur skeleton of a civilization that had disappeared in a catastrophe it had brought upon itself — taking Benjamin with it.

The Arcades

Modernism, seen in a Benjaminian light, is the attempt by the imagination to dominate reality dialectically transformed into the subordination of the imagination by capital. It is a process that involved the acclimatization of the masses to the spectacle, which took its early forms in the various -ramas, a long list of which, parodied by Balzac in *Père Goriot*, is given in Convolute Q — georama, diorama, panorama, etcetera.[28] The illusion created by the technology for their audiences is a surround of images — a map of France or of the world, lives of famous people in condensed and simplified versions, viewed in sections as the diorama wheels rumbled in their grooves. Benjamin had declared that '... technology is not the mastery of nature but of the relation between nature and man. Men as a species completed their development thousands of years ago; but mankind as a species is just beginning his.'[29] Yet technology, in harness with capitalism, dominated man by the creation of a world of enchantment, the glittering, nefarious phantasmagoria of the arcades. While 'the energies that technology develops beyond this threshold [of human needs] are destructive', exhibiting themselves in war and propaganda, this may be said to have 'occurred behind the back of the last century', which was still unaware of their destructive potential. Like the early twentieth-century Social Democrats, who remained in thrall to the illusions of postivism, who 'saw the past as having been gathered up and stored forever in the granaries of the present', the most grievous shocks were yet to come.[30] But the introductory music had begun.

'Architecture is the most important testimony to latent "mythology". And the most important architecture of the nineteenth century is the arcade' (A 834). The latent mythology of the modern era is the market, with its demented believers in the naturalness of the cycle of production and consumption in its ever-accelerating spin that deepens into the three-dimensional vortex of 'development'. Marx's account, in his Introduction to the *Grundrisse* of the dialectic of production and consumption (completed by distribution), is amplified by Benjamin's recognition that in consumption there is a libidinal appeal that is actually intensified by bewilderment.[31] To be a consumer, one must be dazed into a state of arousal that must be even more powerful than revolutionary fervour, a Parisian disease for which only an addiction to Parisian pleasure was the effective cure. All pleasures were there, to be bought; buying was not only a pleasure in itself, it was a gateway to other pleasures, a brilliant surrogate for freedom. The flâneur

> makes himself available in
> purchasability. In venality of this kind,

[he] outdoes the whore; one might say that he takes the abstract concept of "For Sale"-ness on a stroll through the streets. He fulfills this concept only in his last incarnation: I mean, in the figure of the sandwich man.[32]

Bewilderment can be a pleasant state of shock, in which constant stimulation becomes a form of leisure. Indeed, leisured idleness is the most receptive soil for this entwining plant and the person most luxuriously entangled in its coils is the flâneur, who has fled from the dirt and noise of the street (not yet the boulevard) to the comparative hush and cleanness of the arcade, where his senses can open to the world of rinsed sensations, rather than curl up in disgust at the stench, dung and mud of the narrow thoroughfares and their even narrower pavements. The broad pavements of the boulevards and the department stores with their great glassed fronts eventually ended the dominance of the arcades about 1880, although that dominance and appeal was in fact enhanced for a time by the chaos of urban construction. But for sixty years, as Paris under Louis-Philippe and Guizot became a city of shopkeepers and failed to renew the revolutionary and Bonapartist history of its heroic political age, except as farce — as Marx so memorably described the tinpot dictatorship of Napoleon III — consumerism steadily digested the political and thereafter lived on its meal for two generations while France, the giant of fashion and culture, dwindled into a political pygmy.[33] The 'meretricious Paris of the Second Empire' disappeared briefly in the days of the Commune: 'No longer was Paris the rendezvous of British landlords, Irish absentees, American ex-slaveholders and shoddy men, Russian ex-serfowners and Wallachian boyards.' But this was the Paris overcome in the massacres of May 1871, amid the celebrations of the bourgeoisie, whom Marx believed (rather desperately) to be simultaneously attending upon the obsequies of their own class. 'The Paris

29 *One-Way Street*, SW, 1.487

30 'Eduard Fuchs, Collector and Historian', *SW*, 3.267

31 Karl Marx, 'Introduction to the *Grundrisse*', in Marx, *Later Political Writings*, ed. Terrell Carver (Cambridge, 1996), 133–40

32 'Exchange with Theodor W. Adorno on "The Flâneur" Section of "The Paris of the Second Empire in Baudelaire"', *SW*, 4.208

33 Benjamin often commented on the dual nature or history of Paris: 'Paris is a counterpart in the social order to what Vesuvius is in the geographic order: a menacing, hazardous massif, an ever-active hotbed of revolution. But just as the slopes of Vesuvius, thanks to the layers of lava that cover them, have been transformed into paradisal orchards, so the lava of revolutions provides uniquely fertile ground for the blossoming of art, festivity, fashion' (A 83, C1, 6). On Louis Napoleon's dictatorship, see *The Eighteenth Brumaire of Louis Napoleon*, in Marx, *Later Political Writings*, 31–127.

34 Marx, *The Civil War in France*, in *Later Political Writings*, 195

35 Benjamin translated two volumes of Proust's novel, *À l'ombre des jeunes filles* and *Le Côté de Guermantes*, 'two of the most perfect translations in German', according to Adorno in 'A Portrait of Walter Benjamin', in Theodor W. Adorno, *Prisms*, trans. Samuel and Shierry Weber (Cambridge, Mass., 1983), 230.

of M. Thiers was not the real Paris of the "vile multitude", but a phantom Paris, the Paris of the [renegade] *francs-fileurs*, the Paris of the Boulevards, male and female — the Paris of the rich, the capitalist, the gilded, the idle Paris, now thronging with its lackeys, its blacklegs, its literary *bohème*, and its *cocottes* at Versailles, Saint-Denis ...'[34] This Paris leaves its traces everywhere in Benjamin's Paris; it is a site of carnage and debauch, both of which realities are integral to its incessant parade of its own stylish, fashionable subjectivity, for which the political had become a spectacle. The element of self-regard in this wilderness of mirrors led to the objectifying of the person, most obviously in the trade of prostitution:

> Where doors and walls are made of mirrors, there is no telling outside from in, with all the equivocal illumination. Paris is a city of mirrors. The asphalt of its roadways smooth as glass, and at the entrance to all bistros, glass partitions. A profusion of windowpanes and mirrors in cafés, so as to make the inside brighter and to give all the nooks and crannies, into which Parisian taverns separate, a pleasing amplitude. Women here look at themselves more than elsewhere, and from this comes the distinctive beauty of the Parisienne. Before any man catches sight of her, she has already seen herself ten times reflected. But the man, too, sees his own physiognomy flash by. He gains his image more quickly here than elsewhere and also sees himself more quickly merged with this, his image. Even the eyes of passersby are veiled mirrors. And over the wide bed of the Seine, over Paris, the sky is spread out like the crystal mirror hanging over the drab beds in brothels. (A 877, c°, 1)

Baudelaire

Hell had never seemed more attractive, repetitive and addictive, afflicted by an ennui that was deepened by stimuli designed to erase it. This was especially so in Paris and, in Paris, especially in Baudelaire. It was Baudelaire who captained the ship of death in the pursuit of the new, but oddly not through the crystalline seas of the arcades. His poetry invokes the onset of modernity, but as a demoralization and a debauch. These strange territories of glass and polished marble, chilled by the solitude of crowds, heated by the devouring beat of commerce that sent a rippling erotic appeal through the cavernous ennui of their enclosed spaces, appear instead in the lustrous prose of Proust; a passage from *Du Coté de chez Swann*, says Benjamin,

> shows very clearly how the old Romantic sentiment for landscape dissolves and a new Romantic conception of landscape emerges — of landscape that seems, rather, to be a cityscape, if it is true that the city is the properly sacred ground of flânerie. In this passage, at any rate, it would be presented as such for the first time since Baudelaire (whose work does not yet portray the arcades, though they were so numerous in his day). (A 420–21, M2a, 1)[35]

Yet the flâneur is not an idler, a creature of sensation only; he is an observer who has an empathy with the collective that allows him to feel for its degradation into a crowd, even though the feeling is never untainted by disgust, nor compromised by any flight from solitude. 'The Man of the Crowd' oscillates between anonymity and demonism, although, true to his literary origins in Poe, he can never disentangle the sinister from the absurd elements in his glide through the streets. (But Benjamin disagrees with Baudelaire that this figure could be a flâneur.) Is he an utterly new and evil phenomenon, or is he just a hothouse specimen from the romantic nursery? Baudelaire's *Fleurs du Mal* so combines in its title the elements of the orthodox and the shocking that the '*mal*' loses half the force of the blow it wants to deliver, whatever associations of prostitution or satanism it generates.[36] For the histrionic aspect of the title or of the poems rarely separates itself entirely from a traditional or archaic grounding. However, this grounding can sometimes dispel the merely histrionic and lend to the work a metaphysical weight. 'The concept of the demonic comes into play where the concept of modernity converges with Catholicism' (A 236, J4a, 4). In some simple ways, Baudelaire signals the survival in his work of the ancient religious tradition and of the importance of the survival in it of allegory, a point Benjamin insists on.[37] Baudelaire's title is of a piece with a general transfer of the floral motif to industrial and decorative design in which there is an attempt to give to self-consciously modern materials some of the prestige, even the 'prettiness', of an older convention. Flowers, for instance, grew too abundantly on iron railings, in arts and crafts wallpapers and hand-pressed book ornaments and decorations ever to lose their old-fashioned appeal as 'natural', 'organic' elements, tendrils and fronds surviving in a stark technological world; evil in that context is more like bad taste, it cannot escape modernism's hapless inclination to kitsch, which is part of its rebellion, not against tradition, but against the new materials in which it found itself compelled to inaugurate a revolution in form (iron, concrete, plastic, and the like). 'The life of flowers in Jugendstil: from the flowers of evil extends an arc, over the flower-souls of Odilon Redon, to the orchids which Proust weaves into the eroticism of his Swann' (A 556, S7a, 3).[38] Or, 'It may be supposed that in the typical Jugendstil line — conjoined in fantastic montage — nerve and electrical wire not infrequently meet (and the vegetal nervous system in particular operates, as a limiting form, to mediate between the world of organism and the world of technology)' (A 558, S9, 2). Neurological shock is often imaged in the unexpected circuitries of languid line or

gesture; the nerve is a frond as much as it is a wire.[39] Shock is knowable as such only in leisure; relayed through the feudal 'wiring' of arches and ferns, it is always delayed shock. In such imagery, the 'new' tries to escape from the 'natural' and intricacy of pattern becomes an index of cultural depth and complexity. The iconography of Catholicism or of *ancien régime* architecture is extolled as a lost repertoire of crafts and meanings that hum with a meaning that the stark geometries of iron cannot transmit. Such kitsch is often a central element in the jejune political regressions that, throughout modernism, exploited the idea of, for instance, the traditional building (church or mansion) with all its plasterwork and sculpture, outfacing the inhuman elements of a new dispensation, characterized by mass-production and a banality of the new that exceeded even their own banality of the old. Even the furniture and the pattern of its arrangements in the pseudo-castles or fortress apartments of the middle classes were legible to Benjamin in the light of a derision that he shares with Lukács, whom he quotes to the effect that 'from the perspective of the philosophy of history, it is characteristic of the middle classes that their new opponent, the proletariat, should have entered the arena at a moment when the old adversary, feudalism, was not yet vanquished. And they will never quite have done with feudalism' (A 215, I2, 3).[40]

Benjamin's reading completes Baudelaire's portrait of flânerie. In each case, the flâneur is a self-portrait of the intellectual *in extremis*, attempting (vainly) to recover in the present the past that has been lost, before it is too late. It is too easy to say that it always is too late; nevertheless, recovery is badly delayed; there are always unforeseen complications, the most subtle and decisive of which is that the newly reified world cannot be redeemed in the sense that what preceded it can be restored. There is no question of that. Baudelaire's achievement has nothing to do with restoration, which

36 This theme recurs throughout Convolute J, *Baudelaire*; see A 316ff.

37 Several quotations from Baudelaire himself and from Gautier on Baudelaire emphasize the importance of allegory for the former's poetry. See, for instance, A 308, J43a, 8; A 316, J48a, 7; A 324, J53, 3; and for the relation between allegory and commodity, see A 335, J59, 10: 'The commodity form emerges in Baudelaire as the social content of the allegorical form of perception. Form and content are united in the prostitute, as in their synthesis.'

38 Jugendstil was a style of architectural, figurative and applied art of the late nineteenth and early twentieth century, associated with the periodical *Die Jugend* (Youth). See A 557, S8a, 1: 'Jugendstil is the second attempt on the part of art to come to terms with technology. The first attempt was realism.' Benjamin regarded it as a regressive movement that attempted to restore aura after the conditions for its existence had disappeared. 'Jugendstil forces the auratic' (A 557, S8, 8).

39 See Benjamin on the experience of shock in Baudelaire's poetry, 'On Some Motifs in Baudelaire', *SW*, 4.319–20. See also, on shock in war and in modern work practices, Susan Buck-Morss, *Dreamworld and Catastrophe: The Passing of Mass Utopia in East and West* (Cambridge, Mass., and London, 2000), 101–11.

40 See Georg Lukács, *History and Class Consciousness* (1922), trans. Rodney Livingstone (London, 1971). This book had a profound impact on Benjamin.

41 In A 324–25, J55a, 1, Benjamin quotes from his own work, *On the Origin of German Tragic Drama*, trans. John Osborne (London, 1998).

Benjamin is at pains to distinguish from redemption. As the use of iron had created a new organization of space, so too the combination of iron frame and plate-glass sheeting extended the phantasmagoric world of reflections, of crowds milling within interiors, of motley images and shadows in gaslight, electric light, sunlight, rainlight. The dialectic between open space, fresh air (both associated with the spirit of revolution) and enclosure, interior, the whole city becoming a room (regression, neurosis), dominates much of Benjamin's writing, although it is more pronounced, even hectic at times, in *The Arcades Project* (as in Convolute F, 'Iron Construction' for example). The greenhouse, the winter garden, the train station in their early forms in the first third of the century had become, he claimed, dreary spectacles, for 'no one as yet understood how to build with glass and iron'. But while the engineering problems had long been solved, there was no similar advance in human or social terms; the deadly infelicities of the combination of plants and iron in the pseudo-mythic garden, awoke Benjamin's Baudelairian wince of sexual disgust and social disdain: 'Now it is the same with the human material on the inside of the arcades as with the materials of their construction. Pimps are the iron bearings of this street, and its glass breakables are the whores' (A 155, F3, 2).

Benjamin observed how a great middle-class or aristocratic house could be altered for public use, with all its plushness and comfort retained, even exaggerated, for the use of the general public, as most obviously in the café (Benjamin's own favourite interior/exterior in Paris or elsewhere). Space that belonged to particular classes had now been reorganized for the general masses; that was a benign political implication, reinforced further by the sociability of the café, and the achievement of a public world infused with the warmth of what had previously been the private. Thus the *habitué* of the café or of the arcade, in the person of the flâneur, has a crucial role to play in the phantasmagoric world of late capitalism, as the agent of the awakening from its dreaming existence, imminent because the fantasy has in its intensity reached the point of reversal in which the process of transformation will begin. But this status is erratic; the flâneur can also seem at times to be the wilful representative of a world in which technology and commerce have been awarded the salute that should belong only to genuine social and human progress. But more often, we see in this figure a satiated Faust beginning to tire of the material world he has ransacked and beginning also to become aware, in shock, of the terms of the pact that he has signed; 'the motif of shock emerges in the "scornful laughter of hell" which rouses the startled allegorist from his brooding' (A 383, J90).[41] Benjamin points to what he regards as the matching examples of Proust and Freud, in whose work the moment of awakening from sleep and dream has such strategic importance (as in the opening of *À La Recherche du temps perdu*); these are examples of a generational and historical effort to rethink the relationship between specific individual and generic human experience, one that does not regard these as polarities but as the presiding elements in a dynamic interchange that will have transformative effects on the structure of human thinking about thinking and therefore on everything else. The awakening in shock from a dream is the best example of dialectical reversal, for in it, always imminent but constantly deferred, the communal comes to be known through the individual experience and the individual through the communal. It is remarkable, he observes, how Baudelaire seldom uses the first-person singular and how, in key poems, 'it is kept in the background' (A 317, J49, 3). It is in that representation of subjectivity passing over into a collective voice that the new era dawns. 'The imminent awakening is poised, like the wooden horse of the Greeks, in the Troy of dreams' (A 392, K2, 4).

Allegory and Melancholy

In Benjamin's conceptual grammar, repetition is the signature of hell. Its modern versions are Nietzsche's woeful 'eternal return' and the 'always-the-same' of liberal humanism, both of which deny the possibility of any escape from history.[42] But it also has a home in the myths of antiquity — Sisyphus, Tantalus, Ixion, the Danaids (all myths of eternal punishment) — and it is in this sense that history is understood to be mythical and many of its most attractive formulations (Hegelian, in particular) to be no more than versions of a fate or destiny that awaits its fulfilment — and it is a long, boring wait.

> The belief in progress — in an infinite perfectibility understood as an infinite ethical task — and the representation of eternal return are complementary. They are the indissoluble antinomies in the face of which the dialectical conception of historical time must be developed. In this conception, the idea of eternal return appears precisely as that 'shallow rationalism' which the belief in progress is accused of being, while faith in progress seems no less to belong to the mythic mode of thought than does the idea of eternal return. (A 119, D10a, 5)

Emancipation is, therefore, impossible — it could be denied to some on the sectarian grounds of class, race, gender or religion, or to all on the wider ground of the concept of human nature, which itself is hopelessly dependent upon fate for company. Still, conceptually as well as economically, one can say with Kafka, 'dependency keeps you young' (A 306, J42a, 8). Myth, the old one, and history, the young one, make a terrific pair; their tacit agreement is that they are really one; their appearance of difference is a fake aggression; it conceals their mournful obsequiousness to one another and to the 'fate' that binds them. Fate is not some secret force, but a relation or web of relationships, although in common idolatry it is taken to have some behind-the-scenes existence of its own.

The Arcades Project reworks some of the basic themes of Benjamin's famous study of seventeenth-century German baroque drama, the plays of mourning, *Trauerspiel*.[43] It too dwells on repetition, on the petrified world of German Lutheranism, where subjection to fate, comparable to the pagan belief in the foreordained, had achieved its melancholy post-Catholic intensity. In this world, the symbolic had lost its importance as an expression of religious mysteries; the possibility of the mystical instant, where time and symbol intersect, had disappeared or at least declined. As a consequence, this universe was closed shut. It was in mourning for a lost hope, doomed to an inescapable fate, looking for meaning in a world that presented itself almost entirely in one of two forms — that of material nature and, set within it like a bas-relief on rock, history. History is in time indeed; therefore it cannot be read as myth, from which time has been exorcised. For that which is in time and yet subject to a timeless fate, there is only one available form of representation — allegory. Benjamin explains at length how the romantics had given allegory a bad name by comparing it unfavourably with symbol; in effect they were saying that the goal (unwitting, a desire secret to itself) of allegory all along was to become symbol and that this had finally been achieved in the eighteenth century after much aimless foostering and yearning in the sculpted deserts of the baroque, or in the untidy bric-à-brac of the magician's cell or the alchemist's study. This is precisely what Benjamin wishes to reject, this kind of romantic self-satisfaction that sees the goal of a style, genre, whatever it may be, realized in itself, in its own present. Yet that post-history of allegory, which is dominated by the romantic takeover bid, is inescapably part of our understanding of what allegory is and how it functions, as much as its pre-

42 See the entries on Nietzsche and Baudelaire in A 337, J60, 7 and in A 340–41, J62a, 2.

43 *Ursprung des deutschen Trauerspiels*, hereafter *Origin*

44 *Origin*, 226–27
45 'The Influence of *Les Fleurs du Mal*', SW, 4.96
46 *Origin*, 139
47 *Origin*, 196n.
48 *Origin*, 196

history. In allegory, in the Benjaminian terms which continued to operate in *The Arcades Project*, the material world has gone to the devil. Previously, it had been divided among the pagan deities; but now Satan has arrived as sole ruler.

> With the revival of paganism in the Renaissance, and Christianity in the Counter-Reformation, allegory, the form of their conflict, also had to be renewed. The importance of this for the *Trauerspiel* is that, in the figure of Satan, the middle ages had bound the material and the demonic inextricably together. Above all, the concentration of the numerous pagan powers into *one*, theologically rigorously defined, Antichrist meant that this supreme manifestation of darkness was imposed upon matter more unambiguously than in a number of demons.[44]

This allegorical world is reproduced in Baudelaire; the satanism of his material world is immediately recognizable, presenting itself as novel, then fading almost instantly into banality. This is a more potent energy in his work than the posturing, the diabolism of disaffected groups in which it was a substitute for political conspiracy. In a fragment, written in 1938, Benjamin extended his vision of the seventeenth century to the nineteenth:

> The allegorical mode of presentation is always built on a devalued world of appearances. The specific devaluation of the world of things, as manifested in the commodity, is the foundation of Baudelaire's allegorical intention. As an embodiment of the commodity, the whore has a central place in his poetry. From another point of view, the whore is allegory incarnate. The props with which fashion equips her are her allegorical emblems. The hallmark of genuineness for the commodity is the fetish; for the allegory, it is the emblem.[45]

Clearly, the German world of which *Trauerspiel* is an expression is also a forerunner of the world of modernity in the arcades of Paris; it even has, in its grottoes and catacombs, versions of the arcade and of the passage across the threshold that divides or conjoins interior and exterior (A 214, I1a, 4). The very idea of sovereignty, the centre that creates meaning just in virtue of being a centre, is under question in both universes. The Reformation had ruined the papal centre; kingship, spiritually and politically, had been stunned; it was possible, in the seventeenth century as in the nineteenth, to announce that God was dead. Was it then the consequence that, in modern mode, meaning must be invented, must assume (with tragic gesture) a mask? 'Mourning is the state of mind in which feeling revives the empty world in the form of a mask, and derives an enigmatic satisfaction in contemplating it'.[46]

The condition of mourning or melancholy is aggravated by the asymmetry between it and the political world of the court where sovereignty rests; sovereignty bespeaks order and significance. But that political idea no longer radiates the force it once had into the provinces of philosophy or morality. Authority itself is now flawed. While sovereignty aspires always in speech to the condition of wisdom in the form of the proverb or maxim, 'not to be spoken by servants but by noble and senior characters', and while what it utters is the wisdom of the ancients, *sapientia veterum*, this is now mere repetition.[47] The wisdom of the dead has become dead wisdom; analysis is suffocated in this airless universe. 'It is not uncommon for speech in the dialogues to be no more than a caption, conjured up from allegorical constellations in which the figures are related to one another. In short: as its caption, the maxim declares the stage setting to be allegorical.'[48] But the alternative to the maxim or proverb is the staccato of indecision, all the more excruciating in a prince or sovereign. For to be resigned to fate can produce equanimity and ritual behaviour; but it can also produce anguish, the question always of what fate is, if our actions produce it or are in conformity with it. If the ruler has a weakened belief in his capacity to rule or even in the unquestionable nature of rule, then what?

> The antithesis between the power of the ruler and his capacity to rule led to a feature peculiar to the *Trauerspiel* which is, however, only apparently a generic feature and which can be illuminated only against the background of the theory of sovereignty. This is the indecisiveness of the tyrant. The prince, who is responsible for making the decision to proclaim the state of emergency, reveals, at the first opportunity, that he is almost incapable of making a decision ... the theatrical figures of this epoch always appear in the harsh light of their changing resolve.[49]

This is the world of Hamlet. Hamlet is in almost every respect a character from a German play of mourning. Except that the play *Hamlet* is a tragedy and that he himself is a tragic hero. Benjamin says that the 'object of philosophical criticism is to show that the function of artistic forms is as follows: to make historical content ... into philosophical truth'.[50] The philosophical truth of *Hamlet* is the creation of subjectivity as a historical phenomenon, comparable to that of the Cartesian 'cogito'. However, there is a fundamental difference between the two. For there is, so to say, a good and a bad subjectivity. The bad kind has as its goal 'absolute knowledge'; the good kind, 'truth'. The bad kind is satanic, inexhaustible, Faustian, polarizing the universe into the wholly material versus the wholly spiritual, its realm is that of the polymath, the alchemist, the adept who is willing, even eager, to undergo isolation from God and man; the good kind is redemptive, limited, cleansed of 'the final phantasmagoria of the

objective.'[51] Shakespeare's achievement, in Benjamin's reading, was to open the closed world of the mourning play, to show the melancholic the path out of prison. Thus we can in truth *only* have *Hamlet* without the prince of melancholy, anguish and indecision the romantics celebrated. It is only after his Luciferian fall into subjectivity, illustrated in all the allegories of dumbshow, tyrannic ostentation, intriguers and spies, contemplations on the *memento mori* — 'the fall from emblem to emblem down into the dizziness of its bottomless depths' that the 'turn-about', the reversal comes; 'all this vanishes with this *one* about-turn'.[52] 'Only Shakespeare was capable of striking Christian sparks from the baroque rigidity of the melancholic ... this drama will also be recognized as the unique spectacle in which [the ascendancy of Saturn and marks of *acedia*] are overcome in the spirit of Christianity.'[53]

Hamlet is both an allegory and an instance of a redeemed social world. In this particular tragedy (and in tragedy as such) we witness a reversal — of the double helix of the automatism of myth and fate and the fall of the subjective rebel spirit — and the redemption from that endless melancholy, that hell of repetition, by a martyr-saint who has brought the generic fate of his kind to a culmination in himself, and who is on that account the tragic hero. Hamlet is an observer of the world and he finds, as is proper to the melancholic, that the world is marked by decay, that everything human or historical is written in the natural world under the sign of transience; thus he 'cannot find satisfaction in what he sees enacted, only in his own fate. His life, the exemplary object of his mourning, points, before its extinction, to the Christian providence in whose bosom his mournful images are transformed into a blessed existence.'[54]

Benjamin's book was published in 1928. Some four or five years later, Carl Schmitt, the legal philosopher and historian, later

49 *Origin*, 70–71
50 *Origin*, 182
51 *Origin*, 232
52 *Origin*, 232
53 *Origin*, 158
54 *Origin*, 158

55 Carl Schmitt, *Hamlet or Hecuba: The Interruption of Time in the Play*, trans. Simona Draghici (London, 2006)

56 In 'Curriculum Vitae (III)' of 1928, Benjamin names Schmitt as one of the basic influences on his book. See *SW*, 2.78.

57 Carl Schmitt, *The Concept of the Political* (1932), trans. George Schwab (Chicago and London, 1996), 72

58 Schmitt, *Hamlet or Hecuba*, 146–47

59 *Origin*, 228–29

to be known as a leading apologist for and theoretician of Fascism, began a response to it, although this was not published until 1956 as chapter 3 of a book on *Hamlet*, including a section on 'The Source of the Tragic' with an appendix on Benjamin's treatise.[55] Benjamin had sent Schmitt a copy of his book in 1930, with a letter of thanks for the help Schmitt's definition of sovereignty had been to him.[56] Schmitt's work on Shakespeare extended his general critique of liberalism and its subjugation of 'state and politics', as a consequence of which 'every political concept' has 'a double face. Thus the political concept of battle in liberal thought becomes competition in the domain of economics and discussion in the political realm.'[57] In brief, Schmitt's essay sees *Hamlet* as a world-historical play, in which Hamlet, the traditional man of action, the avenger, is distorted into the indecisive man of contemplation by the scale of the historical 'emergency' choice that he faces in the England of that time, caught between Catholicism and Protestantism. The choice is between the Europe of the new State, the system that puts an end to religious wars and creates the 'political' as the new form of dominant power, on the one hand, and, on the other, the Protestant English turn away from the Continent towards the maritime empire, from land to sea. This was the 'barbaric' political system that chose the reformed faith, got rid of the Stuarts, and, in the century between 1588, the defeat of the Armada, and 1688, the date of the Glorious Revolution, became a world power. It is part of Schmitt's general theory of the tragic that it must have a dimension in historical reality, that as a dramatic form it must operate in the public sphere in relation to an audience (and thereby refuse the subjectivity of the lyric and the opportunity that gives for the declaration of the aesthetic as an autonomous realm). Without that historical dimension, tragedy cannot be achieved; this was the defect in the German *Trauerspiel*. Thus the sea that whispers around the base of the castle of

Elsinore is the imperial sea that will be ceded to England in the Treaty of Utrecht in 1713, when the Stuarts are finally written out of English history; *Hamlet* is the play in which the prince detaches himself from a feudal past and brings about the future, the time that is implicit in that past but which can only be realized in him and in the form of art that is tragedy. Hamlet himself becomes a mythical figure, but precisely as the embodiment of a historical transition, not as the hero of romantic subjectivity which he became in German romanticism first and later everywhere.

This reading is strongly marked by Benjamin's work, although its political direction is evidently different. Both readings emphasize the importance of the allegorical features of the play; Schmitt approvingly quotes:

> Every elemental utterance of the creature acquires significance from its allegorical existence, and everything allegorical acquires emphasis from the elemental aspect of the world of the senses. ... the drama of fate flares up in the conclusion of the *Trauerspiel* as something that is contained, but of course overcome, in it.[58]

This is the element that Benjamin says is no more than glimpsed in the *Sturm und Drang* period and that remains important in Baudelaire (A 352, J69a, 4).[59] But Schmitt misses a crucial nuance in Benjamin's analysis, although his essay helps to illuminate it. Benjamin does not correlate the 'elemental' with the 'reality' of the world, as Schmitt sees it. For Schmitt — and in his view this had to be true of any Marxist — the dominant category of everything was a political 'real', according to which, in this instance, the maritime empire of England is the implicit future of Shakespeare's play. This is actually to say that there is an ordained fate in human affairs and the peculiar power of art is to in some way embody that — perhaps this is how it becomes timeless — whereas German plays of mourning of this period did not have that capacity and are therefore not 'art' in the same sense. This seems close to Benjamin, even though in retrospect it seems clear that Schmitt was in effect writing an apologia for the oncoming German Empire in 1930s Europe, legitimating it as part of the fate of history and also indicating a certain shared world destiny with the Teutonic English cousins. But this is not the main ground for distancing Schmitt from Benjamin.

That ground is their different conceptions of allegory. For Benjamin, it is the counterweight to that subjectivity (Schmitt would say 'individualism') which he regards as one of the cultural achievements of bourgeois civilization and, because it became (or always was) so Faustian, its central disaster. The arcades in Paris were the hell it created and the whole gallery of figures of the damned, those in whom the nature of damnation was distilled in most identifiable form and who also still had in them some fading pinpoint of recognition about their fate, were the figures from the modern emblem book. Their sojourn through the arcades was a sojourn in a world of objects in which they had become automatons, while being perfectly assured of their autonomy. Theirs was a diabolic possession. This is a theological equivalent of commodity fetishism, the process in which the person as subject becomes the object of his own desire, the desired object becoming inevitably the stimulant of further desire, in an endless acceleration (A 207, H2, 6). Even the emancipatory element that could be perceived in the collection of objects, whereby they were acquired for something other than their use function, has its sinister side. Toys, robots, children in gothic tales, objects in which a 'time' was entrapped — like childhood, for instance — all share in this quality of petrifaction; they are all allegorical subjects and, therefore, it is only in the recovery of their innocence

as objects, rather than as items in a register, list, treasure hoard, that freedom is possible. Then the reign of Satan in the world comes to an end.

As the condition of subjectivity intensifies, it becomes more, not less, susceptible to allegorical description. In more modern idiom, it becomes the stereotype. In earlier literature it was the avenger, the courtier, the tyrant, the intriguer, the favourite son, the enchanted princess, etcetera. In Benjamin's Paris the allegorical figures are now new stereotypes — the collector, gambler, forger, dandy, man of the crowd, the flâneur. Subjectivity culminates in the stereotype and its culmination is announced by technology, in the arcades of Paris, in the endless self-repetition of the halls of mirrors. 'One encounters an abundance of stereotypes in Baudelaire, as in the Baroque poets' (A 337, J60a, 3). Typically, it must have seemed, this world signed its death certificate in the treaty that ended the First World War in the Hall of Mirrors at Versailles.

But there was the 'turn-about', the moment after allegory, when the world of objects would be freed of its satanic domination, and the creaturely world again become mute, no longer obliged to represent something not itself. Subjectivity would incandesce into the collective. The nineteenth century would awake from its dream.

> Every age must strive anew to wrest tradition away from the conformism that is working to overpower it. The Messiah comes not only as the redeemer; he comes as the victor over the Antichrist. The only historian capable of fanning the spark of hope in the past is the one who is firmly convinced that *even the dead* will not be safe from the enemy if he is victorious. And this enemy has never ceased to be victorious.[60]

60 'On the Concept of History', *SW*, 4.391

Albrecht Dürer
Melencolia I
1514
engraving
24.1 x 18.9 cm

61 In the vast literature on
the German recovery
of pagan antiquity in
Renaissance art, the
most comprehensive
work is Erwin Panofsky,
*Studies in Iconology;
Humanistic Themes
in the Art of the
Renaissance* (London,
1992); Aby Warburg,
'Dürer and Italian
Antiquity', an essay of
1932, is to be found
in his *The Renewal
of Pagan Antiquity*,
trans. David Britt (Los
Angeles, 1999).

Melancholy Angel

Albrecht Dürer's engraving *Melencolia I* had
a great appeal for the French romantics in
particular, as a depiction of the melancholic
artist confronting the limitations either
of his powers of expression, or of the
technology available to him, or of the
limitations of his historical time. Although
these themes were otherwise appealing to
him, Benjamin shows more interest in the
readings of his more recent times by Erwin
Panofsky, Aby Warburg, Alois Riegl and
others.61 In Warburg's reading in particular,

the engraving represents the collision of two forces, Saturn and Jove. Saturn's is the realm of melancholy, and its various emblems, from the polyhedron to the stone to the dog, are dispersed within it; for in sadness, everything is dispersed. Jove can be read as the other, triumphant force here, human energy and intelligence overcoming a world disheartened by absurd but potent beliefs. Humanism dismisses the *disjecta membra* of the religious tradition and the apparent senselessness of the world subject to it. So, *Melencolia I* shows a historical transition taking place. The old world of Saturn comes to an end: the reign of Jove has begun. In the Jovian dispensation, human will and intelligence take over. Benjamin doubles this reading, accepting it at one level, cancelling it at another, folding each into the other. For if reason triumphs over magic, still the signs or effects of ancient petrifaction have not gone away; the engraving allows us to see the two worlds, not according to the logic of an inevitable progress in which one surpasses the other, but in a dialectical relation wherein the triumph of Saturn and the triumph of Jove are both present. This Angel is not merely disheartened by the limitations of the technology or the belief system (allegory) available to her. She is disheartened by the future. The great project of modernity that began in the Renaissance became modern capitalism and led to the construction of hell, a brilliant and appalling achievement. Alternatively, the angel in this engraving is earthbound by melancholy, a humour associated with the earth and with stone, and is stricken by the realization that this reveals the reality of a creaturely condition we cannot fly beyond.[62] All wings, like all such transformative hopes, are wax.

Is this an occasion, though, when Benjamin obliquely addresses the question of what went wrong with the greatest of all opportunities for human emancipation in Russia? Like all at the Frankfurt Institute, he was so intellectually and morally

convulsed by the coarseness of Fascism as a political philosophy, that he read it only as a pathology. But then, they read capitalism as one too, both in its structure and in its effects. The failure of socialism/communism in Russia offered a rich harvest of pathologies, but it was never gathered into any Frankfurt granary. In Benjamin's interpretation of the Dürer engraving, perhaps the October Revolution is coded as the Renaissance. In each case, a brilliant achievement and hope turned to nightmare. Jove's triumph is a delusion, for it does not abolish the world of Saturn. It restores it, *through Jove's own success*. This is the more disheartening because the bogus enchantments have now become more effective, for they have absorbed technology, the product of reason. Similarly, reaction absorbs revolution and becomes correspondingly more powerful; could anything truly revolutionary be retrieved, ever?

Benjamin had said yes to this question, long before he became a Marxist. Part of the hidden history of the allegorical object becoming a commodity fetish is embedded in the transition from Christianity to capitalism, which Benjamin sees, in a Nietzschean light, as a passage from a religion to a cult. In the sketch or fragment that he wrote in 1921, 'Capitalism as Religion', he says: 'Capitalism is a religion of pure cult, without dogma. Capitalism has developed as a parasite of Christianity in the West … until it reached the point where Christianity's history is essentially that of its parasite — that is to say, of capitalism.'[63]

The fetish is a characteristic product of a parasite; that is, parasitism is in the nature of capitalism; it gradually reproduces, as what it calls natural, the digested replica of the world that it feeds on. This is phantasmagoria. It is a mystification that is successful because it claims it is the consequence of demystification. What made the October Revolution different was the ambition it had to recover the real world. In

62 For an interesting variation on these readings, see Beatrice Hanssen, *Walter Benjamin's Other History: Of Stones, Anima.ls, Human Beings and Angels* (Berkeley, Los Angeles, London, 2000), 159–62.

63 *SW*, 1.289

64 Jacques Derrida, 'Force of Law: The "Mystical Foundation of Authority"', in Drucilla Cornwell, Michael Rosenfeld and David Gray Carlson, eds., *Deconstruction and the Possibility of Justice* (New York, 1992), 3–67; see also Eleanor Kaufman, '"To Cut too Deeply and Not Enough": Violence and the Incorporeal', in Creston Davis, John Milbank and Slavoj Zizek, eds., *Theology and the Political: The New Debate* (Durham and London, 2005), 350–65.

65 *SW*, 1.251

66 Benjamin's status as tragic victim of Fascism, culminating in his suicide in the border village of Pau in the Pyrenees, has inevitably been treated as a gift to fiction by at least two novelists: Jay Parini, *Benjamin's Crossing* (New York, 1997) and Bruno Arpaia, *L'Angelo della Storia* (Torino, 2001), *The Angel of History*, trans. Minna Proctor (Edinburgh, 2006).

his celebrated essay, also of 1921, 'Critique of Violence' (which was subject to an almost equally celebrated reading by Derrida in 1992), Benjamin distinguishes between 'mythic violence' and 'divine violence'.[64] The first serves law and the state, the notion of sheer survival under certain conditions, as when the state demands of its subjects that they sacrifice their lives for it. The second serves life, not as survival alone, but as an adventure in realizing possibility. It does not demand sacrifice, it accepts it.

The proposition that existence stands higher than a just existence, is false and ignominious, if existence is to mean nothing other than mere life … if the proposition is intended to mean that the non-existence of man is something more terrible than the (admittedly subordinate) not-yet-attained condition of the just man.[65]

Benjamin repudiated that proposition when he committed suicide.[66] ■

'Keep goin'. Gotta keep goin'.'
Remembering Robert Altman

Stephen Rea

When Robert Altman died on 20 November 2006, the obituaries were almost unanimous in remembering him as a cantankerous, wayward maverick, the suggestion being that his movies were mostly haphazard, uneven curiosities, punctuated by occasional explosions of brilliance. Without question, he was a colourful, shit-kicking, dope-smoking, two-fisted drinker (retired). But to conclude that the intricate chaos and seemingly random turmoil he uniquely captures in his movies is the result of anything but a massive vision, a sophisticated grasp of structure, and a high moral sense, would be a serious mistake. He was the genius of American cinema who was never let preside.

Robert Altman in London, 1994. Photograph: Steve Pyke/Getty Images.

Altman's approach and method, his spirit and presence, were anathema to the arch-conservative studio heads in Hollywood. His first (and biggest) hit movie *M*A*S*H* (1970) only got made because the Fox execs were looking the other way, believing it to be a cheap movie that would 'just play in drive-ins'. Though set in the Korean War, all the political attitudes of the film were about Nixon and Vietnam. The TV spin-off (whose intentions were the opposite of the movie's and in which Altman had no hand or part, and which he regarded as obscene, given America's continued involvement in Vietnam) was an early example of the industry's exploitation of Altman's originality. His live-action version of the cartoon *Popeye*, regarded as weird in 1980, was followed by a wave of imitations (*The Flintstones* [1994], *Scooby-Doo* [2002], etcetera). His enthusiastic shattering of the conventions of camera movement — the use of slow zoom, two camera set-ups, cutting from moving shots to static shots — were eventually adopted by lesser practitioners.

During the shooting of *Prêt-à-Porter* in 1994, I stood beside him in the huge hotel lobby where he was about to attempt to convert the real-life mayhem of a team of headstrong actors into the controlled chaos that would introduce, one by one, each of the characters who would appear in the movie. He turned to me and said glumly, 'Who do I have to fuck to get off this movie?' But within half an hour, he had it choreographed — a typically exhilarating signature shot. And if anyone thinks there was anything aimless or unplanned about it, they know nothing about shooting a movie. It was sheer dogged artistry.

He was frequently misunderstood, despite going to lengths to explain himself with an impressive patrician authority. I saw him give a serious dressing down to

Robert Altman chats with news anchor Tom Brokaw on the floor of the Democratic National Convention in Boston, Massachusetts, 27 July 2004. Altman was taping *Tanner on Tanner*, a three-part TV film for which Brokaw did a cameo appearance. Photograph: Scott Olson/Getty Images.

a Democratic congressman in Orso's restaurant in New York for failing to deliver on election promises, and also the glazed expression on the face of an MGM executive, as Bob pointed out to him that 'All *you* care about is the money. All *I* care about is the movies.'

The combination of continual experimentation, determined criticism of America and his interest in ideas rather than plot made him a provocative figure to the movie establishment. Elliott Gould and Donald Sutherland tried to have him fired from *M*A*S*H*, fearing for their careers, as what they thought was their star vehicle was transformed into an anarchic ensemble piece. The big man was deeply wounded. And of course ultimately the movie provided Gould and Sutherland with enough street-cred for several careers.

In *Brewster McCloud* (1970), he parodied the car chase from *Bullitt* (1968), which he regarded as irresponsible because the audience weren't required to care about any of the people who died as a result of Steve McQueen's driving. John Wayne described Altman's radically different western *McCabe & Mrs. Miller* (1971) as 'corrupt'. But then Wayne also thought *High Noon* (1952) was a communist plot. Nice one, Duke. And Burt Lancaster said, 'Altman isn't a director — he didn't give me any directions.' But that was not the way he worked. He created an atmosphere where actors could expand. On *Prêt-à-Porter* I proposed tentatively that I might change a line. He said, 'Say whatever you like.' On another occasion he said to me, 'On your entrance, I need you to stand *here*. Then to move *here*. After that, it's entirely up to you. We'll follow you.'

Kansas City (1996), a great film, was largely ignored; it is critical of America — its corrupt voting system and violence, which he depicted casually rather than sensationally. That was enough to have it dismissed. But the movie, set in the 1930s, is a homage to a great era in American music. And the central relationship between the two women exposes the popular hit *Thelma and Louise* (1991) as sentimental escapism.

All Altman's movies have some element of innovation. I love the continuous druggy soliloquy of Elliott Gould's Philip Marlowe in *The Long Goodbye* (1973), replacing the routine Chandlerian voice-over. But out of an astonishing extensive canon of work, I imagine most people will look to *Nashville* (1975), a transforming moment

in American cinema, and *Short Cuts* (1993) — sublime achievements in a huge career. '*Nashville*,' he said, 'was like trying to paint a mural where the houses kept moving.' It is a political film with a panoramic view of America using country and western music as a metaphor. Pauline Kael described it as 'the funniest epic vision of America ever to reach the screen'. *Short Cuts* is an inspired adaptation of eight Raymond Carver short stories in a kaleidoscopic tragic-comic view of Los Angeles. Aficionados of Carver disputed its fidelity, but somehow that misses the point. It is pure Altman — the use of the camera, the superb editing, the command of an epic narrative and unexpectedly brilliant performances.

Most people don't look on *Prêt-à-Porter*, Altman's take on the fashion industry, as a shining example of his work. But I don't care. It is the only time I worked with him and I loved every minute of it. I was in Paris with him and his fabulous wife, Kathryn, and you'd learn more in a day and a half with Altman than you would in a lifetime with almost anyone else. There's a scene near the end of the movie where all these nude models parade on the catwalk. As we were about to shoot, Bob said, 'Well, after all, clothes are about nakedness.' Maybe it wasn't a huge informing idea, as informing ideas go, but I'm certain that his belief in *some* idea was what lifted his films onto a different level. That and the fact that he wanted to see it expressed through a whole society, not just through the anger of one central existential hero. And that he didn't believe there were any rules about how to achieve that.

I visited him in New York in April 2006. He'd just finished *A Prairie Home Companion* and he was quite ill. But he was planning another movie for the fall. 'Another movie?' I said. 'Oh yes,' he said. 'Keep goin'. Gotta keep goin'.' ∎

31

An Interview with Tim Robinson

Brian Dillon

Since the early 1970s, the writer, artist and cartographer Tim Robinson has essayed a varied and suggestive series of projects that aspire to and risk what he calls 'the good step' across the complicatedly overwritten territory of Connemara and the Aran Islands. Born in Yorkshire in 1935, Robinson studied mathematics at Cambridge and worked as a teacher and artist in Istanbul, Vienna and London. In 1972, exasperated by an art scene in which he had begun to acquire some success, he left London for Inis Móir, the largest of the three islands. The first practical manifestation of his relationship with his new home was a map, completed in 1975. In 1986, he published *Stones of Aran: Pilgrimage*, in which he explores the history and topography of the island's perimeter ('the sea', he had been informed on arrival, 'goes all the way round the island'). The book's companion volume, *Stones of Aran: Labyrinth*, published in 1995, is an investigation of the interior. Since then, he has written *Setting Foot on the Shores of Connemara and Other Writings* (1996), the essay collection *My Time in Space* (2001), a book of fictions, *Tales and Imaginings* (2002), and most recently *Connemara: Listening to the Wind* (2006), the first volume in a projected three-volume work. With his wife Máiréad, he continues to publish maps and books under the imprint of Folding Landscapes, based at his home in Roundstone, County Galway.

Tim Robinson, 2005.
Photograph: Penguin

BRIAN DILLON: *Your career as an artist in London in the sixties already suggests that you were fascinated not only by a certain kind of relationship between the individual and the landscape, but particularly by the notion of a mobile landscape, of which the coast is the perfect example. Is this what you found when you first moved to Aran?*

TIM ROBINSON: The decision of my partner M. and myself to leave London for the Aran Islands in 1972 was a drastic response to a conjunction of practical and psychological problems. Our landlord had bought us out of our comfortable West Hampstead flat, and the trying business of searching for an equivalent seemed at best to promise nothing more than a continuation of everydayness; I was turning away from the public world of the visual arts in which I had invested my creativity for the previous decade and needed solitude and silence in which to concentrate on writing; we both wanted change, another throw of the dice. Underneath all that was a sense, not uncommon at that period, that the culture of the city, rich and heady as it might be, needed to be brought into relation with the countryside. The environment was becoming an issue; symptomatically, various visual artists were undertaking journeys and siting constructions in rural areas and remote wildernesses. I found myself taking long walks through the suburbs of north London, navigating by the sun or by distant glimpses of the steeples of parish churches in Kilburn, Neasden and Harlesden (which I identified with Proust's bell-towers of Martinville). A couple of years earlier I had exhibited a series of large geometrical abstract paintings suggested by the most generalized residue of my experiences on a walking tour in Provence: they had titles like *Windward* and *Towards the Sun*, they were intensely directional, and now they look to me like street signs saying 'Out of Here!' Another artwork of those last London years was *Moonfield*; it was shown in a large gallery, in almost total darkness, and consisted of a hundred or so flat geometrical shapes, white on one side and black on the other, scattered on a black floor; initially they lay black side up and were quite invisible, but as people found them with their feet and turned them over and rearranged them, a ghostly lunar landscape came into existence. Later on this seemed to have been a premonition of the great horizontal sheets of limestone surrounding the cottage we occupied on the Aran Islands, a thousand shades of grey by daylight, silvery by moonlight, black and glittering in rain. Another project planned during those last London years, but never realized, was for a concrete floor moulded into a shallow wave formation, the distance from wave-top to wave-top being a good stride, the regularity of which would impose a rhythm on whatever additions were brought to it — dance, water, a scattering of measuring rods, oblique candlelight, etcetera. In Aran (as I'll call the islands, for convenience), I found landscape-sized areas disconcertingly reminiscent of that

abandoned project: acres of flat rock riven by systems of parallel fissures, which force a regularity, or at least a degree of forethought, upon one's steps.

Perhaps you can trace some of the history and motivation of the Folding Landscapes project?

Coming to Aran was the great good step in my life. A hundred other islands of Britain or Ireland might have given us adventure and mental stimulation, but I doubt if any of them combine so many profoundly individual and fascinating features as Aran. I have hinted at its extraordinary glaciated limestone-karst geology; its flora and the bird-life of its great cliffs, its archaeology — neolithic tombs, Iron Age stone cashels, early Christian oratories — its still lively Gaelic language, its folklore and country ways, are all equally intriguing. The projected novel I had brought with me was soon swept out of mind by the flood of words in which I recorded my day-by-day discovery of the islands, in volume after volume of diary. When a local lady, seeing that I was spending all my time walking and taking notes, suggested that I make a map of the islands, the idea seemed so right, as a way of recording and integrating my findings and sensations, that I started to plan the work that same night. The only detailed maps available at that time were the Ordnance Survey sheets at six inches to the mile, which had last been updated in 1899 — topographically very accurate but rather blank so far as placenames went. I took these as a basis, and spent a long summer walking every path, marking in every house, collecting information of all sorts from everyone I met, leaning over the cliffs to sketch their ledges and overhangs. It was an exhausting struggle against rain and wind, but by the end of it I felt that the islands had been so deeply etched into my very being that I could have printed off an image of them by rolling on the paper. The islanders

Elizabeth Rivers
... an old man with a tree trunk across his shoulders
1947
print wood engraving
6.2 x 7.9 cm
National Library of Ireland

were deeply interested in my progress, and as I had begun to learn Irish and was particularly interested in the oral history and placelore of which they were the sole custodians, the map took on some aspects of a communal creation. Looking back on it now, that first attempt at a map was a crude production; since then I have published two more versions, the latest with a 'companion' book explaining the Irish placenames and summarizing the islands' history; and that is as far as I can go, in the medium of cartography, towards creating an adequate, if not a worthy, image of Aran.

Cartography is, for you, then, a matter of recording something of your own passage across the landscape, or around the perimeter of the island?

One of the satisfactions of do-it-yourself cartography is carrying through the whole of the process, from choosing the area to be mapped, deciding on the parameters of scale and sheet size, exploring the terrain, doing the drawing, overseeing the printing, and finally selling the maps — activities normally spread between people who never meet. Creatively, the important identification here is between the person who explores the terrain and the person who does the drawing; this brings the process into the realm of art and makes cartography a mode of expression of a lot more than topographical fact. In terms of our life on the islands, the most gratifying closure of the circuit of action was carrying a pile of the finished product into the little shop run by the elderly lady who had first suggested the map.

As soon as I had done this I rewarded myself with a trip to the Burren, the limestone uplands of County Clare, which lie just east of the islands. I had read about its extraordinary flora, with its mixture of Mediterranean and arctic-alpine species, and I soon found that it was equally remarkable in its geology and archaeology. But it is

a complex area sprawling over hills and valleys, a glacially carved plateau, and there is no point from which one can get an overview of any large proportion of it. Instead, a moment of time came along that revealed the possibility of mapping it, of grasping and expressing some unity in it. M. and I went for a long hike one beautiful autumn day, and as we were crossing a pass between two valleys we heard the echoing cries of men and barking of the dogs and saw a long file of cattle winding along a the track that diverged from ours and climbed to the uplands. An unusual feature of the farming life of the Burren is that the cattle are pastured in the lowland meadows, near the farmhouses, for the summer milking and calving season, and spend the winters on the barren-looking uplands, grazing the thin but nutritious herbage that grows among the rocks. In accordance with tradition, the cattle are moved to the winterage on or near the first of November, and brought down again around the first of May, these two dates being those of the ancient festivals of Samhain and Bealtaine. The fact that, without knowing anything about it, we had witnessed a trace of one of these two ancient rites of the Celtic year, swung open a door for me into the past and the particularity of the Burren. But during the following year I often felt that door closed against me, as I struggled physically with dense thickets of hazel scrub in search of megalithic tombs, and psychologically with the region's lonely crags and gloomy legends and rampant

Elizabeth Rivers
*With wind and rain this
journal opened ...*
1947
print wood engraving
5.7 x 7.7 cm
National Library of Ireland

superstition. I am proud of the map, which looks like a model of clarity, but I am conscious of how much personal darkness is unexpressed in it.

By 1984 we had been living on Aran for most of each of twelve years; I had mapped the islands twice, completed the Burren map, and was beginning on a map of the south Connemara coast; my aim was to map all the land visible from Aran, as if that were a necessity in order to find my feet in this destabilizing new world. But it was time to make something more structured and practical and economically supportive than a cottage hobby out of this almost ritualistic and magical activity of mapping. We moved to Roundstone in the west of Connemara, where we rented a studio and a little house, and M. set up Folding Landscapes, which still continues to publish and distribute the maps and a few related books. The south Connemara map spread to become a map of the whole of Connemara, which

took seven years to complete and was not published until 1990. Since then I have concentrated on writing, using the maps as a way of ordering and storing experience and information.

Was the cartography always meant to be an adjunct to writing?

Whatever its mental and physical demands, cartography is a welcome relief from and evasion of the task of writing, and I do regard the making of those three maps as a detour — a very fulfilling one, if inordinately lengthy — in my life as a writer. In London I had written a good deal — a novella, and a number of short fictions that I felt little drive to publish at the time and that didn't see the light of day until recently — and in Aran I had begun the two-volume study of the biggest of the three islands eventually published as *Stones of Aran, Part 1, Pilgrimage* and *Part 2, Labyrinth*, in 1986 and 1995 respectively. It is a very personal work despite its pretensions to objectivity and comprehensiveness, and its pervading imagery of the step taken across difficult and complicated terrain derives from my feelings about our right relationship to the Earth. Since then I have written *My Time in Space*, a collection of essays responding to a retrospective realization that everything I've done has had to do with space of some sort, whether it was my mathematical studies at Cambridge, my geometrical abstracts and installations, the cartography, the topographical writings, or my avid popular-science reading on the cosmos. Now I'm engaged on work on Connemara, the first volume of which has appeared, and at the same time I have been drawn into visual art again and am experimenting with two or three projects, each with some reference to real or psychological topographies.

A few years ago I dug out some artworks I'd made in the year we left London for Aran but never shown to any but a few visitors to my studio. One of them was a slim white wooden rod a yard long, suspended vertically by a multitude of coloured threads attached to its upper end, which at the time I'd seen as marking a stride taken towards the centre of the earth. The others were bundles of slim rods of various lengths, marked with black bands on white, that lay scattered on the floor, and now look to me like measuring rods; the rediscovery of these works with their references to walking, to the step, to mapping, was rather shaking; was it impossible to step free of one's circle of obsessions, even by uprooting oneself in the middle of a career, taking up a new medium of expression, and leaving the centrality of the city for somewhere as marginal as possible? I used these old works together with quotes from the more recent work done in Ireland in an installation called *The View from the Horizon*, shown at the Irish Museum of Modern Art in 1997, which explored the necessity and apparent impossibility of stepping free of one's own

personal network of metaphors. So I think the answer to the question as to whether the cartography was always intended to be accompanied by writing is that the connection between them and the work in other media has been at a level below free will and has manifested itself in a web of dreamlike correspondences.

The islands seem to have been subject to several sorts of misinterpretation, especially when it came to naming their geological features. Even inhabitants of one island would often remake the names of another. You write that 'offshore usage re-creates the surrounding landscapes; like a poet I know who finds his lines by glancing along titles on library shelves, so the fisherman low among the waves raises his eyes and picks words off the land with which to write sentences on the sea'. The process is especially obvious with the earliest Ordnance Survey maps.

The first Ordnance Survey maps of Ireland were made for use in such financial and legal contexts as the setting of rates and rents and the assigning of leases. There was, however, a section of the OS, set up in 1835, called the Topographical Department, which was charged with the collection of information on what would now be called 'Heritage'. It was headed by George Petrie and among the scholars working for it was John O'Donovan; these were among the great names in the transition from antiquarianism to archaeology, and the study of the ancient manuscripts and annals of Ireland. The department took on such a life of its own and showed so much energy and enthusiasm in its researches that the authorities soon recalled the OS to a stricter adherence to its more mundane aims, but in the meantime John O'Donovan travelled the remotest corners of Ireland, describing ancient monuments in copious letters to the OS and collecting placenames from Irish speakers and from written sources. However, the policy of the OS was to anglicize these names; that is, to spell them out according to the phonetic system of the English language. This was a process that had been going on piecemeal since the earliest days of the English colonization of Ireland, but now it was being implemented systematically. As a result, over most of Ireland the placenames have lost their subtlety of sound (to take the most basic and omnipresent example, there is a world of difference between the slightly silly-sounding element 'bally', meaning 'a settlement', and the subtle swerving phonemes of its Irish original, *baile*) and have been rendered meaningless, thereby shedding their load of historical, mythical and descriptive content.

But Irish is still alive and well in Aran, and although at first I had no knowledge of the language, I soon realized that the map-names were a travesty and often lent the prestige of the official to glaring errors of transcription and interpretation, and that most placenames in daily use had never been written down. So it became my intention to try and undo this historical insult to the language and its speakers; there was an element of post-colonial reparation in

undertaking this task. Of course I soon found that my slow-growing command of Irish was inadequate and I took to consulting experts (as I also did in the fields of archaeology, botany, etcetera.). Tomás de Bhaldraithe, the leading lexicographer, and Tomás Ó Máille, the professor of Irish at University College Galway, and the staff of the Placenames Department in the Ordnance Survey, were my principal and most generous mentors, and with their help I am proud to have restored some thousands of names to the map record of the areas I have covered.

Although my own maps are based on the mensurational work of the OS and there is no way I could have carried out what was indeed the work of an army of men, there are several practices of official or professional cartography I felt free to depart from if they did not suit the nature of the terrain I wished to express. A most impressive and characteristic feature of the Aran Islands is the superb range of vertical or overhanging cliffs facing the Atlantic; on OS maps they are reduced to little more than a line because of the insistence on a standard overhead view; I preferred to show the cliffs in a seagull's-eye perspective, with their principal ledges (many of which had names, as the cliffmen of old used to go down them after seabirds), even if I had to sacrifice a little accuracy in the coastline in order to meld the cliff view with it. When I started on the map of Connemara, I found that it sat better on the paper if the edges of the sheet were not aligned with the national grid in the standard manner. I remember vividly imagining I was taking the landscape in my hands and turning it a little when I made this decision; that feeling was like a realization that the region did form a graspable unity, and that therefore it was, in a deeper sense than the usual, mappable. The question of what the cartographers call 'ornamentation' was crucial for me. The word has connotations of superficiality and the superfluous, but I wanted whatever

Elizabeth Rivers
Books!
1947
print wood engraving
5.3 x 8.2 cm
National Library of Ireland

symbolism I used to indicate rocks, sandy beaches, mudflats, etcetera, also to convey something of the experience of treading those terrains. So my maps are covered with minute flecks and twirls and dots of ink, the day-long execution of which became an almost trancelike reminiscence of the act of walking across the very spot I was now drawing. Again, the idea of the step underlay this practice, and the urge not to alienate the foot from the hand, or the body from the mind.

You note that J. M. Synge seems not to have noticed some of the most beautiful or alarming features of the islands. Can you speculate as to why that might have been? Of course, Synge has a particular interest in language and custom, but I wonder whether there is not a more general distinction to be made between two sorts of romanticizing (or Romanticizing): a geological Sublime and a cultural Picturesque?

Synge's *The Aran Islands*, based on his experience of spending a few weeks on the islands in each of a few years from 1898, is

a very well-shaped work, apart from some folkloristic overburdening of its last section. Presumably he excluded some geographical material in order to focus on the people, and the fascination and enigma of the book is the conflict between realism and romanticism in their depiction, and how shallow Synge's commitment to his subject matter makes such aesthetic distinctions appear. Nevertheless, it is disconcerting to find no mention of such amazing features of the islands as the great block-beaches of countless huge boulders pushed inland and assembled into rampartlike ridges by waves that must have broken over the tops of hundred-foot-high cliffs. The famous prehistoric stone cashels or ringforts too are scarcely alluded to, even the most impressive one almost overhanging the cottage he lodged in. However, in his private notebooks there is a remarkable passage in which, having walked across to the Atlantic shoreline for the first time, he describes his first sight of 'the magnificent waves towering in dazzling white and green before the cliff'. He likens the experience to that of a man with a fully educated perception of music, but quite ignorant of it, on hearing a Beethoven symphony for the first time, that of a man

Elizabeth Rivers
*... beauty of bog and
mountain*
1947
print wood engraving
3.3 x 6 cm
National Library of Ireland

'with full power of appreciation' standing before a woman for the first time, and that of a man knowing nothing of death who comes across a corpse. These impossible scenarios imply that the soul is as deeply open to the profundities of nature as it is to art, sex and death; Synge's brief wrestling with this personal experience is in its honest inadequacy more engaged and engaging than a recourse to a theory of the Sublime.

With regard to Robert Flaherty's film Man of Aran *(1934): it would be easy to see it as a film that merely sets cultural quaintness against implacable Nature: but as you point out, it's also, at its most apparently abstract moments (the storm scenes, especially), a film about substance, about air, water and rock. I wonder if you can say something about how you see the relationship, in your writing and mapping, between cultural history and the physical palpability of the coastal landscape?*

Flaherty depicts the physical world as nameless, uncharted and extrahistorical, and his archetypal Man of Aran and his family as engaged in an epic struggle against the elemental forces of Nature rather than in an ecological relationship with them. But despite the extremity of its setting, Aran life was ingenious in its accommodations with rock and wave and wind; ironically, it's only in our foolish present days that Araners build on higher ground, for the sake of a view, instead of tucked into the lee of scarps, and suffer the consequences of battering wind and rain. I'm intrigued by the intimacy of relationship of past generations with the shore, as evidenced by the close weave of placenames covering even the ledges of the cliffs, as mentioned earlier. Such geological determinations of cultural forms as the basis of commerce between the populations of the Connemara littoral and the Aran Islands being the different properties of granite and limestone interest me too. (Aran's fissured limestone is dry and carries a sparse but fertile soil, whereas granite is impervious and gives rise to acidic soil and to bog; hence the export of turf to Aran, in return for potatoes — and even for gravestones! — has been the saving of Connemara, to the point of the denudation of its own land.) The fissures of Aran, running largely north–south and enlarged by weathering into clefts many feet deep and several inches wide, have imposed their directionality on paths, field walls and settlement patterns; since their formation is probably related to the slow pulling-apart of Europe and America over the last two hundred million years, I think of the Aran farmer following a stone-walled track between his fields as walking arm in arm with the Atlantic. I also like the fact that the incredibly tortuous and indented Connemara coastline was evidently designed by God with smuggling in mind, so that even poor fisherfolk could go to worship Him in fine silk hats from Guernsey. These connections are rich hanks of threads in the web of causality.

You warn at one point in Stones of Aran *against the application of 'overluxuriant metaphors' to inhuman reality. I was reminded by that passage that one of John Ruskin's first examples of the pathetic fallacy is from Charles Kingsley's* Alton Locke: *'They rowed her in across the rolling foam — / The cruel, crawling foam'. Is the danger (if that's what it is) greater with a seabound and vanishing territory?*

Living on an island, a little habitable space in the midst of a rampant wilderness, forces a metaphorical or allegorical dimension into everyday space, as does living within sight of the edge of a cliff subject to unpredictable collapses. At least, so it did for me, though many an islander might have been amused

by the idea. But I also relished the island's deep anteriority to all human interpretations of it. I suppose a lot of *Stones of Aran* is taken up with the ironic juxtaposition of non-human reality and meaning; which of these two is the island and which the ocean? In the remark you allude to I was underlining a passage in which I describe a beach on which the waves subscribe themselves in the shape of the tideline, seabirds imprint their signatures on the wet sand, etcetera. I claim there that we (humans) are the only sources of meaning 'at least on this beach of the universe'. Many would disagree profoundly, but for me this is a most probable fact, on which I'd found my attempts to understand how things are. However, the metaphors I complain of are almost unavoidable, useful and not harmful if kept on the reins of scepticism. A related question comes up for me when I reread other passages, written at various times, in which I seem to be suggesting that Space is our unrecognized god, or that the Earth is an object of worship; I suppose in fact I'm using an established persuasive shorthand here for directing our powers of attention and care, for I have no supernaturalist beliefs about the Earth or anything else including Nothing. The geopoeticist Kenneth White suggests that the word 'sacred' might be given a rest for a few generations — but despite its unwanted millennial baggage, I don't know how to do without it. It's an unsettled and unsettling question for me. ■

Twilight on Old Stones

Tim Robinson

Lingering elegiac evenings of the summer solstice, when the parted day slips behind the mountains to the north like a child hiding behind a sofa, are the best for exploring the lanes of Ballynakill. Elements of this little world apart that might not be noticed at other times become quietly insistent on presenting themselves, and those prominent by daylight sink back into obscurity.

The roofless gables of the medieval chapel of St. Ceannanach (from which the parish is called Baile na Cille, the settlement of the church) are less distinguishable from the dark profiles of trees in the graveyard behind it, whereas, by day, the ruin, one corner of which touches the roadside wall, seems to rest an elbow on it and lean out like an old farmer eyeing the approaching passer-by; you know you will not get past without having to listen to some inconsequential local history. 'Did you ever hear of Strong Ned?' he might say. 'That's Éamon Láidir in Irish. He was an O'Flaherty; his grandfather had the land round here until Cromwell hanged him and gave it to the Martins. Nimble Dick Martin used to come round for the rent with his servants, all armed, and Ned would drive them off all by himself. He was seven feet tall. When he died he was buried just where I'm standing now. People used to come and see his great big bones; they were on show in a sort of shelf in the church wall …' But in the evenings the stories that make themselves heard are less easily understood and of much older origins. At the further end of Ballynakill Lake, which lies at the foot of the meadowed slope south of the chapel and stretches for over a mile to the west, the attention of the belated walker might be caught by two white shapes on a low hillock; at first glance they might be swans asleep. Two stones, in fact, strangely luminous in the gloaming, one of a pyramidal shape and about a yard high, the other a stubby block of the same size but fallen on its side. A little farther on a lane leads to the south, climbing around some curious little hills, a moraine left by the glacier that once pushed through the Ballynakill valley to Cleggan Bay. It is because of these hills that the area is called Sheeauns, or in Irish, Na Siáin, the fairy mounds; there is Sián Fada, the long fairy mound, Sián Mór and Sián Beag, the big and small fairy mounds, Conroy's Sián, topped by a circular cattle shelter that the long-departed Conroy built up out of the ruins of an ancient ringfort, and Sián na Cuaiche, the fairy mound of the cuckoo; I have never seen a place more conducive to the fairy faith. The lane continues past a few cottages, then the sound of a stream hidden in an overgrown gully begins to accompany the way, and after a little bridge and a bend to the west, one sees another stone gleaming in the twilight, a stout pillar about five feet high, among gorse bushes on a corner of rough land overlooking the stream. What are these ghostly stones that seem to come out at night?

Of course, the archaeologists have noted them in all the daylight science can cast on

An Gearrán Bán.
Photograph: Tim Robinson.

them, and determined that they are Bronze Age monuments, dating from between 2500 BC and 1000 BC. I will approach the questions of their concentration in the Ballynakill area, their significance to our age, and the less answerable one of their significance to those who erected them, through an account of my first sight of one of their sort, in the townland of Garraunbawn, another maze of lanes and fields and little hills a mile or so to the east of the old chapel of Ballynakill. At the time of my visit I had already gathered into my mind a number of bits of information about this place, fragmentary but intriguing, like shards of some antique decorated vessel. According to the experts I had consulted at the Ordnance Survey, 'Garraunbawn', the official townland-name, is an anglicization of the Irish 'An Garrán Bán', the white or fallow thicket, *garrán*, a shrubbery or thicket, being a common element in placenames. However, I had also dug out of the OS archives the 'field name books' kept by the surveyors who first mapped this area in 1839, and in one of these was a note saying that the Irish name of this place was 'An Gearrán Bán', the white horse. *Gearrán*, a gelding or small horse, is close in sound to *garrán*, and the difference between them — that subtle deflection of the g towards a *gy* — is lost, like so much else, in anglicization. Further, the old name book stated that the townland took its name from that of a rock, although it did not record the location of this rock. There was also a story I'd heard from a nonagenarian gentleman, formerly of Garraunbawn House, about a white horse that came up out of Garraunbawn Lake; a man caught it and saddled and rode it, and then took the saddle off and hung it over a rock, while the horse galloped away and plunged into the lake again. The mark of the saddle, my informant had heard, was still to be seen on the rock, but unfortunately he didn't know exactly where this rock was. Another hint had come from an archaeologist who told me that there was a Bronze Age standing stone on the

top of a small glacial hill or drumlin in Garraunbawn; in fact such a hill occupies most of the area of the townland.

I remember that it was on a particularly beautiful evening that the thread of my explorations led me through Garraunbawn. I pushed my bike up the lane, sunk between banks rich with wildflowers, that crosses the hill and, just at the top of the slope, I glanced through a gap in the hedge. There, in a meadow that fell away towards Ballynakill Bay and the vista of mountains beyond, was the standing stone. It was a stumpy boulder set on end, about five feet high, of milk-white quartz dappled with grey lichen, and in the twilight it looked exactly like the rump of an old white horse, peacefully grazing. I had previously noted a quartz vein exposed on the shore of an island in the bay below, from which big lumps of quartz had rolled out as the coast was cut back by the waves; perhaps some Bronze Age people rafted such a boulder across and lugged it up half a mile of hill to install it here. No doubt until the building of Garraunbawn House in about 1850 it was the most prominent object in the neighbourhood.

In fact I am sure that the stone is the mythical white horse itself, that the surviving version of its story, in which the man hangs the saddle over the stone, is an impoverished one, an attempt to mitigate the magic of an older tale and that in the eclipsed version the horse was metamorphosed into the stone. So, at that moment, looking through the hedge at the old stone horse cropping the grass on the hilltop, I could tie together a geological and an archaeological strand of Connemara's prehistory, and follow the efforts of later generations to make sense of that mysterious stone, first by means of a legend of an otherworldly horse, and then by tidying up that story already half forgotten and fossilized in a placename, which itself was later to be misunderstood and gelded by officialdom. For this place is not An Garrán Bán, the fallow thicket, but An Gearrán Bán, named from its ancient, perhaps totemic, white horse of stone, which has been ridden over the millennia by various meanings we can only guess at. The stone itself is as it always was and as a physical object needs no restoration; the restoration of its meaning as a contemporary monument, an icon of the locality's specificity, is the task of the topographer and a touch in the restoration of our eroded modern consciousness of place. But what of its original significance in the life-world of those who set it up? If anything can be recovered of that, it is only in the context of a wider enquiry into the prehistoric remains of Connemara.

At the time of my beginning to map the region, the prevailing opinion among archaeologists was that, compared to the riches of the Burren and the limestone plains east of the Corrib, not much was to be expected from these unwelcoming boglands beyond the half-a-dozen megalithic tombs and a similar number of standing stones recorded by nineteenth-century antiquarians, mainly in the area of Ballynakill. This view was soon to be confounded by the work of the Galway Archaeological Survey (GAS) team, emanating from the National University of Ireland in Galway and, in particular, the discoveries made by one team member, the indefatigably enthusiastic Clifden archaeologist, Michael Gibbons. The synchrony of the GAS's and my own campaigns in Connemara was productive; all the GAS finds went onto my own map, and the sites that I stumbled across myself or was directed to by local farmers or by placename evidence, were all promptly visited, verified and recorded by the specialists. It was an exciting time for me, mentally and physically stretching. One day, in the village street of Letterfrack, I saw Mike Gibbons sitting in his car, wrestling with the big sheets of the 1898 six-inch OS map; he told me that he had heard that turf-cutting had begun in an area of previously untouched bog, and he was off to see if any archaeology had been unearthed. I immediately abandoned the

rather tedious sketch-mapping of houses and shops I'd been engaged upon and joined him. We took the main road south-westward for about four miles and left the car in a turf-cutters' track leading off to the east, in the townland of Crocnaraw (Cnoc na Rátha, the hill of the rath — and we had already checked out the dilapidated little cashel-like enclosure from which it presumably derives its name). After a few hundred yards the track ended in a welter of mud and we turned to climb the small bog-covered hill ahead; I soon diverted to go and talk to some turf-cutters at work nearby, while Mike raced for the summit. Soon he came striding down to tell me that there were white stones up there. We went up together. A fresh turf-bank had recently been opened, a trench running across the rounded top of the hill, some six feet wide and a few feet deep, cutting down through the bog-stuff to bedrock — and there, gleaming in its blackish depths, were two massive chunks of white quartz. One stood on end, to a height of about four feet, and the other, a little larger, was prostrate and still partly embedded in the peat. Evidently they had been set up before the bog began to form, and had probably been lost to sight for thousands of years. Elated by the discovery, we looked around us, seeing the countryside, as it were, through the stones' eyes. Two miles to the north-east at the head of Ballynakill Bay was Rosleague (in Irish, Ros Liag, standing-stone headland), where we already knew of a standing stone now hidden in recent forestry and a stone pair in a gorse-grown field. In Roscrea, a little nearer in the same direction, was a well-known standing stone, a thin slab of schist set on edge, while just over a mile to the north was Garraunbawn and its stone. How many such monuments would be visible from the one we were standing by, were it not for trees and hedges? About a mile to our south-west, out in the bog on the further side of the road, was a small drumlin; we ran across and panted up to its summit — and there, just showing through the well-grazed heather and grass, was what looked like the top of a

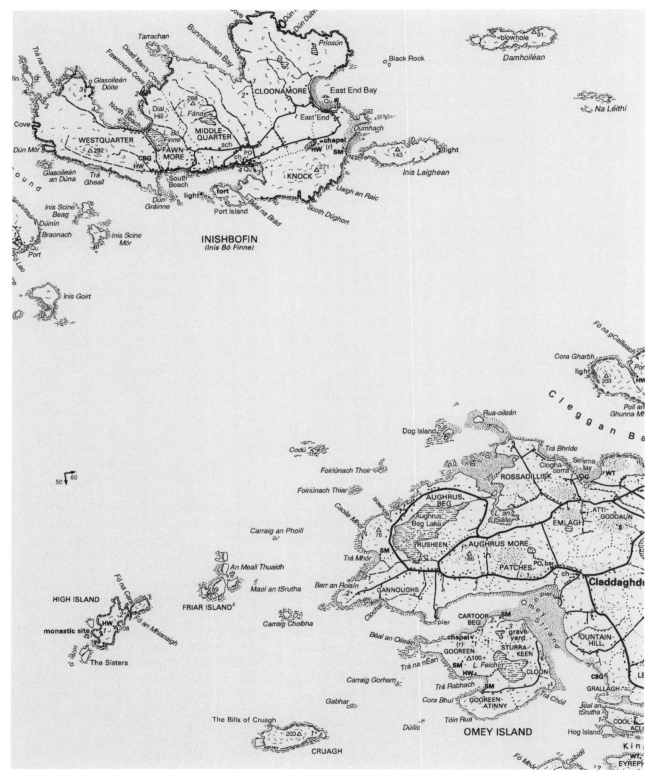

Detail of Tim Robinson, *Connemara, Part 2: A One-Inch Map …*
(Roundstone: Folding Landscapes, 1990)

SCALE
One inch to the mile (1:63360)

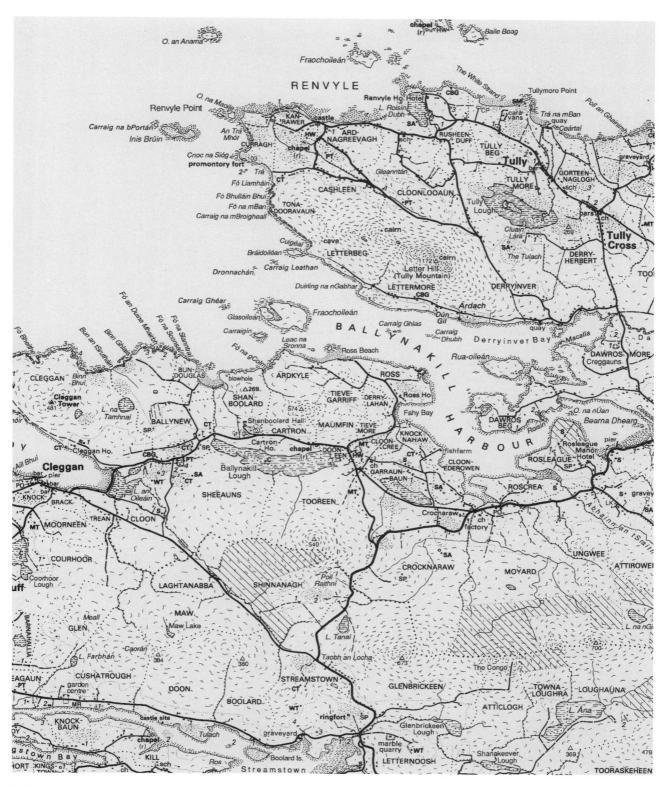

KEY
C crannóg or lake dwelling **CBG** children's burial ground **CT** court tomb **HW** holy well **MR** mass rock **MT**
unclassified tomb **PT** portal tomb **S** standing stone **SA** stone alignment **SP** stone pair **WT** wedge tomb

block of white quartz, still entombed in peat. Later on that summer I went up to the top of yet another drumlin three quarters of a mile to the south of this last, and found the edge of a horizontal slab of rock showing in the side of a new turf-bank there, a yard or so below the bog surface, which could well have been a thin standing stone like that of Roscrea, fallen or overthrown during the period of bog-growth.

The current reckoning is that, west of the Corrib, there are about eighteen single standing stones like that of Garraunbawn, ten stone pairs like that of Crocnaraw, and five rows of four or more stones, including the prominent Finn Macool's Fingers, on a drumlin summit near Tully Cross, and the six-stone row I found on the crest of a moraine in Gleninagh, a valley of the Twelve Pins. A large majority of these single and multiple standing stones are in the north-west, roughly between Clifden and Renvyle, and it is now recognized that they amount to one of the richest concentrations of such monuments in Ireland. This area is deeply penetrated by narrow bays reaching to the foothills of the Twelve Pins, cut by the sea into the lowland of soft schists and marbles. These lime-rich rocks, together with the drifts of till raked out of the mountains by the glaciers of the last Ice Age and deposited here, make this the most inviting part of Connemara to settlers; it was so in the late Stone Age and is so today. None of these sites has been excavated or accurately dated, and it is only because of their similarity to datable monuments elsewhere that they are assigned to the Bronze Age; however, studies of the pollen grains preserved in lake sediments in the area point to an increase in clearance, cattle-raising and crop-farming in the later Bronze Age, and so it is not unlikely that most of these stones were set up in that period.

As to their purpose, both of the stone rows mentioned above are aligned with dips in the horizon into which the sun appears

to set on the shortest day of the year, and no doubt some ceremony was involved in the observation of this phenomenon, which would have been of great practical and spiritual significance. While the standing stones perched on hilltops and glacial ridges, like the two mountain-top cairns also known from this vicinity, may have marked important burials, indicated boundaries, or focused religious rituals, their siting primarily suggests the outward gaze from a lofty centre, the eye of dominance — first cousin, I am forced to admit, to the eye of acquisitive enquiry and competitive discovery with which Mike and I swept the landscape that day from the top of Crocnaraw. To me it looks as if the Bronze Age people or peoples took mental command of territory through their highly visible monuments, triangulating their claims as tightly as the Ordnance surveyors of the imperialist nineteenth century. If so, there is a sorry connection between the will to power these monuments hint at, and the exploitation and depletion of the soil that contributed to the beginning of the formation of bog in about 1200 BC — the slow black tide that would swallow up their sacred stones, not to be revealed again until our own exploitative, turf-cutting times.

But if the world was already old in worldliness in those ancient times, it was as provoked by mysteries as it is still. What did the Bronze Age farmer make of the numerous structures, like chambers or tables made of massive slabs of rock, that stood in his fields or by his paths, just as one finds them in people's gardens or behind roadside walls in today's Ballynakill? In the nineteenth century, antiquarians regarded them as druids' altars, and one or two are marked so, in the evocative Gothic print reserved for ancient monuments, on old Ordnance Survey maps. For country folk such a structure was Leaba Dhiarmada is Ghráinne, Diarmuid and Gráinne's Bed, and everyone knew how Diarmuid ran off with Fionn Mac Cumhail's betrothed, Gráinne, and the pair were hunted all around Ireland by Fionn and his warrior band the Fianna, so that they never slept in the same place twice and built a new bed for themselves every night. That was a legend from Celtic times, the pre-Christian Iron Age, and what theories or stories the Bronze Age, a thousand or more years earlier, had to explain those monuments is of course unknown and unknowable. Unlike the Bronze Age monuments, they occur mainly in valley bottoms and by the seashore, and we now understand them to be Neolithic tombs dating from the earliest days of settled, agricultural society, around 4000 BC.

No fewer than thirty-two such tombs have been found in north-west Connemara, nineteen of them recent discoveries of Mike Gibbons. I visited most of them with the GAS team, who sometimes were accompanied by more senior visiting archaeologists such as the late Seán Ó Nualláin of the Ordnance Survey. I became fond of Seán, a plain-spoken, practical-looking and unacademic man, though my first contact with him had not been auspicious. When I was mapping the Burren in 1976, and lugging with me the weighty County Clare volume of the *Survey of the Megalithic Tombs of Ireland*, co-authored by Seán and the eminent Professor Ruaidhrí de Valera, I found I had wasted two days crashing around in dense hazel and bramble scrub looking for tombs, which, according to the map references in this magisterial tome, were in certain overgrown fields, whereas in fact they were in other overgrown fields nearby. I wrote to the OS about this, and received a polite acknowledgement from Seán, regretting the mistakes and thanking me for my contribution to the pursuit of truth. During the Connemara campaign, Seán told me that he had been a humble recruit in the OS, and archaeology had not entered his head until one day he had been detailed to assist 'this professor-fellow', Dr. de Valera, with his Megalithic Survey and found himself travelling round the country visiting every

known megalithic tomb in most eminent intellectual company. By degrees he became a collaborator in the work and, after the death of the professor, standard-bearer for the Megalithic Survey and the theoretical classification of tomb-types it had developed.

This theory recognized four types of tomb, which in those days were known as court cairns, portal dolmens, wedge-shaped gallery graves and passage graves, and nowadays are more crisply referred to respectively as court-tombs, portal-tombs, wedge-tombs and passage-tombs. Newgrange is the supreme example of the last type, with its long passage leading into a burial vault deep within a huge cairn; so far nothing like it has been identified in Connemara, though one or two hilltop cairns might conceal smaller versions. The other sorts of tomb were also originally covered in mounds of clay and small stones, but have largely lost this covering through the centuries of weather, and their now exposed vaults look like more or less collapsed chambers made of boulders and slabs of rock. Court cairns are so called because at one end, usually to the east, of the cairn was a semicircular open area defined by upright set stones, giving access to a vault of one or more chambers. Portal-tombs have two tall stones flanking the entrance to the vault, which is usually of one chamber and roofed by a sometimes enormous slanting stone propped on the portal stones and a lower backstone. Wedge-tombs have a vault that is wider and higher at the front, invariably western, end. According to de Valera, each type is associated with a characteristic range of grave-goods and has a particular distribution within Ireland. Court-, passage- and portal-tombs are largely confined to the northern half of Ireland and may represent successive cultural influences or population movements from northern Britain, while wedge-tombs are found particularly in the south-west and were considered to have been introduced from Brittany, late in the Neolithic period. Connemara was peripheral to this overview of megalithic culture, the few known wedge-tombs there being seen as conforming to 'rather small and poor types' constituting 'a poor coastal diffusion of no great significance'.

This fourfold theory did not suit the young Turks of Connemara, excited by the discovery of a number of tombs that the de Valera scheme would relegate to the mongrel or anomalous classes, but that included some impressive and fairly well-preserved monuments. Their own emerging opinion was that the Connemara tombs, in their simplicity, variety and apparently ecumenical intermingling, represented indigenous and early variations of the Neolithic burial-cult, rather than the work of various cultures at various times. The finds of monuments were being paralleled by those of the Galway palaeoecologists, whose studies of the fossil pollen record in the Ballynakill area had revealed the onset and flourishing of settlement and farming during a 200-year period centring on 4000 BC; Mike Gibbons and his colleagues held that the wedges and some small 'unclassified' tombs, as well as the court- and portal-tombs, were built during that early and vigorous phase of the Neolithic. So it was an argumentative occasion when Seán Ó Nualláin was conducted on a tour of the recent discoveries by the GAS team. In the absence of radiocarbon dates or of funds for proper archaeological digs, all depended on visual inspection, mental reconstruction and stylistic categorization of the tombs; in each case the present position of every stone had to be accounted for in terms of the original form of the tomb and its mode of collapse. Seán was particularly physical in this exercise of the imagination; to see him miming the manhandling of a leaning pillar of stone back into what he thought should be its rightful place was to see the tomb-builders themselves at work. Whether he succeeded in propping up the fourfold theory, I am not so sure. The final outcome of the GAS campaign, the *Archaeological*

Inventory of County Galway, employs the standard categories, listing 12 court-tombs, 4 portal-tombs and 6 wedge-tombs for Connemara, sharing out 11 question marks among these determinations and noting that in a number of instances 'the classification lines are blurred' and that others 'cannot be considered as classic examples of their category'; another 9 tombs, most of them robbed beyond recall of their stones, are left unclassified. Connemara has shaken but not yet overthrown the fourfold dogma, I think.

But however vague their theoretical status, the cumulative psychic presence of the tombs in Ballynakill is massive. Some, like the court-tomb near the shore west of Cleggan House, with its thick tortoise-backed roofstone, on stubby stone legs, or the unclassified tomb on the opposite shore of Cleggan Bay in Knockbrack, which has a rather narrow roofstone eight feet long, delicately poised, as if about to take flight, on the points of its few remaining uprights, stand in open land but seem to disassociate themselves from their surroundings and yearn towards the western sea horizon. Others have to be sought out in fields and thickets; one probable portal-tomb in Ballynew, by the road that leads toward the chapel of Ballynakill, crouches as if it were seeking for shelter under a gorse-bush behind the roadside wall, and the casual passer-by would not know it is there — but step over the wall and down into the hollow of the field, and the dozy weight and resigned slant of its displaced roofstone leaning against the darkly cavernous chamber will make you remember it in future. Those who brought these great stones together thought much about death; they perhaps debated as to whether entrance to the house of death should be from the east or the west, that is, how the cycle of life and death interlinks with those of the sun, stars and moon. These were collective burial places; none of the Ballynakill tombs has been excavated, but elsewhere similar tombs have been found to hold the cremated remains, or in some cases the disarticulated bones, of a number of persons. The grave-goods interred with them — pottery, tools, ornaments — indicate a belief in an afterlife in which such things would continue to be goods. Only the great would be accommodated so grandly and at such expense of communal effort. What of the common people? Their traceless burial places must be all around us, in every ditch and field and the foundations of our houses. Thousands of years of impious robbery and mindless weather have undone the forethought for survival of even the rich and famous. The dark hollowness of the tomb under the roadside gorse-bush says, 'There is nobody here, and you shall be nowhere too'.

But perhaps the Bronze-Agers saw things differently from their Stone Age ancestors and placed their trust in monuments to life rather than death. They practised unobtrusive single burials; a Ballynakill farmer has shown me a box made of stone slabs, big enough to hold a crouched body, torn open by a JCB in the sidebank of a newly dug roadway — one of their 'short cists'. In general their standing stones are not known to be associated with death. Some at least of the alignments of several boulders, and perhaps of the stone pairs, point out the midwinter sunset, but this event marks the winning-through to the halfway mark in survival of the season of shortage, a cause of celebration. The quartz stones, which seem to radiate light and call attention to themselves from afar, may have been as territorial as birdsong: 'We are triumphantly here, this hilltop and this lowland it oversees are ours.' And sometimes in the hush of midsummer half-light the glimmering stones of Ballynakill whisper to the imagination, 'You cannot see us, but we are still here.' Ghosts and fairies are moods and modes of one's feeling for the Earth; they wax and wane with our desires and delusions. The glimmer of white quartz, dim afterlife of its daytime brilliance, may persist throughout a long summer evening, but will succumb to the black rainy nights after Hallowe'en. ∎

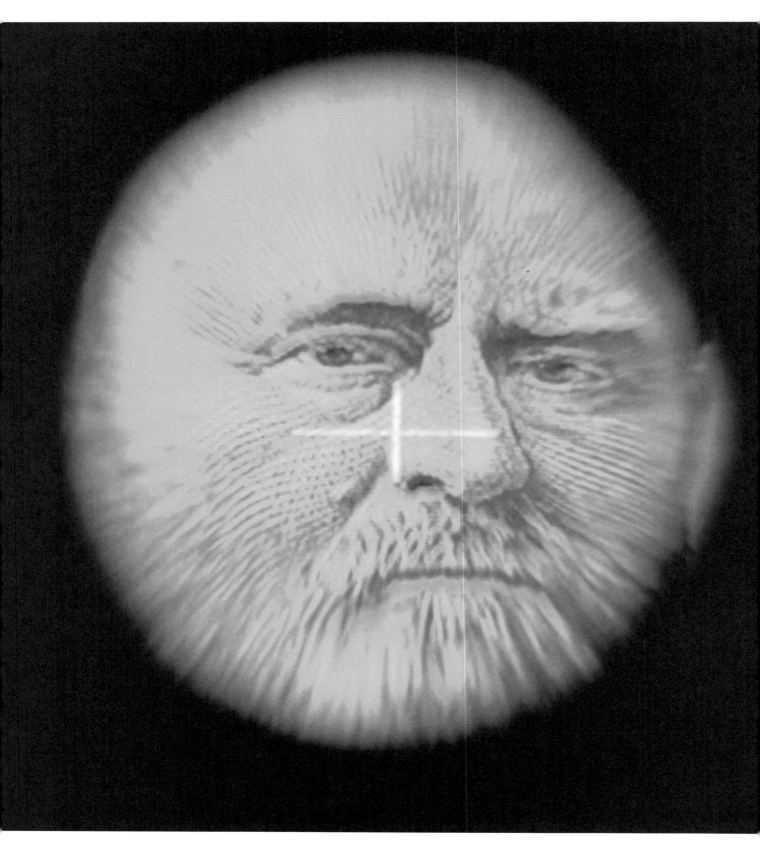

War, Counterfactual History, and Alternate-History Novels

Catherine Gallagher

'What if Grant had been drinking at Appomattox?' asked James Thurber in the *New Yorker* in 1930. That might have changed the history of the entire nation, he excitedly opined, and then went on to outline a ludicrous scenario in which the blotto Grant rises unsteadily and hands over his own sword to Lee when that general comes to surrender. Oops!

1   Mike Resnick, ed., *Alternate Kennedys* (New York, 1992)

2   Ward Moore, *Bring the Jubilee* (London, 1981 [1952]), all quotations are from this edition; Philip K. Dick, *The Man in the High Castle* (New York, 1974 [1962]), all quotations are from this edition.

Ulysses S. Grant on the fifty dollar bill, seen through the viewfinder of a television camera, 28 September 2004. Photograph: Mark Wilson/ Getty Images.

Thurber was satirizing a little spattering of lately published counterfactual historical essays reversing the outcome of the Civil War, the most notable of which was Winston Churchill's playful 'If Lee had not Won the Battle of Gettysburg'. In 1930 such suppositions were rarely seen in reputable publications, and so they were an obvious target of ridicule.

Today, though, counterfactuals (that is, hypothetical propositions that are contrary to the known facts of the historical record) are frequently used to initiate exercises in historical speculation, which are sometimes called 'what if' histories. Counterfactuals, we are told by historians who use them, must be plausible and should appear as real options in the historical record, and even when they are used to launch elaborate narratives, which are sometimes called 'alternate histories' or, more grammatically, 'alternative histories,' or (neo-logistically) 'allo-histories', plausibility should be maintained. We have all encountered these allo-histories, in which a slight change in circumstances sets off a chain reaction that takes the course of history in a direction dramatically different from that of actual events. Think, for example, of the annual November speculations in American newspapers about how United States history might have been if JFK had survived Oswald's

bullets. Although many newspapers dropped this feature after the fortieth anniversary of the assassination in 2003, you can still indulge your counterhistorical appetite for them in a volume entitled, simply, *Alternate Kennedys*.[1]

In this essay, the nature and history of allo-histories will be examined, as well as their kinship with a form of fiction — the alternate-history *novel* — that began to appear in the US in the 1950s and has grown by increasing magnitudes in each decade since. Three questions will be put to these two forms. First, why do most of them postulate a counterfactual outcome to a war? Second, why has their bulk and prestige grown with such rapidity in the sixty years following the Second World War? And, third, why do so many of them conjecture that the US lost wars it quite decisively won? The novels under examination are Ward Moore's *Bring the Jubilee* (1952) and Philip K. Dick's *The Man in the High Castle* (1962), and it will be the refrain of my argument that the novels tell us more about the reasons for our counterhistorical imaginings than do the allo-histories themselves.[2]

In an attempt to explain why most counterfactuals tell alternate stories of wars, it is necessary first of all to look more closely at counterfactuals in history. The history of allo-history certainly bears out this generalization. Isaac D'Israeli, the nineteenth-century English writer and father of the Prime Minister Benjamin Disraeli, is normally said to have inaugurated the genre of alternate history, and he was the first to call attention to it in an 1823 essay titled 'Of a History of Events which have not Happened'. His first and most prominent examples are military.[3] The Roman historian Livy, he points out, indulged in a lengthy speculation beginning with the counterfactual that Alexander the Great might have invaded Italy. And in Book IX of Livy's Roman History, we probably do find the first self-conscious and detailed use of alternate history.[4] Disdaining the Greek supposition that Alexander could have interrupted the growth of the Roman Empire, Livy shows where the Macedonian army would have invaded and ranged itself, where the Roman armies would have been at that moment and how many allies they could call upon. He even compares the two forces' weapons and modes of warfare, and, of course, he compares Alexander's generalship with that of the contemporary Roman generals he would have encountered as he tried to make his way to Rome. The point of the exercise was not only to praise the superiority of Roman armies, but also to bring into comprehensive view the full might of dispersed Roman forces in the time of Alexander.

D'Israeli recommended the use of such counterfactuals in military history precisely for their ability to present new perspectives on the facts, but he had a second motive for proposing their development into longer alternate histories. He thought such exercises, by stressing the contingencies of events and teaching analytical methods, would wean people from believing that the fortunes of war are decided by supernatural powers, be they interfering classical gods or the special providences of Christians,

Muslims, and Jews. D'Israeli, in other words, suggests that the ability to think counterfactually and to construct alternate histories of important wars measures the extent to which a nation's historians have joined secular discipline and have truly broken with the concept that divinely decreed necessity shaped the national past. He thus places counterfactualism at the heart of the modern historical enterprise, in which secular contingency replaces providential necessity.

D'Israeli suggested yet another reason for the mutual attraction between alternate history and military history. In describing Livy's counterfactual digression, D'Israeli describes the historian's behaviour in terms appropriate to a general: Livy 'arranges the Macedonian Army', has a 'momentary panic' when Alexander first comes into Italy, 'cautiously counts the allies', 'descends' to inspect the weapons, and finally 'terminates his fears' by 'triumphantly' 'bringing forth' the Roman generals. D'Israeli thus playfully indicates a special congruence in military history between historical actors and historians. In 1823 he could point only to the ancient example of Livy's digression, but ten years later the first detailed, book-length allo-history appeared in France: *Napoléon et la conquête du monde* by Louis Geoffroy, which opens with Napoleon's decision not to retreat after the burning of Moscow but instead to march on St. Petersburg. This improved strategy allows the emperor to proceed, through several hundred pages of crafty negotiations and imaginary campaigns, to the subjugation of all the world's peoples to a universal, but nevertheless French, monarchy. The delight of applying Napoleonic tactics better than Napoleon himself had done is conspicuous in Geoffroy's exuberant style and his unwillingness to miss any of the apocryphal Napoleon's brilliant military and diplomatic manoeuvres.

Although the first allo-historians, Livy and Geoffroy, gave themselves unusual

3 Isaac D'Israeli, 'Of a History of Events which have not Happened', in *A Second Series of Curiosities of Literature: Consisting of Researches in Literary, Biographical, and Political History; of Critical and Philosophical Inquiries; and of Secret History* (London, 1823), 253–68

4 Livy, *Historiae Romanae with an English Translation*, 14 vols. trans. B. O. Foster (Cambridge, Mass., 1919–67), vol. 4, 227–41

Leesburg, Virginia: The Confederate Army 1st Louisiana Tiger Rifles march to camp during the First Manassas Civil War Re-enactment, 3 August 2001. Approximately 20,000 people participated in the re-enactment of First Manassas, known as Bull Run to the Northern Union States, the first major battle of the US Civil War on 21 July 1861. Photograph: Paul J. Richards/AFP/Getty Images.

latitude in imitating military planners, their behaviour was not greatly different from normal military historians. The general looking forward and the historian looking backward both assess the dangers, the options and their consequences, and both must have plenty of contingency plans in mind. Military historians routinely reproduce the calculations and decision-making of commanders, entering deeply into their modes of speculation, in addition to describing the course of events. Moreover, since the archives of *modern* wars, especially, bulge with unused plans, even normal historians are drawn into numerous 'virtual' battles and campaigns that were thoroughly conceived and in some cases (such as that of the invasion of Japan's home islands to end the Second World War) meticulously prepared for, but never actualized, and these potential battles not only fill out regular military histories but also inspire the alternate historian. The fullness of modern historical war records, in other words, creates a thick penumbra of possibilities surrounding the actual events, and curiosity about those possibilities grows with their elaboration. Hence there is, for example, a thorough account of how Germany's 1940 invasion of Britain would have played out, based on both the German battle plans and the British defence preparations. The education of military leaders, moreover, encourages the alternate-historical imagination, stressing as it does exercises from which students in military schools (and now in some public schools) learn both strategy and the history of warfare. Working with computer models and simulations of past battles and campaigns, students now subtly transform particulars to see what might be learned from modified chains of events. Eventually these students will be able to produce some of the thousands of military scenarios, the imaginary wars, that fill the drawers and the hard drives of the Pentagon. In short, no enterprise in Western culture puts the question 'What if?' to both the future and the past more insistently than the military.

Despite the importance of counterfactual imagining in both the conduct and the history of warfare, fully fledged allo-histories like Geoffroy's used to be primarily the province of journalists and the writers of popular, rather than academic, history;

indeed, one of the early twentieth-century collections of alternate histories, which appeared in 1931, was subtitled *Lapses into Alternate History*. But today, quite respectable historians seem free to describe (sometimes in elaborate detail) how it might have been if only this or that battle had ended differently, this or that assassination had been prevented, this or that dictator had never been born. In the 1960s and 1970s counterfactualism became a debated topic among academic historians rather than just a trivial pastime, what E. H. Carr once dismissively called 'the parlour game of might have beens'. New statistical techniques developed in the sixties gave a boost to counterfactual arguments in (of all places) social and economic history, allowing, for example, Robert Fogel to calculate that, had the US railways not been built, the Gross National Product in 1890 would have been only slightly lower than it actually was.[5] Geoffrey Hawthorn, whose essays in *Plausible Worlds* come closer to narrative allo-histories, statistically undid the Black Death and imagined the cultural and intellectual effects of the demographic alteration in Europe.[6] Although counterfactual speculations remain highly controversial among historians, the technical virtuosity of such studies has gained them new respect, and historians now at least discuss counterfactuality with the gravity appropriate to methodological issues.

The objections remain, however, and to give a better idea of them, a clearer description of the structure of counterfactual speculation is necessary. Because allo-histories trace out, by some statistical or narrative process, the trajectory of untaken paths, their chronotope, their temporal pattern, resembles a bifurcating line — something like a capital Y. Time's arrow points upward, through a unified root or trunk of historical development to a juncture at which a rupture occurs and the branches diverge; the juncture is the critical moment (sometimes called the nexus) imagined by

the historian. Branch A (actual history) is generally taken for granted as the implicit comparative ground against which Branch B (counterfactual history) comes into view. For historians who oppose counterfactual history (and there are many), its most objectionable trait is its assumption that history could be conceived as a completely unified actuality at Time 1 and then reconceived as branches at Time 2, even though Branch B is understood to be merely in the conditional mood. The philosopher Benedetto Croce saw in this problem of the logical transition from Time 1 to Time 2, an illicit division of historical material into the necessary and the contingent:

> Under the sign of this 'if', one fact in a narrative is graded as necessary and another one as accidental, and the second is mentally eliminated in order to espy how the first would have developed along its own lines if it had not been disturbed by the second.[7]

Croce, in other words, objected to the fact that the stem of the Y is simply given as necessary, in the sense that all past events are 'necessary' because they happened, whereas something conceptually deletable, and therefore *historically* contingent (an oxymoron, according to Croce), is posited at the Y's juncture.

Croce may have misunderstood the type of analysis counterfactual historians undertake, but his criticism nevertheless helps us to understand why so many of these exercises take war, with its demonstrably contingent events, as their cruces. The preference for the combination of contingency and world-historical importance draws writers of allo-histories to all that is unpredictable, even implausible, in wars: to crucial battles between well-matched forces (such as the battles of Waterloo and Gettysburg), or to such mere (from a human point of view) randomness as the outbreak of the mysterious disease that decimated the

5 Robert W. Fogel, *Railroads and American Economic Growth: Essays in Econometric History* (Baltimore, 1964)

6 Geoffrey Hawthorn, *Plausible Worlds: Possibility and Understanding in History and the Social Sciences* (Cambridge, 1993)

7 Benedetto Croce, '"Necessity" in History', in *Philosophy, Poetry, History: An Anthology of Essays*, trans. Cecil Sprigge (London, 1966), 557. For a more up-to-date discussion of the uses and problems of counterfactual history, see 'Counterfactual History: A Forum', *Historically Speaking: The Bulletin of the Historical Society*, 4, 5 (2004), 11–32.

8   Niall Ferguson, *The Pity of War: Explaining World War I* (New York, 2000)

9   Robert Cowley, ed., *What If: The World's Foremost Military Historians Imagine What Might Have Been* (New York, 2000), xiii

Assyrian force laying siege to Jerusalem in 701 BCE. What if that enigmatic microbe had not appeared then and there, would there have been Judaism, monotheism, Christianity, Islam? To be sure, a growing number of these studies are now focusing on momentous *decisions*, implying that human agents are, at Time 1, undetermined in their choices and faced with real options, which the historian should try to re-create, along with their probable alternative consequences. In these allo-histories, conscious human deliberation, rather than accident, provides the contingency effect and allows for the branching at Time 2. Histories such as Niall Ferguson's *Pity of War* use counterfactuality (suppose that diplomat A had played his cards differently) to illustrate that human decision-makers, not wholly constrained by external conditions, shaped history at certain junctures and could have shaped it otherwise.[8] In the wake of the US elections in November 2006, Americans are intensely engaged in counterhistorical exercises about who is responsible for having misled US citizens into the disastrous war in Iraq. And these arguments regarding pre-war decision-making must also be counted among the military stories. The vast majority of allo-historians, though, are less interested in policy than in tactics and they prefer a tight nexus, so they tend to develop the implications of the alternate outcome of a single battle, the vagaries of the weather, or the accidental death, assassination, or failure to be born of a single world leader whose presence or absence would change our military history. As Robert Cowley, the respected historian of the Second World War, has pointed out, 'Nothing is more suited to "what if" speculation than military history, where chance and accident, human failings or strengths, can make all the difference.'[9]

We have, then, several reasons for the predominance of war stories among alternate histories. Wars are believed to be full of unpredictable turning points, meeting the criteria of both contingency and plausibility;

wars have long-range and wide-spread ramifications that affect all citizens in the nation, meeting the criterion of self-evident significance; and military histories themselves often stress not only the importance of contingency but also the vastness of the catalogue of alternatives used in planning. Add to these the obvious advantages that 1) most people know who won the major wars their countries fought, so readers will not become confused, and 2) readers are often attracted to histories with plenty of hectic and lethal action, and the predominance of military allo-histories seems almost inevitable. Assembling pieces of the post-war context allows us to see what stimulated the counterfactual imagination in the last half of the twentieth century. First, the development of alternative scenarios is an increasingly important activity in military institutions; we might also speculate that the Cold War draft, which gave a large percentage of young American men a taste of war-game training (many of them as non-commissioned officers), might also have helped spread those habits of thought into the civilian world. Meanwhile, among professional historians, breakthroughs in statistics and computing technology were eroding the resistance to counterfactualism in other fields of history, which seems to have encouraged more academic military historians to try alternate-history speculations.

※

Not all wars are equally interesting to alternate-history writers, however, and Americans seem fixated on two in particular: the Civil War and the Second World War. The remainder of this essay will be given over to analyses of one alternate-history novel dealing with each war: Ward Moore's *Bring the Jubilee*, which is concerned with the Civil War; and Philip K. Dick's *The Man in the High Castle*, which is concerned with the Second World War. The analyses will be used to continue elaborating the post-war context and as an aid to answering the second and third questions about what drove the genre's proliferation and why writers kept returning to the fantasy that the US lost both wars. The answers to those questions, as noted earlier, seem especially visible in the alternate-history *novels*. And so an outline follows of the differences between the sorts of allo-histories mentioned so far, and the novels that begin with similar premises, moving very fast through the most obvious generic differences and then slowing down when the structural distinctions that call for discussions of these particular novels and their contexts are reached.

The narrator's persona is probably the reader's first signal of generic difference. Allo-history writers normally pretend to be writing histories and imitate the historian's conventional expository style. Often they lay down rules in opening paragraphs, as in this introduction to an essay by Civil War historian Stephen Sears: 'Without improbably distorting actual events ... and without putting unspoken words into the mouths of the actors, then, imagine that this ... critical Civil War moment ... turned out [differently].'[10] He then goes on to narrate the allo-history in the past indicative. Allo-historians recount the action from the most objective perch possible, eschewing any stationary participant's point of view, and they base all conclusions about private consciousness on the (real or pretended) historical record. Kenneth Macksey's *Invasion*, for instance, starts off with a god's-eye view of England in the early days of the supposed German invasion by citing passages from the invented diary of a crew member in a German reconnaissance aircraft.[11]

The novelists, on the other hand, use the characteristic narrative features of fiction. Their narrators have full access to other consciousnesses; they frequently manipulate point of view and focus; they use free indirect style, along with its peculiar tenses, etcetera. These conspicuous differences conform to the genres' separate purposes.

Alternate-history novels attempt to create a complete alternative reality, presenting in detail the social, cultural, technological, psychological, and emotional totalities that result from the alteration, which is why they are often called 'alternate *world* novels'. The historical alteration in the novels permeates to the level of commonplace individual lives, where habits of thought, modes of speech, and routines of daily life are registered.

And, it almost goes without saying, in the novels the private and subjective ramifications of the alterations are explored through the normal novelistic devices of creating fictional characters integrated into plots that layer personal and national history. Allo-histories, on the other hand, seldom strive to imagine an entire social world, and they normally get along without fictional characters, although they sometimes provide historical personages with new scripts, taking care to remain true to the personalities as depicted in the history books. We might say that the novels give readers of alternate histories the same things that historical novels give readers of regular histories: a sense of what human qualities would be encouraged or discouraged; of how things would look, smell, taste, sound, and feel; how the alternate power relations and technologies would be experienced; etcetera. For example, Robert Childan in *The Man in the High Castle*, is an American businessman who caters to the alternate San Francisco's upper class: wealthy Japanese occupiers who buy 'Americana', the scarce remnants of pre-war popular American culture, like Mickey Mouse watches, Civil War posters, and old jazz records. Childan behaves obsequiously and strives to imitate what the book presents as refined 'Japanese' attitudes and manners. He speaks and even thinks in a 'Japanese' English idiom, from which articles and prepositions are frequently dropped. Usually suffering from acute feelings of anxiety and insecurity in relation to his Japanese customers, he is easily shamed, but occasionally vestiges of

10 Stephen Sears, 'The Confederate Cannae and Other Scenarios: How the Civil War Might have Turned Out Differently', in Cowley, *What If*, 241

11 Kenneth Macksey, *Invasion: The German Invasion of England, July 1940* (New York, 1980), 11–13

Edward, Duke of Windsor (1894–1972) with Nazi officers after his abdication. Photograph: Central Press/Hulton Archive/Getty Images.

his pre-conquest sense of racial superiority emerge. Childan is a portrait of the typical American forced to behave as the occupied Japanese actually did — politely — while suffering personal and national shame. The hero of *Bring the Jubilee*, Hodge Backmaker, also registers the subjective state of the conquered. He struggles against the backwardness, racism, anti-intellectualism, and perpetual indebtedness of the citizens in the conquered twenty-six United States of America. Like his fellow-citizens, he is emotionally numb but at least he has inherited from a maverick grandfather some intellectual ambition, which is almost impossible to satisfy in an early twentieth-century US without proper universities, publications, or transportation. Robert Childan and Hodge Backmaker, in short, are supposed to embody their allo-historical situations. You now have some plot information, but the argument in which it was wrapped is simply this: allo-histories

adhere to the conventions of history-writing and alternate-history novels conform to the conventions of novels.

Structural dissimilarities also follow a pattern, and in the course of examining them, the second question will begin to be answered: Why does the novelistic genre, almost unknown until the 1950s, become rapidly popular after the Second World War? Without giving away too much, let me anticipate my conclusion now by saying that both these novels can be read as attempts to assess just what it was the US won in that war. They were popular and are durable because they ask important questions — such as, are the American people living according to the principles for which they fought? And have they achieved the peace they anticipated?

Both alternate-history forms, as mentioned earlier, contain a crucial single moment, which serves both as a nexus linking the accepted past with the hypothesized alternative and as a point of departure separating the true from the altered. But the novelists and allo-historians use the pattern quite differently. Most noticeably, the novelists often accord both of the branches of the Y equal ontological weight inside the fiction. Instead of merely claiming, as the historians do explicitly or implicitly, that both branches are equally *plausible*, the novels often present them as equally *true* within the diegesis. That is why they are often categorized as fantasy or science fiction. The alleged equivalence of the prongs of the fork is easiest to see in Moore's *Bring the Jubilee*, where the first sentences present the entire narrative as the solution to a temporal enigma: 'Although I am writing this in the year 1877, I was not born until 1921. Neither the dates nor the tenses are error — let me explain: ...'[12] The explanation is that Hodge, seeking community and enlightenment, takes refuge from the chaos, bitterness, and depression of the conquered US on a commune in Pennsylvania founded two generations earlier by a former officer in the Confederate Army. There he becomes a historian of the Civil War, or as it is called in the alternate reality, the War of Southron Independence; he has a long, tortured relationship with a neurotic but brilliant physicist (this novel's version of a 'mad' scientist) who eventually figures out how to interface the space–time nexus with the matter–energy nexus, sending Hodge back in time to the Battle of Gettysburg, where he is careful to 'do nothing' to change the outcome. Ironically, by doing nothing, remaining silent when asked a crucial question about whether or not Union troops have moved up to the Round Tops that overlook the field, Hodge starts a panic among the Confederate troops, who were just about to occupy that high ground themselves. They not only beat a disorderly retreat from the orchard, leaving the little hills available for the Union forces, but also cause the accidental death of their commander, who happens to be the grandfather of the physicist. So no physicist, no time machine, and Hodge is therefore stranded in an 'elsewhen' (otherwise known as 'OTL' or 'Our Time Line'). We should note that although Moore's means of conveying his protagonist to the battle is certainly fantastic, what happens to him there is highly plausible. More to the point, however, is that the fiction represents both alternatives as solid realities. The rupture in the chronotope does not cancel the diegetic fact that Hodge inhabited the ATL (or Alternate Time Line).

Philip K. Dick's use of the two branches of the Y pattern is subtler than Moore's. In fact, one might argue that it is gratuitous, but we often see obedience to a formal imperative most clearly in fictional events that have no apparent reason for being there. In one such scene, Dick has his protagonist, Mr. Tagomi, accidentally transport himself into the actual San Francisco of 1962. Confused, Tagomi at first reflects: 'Mad dream. ... The whole vista has dull, smoky, tomb-world cast. Smell of burning. Dim gray buildings, sidewalk, peculiar harsh tempo in people. And ... no pedicabs. ... Only cars and buses. Cars like brutal big crushers, all unfamiliar in shape.'[13] Contemporary readers of *The Man in the High Castle* would have known Tagomi had stumbled into our world because one of the first sights he sees is a 'hideous misshapen thing on the skyline. Like nightmare of roller coaster suspended, blotting out view. Enormous construction of metal and cement in air.'[14] This satiric description of San Francisco's despised Embarcadero Freeway (finally torn down after the 1989 earthquake), combined with the concentration on dirt, smog, anxiety, noise, and incivility in Tagomi's perceptions, not only undercut the reader's assumption that real history is superior in all respects to the imagined alternative but also materialize the other branch of the alternate-history chronotope.

12 Moore, *Bring the Jubilee*, 1
13 Dick, *The Man in the High Castle*, 222
14 Dick, *The Man in the High Castle*, 222

15 Jorge Luis Borges, 'The Garden of the Forking Paths', in Donald A. Yates and James E. Irby, eds., *Labyrinths: Selected Stories and Other Writing* (New York, 1964), 26

16 Moore, *Bring the Jubilee*, 142

This Y-shaped chronotope in which the branches are equally plausible is familiar to contemporary readers from a couple of other contexts, which are here quickly described in order to fill out the intellectual world of these novels. Popular science fans might recognize an illustration of Hugh Everett's 'superspace', in which parallel realities proliferate. Dick borrows in this passage from the 'multiverse' explanation of the behaviour of quantum entities. Based on the mathematics of quantum mechanics, the theory is one of a number used to explain the uncanny behaviour of quantum entities when their wave-functions 'collapse' and the various possibilities they contain are resolved into a single outcome. The multiverse interpretation of their behaviour holds that *all possible outcomes always occur, each one in a separate universe,* but our observation is limited to the one outcome in the universe we inhabit. Given the overlapping readerships of popular science and science fiction, it is not surprising that Moore and Dick would make gestures toward multiverse theory.

We can see the same bifurcating time lines, moreover, in post-modernist formal narrative experiments of the sort that Jorge Luis Borges inaugurated in 'The Garden of the Forking Paths' in the late 1930s (not long after the multiverse theory was first developed). Borges's story (like Dick's) deals with a spy who knows the target of an air attack and is on an assassination mission. When he confronts the man he's supposed to kill, however, the spy becomes uncertain, and his target relieves him by letting him know that he is not in a traditional story where 'each time a man is confronted with several alternatives, he chooses one and eliminates the others'. Instead, he is in a story where 'he chooses — simultaneously — all of them. *He creates,* in this way, diverse futures, diverse times which themselves also proliferate and fork.'[15] *The Man in the High Castle*, imitating Borges, even hints at a proliferation of universes

by furnishing the alternate reality with a novelist who has written an alternate-history novel, called *The Grasshopper Lies Heavy*, in which the Allies won the war. Placed in these contexts, it would seem that the alternate-history novelists, although they parted ways with the allo-historians by affirming the equal reality of each alternative, were nevertheless keeping respectable intellectual company in the 1950s and 1960s.

They also had, though, what seems to be a more urgent reason for maintaining the parity of the alternatives: both works emphasize that their alternate worlds closely resemble some important aspects of current American reality. The defeated US in *Bring the Jubilee* is a nightmare version of the worst aspect of the Southern states during and after the Great Depression. It is a rural society in which most farmers are share-croppers; it is obsessed with racial separation, a fact that one character explains as the natural consequence of having 'lost a war, the most important war in our history' to end black slavery; African Americans were therefore viewed as the source of all the impoverished whites' misery.[16] The US is plagued by lynchings, is isolationist and narrowly provincial. Politically, its voters veer between electing oligarchic 'gentlemen' who sell them out, and demagogic 'populists' who cater to all of their prejudices. There is even a terrorist organization, like the Ku Klux Klan, which abducts and murders blacks and interfering foreigners. The educational system lags far behind the standard of the industrial South, where the wealthiest families send their sons to college. To be sure, the alternate Northron America is not an exact replica of the actual South, but an allegorical exaggeration, just as the novel's Southron America, with its emancipated but disenfranchised blacks, its advanced technologies, military and industrial imperialism, and international ambitions, is a caricature of the North. But the similarities are pointed enough to make the reader think that the alternate world in which Hodge grows up is really the South of OTL. In order to read the novel as the social commentary it clearly is, in other words, we have to recognize that both branches of the fork are simultaneously 'true': there is a world like Hodge's, and that world is the South. We might, therefore, see another chronotope shadowing the alternate-history/ actual-history bifurcation: the history of the US up until the failure of Reconstruction is figured in parallel lines, one for slave states, one for free. At the end of the Civil War there is a brief period of conjunction, after which there really are two countries with different time lines: one relatively static and the other more progressive. The ending of Hodge's narrative, supposedly written in OTL 1877, makes this point obvious: 'There are rumors of a deal between northern Republicans and southern Democrats, betraying the victory of the Civil War … in return for the presidency. If this is true, my brave new world is not so brave. … It may not be so new either.'[17] These last words of Hodge Backmaker provide an answer to the third question — Why imagine that the US lost the Civil War? — for they convert the alternate-history speculation, that perhaps the South was not defeated, into a historical fact.

Moreover, the novel's main themes point directly to the most widely publicized ways in which the South defeated its defeat: racial separation and educational deprivation. The one political sentiment that engages Hodge's passion is civil rights for black Americans, and the abiding ambition of his life is to acquire an education, and the novel gives us a complex interweaving of these two strands of the plot, too complex to be outlined here. Suffice it to say that Hodge's poverty threatens to deprive him of an education, while consorting with a black man ostracizes him socially. The joining of these two issues registers the immediate context of the novel's composition and publication (in 1950–52). A number of widely discussed legal cases

challenging Jim Crow laws came before the Federal courts in those few years, and the most pivotal charged that African Americans in many Southern states were denied an education equal to that of their white fellow-citizens. In the case of *Sweatt v. Painter*, a suit involving the University of Texas Law School in 1950, the U S. Supreme Court ruled in favour of the anti-segregationists, and that was the prelude to the court's landmark ruling in the case of *Brown v. Board of Education*. The last sentences of *Bring the Jubilee* acknowledge that historical turning points can be reversed, and therefore a real-life version of time-travel does exist. Replete with allusions to the turning point in North/South and black/white relations taking place at the moment of its production, Moore's novel seems to be both celebrating and issuing a warning: that we will have to be vigilant lest history repeat itself by *again* reversing itself.

In summary, unlike the allo-historians, the alternate-history novelists posit the ontological parity of the forks of the Y in order to indicate that their alternate worlds actually refer to our social reality and, in doing so, they reveal the contexts for the appearance of the form in the 1950s and 1960s. Indeed, one science-fiction writer has gone so far as to claim that alternate-fiction novels appeared in America in the last decades of the twentieth century because that was the period in which American history began to be reconceptualized in the light of the experience of ethnic and racial minorities.[18] *Bring the Jubilee* is certainly an important piece of evidence for that thesis.

But there are other contexts as well, which might best be viewed through another of the *structural* differences separating alternate-history novels and allo-histories: they deploy the convention of the nexus very differently. Alternate-history writers put their nexus in prominent places: it might come in the middle of the work, the narrator moving toward the point of departure for

17 Moore, *Bring the Jubilee*, 192
18 Brian Stableford, quoted in Eric B. Henriet, *L'Histoire revisitée: Panorama de l'uchronie sous toutes ses formes* (Amiens, 2004), 112.

Plans for a German invasion of Britain. Photograph: The Art Archive.

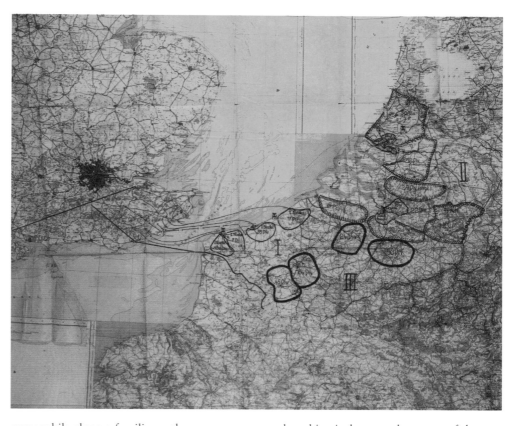

19   James M. McPherson, 'If the Lost Order hadn't been Lost: Robert E. Lee Humbles the Union, 1862', in Cowley, *What If*, 232

20   McKinley Kantor, *If the South had Won the Civil War* (New York, 2001), 13

some while along a familiar path, even covering the very ground of the nexus itself before backing up slightly, as does James McPherson in a Civil War narrative: 'The odds [he announces] against the [actual] sequence of events [just recounted] must have been a million to one [these have to do with the loss of General Lee's Special Order No. 191]. Much more in line with the laws of probability [McPherson continues] is the following scenario'.[19] Or they might begin with the nexus, as does McKinley Kantor: 'The death of Major General U. S. Grant came as a sickening shock to those Northerners who had held high hopes for a successful campaign in the West — for the reduction of Port Hudson and Vicksburg and the freeing of the Mississippi River from Confederate domination'.[20]

Allo-histories do not, like *Bring the Jubilee*, conceal the departure until the end, making it the central mystery of the book. Moore, however, uses the nexus as the climax, the moment we have been waiting for throughout the novel in order to make sense of his 'preposterous' opening sentence. Dick pays almost no attention to the nexus moment in *The Man in the High Castle*, but he nevertheless seems to recognize his generic obligation to produce one. He casually slips the nexus into a conversation that takes place well into the novel. At the point of its identification, all the major characters have been introduced, our attention is focused on their parallel but intertwining plots, and we may even have given up the expectation of a counterfactual nexus, so its appearance seems almost a gratuitous narrative sidebar. Moments in which characters must tell each other the history they are all tacitly supposed to share are by definition annoyingly contrived. Dick tries to minimize the awkwardness by presenting the departure moment during a counterfactual speculation voiced by a minor character who seems to have been introduced mainly to offer it, although she is merely giving the summary of the plot of the novel-within-the-novel, *The Grasshopper Lies Heavy*, which later also diverges from actual events: '[The] theory is that Roosevelt would have been a terribly strong President. As strong as Lincoln. ... [If] Roosevelt isn't assassinated in Miami; he goes on and is reelected in 1936, so he's President when Germany attacks England and France and Poland.'[21] The nexus — the assassination of Roosevelt — is predictable, but it still needed to be stated.

In these quite different ways, Moore and Dick signal that their novels will concentrate on the world produced by a Confederate or an Axis victory rather than on *how* those victories came about. Whereas the allo-histories are often war stories in the most concrete sense, the best of the novels tend instead to ponder life in the aftermath. And this brings us once again to the third question about why victory is imaginatively turned into defeat: Why in the post-war period did we begin imaginatively to snatch defeat from the jaws of victory? Previously, allo-historical imaginings often took the wishful form of 'if only' fantasies, like Geoffroy's apocryphal Napoleon or any one of the pro-Confederate replays of various battles that were published between 1905 and 1930. In the post-Second World War period, we see a rise in the percentage of 'what if' speculations written on the assumption that the alternative was not preferable. No doubt in the first decades after the war, especially as the public gained a clearer sense of the horrors perpetrated by Nazi Germany, imagining an Axis victory allowed some Americans to express their new sense of the extent of the disaster averted; as in the wake of a traumatic near-encounter with death, people talk over how close they came to annihilation. No doubt, too, writers who drew dystopian portraits

of life after a Confederate victory, like Ward Moore, were also partly motivated by a desire to prove that *it could have* happened in the US: in his alternate Americas there are massacres and expulsions of Jews and Asians, as well as African Americans.

If the emotional tone of some alternate histories and alternate-history novels is relief, though, the most widely and continuously read of the novels, as has been demonstrated in the case of *Bring the Jubilee*, keep a strong sense of the continuing presence of the danger. In the aftermath of the most destructive and world-altering war ever fought, these novelists keep alive the issue of who wins the peace. Moore strongly suggested that the South, after a short interval, succeeded in becoming a separate polity, and Dick also points, at the conclusion to *The Man in the High Castle*, to a similar irony regarding the aftermath of the war in the Pacific. In that novel the Japanese rule is already threatened by their former allies', the Nazis', lust for world domination. The Germans are about to attempt to annihilate their Asian allies in a sneak nuclear attack. The fantasy, therefore, makes America's nuclear attacks on just two cities look benign in comparison to what the Nazis *would have done*. Moreover, the thesis that the Japanese were winners as well as victims harmonizes with the consensus view in both countries by the 1960s: that Prime Minister Shigeru Yoshida was prescient when he claimed that it was possible to lose a war and yet win a peace. *The Man in the High Castle* illustrates the corollary point: that it would have been possible for Japan to win the war and yet lose the peace. At its ending, Dick reveals that the alternate-history novel-within-the-novel, *The Grasshopper Lies Heavy*, in which America and Britain are imagined to have won the war but also to be fighting each other ten years later, possesses 'inner truth': in some 'essential' way Germany and Japan lost the war. Extrapolating (as we are clearly supposed to) to the alternate-history novel we are reading,

21 Dick, *The Man in the High Castle*, 61

it follows that its 'inner truth' is that, in some 'essential' way, the Allies lost the war. They lost, the novel implies, because seventeen years after the cessation of the Second World War, before and during the Cuban missile crisis, the victors appeared to be on the brink of mutual destruction through nuclear war. Dick implies that America and the Soviet Union lost the war because they never really ceased to be at war. If American citizens thought that winning the war would give them peaceful security, their expectations were disappointed. It was the winners, not the losers of the Second World War, the novel bitterly concludes, who were condemned to permanent states of war.

These novels remind us that the era of the Cold War, containing the struggle to end segregation, was a prolonged aftermath like none before it; amidst Americans' guilt, fears, anxieties, consciousness of gross racial injustice, continuing wars and constant alerts at home about how to protect themselves against the nuclear genie they had let out of the bottle, it was difficult for many fully to realize that they were supposed to be in a period of unprecedented peace and prosperity. Counterfactual narratives in which *just* wars are refought and lost were ways of coping with their difficulty. And within those texts, the alternate-history novels especially reveal the troubled historical situation that produced them. These novels are powerful reminders that, despite the unconditional surrender of America's enemies, justice and peace still eludes its people. ■

Why Irish History Starved
A Virtual Historiography

Guy Beiner with **Joep Leerssen**

The emergence of a 'New Irish History' has been hailed as a 'historical revolution'. Here **Guy Beiner** and **Joep Leerssen** debate the development of historical scholarship in Ireland and, in particular, the rejection of antiquarianism by professional historians.

1 Niall Ferguson, 'Virtual History: Towards a "Chaotic" Theory of the Past', in Niall Ferguson, ed., *Virtual History: Alternatives and Counterfactuals* (London, 1999 [1997]), 1–90

2 Ferguson, 'Virtual History', 87, 64; the emphasis is in the original.

Paul Mosse
Catacomb
2004
acrylic, plywood, sawdust, glue, wire, foam
105 x 107 x 22 cm
courtesy of the artist and Green on Red Gallery

BEINER: The temptation to indulge in counterfactual speculations is tantalizing. What if there had been no 'Protestant wind' in 1796 and the French had landed in force at Bantry Bay? Or if O'Connell's monster meetings had succeeded in repealing the Union, if the masses had rallied to Young Ireland's confederate flag and risen in 1848, if one of the Home Rule Bills had successfully passed, if the anti-Treaty irregulars had defeated the Free-Staters in the Civil War and declared a republic in 1923? The possibilities are endless, but perhaps the only viable counterfactual is: what would have happened had the study of Irish history developed in a radically different direction?

In a ninety-page essay on 'virtual history', Niall Ferguson forcefully presented a (perhaps overstated) case for the value of historical counterfactuals. Counterfactuals can undermine teleological thinking and offer an escape from the pitfalls of historicist determinism by reminding us that the past was, to borrow from Jorge Luis Borges, a 'Garden of Forking Paths' (*Jardín de senderos que se bifurcan*). Virtual history is useful in reminding us that things *could* have been different. However, it is not clear that historians can actually sketch out the development of alternative pasts. Chaos theory, which examines stochastic behaviour

in deterministic systems, may appear to offer new possibilities for historians straddling the dilemma of contingency and causation, yet such analysis, as Ferguson concedes, inevitably results in 'unpredictable outcomes even when successive events are causally linked'.[1] The possibility of writing 'chaostory' is undermined, in practice, by the infinitude of incommensurables, environmental and human. For all their knowledge of the past, historians have a dismal track record in predicting future outcomes (the collapse of the Iron Curtain may serve as the ultimate cautionary case). Moreover, academic historical training does not encourage its practitioners to imagine anything beyond the boundaries of what is already familiar. Historiography, on the other hand, is perhaps one of the few fields in which historians are consciously aware of practically all the conditions and determining factors. It could therefore be reasonably argued that the only feasible form of virtual history is virtual historiography.

Ferguson was interested in a quasi-factual, counterfactual history of '*how it actually wasn't* — but how, to contemporaries, it might have been', as opposed to a focus on that history of *mentalités* and historical consciousness characteristic of the new cultural history; this, he avers, 'represents a relapse into antiquarianism'.[2] But we find that it is the spectre of antiquarianism which was taken to be a threat at the very moment of the professionalization of history. Irish historians have been told that 'we are all revisionists now', but is that, in the words of *A Memorable History of England*, a 'Good Thing'?[3] Small as it is in size and population and despite its peripheral location on the outskirts of Europe, Ireland's cultural contribution to the world is truly remarkable. Ireland has been repeatedly and innovatively 'invented' in its art. Historians have undeniably written many fine works and contributed much to a better understanding of Ireland's past, yet it is hard to think of Irish historians who have made international innovations that have changed the way we understand history.

On the other hand, historians who took an active part in the professionalization of Irish history, or who see themselves as the inheritors of its legacy, have frequently described the process as a 'historical revolution'. This self-congratulatory tone could be tempered by some Burkean reflections on the historical 'revolution' in Ireland. Tradition was so thoroughly consigned to the dustbin that a reading of the 'revisionist debate', which rarely shows any long-term historiographical awareness, raises the question if there was *any* history writing of value in Ireland prior to the launch of *Irish Historical Studies* in 1938. W. E. H. Lecky, of course, stands out as the only Irish historian to have made it to the centre stage of British historiography. At least in some ways, this great Victorian champion of rationalism, an unreconstructed liberal (and as such, extremely wary of democracy and deeply suspicious of the masses) and a pioneer of archival research into the Irish State Papers, anticipated what would later be known as the 'New Irish History'. Seen in this light (and there are other facets to Lecky), he is a precursor of and not an alternative to academic historiography in its current form. We are routinely presented with a Whiggish interpretation of Irish

historiography that begins with Lecky, then undergoes a 'glorious revolution' in the 1930s and is then reinvigorated by the missionary spirit of iconoclastic revisionism in the 1980s. This, in its triumphalism, has consigned all other voices to the kind of roles once attributed to 'Jacobite reliques'. Here, unmistakably, is a teleology waiting to be questioned. As in the 'Whig version of the course of history', here too can be found 'certain methods of historical organization and inference — certain fallacies to which all history is liable', which Herbert Butterfield famously deplored.[4]

Kevin Whelan has criticized the Irish historical revisionism of the 1930s for being parochial, denouncing it for its 'insulation from the intellectual revolt in historiography spearheaded by Marc Bloch and Lucien Febvre in France, and signalled by the advent in 1929 of the innovative journal *Annales*'.[5] The historiographical counterfactual in this critique assumes that if the professionalization of Irish history had taken its direction from the University of Strasbourg and subsequent historical developments in Paris rather than from the Institute of Historical Research in London and Peterhouse College in Cambridge, it would have been at the cutting edge of European historiography. Yet that too would have been a form of mimicry. In contrast, the various novel artistic movements in Ireland seem to have sprouted out of a creative engagement with long-standing traditions. Nowhere has it been considered what would have happened if a distinctly Irish historiography had emerged from indigenous antiquarian traditions of writing history. Under the surface, there appears to be an a priori assumption that any such evolution would have been inherently sectarian and ridiculously amateurish.

Leerssen: But then again ... 'what if' ain't history, and we should be wary of the metaphor of Forking Paths. That metaphor describes plot lines, not events, and there

3 Roy Foster, 'We are All Revisionists Now', *Irish Review*, 1 (1986), 1–5. See W. C. Sellar and R. J. Yeatman, *1066 and All That: A Memorable History of England* (Stroud, 1993 [1930]). This witty parody of English schoolbook history, 'comprising all the parts you can remember', lists 103 'Good Things'. It only includes several passing references to Ireland, such as ridiculing 'Blood-Orangemen' for being 'so loyal that they are always ready to start a loyal rebellion', while commenting that after the Battle of the Boyne 'the Irish who remained were made to go live in a bog and think of a New Question'; see 87–88.
4 Herbert Butterfield, *The Whig Interpretation of History* (London, 1931), v
5 Kevin Whelan, 'The Revisionist Debate in Ireland', *boundary 2*, 31, 1 (2004), 185

6   Reinhart Koselleck,
     *Vergangene Zukunft.
     Zur Semantik
     geschichtlicher Zeiten*
     (Frankfurt, 1979)

is a specious fallacy in the notion that the Course of History (a term which is itself a descriptive extrapolation from historical narrative, not a description of the past) would have Turned Out All Different if a certain event had panned out otherwise. Most of us nowadays see our world as a chaotic welter of free-floating contingencies — the 'butterflies and hurricanes' paradigm; but that is only one way of looking at things.

Anyone with a word processor can check this out. Take a long document with a 'tight', densely filled and heavily footnoted page layout. One might expect that by adding or deleting a word or even a sentence, the different line-breaks, paragraph-lengths and page-breaks would ripple throughout the rest of the document, possibly having a knock-on effect that will eventually cause the document to occupy one or two pages more, or less. However, contrary to that expectation, you will find that invariably, after one or two pages, the document will retain its original page-breaks despite the alteration. In other words: alterations do not necessarily spread into widening chain reactions. Not all hurricanes are caused by fluttering butterflies, and many a flutter failed to became a storm. There is a noticeable tendency for surface destabilizations to be buffered back into the inertia of a default state.

So too with the course of history. We tend to read Borges's story of the 'Garden of the Forking Paths' too much through the eyes of Robert Frost, whose 'path not taken' stands for an irreversible life-choice. But although single choices and incidents may later be remembered and invested with symbolism (or 'importance', or 'meaning'), they rarely make 'all the difference' in the larger scheme of things. Indeed Borges's story argues precisely that point: the entire 'Forking Paths' episode is only a footnote to the fact (related in the story's opening paragraph) that a battle scheduled for 24 July 1916 was postponed for five days, owing to torrential

rains; the narrator comments that the delay 'lacked any special significance'.

One of the first things first-year history students learn is to avoid 'monocausality': the idea that important historical situations can be adequately explained from one single cause. They are always the outcome of many contributory causes, which hang together and interact in complex ways. 'What if' history is monocausality in reverse: it presupposes that the alteration of one single event might have overturned the entire complex web of manifold causes and their interrelated effects.

I don't want to stumble into the opposite error — that of determinism, the idea that human agency and choices are insignificant in the preordained scheme of developments — but the case against the Path Not Taken model needs to be made. In history, there are *no* Paths Not Taken. Everything has been attempted, all scenarios have had their zealots and proponents, all arguments have been raised, and even the models and ambitions that failed to achieve dominance in actual practice are still there for us to resuscitate and retrieve. History is not just a successive series of events; it is also a cumulative growth of models, outlooks, examples. We cannot re-enact past events, but we can still read the books that have come down to us.

As Reinhart Koselleck reminds us, history is not just the track record of how things turned out the way they did; the task of the historian is also to reconstruct the hypothetical scenarios that were present and operative in the past, as models of inspiration or fear, without ever having been realized (say, the possibility of a Union between Great Britain and Ireland in the 1720s, or of a Redmondite or 'Dual Monarchy' settlement in the 1910s).[6] The past carries within itself, within the experience of its actors and protagonists, a plethora of potential futures, none of which can be neglected by the historian. Within that overwhelming multiverse of 'past futures', the fictitious counterfactual option of Hitler having died at birth, Napoleon having won the Battle of Waterloo, or Trinity College Dublin historians having become *Annales* adepts in the 1930s, becomes a piece of flippancy. It confuses two modes of irreality: the fictional and the potential.

In setting up a Paths not Taken model, we run the risk of losing ourselves in a poetically binate rhetoric. On the one side, we see history as it turned out to be: academic, jejune, factualist, revisionist, "liberal"-elitist. On the other side, we are given all the lost opportunities, creative, poetical, the lost heritage of antiquarianism, democratic. That schematization is loaded from the outset. For one thing, Lecky deserves to be remembered for the victory he won in his showdown with James Anthony Froude, not to mention his multivolume *History of European Morals from Augustus to Charlemagne* (1869) which places him in the company of intellectual historians such as Henry Hallam, Henry Thomas Buckle and Leslie Stephen.[7] For another, the rule of the *Annales* school, here cited by Whelan as a comment on the parochial tweediness of the TCD historians, resulted in the profession's stultifying and arid preoccupation with economic infrastructures and demographics throughout the mid-twentieth century. I cannot imagine that its adoption among Irish historians (who in any case were far from ignorant of that approach) would have constituted a 'Good Thing'. I am very certain, on the contrary, that being a revisionist is a Good Thing. More than that, it is an indispensable thing. It is for the historian what Salvadore Dali said about being modern: not an aspiration, but an unavoidable condition. All history-writing is by definition revisionist; that's what makes it different from novel-writing, that's what makes it an academic field of research rather than just a genre in *belles-lettres*.[8] If we see no reason to revise previous histories, we can just reprint the old ones and close down our departments. Is that what we want: just reprint the Good Old Boys, return to the days when it was still Fun and we did history to reaffirm our certainties as to who were the Good Guys (us) and who the Bad Guys (them)?

Faced with the multifariousness, the contradictions and the clashes of the present, I perceive everywhere a tendency to represent the past as a situation of homogeneous integrity, something unitary, at least in the moral terms of who mattered, who was the Hero of the Tale, the protagonist we identify with. What history (as opposed to antiquarianism) shows, is that the past was at least as fraught, contradictory and torn as the present, and that understanding the past means trying to enter into alien points of view, even those of the Bad Guys. The danger of a new Antiquarian Turn is that it leads us into an a-critical direction. Nietzsche, when distinguishing three different modes of history-writing, identified them as monumental, antiquarian and critical. None of us these days is much into Monumental History (although the celebratory mode is still with us, from Christy Moore's execrable song 'Irish Ways and Irish Laws' to the movie *Michael Collins* (1996) and the more popularizing publications in Eason's or Waterstone's); but going antiquarian must not mean that we can use it as a pretext to become less critical. Are we, by any chance, nostalgic for a Paradigm Lost, like a path not taken in the woods on a snowy evening?

Beiner: There is a Kuhnian logic in labelling antiquarianism a 'lost paradigm' (on a par with, let's say, pre-Copernican astronomy). Is antiquarianism essentially antiquated, an outdated practice which by its very nature could not have survived into modern (let alone post-modern) times? Just as historiography follows developments in the study of history over time, antiquarianism

7 See my *Komparatistik in Grossbritannien. Eine Einführung* (Bonn, 1984), 57.

8 On the distinction between history and fictional narrative, including the agonistic element that makes historians 'rewrite' in an 'against-their-predecessors' mode, see Ann Rigney, *The Rhetoric of Historical Representation: Three Narrative Histories of the French Revolution* (Cambridge, 1990), and *Imperfect Histories: The Elusive Past and the Legacy of Romantic Historicism* (Ithaca, 2001).

9   Clare O'Halloran,
    *Golden Ages and
    Barbarous Nations:
    Antiquarian Debate
    and Cultural Politics in
    Ireland, c. 1750–1800*
    (Cork, 2004), 3
10 Arnaldo Momigliano,
    'Ancient History and the
    Antiquarian', *Journal
    of the Warburg and
    Courtauld Institutes*,
    13, 3–4 (1950),
    285–315; Arnaldo
    Momigliano, *The
    Classical Foundations of
    Modern Historiography*
    (Berkeley, 1990)

also has an 'antiquariography', which shows it to be a constantly evolving field, influenced by cultural trends that are part of a wider international intellectual discourse. Though antiquarians may have championed a static, or spatial, conceptualization of history, the practice itself was by no means static but under continuous development. In a sense, antiquarians were also 'revisionists'. Antiquarianism responded to an internal crisis in the nineteenth century by effectively undergoing an overhaul and introducing more rigorous self-criticism into its scholarship. Moreover, antiquarians in Ireland were in constant dialogue with scholars across Europe and were informed of shifts in wider cultural–scholarly trends. It would therefore be 'virtually a-historical' to contemplate eighteenth-century or early nineteenth-century scholarship persisting unchanged into today's world.

For example, Protestant antiquarianism in Ireland was originally an Anglican affair and there was apparently little, if any, Irish Presbyterian antiquarian writing in the eighteenth century.[9] However, this was clearly not the case for the thriving nineteenth-century Presbyterian antiquarian scene in Belfast and its environs, which emerged in the middle of the century and went through a transformation around the *fin de siècle*. Significant developments in the scholarship of northern antiquarianism are evident from a comparison between the first series (1853–62) and second series (1894–

1911) of the *Ulster Journal of Archaeology* (and its many monographic offshoots).

Part of the virtual challenge is to envisage how antiquarianism would have continued to evolve had it been given a chance. Contemplating the perseverance of antiquarianism should therefore not be a sweeping negation of the professionalization of Irish history, but rather an exercise in imagining other ways of professionalization. Arnaldo Momigliano is particularly insightful in this context, as his take on the emergence of modern history is not one of a Rankean rupture with an antiquarian past but of a convergence (that pre-dates Leopold von Ranke) of classical traditions of history and antiquarianism, which he characterized as a reclamation of a lost Herodotean historical tradition that transcended the limitations of the predominant Thucydidean tradition of political-diplomatic-military history.[10] The notion of a rediscovery of an ancient historical tradition rather than a new invention is of course in line with the self-perception of antiquarians, who regarded their practice as a relic of antiquity (though Varro's *Antiquitates* would be the appropriate classical model, rather than Herodotus).

The decline of antiquarianism and the rise of professional history is part and parcel of the same process. However, since antiquarianism continued to flourish into the early twentieth century, one should be weary of setting a premature 'time of death'.

David Quinn
vent
2005
mixed media on panels
14 x 10 cm
courtesy of the artist and the
Kevin Kavanagh Gallery

Phillipa Levine has portrayed the officials of the Public Record Office in London as the first practitioners of professional history and suggested that the use of archives may distinguish between professional historians and antiquarians. Yet she observed that in the early years archives were frequented by antiquarians.[11] Furthermore, was it not J. T. Gilbert, an antiquarian, who set up the Public Record Office in Dublin? It would be more accurate to claim that, unlike positivist historians, antiquarians did not confine themselves to the archive but enthusiastically engaged with a wide range of sources that were later pushed out of Irish historical studies, such as Gaelic (Irish language) literature, material objects and oral traditions.

Ciaran Brady's survey of Irish historical revisionism noted that the Ulster Society for Irish Historical Studies and the Irish Historical Society — the flagships of what was to become the 'New Irish History' — made a point from the outset of discouraging antiquarian studies.[12] This conscious determination to reject antiquarianism is the historical moment that begs to be revisited. There is of course a long history of historians denigrating antiquarians but this exclusion from the respectable halls of a newly institutionalized academy dealt antiquarians a knockout blow from which they could not recover. In the early twentieth century historians and antiquarians could still make common cause in seeking to preserve archival records.[13] Later on, such co-operation was no longer tenable. For example, J. C. Beckett's introductory comments to one of the volumes of the *New History of Ireland* exemplify the demonization of antiquarians as those who 'impeded rather than advanced the cause of scholarship'.[14] Such rhetoric from the mouth of an assertive new historical establishment marks antiquarians' fall from grace — the transition in their image from torch-bearers of erudition to Luddite saboteurs. The important

contributions of antiquarians were all too readily dismissed and forgotten.

Seen in this light, the professionalization of the study of history can be construed as a colonization of the past by metropolitan-trained historians — a ruthless power struggle in which antiquarians (among other long-established interpreters of history) were ousted. In the name of modernity and progress, indigenous historiographical traditions were laid to waste and, in consequence, Irish history in this 'post-colonial' condition is all the poorer for its rejection of antiquarianism. To be fair, there may be another, more rounded, way of looking at the issue: perhaps remaining antiquarians also retreated in face of the political developments of the early twentieth century. The case of Francis Joseph Biggar, the iconic antiquarian of the period, is instructive, as partition seemed to deal a death blow to his life's work. All the same, antiquarians were marginalized and no longer treated with respect.

In practice, antiquarianism did not disappear wholesale but mutated into new forms. Its stubborn survival is comparable to the case of the so-called decline of magic (as charted by Keith Thomas), which seems to have gone underground only to later re-emerge in the guise of modernist spiritualism, New Ageism and a widespread fascination with the paranormal. Similarly, neo-antiquarianism crops up in various popular (if not populist) presentations of pseudo-science and sham-history. Nonetheless, not all remnants of antiquarianism have been co-opted by cranks and subsumed into counterculture (or perhaps post-modern popular culture). Old-style antiquarian erudition evolved into a wide range of recognized scholarly disciplines. Archaeology is the widely acknowledged heir apparent of antiquarianism but it does not stand alone. First of all, this pedigree could be extended to ethnological studies

11 Philippa Levine, *The Amateur and the Professional: Antiquarians, Historians, and Archaeologists in Victorian England, 1838–1886* (Cambridge and New York, 1986)

12 Ciaran Brady, 'Constructive and Instrumental: The Dilemma of Ireland's First "New Historians"', in Ciaran Brady, ed., *Interpreting Irish History: The Debate on Historical Revisionism 1938–1994* (Dublin, 1994), 4

13 See R. D. Edwards, 'An Agenda for Irish History, 1978–2018', in Brady, *Interpreting Irish History*, 56.

14 See J. C. Beckett, 'Introduction: Eighteenth Century Ireland', in T. W. Moody and W. E. Vaughan, eds., *A New History of Ireland*, vol. 4, (Oxford, 1986), lx–lxiv.

15 Momigliano, *The Classical Foundations of Modern Historiography*, 155

16 See Diarmuid Ó Giolláin, *Locating Irish Folklore: Tradition, Modernity, Identity* (Cork, 2000), 35–37.

17 See Gillian Doherty, *The Ordnance Survey: History, Culture and Memory* (Cork, 2004).

18 E. Estyn Evans, *The Personality of Ireland: Habitat, Heritage and History* (Cambridge, 1973)

19 See for example, Roy Foster, 'History and the Irish Question', in Brady, *Interpreting Irish History*, 128–29.

20 *Irish Press*, 3 April 1935; *Irish Times*, 3 April 1935

21 Aidan Clarke, 'Robert Dudley Edwards (1909–88)', *Irish Historical Studies*, 26, 102 (1988), 126–27

of material culture and to sub-areas of archaeological specialization which have practically become fields in their own right, such as numismatics and epigraphy. Writing in the early 1960s, when structuralism was in fashion, Momigliano identified sociology as the 'refurbished form of antiquarianism which our age requires'.[15] There are also other legitimate progeny. The study of folklore can partly trace its roots to the field trips of antiquarians who interviewed locals and documented popular customs in works such as John Brand's *Observations on Popular Antiquities* (1777), which annotated Henry Bourne's *Antiquitates Vulgares* (1725).[16] Perhaps the most dynamic exponents of contemporary antiquarian scholarship can be found in local history societies and their journals. It could be reasonably argued that some of the most exciting work in Ireland is happening on a local level but is rarely acknowledged on the centre stage of Irish Studies. This would strongly suggest a need to reconsider prevalent notions of centre and periphery in the mental geography of Irish historical scholarship.

With local geography in mind, it is worth revisiting the historical and ethnographical work of the Topographical Department of the Ordnance Survey of Ireland, in which antiquarian scholarship for a time flourished again.[17] Here we can find a possible starting point for an alternative direction for Irish studies, one which could take into account all the elements that E. Estyn Evans would later prescribe in his *Personality of Ireland*, a trilogy of regional studies that examined habitat — 'the total physical environment', history — 'the written record of the past', and heritage — 'the unwritten segment of human history'.[18] It is too readily assumed that the pioneering scholarly initiatives introduced by the Ordnance Survey were doomed to fail on account of embedded sectarian politics.[19] Though this exercise in applied antiquarianism was terminated by the authorities in 1842, it survived in

memory as an inspirational model. Upon inaugurating the Irish Folklore Commission (1935), the Minister of Education, Tomás Ó Deirg, described the collecting of folklore under the aegis of the state as a continuation of 'work abandoned 100 years ago' by the Ordnance Survey.[20] The institutionalizing of Irish folklore, which documented thousands of oral traditions of significant socio-historical interest (*seanchas*), was contemporaneous with the professionalization of a kind of Irish history that made a point of dismissing oral tradition. Both these developments were happening in tandem in the halls of University College Dublin in the mid-1930s.

The rejection of folklore would appear to be part of a calculated policy, which required that historians disavow any proclivities that might appear to conjure up associations of antiquarian excesses. Seeking to explain the noticeable 'disjuncture' between the flamboyant personality of Robert Dudley Edwards (who alongside T. W. Moody was a pillar of the New Irish History) and his restrained writing, Aidan Clarke noted that his characteristic

> ability to see unlikely consequences, to make intuitive connexions, and to draw startling inferences; the eagerness to explore irreverence, disturb complacency and contemplate the outrageous; the delight in jibes and oracular utterances — were all attributes of precisely the kind that were eschewed by the disciplinary canons that Edwards and Moody imported into Irish historical scholarship and promoted thereafter.

This led Clarke to wonder whether 'the reformers were not too literal and mechanistic in their exposition of the creed, too intolerant of the undocumented statement, too unappreciative of the contribution that the historian himself can make to the understanding of the past'.[21]

James Dixon
Arlin Point
1966
mixed media on board
The Anthony Petullo
Collection

Let us imagine that Irish history had not purged itself of antiquarianism but had developed in dialogue with long-standing indigenous historiographical traditions. In such a scenario, I would like to suggest that the Irish language would be prominent; oral tradition would be accorded respect; investigations of material culture would be integrated into historical work; local studies would be to the fore; and there would be a readiness to transcend rigid disciplinary boundaries. In its multifaceted inquiries, antiquarianism offered a model for the currently lionized interdisciplinary ideal. (More often than not, this is a guise for crude and half-hearted multidisciplinary incursions.) The old–new Irish history that would emerge by integrating antiquarian and professional traditions would not necessarily be outlandish or quixotic, though it would be distinctly Irish, without succumbing to insularity or parochialism. It would still maintain contacts with and absorb influences from other historiographical traditions. It would not be a question of unreconstructed

antiquarianism replacing scientific history but of an emerging synthesis, which could also allow for creative combinations between antiquarian–synchronic and historical–diachronic (or chronological) analyses.

In turn, interactions with historians could reduce antiquarian credulity and perhaps also cure antiquarianism of its predisposition to flowery language and its obsession with trivial minutiae. At the same time, antiquarianism could also offer history a bridge to literature. Nineteenth-century writers of historical fiction regularly consulted antiquarian scholarship and adopted an 'antiquarian impulse' for reconstructing the past in picturesque detail. Walter Scott is a prime example; although *The Antiquary* (1816) is often cited as a parody of antiquarianism, behind the humorous depiction of Jonathan Oldbuck of Monkbarns there is a noticeable reverence. After all, Scott himself was an unabashed antiquarian (as was made clear in the well-advertised case of his discovery

22 Levine, *The Amateur and the Professional*, 14

23 See my article 'Celticism', in Terence Brown, ed., *Celticism* (Amsterdam, 1996), 1–20, and *Remembrance and Imagination: Patterns in the Historical and Literary Representation of Ireland in the Nineteenth Century* (Cork, 1996).

24 Mairéad Carew, *Tara and the Ark of the Covenant: A Search for the Ark of the Covenant by British-Israelites on the Hill of Tara (1899–1902)* (Dublin, 2003); Máirín Ní Cheallaigh, 'Perceptions of Archaeological Monuments in Nineteenth-Century Ireland: A "Past of Excessive Human Thought and Action"', unpublished PhD thesis, University College Dublin, 2005; Lesa Ní Mhungaile, 'Joseph Cooper Walker (1761–1810): Beatha agus Saothar, Historical Memoirs of the Irish Bards', unpublished PhD thesis, National University of Ireland, Galway, 2001; John Waddell, *Foundation Myths: The Beginnings of Irish Archaeology* (Bray, 2005).

25 Rosemary Sweet, *Antiquaries: The Discovery of the Past in Eighteenth-Century Britain* (London, 2004)

26 Paul Veyne, *Comment on écrit l'histoire, suivi de Foucault révolutionne l'histoire* (Paris, 1978)

of the Scottish crown jewels). The mediation of antiquarianism in establishing a closer relationship with historical fiction could have served to circumvent some of the recent historiographical conflicts, which wearyingly pitted historians against literary critics. Irish scholarship in general would be enriched by the enthusiastic passion for learning, characteristic of antiquarians, exemplified, for instance, by Thomas Crofton Croker, who would regularly attend meetings of two or three learned societies in an evening and, like so many other prominent antiquarians of his time, exhibited an astonishing range of knowledge.[22] Above all, historical inquiry would be enthused and empowered by imagination. Hence such a virtual historiography pre-empts the need for virtual history, as counterfactual speculation would already be embedded in it.

Leerssen: To the extent that history is an academic discipline, it is subject to a progressive logic, involving paradigm shifts. We can read Sir Thomas Browne, Gibbons or Michelet as literature, but their compelling power as scholars has been ceded to younger generations. Even so, old paradigms never die. Even the discarded historical models remain latent and available, and can be susceptible to reactivation. The orientalist speculations of antiquarians in the Charles Vallancey and William Betham mode may have been ousted by the new paradigm represented by George Petrie, but it kept a tenacious existence among non-academic believers, was kept alive by a fringe following of Freemasons, theosophists and British-Israelites, and indeed, through the remarkable stepping-stone of Robert Graves's *The White Goddess*, has resurfaced again in a New Age context.[23]

What do we make of this? To begin with, it means that antiquarianism is still with us as something that *has* a history. Any history of ideas or history of *mentalités* will need to study, not just how people in the past envisaged their future, but also how they envisaged their past. The antiquarian view of the past, as a cultural presence, is part of any cultural history worth its salt. In Ireland we have many excellent examples of this historical interest in the antiquarian past. Clare O'Halloran's work has been mentioned; one could add the great work now being done in the field of Irish Studies, in particular in Irish archaeology.[24] This new interest in antiquarian models is part of a Europe-wide growth in what has been called 'identity history' or 'remembrance history'; Rosemary Sweet's work on English antiquarians is a case in point.[25] Indeed, the rediscovery of antiquarianism is part of a general 'cultural turn' in the historical sciences, which was, ironically enough, a rebellion of the post-Foucault generation against the older *Annales*-style preoccupation with social and economic infrastructures. Much as sociology went through a 'cultural turn' following Bourdieu, so the historical sciences went through a cultural-cum-anthropological turn following Foucault — a shift first spotted by Paul Veyne and made famous in the work of scholars like Robert Darnton, Nathalie Zemon Davis, Carlo Ginzburg, Emmanuel Le Roy Ladurie, Keith Thomas and Marina Warner.[26] That particular turn has certainly affected Ireland. However, in Ireland, as elsewhere, it has tended to manifest itself around the fringes of the established historical departments. The rise of Irish Studies is a case in point, and the work of both of us would fall into that category.

So the crux becomes: what do we call *history*? The historical university departments continue to stress archive-based research in the social, political and economic fields. If anything, this particular topical and methodological restriction seems to be what you denounce as 'starvation'. The problem is one of perception rather than practice: so much historical research, which works on other corpuses of material from other cultural fields (like folklore, literature, the arts, scientific thought,

Church history, legal history, historical geography, etcetera), is flourishing, but tends to be ignored as *history*. This is regrettable. It offers us a meagre idea of what the term *history* stands for. There is no denying that historians tend to direct their acumen to dry, factualist topics and pretend that there is no proper 'history' outside that narrow ambit. But it also means that scholars in the para-historical specialisms often work, heedless of the achievements that history *does* have to offer (with its high standards of source criticism, even-handedness, openness to diachronic variability, avoidance of presentism, etcetera).

This recalls the previously mentioned connection between the growth of academic history and the growth of revisionism. It is significant, and regrettable, that on the whole there are more 'narrow-historians' in the revisionist camp (that is to say: alumni of academic history programmes working in history departments), while the anti-revisionist camp has a higher representation of practitioners from the para-historical disciplines (literary history, historical sociology, art history, media studies, historical geography). There is no need for the fault lines to have run that way, but it does create institutional as well as ideological barriers to interdisciplinary exchange and dialogue: ideally, history should embrace all aspects of 'the way in which a society takes reckoning of its past' (to quote Huizinga's famous definition).

Beiner: Must we necessarily define antiquarianism in opposition to history? In a similar way, David Lowenthal has argued that 'heritage and history rely on antithetical modes of persuasion' so that 'heritage and history are closely linked, but they serve quite different purposes'. Such an approach inevitably reaches the conclusion that heritage is essentially 'bad history', or as put by Lowenthal: 'heritage everywhere not only tolerates but thrives on historical error'.[27] But this is not the only way of

looking at the issue. Raphael Samuel, for example, rejected the standard dichotomy and presented in his *Theatres of Memory* a plea for the inseparability of popular and academic history.[28]

There may be, as you have argued elsewhere, a qualitative distinction between 'situational' antiquarianism (with its spatial conception of the past) and *événementiel* history, separated by contrasting spatial and temporal modes of engagement with the past. However, antiquarians did not ignore time; in fact chronology was one of the main interests of classical antiquarianism.[29] They were also preoccupied with writing biographies, which inexorably follow changes over the course of a lifetime. When R. R. Madden chose to write the history of 1798 through his monumental *Lives of the United Irishmen*, he opted for an unusual history, which does not conform to a standard narrative. The outcome is a work of history achieved in an antiquarian genre. There were many other such 'transmuters' — antiquarian historians and historians who engaged in antiquarian pursuits. The more we probe the distinction, the less certain we become about its validity and begin to speculate whether it is not a specious schematization, imposed in order to simplify and regulate a hybrid situation. Instead of clearly demarcating two fundamentally dissimilar studies of the past, we may have to be content with differences in emphases, by which antiquarians showed a preference for the study of cultural production (as opposed to high politics) — subject matter which is more amenable to thematic (as opposed to sequential or temporal) study.

Its polymathic scope has allowed antiquarianism to defy the standard boundaries and perils of compartmentalization; it has been engaged with poetry, historical fiction and historical writing, painting, archaeology, natural history, biology, geography, philology, musicology, folklore, and social reform

27 David Lowenthal, *The Heritage Crusade and the Spoils of History* (Cambridge, 1998); quotations respectively from 12, 194, 6.

28 Raphael Samuel, *Theatres of Memory*, vol. 1: *Past and Present in Contemporary Culture* (London, 1994), vol. 2: *Island Stories: Unravelling Britain* (London, 1998)

29 See Anthony Grafton, 'Tradition and Technique in Historical Chronology', in M. H. Crawford and C. R. Ligota, eds., *Ancient History and the Antiquarian: Essays in Memory of Arnaldo Momigliano* (London, 1995), 15–31.

30 Samuel, *Theatres of Memory*, vol. 1, 250–73, 271; see also 16–17.

31 See for example Stuart Hannabuss, 'How Real is Our Past? Authenticity in Heritage Interpretation', in J. M. Fladmark, ed., *Heritage and Museums: Shaping National Identity* (Dorset, 2000), 351–65.

32 The National Museum in Ireland is a case in point. See Elizabeth Crooke, *Politics, Archaeology and the Creation of a National Museum in Ireland* (Dublin, 2000).

(which can also be defined as a scholarly, if not scientific, field in the terms of the period). This was not interdisciplinarianism *avant la lettre*, rather it was characteristic of the much more fluid situation that preceded the modern delineation of disciplines. History wilfully separated itself from its traditional partner and was elevated by its newly acquired professional status so that subsequent collaboration could only be contemplated on unequal terms. There was, however, an unacknowledged price to be paid for this self-imposed exclusivity.

Samuel provocatively asked fellow-historians: 'Do we not require of our readers, when facing them with one of our period reconstructions, as willing a suspension of disbelief as the "living history" spectacle of the open-air museum or theme park?'[30] Historians relying solely on a restricted concept of history have often discovered that they are insufficiently equipped to present convincing reconstructions of the past and therefore the new wave of cultural micro-histories (by such innovators as Ladurie, Zemon Davis, Darnton, and Ginzburg) moved in the direction of a *rapprochement* with antiquarianism. This may seem to be a pioneering historiographical move forward and yet it can also be seen as a step backwards towards scholarly engagements that were once readily available and, had it not been for the professionalization of the discipline, may have been part and parcel of modern historiography (though this would depend on a conceptualization of 'modernity' that is not defined in opposition to 'tradition'). Historiographical revolutionaries can therefore also be considered reactionaries.

In the context of the conflict between history and antiquarianism, it is necessary to push forward 'the time of death' of 'respectable' antiquarianism. In spite of growing condescension and denigration from professional historians, antiquarianism remained a distinguished preoccupation

through the entire nineteenth century and into the early twentieth century. For this reason the Irish case, with its historical professionalization dated to the 1930s, is pertinent. This time line does not confirm a liquidation of antiquarianism corresponding with the rise of historicism on the one hand and the historical novel on the other, but rather a period of co-existence and interaction, in which the former was on the wane while the other was waxing. This dating is also true for the splintering of antiquarianism into separate scholarly fields, as antiquarians continued to pursue wide-ranging investigations over this period. The transition was therefore an evolutionary paradigm shift rather than a revolutionary moment.

The innovation and success of the historical novel can be partly explained by its accessibility, in contrast with the arcane erudition of antiquarians, who, as Scott jokingly noted, 'wrote essays on medals in the proportion of twelve pages to each letter of the legend'. This difference between the two is more a matter of form than content. The historical novel is an achievement of style, which accommodates the 'suspension of disbelief', that antiquarians employed in reconstructing the past. This relates to current debates on heritage and the constructed category of 'authenticity', which is at the heart of antiquarianism.[31] Antiquarians not only uncovered, restored and collected monuments — they authenticated them. Antiquarians generally preferred to preserve the heritage artefacts they restored in private possession but when they experimented with public exhibitions they laid the foundations for yet another modern field — museology.[32]

When Robert McAdam and his fellow antiquarians in Ulster advertised an 'Exhibition of Objects of Antiquity and Irish Historical Reliques', held in Belfast in September 1852, they boasted that 'Surrounded by such a collection of memorials from all parts of Ulster, the visitor could, for the first time, realize in some degree, the very different states of society which have prevailed in Ireland, and of which our historians convey a very feeble idea.'[33] Note the antiquarians' disregard for historians at a time when the two practices could still apparently address each other on equal terms. Later in the century, Francis Joseph Biggar purchased the Norman castle of Ardglass and turned it into a heritage site open to the public (which he later put in the custody of the government of Northern Ireland). To quote a contemporary visitor: 'Everywhere around one's eyes are feasted on rare antique objects of priceless value.'[34]

This kind of 'living history', facilitated by staged authenticity that locates 'genuine' artefacts in reconstructed settings, is of course antithetical to a history that thrives on the 'death of the past', as famously advocated by J. H. Plumb.[35] The widespread desire today to reclaim an intimate and vital relationship with the past is part of a contemporary obsession with remembrance and commemoration or, as labelled by Jay Winter, a 'Memory Boom' that has become 'the historical signature of our own generation'.[36] Pierre Nora has diagnosed this phenomenon as a reaction to a growing sense of 'the acceleration of history' caused by the passing away of 'living memory' and the last remaining vestiges of tradition. Instead of the familiar academic history that was constructed in opposition to memory as a discipline that aspired to scientific status, his innovative historiographical model of *lieux de mémoire* that are located 'between memory and history' can be read as a reformulated antiquarian approach to the past.[37] Historians may have appeared to have emerged victorious in the first round of their struggle against antiquarians but they now find themselves overwhelmed by new manifestations of antiquarianism with which they need to come to terms.

It is evident today that professional academia does not have a monopoly on authoritative knowledge on the past. One could argue that this has always been the case. Historians (alongside other scientists) may beg to differ, but ultimately the snobbish dismissal of 'amateurs' has not played in their favour. Moreover, the conscious breakaway from the rich tradition of antiquarianism in Ireland can serve to explain the underperformance of contemporary historiography or, in other words, why Irish history starved.

Leerssen: Let us not, in denouncing academic snootiness, over-glorify anything non-academic. The realization that academic scholarship has no binding authority in the real world should not mean that academics must therefore prostrate themselves before the Real World's Last Word. Do immunologists have to endorse or condone homeopathy because that's what scores with the self-medicating drugstore customers? I remember an eminent colleague of ours giving a highly informed lecture to an audience combining fellow-academics and sponsors from the Irish-American business community — only to have to face, at question time, queries from a sponsor as to Irish holiday recommendations.

What do we mean when we speak of 'authoritative knowledge', even whilst denying academia a monopoly to that quiddity? The *American Historical Review* felt called upon, a while back, to start reviewing historical blockbuster movies like *Michael Collins*, *Braveheart*, etcetera, because they realized that it was a hugely important mode of society's collective preoccupation with the past. Some of that was in the sniffy 'they got it all wrong' mode, but even this urge to correct errors is interesting and should not be dismissed. We do not quarrel with Tolkien when he tells us elves have grey eyes, because Middle Earth is his creation and he can give his elves' eyes

33 PRONI D2930/4/4
34 J. K. Owen, *An Irish Chieftain of To-Day* (Belfast, *c.*1910), 9
35 J. H. Plumb, *The Death of the Past* (1969). For an Irish equivalent see Roy Foster, 'Theme-parks and Histories', in his *The Irish Story: Telling Tales and Making It Up in Ireland* (London, 2001), 23–36.
36 Jay Winter, 'The Generation of Memory: Reflections on the Memory Boom in Contemporary Historical Studies', *Bulletin of the German Historical Institute*, 27 (2000), 69–92
37 Pierre Nora, 'Between Memory and History', in Pierre Nora, ed., *Realms of Memory: Rethinking the French Past* (New York, 1996), vol. 1, 1–20. See also Pierre Nora, 'Reasons for the Current Upsurge in Memory', *Eurozine* (April 2002); http://www.eurozine.com/articles/2002-04-19-nora-en.html.

Hughie O'Donoghue
A Long Time Gone
2006
oil, mixed media on wood
construction
private collection

any colour he damn well chooses. All we do is follow the story, on his terms. But with history, the past is Out There, and we readers have as much a title to it as anyone else. So historians are congenitally cursed with *far less* authority than the fictional novelist. In the case of reading history, the suspension of disbelief is, *pace* Samuels, by no means a willing one, rather a grudging one. We reserve the right to second-guess, to disagree.

Ironically, therefore, the carping historian who criticizes popular historical narrative (like a movie review in the *AHR*) for getting the facts wrong — is treating that narrative as history, not as fiction. That being said, everyone will realize how quixotic the idea is: academic history to legislate for popular remembrancing. So the 'authoritative knowledge' that, as you claim, was claimed by academic historians, is unauthoritative in a double sense. It cannot legislate for what people think, and it cannot coerce the reader's reactions.

If the word 'authoritative' has any meaning in this context at all, it must be in the very old-fashioned sense that it is knowledge underwritten by third parties — authorities. That is the very definition of academic knowledge, as opposed to general

knowledge. Academic knowledge is to know, not just a given fact or piece of information, but also to know where you obtained that knowledge. It is meta-knowledge: knowledge that is aware of its provenance.

Now here's an article of faith. I can only assert it, no more, but I feel very deeply about it. Given a choice between general knowledge and academic knowledge (as defined above), I consider academic knowledge epistemically superior. It is not perfect but it is more transparent, less easily confused with *doxa*, ideology or unproven belief. And while I cannot and would not want to enforce the social superiority and authority of academic knowledge, I do firmly hold fast to the superior epistemic quality (call it 'authority') of academic knowledge. That's why I'm a Darwinist rather than a Creationist. To the extent, then, that the development of antiquarianism into academic history involved a shift towards the epistemic standards of academic knowledge, I do not consider that a matter of history 'starving', but rather shedding some flab and acquiring some muscle tone.

Is there such a thing as Bad History? Yes, like bad engineering, bad medicine, bad chemistry. The risk of going Bad keeps Good

History on its toes. Is there such a thing as Bad Antiquarianism? No. Because with antiquarianism, like free jazz, Anything Goes. Antiquarianism lacks quality control.

Beiner: Did professionalization result in the starvation of Irish history or did it rather implement an athletic diet that can be credited with a loss of excess flab and the acquiring of muscle tone?

Despite all their peculiarities and oddities, the invaluable contributions of antiquarians cannot be overlooked. Even if antiquarian preoccupation with time can be branded as essentially a-historical, it would be inaccurate to sum up, for example, J. T. Gilbert's monumental volumes merely as a situational chronology when they are laden with *événementiel* references that accumulate into an incomparable history of Dublin.[38] If we acknowledge the range of scholarly depth and innovation of such luminaries as Petrie, then we cannot but echo the despair of an American scholar who pertinently asked, 'Why is there no archaeology in Irish Studies?'[39] The same can be said for the other fields that brilliant antiquarians like Petrie pioneered but were subsequently brushed aside to the margins of Irish Studies and were, by and large, completely ignored by historians. Contrary to a common misconception, antiquarianism was not synonymous with a simplistic lack of critical thought and did not peddle its ware to a credulous public. Excluding forays into historical fiction and folktales, the great bulk of antiquarian writing was primarily circulated within esoteric erudite circles. The impassioned debates and controversies among antiquarians (such as the furore over the origins of the Round Towers in Ireland) were all about subjecting scholarship to rigorous peer criticism.

At its best, virtual historiography should not be concerned with Irish history merely catching up with current historiographical trends and enhancing its engagement with sources drawn from popular culture. It is about envisaging a 'road not taken', revisiting the deliberate dismissal of an alternative historiography which in this case 'has made all the difference'. This does not refer to the emergence of a local variation of a history of *mentalités* grounded in Ireland but of an *Irish* history that redresses the shameless rejection of 'native' resources (such as Irish language, material culture, and oral history) and of indigenous historiographical traditions, which are not only to be found in antiquarian scholarship but also in vernacular folk history.[40] In Nietzschean terms, this would not be a case of a hackneyed rendition of revived 'antiquarian history' replacing academic 'critical history' but of the formulation of a new–old history, which would synthesize antiquarian, critical and monumental (or commemorative) modes of history into a multilayered and multifaceted exploration of the past. The feasibility of fulfilling such an aspiration in today's world may seem to be questionable. Such attempts were made in the past but were extinguished by the professionalization of history, which effectively starved Irish history, or deprived it of ingenuity. For all its muscle tone, the writing of Irish history is at best a third-rate player in an international arena, as opposed to other areas of Irish creativity, which have remained within an Irish tradition, or are in dialogue with tradition, and yet time and time again have won international laurels and have been widely recognized both by popular and academic standards for their outstanding merits and resourcefulness.

Leerssen: When exactly and how exactly did we pass those paths converging in the snowy woods? Was the Ordnance Survey still an antiquarian enterprise or already a manifestation of the new statistical–empirical phase of history and archaeology? Its popular commemoration has been famously distorted, first in Douglas

38 See T. J. Gilbert, *A History of the City of Dublin*, 3 vols. (Dublin, 1978; facsimile of 1st edn. 1854–59).

39 See Charles Orser 'Why is there no Archaeology in Irish Studies?', *Irish Studies Review*, 8, 2 (2000), 157–65.

40 For a critical examination of Irish traditions of vernacular historiography, see Guy Beiner, *Remembering the Year of the French: Irish Folk History and Social Memory* (Madison, 2006).

41 Starting of course with John Andrews, *A Paper Landscape: The Ordnance Survey in Nineteenth-Century Ireland* (Oxford, 1975).

42 Nicole Belmont, *Aux sources de l'ethnologie française: L'académie celtique* (Paris, 1995); Mona Ozouf, *L'École de la France: Essais sur la révolution, l'utopie et l'enseignement* (Paris, 1984)

43 For example, see Stephan Jordan, *Geschichtstheorie in der ersten Hälfte des 19. Jahrhunderts. Die Schwellenzeit zwischen Pragmatismus und Klassischem Historismus* (Frankfurt, 1999). I have dealt with these issues more extensively in my articles 'Literary Historicism: Romanticism, Philologists, and the Presence of the Past', *Modern Language Quarterly*, 65, 2 (2004), 221–43, 'Ossian and the Rise of Literary Historicism', in Howard Gaskill, ed., *The Reception of Ossian in Europe* (London, 2004), 109–25, and 'Historisme en historicisme', *De Negentiende Eeuw*, 30 (2006), 110–17.

Hyde's lecture on 'The Necessity for De-Anglicizing Ireland', and then by Brian Friel in his *Translations*, and its importance is only slowly being retrieved by, dare I say it, *historical* and revisionist reappraisal.[41] More to the point, it should be seen in the context of those state-led total-inventory projects that all of them seem to have taken their cue, directly or indirectly, from the Parisian *Académie celtique* in 1806, itself probably influenced by the Napoleonic description of Egypt.[42] Its empirical procedures stood at odds with the speculative antiquarianism of the preceding generation, the Vallanceys, Bethams and Henry O'Briens. There is, then, a first anti-antiquarian moment in the decades of romantic historicism. The rise of historicism (Savigny, Grimm, Ranke, Thierry, Michelet) is one of the contributing causes to the decline of antiquarianism; it is this that causes Scott's attitude to antiquarianism to be so full of mixed-feeling irony.[43]

Still, much of what you seem to consider the prelapsarian, vibrant, inclusive and 'antiquarian' form of doing history survives throughout the nineteenth century and the definitive narrowing down of history to the archive-driven investigation of social, political and economic history only occurs in the twentieth century. And indeed, none of these paradigm shifts is absolute. The tradition of intellectual history continues, and is graced by names such as Burckhardt and Huizinga. If we allow our gaze to dwell on the fields adjacent to 'narrow history', we encounter names such as Paul Hazard, Paul

Van Tieghem, Mario Praz, Albert Béguin, Ernst Gombrich, Ernst Robert Curtius, Lewis Mumford, Eduard Dijksterhuis; all this before the post-Foucault 'cultural turn'.

Strikingly, of course, I can find no Irish names to include in that list. That would indicate that the problem is at least in part one of Irish academic provincialism. In the nineteenth century, we see Trinity scholars such as Lecky, Dowden and Hutcheson Macaulay Posnett (a pioneer of comparative literature, with affinities to E. A. Freeman and Walter Bagehot) continue a sociologically and anthropologically inspired style of intellectual history. That tradition, too, gets etiolated in the course of the twentieth century. And one of the contributory causes, I would suggest, lies (alongside the rise of 'academic history') in the nationalistically introspective, indeed self-obsessed, climate of the Free State and the early Republic, which was concerned only with its own identity, its own past, its own nationhood, and which turned its back on the wider academic world.

I would therefore argue that a return to the vibrancy of an interdisciplinary 'broad history' cannot take place without a simultaneous growth towards a new internationalism. A wholesome example to that effect is offered by the field of Irish folklore, which, as I have learned from Diarmuid Ó Giolláin, is now thriving, thanks to intense contacts with, and theoretical impulses from, folklore studies worldwide. ∎

Trajectories of Identity Change

New Perspectives on Ethnicity, Nationality and Identity in Ireland

Jennifer Todd

The cultural social sciences work at the point of intersection of social structure, institutional change and change in mass public perceptions and collective identities. They look for the links between power relations, collective action and social and symbolic boundaries. Marx theorized this for class relations. The most exciting area of the cultural social sciences today, however, is ethnicity, where some of the insights developed in class analysis are used to look at the constitution of ethnic categories and collectivities and the ways the categories of ethnicity and nationality are embodied, manipulated, strategically adapted, and transmitted.[1]

1 For examples, see Michèle Lamont, *The Dignity of Working Men: Morality and the Boundaries of Race, Class, and Immigration.* (Cambridge, Mass., 2000); Rogers Brubaker, *Ethnicity without Groups* (Cambridge, Mass., 2004); Andreas Wimmer, *Nationalist Exclusion and Ethnic Conflict: Shadows of Modernity* (Cambridge, 2002); Richard Jenkins, *Social Identity* (London, 1996).

Detail:
Willie Doherty
Show of Strength I
2006
cibachrome print on aluminum with plexiglass
edition of 3
121.9 x 152.4 cm
courtesy of the artist and the Kerlin Gallery

Ethnic and national identity change is central to this research, for once we move beyond the bare categories of national identity (to paraphrase John Hume, the French who don't stop being French and the Germans who don't stop being German), we see identity shift and identity contest as pervasive. Shifts in the ways of being national — in this context, Irish, or Northern Irish, or British — radically change national boundaries and political action. In turn, political reform, global communications and a changing power balance can shift national and ethnic identifications.[2]

New work in the cultural social sciences focuses on local, familial and everyday modes of interaction, showing how these interact with state institutions and economic structures to form ethnic groups in conflict. In so doing, this work replots the

conceptual landscape and provides a new set of interdisciplinary research questions, which also give us a grasp on the changes in contemporary Ireland, North and South. Four conceptual revolutions have changed the field. Provided below is an outline of the general arguments and their relevance to research on changing identities in Ireland.

Revolution One:
Groups become the Explanandum

The first revolution has to do with the ethnic groups and national communities that enter into conflict. Rogers Brubaker, in a seminal piece, argued that the term 'group' has to be abolished from the analytic vocabulary, that even if ordinary individuals think in terms of ethnic group belonging, analytically we have to explain rather than presuppose group solidarity.[3] Groups and group boundaries are to be explained whether in terms of the benefits (material and cultural) of solidarity, or the work done by ethnic entrepreneurs in brokering alliances and redefining categories, or the internal dynamics of the population where competition is for ownership of 'group characteristics'. What sort of research does this lead to? Brubaker argues for a cognitivist approach, where the researcher looks at how and when individuals deploy the categories of ethnicity and nationality. In this research, the *when* (the interactional context) is highlighted over the *what* (the content of group identity). The picture is one of fluctuation, with ethnicity momentarily highlighted then moving out of focus. Robin Wilson has argued that we should apply this approach to Northern Ireland, believing that if we did so, we would find that ordinary people do not work with the nationalist/ unionist or British/Irish categories so central to official political life.[4] In the South, this approach leads researchers to look at localities, immigrants, gender, youth, anything that people actually talk about among themselves, and this is usually not 'the nation'.

The Irish case, however, shows that we need to qualify the interactional approach. Breaching codes and boundaries in Ireland does not usually lead to explicit ethnic assertion, but rather to silence or a change of topic or worse. In the South, the nation, like sex, is seldom spoken of, and not because either is thought to be unimportant. In a recent set of open-ended interviews carried out as part of research into changing Irish identities, eighty individuals (from a very wide range of social backgrounds) spoke freely of their sense of locality, of class, of religion, of immigration: none volunteered a discussion of nationality or of gender.[5] Were they post-national? Post-gendered? Or did their silence signify that these were still important and disturbing issues? When probed, they talked about nationality, in a set of intersecting, often cross-cutting themes and narratives: national boundaries

remained for the most part salient, but complex, difficult to discuss. A general conceptual conclusion follows. The *when* of ethnicity presupposes the *what*: we need to be able to recognize the turns, the silences, the evasions and what is expressed in them. It also presupposes the *how*: the triggers that change the path of conversation, the meanings given to those triggers, and the reasons they are so powerful.

If 'communities' are the products of convergent interests, ideas and understandings, dispositions to common action, how do individuals themselves understand them? How do individuals interconnect and relate ideas of religion, nationality and community today? Do these understandings converge, and if so, what explains the convergence and the related capacity for solidaristic action? What social mechanisms create and reproduce communal solidarity? The comparative literature gives us some answers. The convergent understandings of ethnicity and nationality may be crystallized in times of trauma.[6] They are stabilized by their emotional hold, which filters out other interests and perceptions.[7] Yet they remain open to incentives for change. David Laitin theorizes the 'tipping game', whereby individuals, worried about peer pressure as well as self-interest, opt for radical change only when each expects that others will too, producing a cascade of change.[8] These themes are directly relevant to the question of how communal solidarity is retained and maintained in Northern Ireland, and the ways in which the 1998 Good Friday Agreement gives incentives for breaching solidarity.[9]

Revolution Two:
Opening Out Ethnicity and Nationality

How are we to understand ethnicity and the related (but state-centred) concept of nationalism? It was once clear. As Walter Connor puts it, ethnicity was understood as

2   Michael Keating, *Plurinational Democracy: Stateless Nations in a Post-Sovereignty Era* (Oxford, 2001); Manuel Castells, *The Power of Identity* (Oxford, 1997)

3   Rogers Brubaker, 'Ethnicity without Groups', *Archives Européennes de Sociologie*, 43, 2 (2002), 163–89

4   Robin Wilson, 'The Politics of Contemporary Ethno-nationalist Conflicts', *Nations and Nationalism*, 7, 3 (2001), 365–84

5   The interviews were conducted in two locations in the Irish state by Theresa O'Keefe for the Identity, Diversity and Citizenship programme, Changing Irish Identities project, in 2003–05.

6   Sudhir Kakar, *The Colors of Violence, Cultural Identities, Religion and Conflict* (Chicago, 1996); Jacques Sémelin, *Purifier et détruire: Usages politiques des massacres et génocides* (Paris, 2005)

7   Roger D. Petersen, *Understanding Ethnic Violence: Fear, Hatred and Resentment in Twentieth-Century Eastern Europe* (Cambridge, 2002)

8   David D. Laitin, *Identity in Formation: The Russian-Speaking Populations in the Near Abroad* (Ithaca, NY, 1998)

9   These are the central questions in Joseph Ruane and Jennifer Todd, *Dynamics of Conflict in Northern Ireland* (Cambridge, 1996) and in our recent joint work, 'The Roots of Intense Ethnic Conflict may not Themselves be Ethnic: Categories,

Communities and Path Dependence', *Archives Européennes de Sociologie*, 45, 2 (2004), 209–32, and 'Path Dependence in Settlement Processes: Explaining Settlement in Northern Ireland', *Political Studies*, 55, 2 (forthcoming 2007).

10 Walker Connor, *Ethno-nationalism: The Quest for Understanding* (Princeton, NJ, 1994), 197; cf. Edward Shils, 'Nation, Nationality, Nationalism and Civil Society', *Nations and Nationalism*, 1, 1 (1995), 93–118, 94–97, 101. For fuller discussion of the points in this paragraph, see Ruane and Todd, 'Roots of Intense Ethnic Conflict'.

11 Benedict Anderson, *Imagined Communities*, rev. edn. (London, 1991), 6; John Hutchinson and Anthony D. Smith, eds., *Ethnicity* (Oxford, 1996), 6–7

12 This quasi-ethnic view has echoes in other Protestant minorities, see Joseph Ruane, 'Majority-Minority Conflicts and Their Resolution: Protestant Minorities in France and in Ireland', *Nationalism and Ethnic Politics*, 12, 3–4 (2006), 509–32.

13 Richard Bourke, 'Antigone and After: Ethnic Conflict in Historical Perspective', *Field Day Review*, 2 (2006), 169–94

a 'sense of kinship' that infused a nation: a 'sense of shared blood' was to be found 'at the core of ethno-psychology'.[10] Now the concepts have been opened out. Ethnicity — to the extent that it is a distinct category from religion, class, or other collectivities — refers to a group inherently limited in space and continuous in time, a spatially distinctive 'people', which is thought of as stretching back into the past and moving into the future, and is typically associated with a symbolism of origin and a set of origin-myths.[11] This sense of 'peoplehood' is, however, a thin category, presupposing not just a multiplicity of peoples, but peoples who define their specificity in different ways. It requires to be filled by other content (linguistic, genealogical, cultural, political, religious), and the set of beliefs, interests and institutional practices that comes to fill it defines the specific ethnicity in question. Ethnicity thus exists on a continuum with other categories, overlapping with religion and class, sliding into a wider sense of commonality with co-religionists abroad, or alternatively, when the ties of religion to institutional practice and theological belief are loosened, religion itself may imperceptibly become ethnicized.

Some groups may not think of themselves as 'a people' at all. And there is no specifically 'ethnic' content that can tell us whether or not they do. Research has to look at the ways in which collectivity is constructed. Free Presbyterians, for example, use an imagery of 'shared blood', which defines a group that never is quite bounded territorially or continuous in time. A favourite hymn in this denomination is 'There is Power in the Blood', which, while explicitly referring to the blood of Christ, implicitly also refers to the blood of believers, has resonances with the 'spilled blood' of Ulster Protestants in the world wars and in the more recent 'war with the IRA', and has more specific reference to the blood of the Protestant martyrs, pictures of whose suffering are prominently displayed

in Martyrs Memorial Church in Belfast. A sense of 'blood-belonging' thus links contemporary Northern Irish Protestants not just to those massacred in the twentieth century because of their loyalty to Britain, but also to those massacred in Ulster in 1641 because of their religion and settler status, as well as to those Protestants (mostly of southern French origin) massacred in Paris some seventy years earlier and in the Cévennes some sixty years later. Here the metaphor usually thought of as typical of ethnic identity is used instead to trace a religious continuity that almost ethnicizes but not quite.[12]

The ethnic dimension of conflict in Northern Ireland, as elsewhere, is always contested and fluid, as Richard Bourke has argued.[13] How far unionists fight for 'their ethnic group', or for their religious values, or for a state to correspond with their idea of nationhood is decided in part by the contention between subsections of unionists, loyalists and Protestants. Is the Northern Ireland conflict an ethnic or an ethno-national conflict? It is a multi-determined one where meanings, the contents emphasized as specific to the group and thus the precise boundaries of the group, are themselves in contest.

Equally, the concept of nationality has been opened. We are still Irish, or Basque, or Ulster Protestant, but it is not possible to read off the meanings of these categories from 'official' national or ethnic discourse. There are numerous ways 'to be Irish' or 'to be Basque', or 'to be Ulster Protestant', quite different from 'official' views, pursued spontaneously by different groups and subsets of groups and individuals, combining differently regional, local, gender, age, class, religious and cultural stances. This means that identifying an 'ethnic' or 'national' identity involves going below explicit discourse, looking not at what people say about 'the nation' but at the way they construct 'peoplehood', if indeed

Willie Doherty
Show of Strength III
2006
cibachrome print on
aluminum with plexiglass
edition of 3
121.9 x 152.4 cm
courtesy of the artist and the
Kerlin Gallery

they do, and the content they give it, which may diverge from official and scholarly categorizations. This phenomenon was evident in our recent research project on the Irish border.[14] On the basis of the scholarly literature, it had been expected that in the Southern border counties a progression from an irredentist nationalism, perhaps still held by some, through a state-centred 26-county nationalism to a new Europeanism would be found, which would have made the Irish border no different from other European borders. Over seventy in-depth interviews, hundreds of school essays and a survey indicated convincingly that the participants did not fit any of these characterizations. Neither the '26-county' state-centred attitudes so prevalent in the Irish media and 'revisionist' scholarship, nor old-fashioned

nationalist irredentism, nor a new European identity were common. What was found again and again was a set of paradoxes.

Respondents provided information about living in Louth, Monaghan, Donegal, past and present. They patiently disclosed their views about the border and the North, what being Irish meant to them and to their parents, how far they saw this changing. They volunteered countless examples of the practical importance of the border in jobs, party system, everyday activity, smuggling, and they freely recounted experiences of danger. They also denied that the border had any impact on their sense of identity and nationality. They even denied that it was close by. In towns not ten kilometres from Northern Ireland, people said they did not

14 Intergenerational
Transmission and
Ethno-national Identity
in the (Irish) Border
Area, funded by the EU
Programme for Peace
and Reconciliation.
Lorenzo Cañás Bottos,
Nathalie Rougier
and I conducted the
interviews; Orla
Muldoon, Karen Trew
and Katrina McLoughlin
conducted the school
essay study and
survey; see www.ucd.
ie/euiteniba. For fuller
discussion of the results
summarized below, see
Jennifer Todd et al., 'The
Moral Boundaries of the
Nation: Nation, State
and Boundaries in the
Southern Irish Border
Counties', *Ethnopolitics*,
5, 4 (2006), 1–18.

15 Rawi Abdelal et al., 'Identity as a Variable' (10 May 2003 version), Weatherhead Initiative in International Affairs, Harvard University, www.wcfia.harvard.edu/misc/initiative/identity/papers/index.htm, accessed January 2005; Richard D. Ashmore, Kay Deaux and Tracy McLaughlin-Volpe, 'An Organizing Framework for Collective Identity: Articulation and Significance of Multidimensionality', *Psychological Bulletin*, 130, 1 (2004), 80–114

16 Karen A. Cerulo, 'Identity Construction: New Issues, New Directions', *Annual Review of Sociology*, 23 (1997), 385–409; Rogers Brubaker and Frederick Cooper, 'Beyond "Identity"', *Theory and Society*, 29 (2002), 1–47; Margaret Somers, 'The Narrative Construction of Identity: A Relational and Network Approach', *Theory and Society*, 23 (1994), 605–49. For a fuller discussion of these issues and their relevance for national identity, see Jennifer Todd, 'Social Transformations, Collective Categories and Identity Change', *Theory and Society*, 34, 4 (2005), 429–63.

17 Erving Goffman, *The Presentation of Self in Everyday Life* (London, 1990 [1959])

live on the border. They saw no symbolic significance to the border. Yet these same respondents had stated that the border had been a source of trauma in the past, for their own parents and grandparents. They had given examples of the differences of North and South: 'The troubles changed everything, everything completely … so many people came from the North to live here, people were afraid, afraid to say what they thought, what they felt'; 'They'd even take over the whole conversation. We were placid, quiet, but they were all gun-blazing.'

These responses are only apparently contradictory. They make sense in terms of the respondents' distinctive construction of national identity and place-in-the-world. The respondents deny the significance of the border through constructing national community as a moral phenomenon and defining themselves as open and peaceful, not closed and oppositional. As one young person wrote: 'We work with each other and are friends with each other'. This everyday civil interaction which cross-cuts the border reconstitutes a different sort of national boundary, one that is founded not merely in institutions but in values and sense of self. A sense of moral values and civility is felt to pervade (Southern) Irish society and to divide the respondents from those who insist on the state boundaries, who reject their openness, deny their good will, and shout them down. This is not an ethnic nationalism — ideologies of Gaelic Catholic Ireland were treated with some irony by many of the respondents — but a moral constitution of the nation. Like other forms of nationalism, however, it is powerful, connecting the collective category of nationality with the sense of self. It defines a moral border, one which excludes Northern unionists threatened by this moral and civilizational expansiveness and Northern nationalists who can not so civilly affirm their Irishness. It is one of the moves in the North–South interactional drama.

Revolution Three: (Re)Building Identity

The third revolution has to do with identity. It is a term that tends to stop thought. Is it something one *has*? Something one *does*? Something one *feels*? Something one *is*? Recent interdisciplinary scholarship has begun to order the ways in which the concept has been used and the different aspects that can be researched.[15] It has thus restored a pared-down concept to analytic usefulness.

For some time now, a 'soft constructivist' consensus has dominated the fields of cultural analysis. Soft constructivism highlights personal variability and new combinations of meanings in identity-categories and moments of choice or intentionality in identity formation. Its major achievement is to have broken definitively with the notion of identity-categories as fixed and defined.[16] This approach emphasizes the fluctuating, relational and situational quality of self-definitions. Identity is not something one *has*, it is not a *thing*. Yet of course identity politics presupposes just this; for example, it is common in the new progressive loyalist politics to hear it said: 'The only thing we have left is our identity', or 'Don't question my identity'.

Those who say this are, in a sense, right to protest that they cannot change their identity, not least their ethnic or national identity, at a whim, and that they do not want intellectuals to define it for them. They are also right to suspect an approach that is simply relational and situational. As identities become plural and open to choice, they proliferate, varying in each situation where a new aspect of self is performed. Identity becomes something one does, as one puts on or takes off different hats. Of course such 'identity-work' goes on, as Erving Goffman has shown so wonderfully.[17] But 'identity-language' classically referred to the stability of the self through a succession of roles; once 'identity' is unmoored from such individual stability, it loses its *raison d'être*. Rogers Brubaker and Frederick Cooper cut the Gordian knot: we should dispense with the term altogether, we can do all that needs to be done talking about identification, self-definition, the preservation of core values, sense of belonging, and thereby one escapes the pitfalls of identity-politics.[18]

Yet there is something to be said for the older term 'identity' when it is seen not as something one has, or does, or feels, but as something one *is*. Being is that place between situation and choice, where we work with given elements — dispositions, values, judgements, emotions — in light of opportunities and aims. These elements are themselves made socially: participation in complex social practices develops dispositions, changes judgements, educates emotions, produces the five senses.[19] They are also embedded socially (in the practices, institutions, opportunities available at any given time) and anchored personally. It is precisely this social and personal anchorage that allows identity to be an independent causal factor in social life, with a different temporality of change than politics or culture, sometimes progressing social revolutions, sometimes inertial, stalling change, making new institutions function just as the old ones did.

Pierre Bourdieu's work on social class provides a model of the anchoring of identity, of the ways in which the power relations of our environment intersect with the categories of our understanding.[20] He has analysed how the *habitus* — the individual's dispositions that give bodily form to collective categories and distinctions — is formed from earliest childhood, as the child situates itself in structured, gendered and differentially pathed social space, and internalizes its objective life-chances in its own subjective expectations and interests.[21] The French bourgeois lady who knows

as second nature how to tie her scarf, what jumpers and make-up and modes of greeting are fine, and who educates her children to negotiate their paths through the drawing room with its small tables and fine china, is creating the materials of class identity as surely as the Kabyle family in the 1950s created the materials of Kabyle identity in the arrangement of the house which reflected the opportunities and life-chances of each gender and led children to internalize a genderized sense of direction.[22] The *habitus* is at the basis of the emotional power of identity, the felt immediacy by which we respond to those who recognize and respond positively to our immediate intuitive distinctions. Most important of all, for Bourdieu, power and opposition are also internalized. Those who control the most progressive parts of the economy, dominate in the academies, and have the power to assert their culture as the rational, progressive, global culture, also develop a sense of ownership of civilizing values, rationality and progress. Their evident material and cultural power provides confirmation of the 'truth' of their belief in their own rationality and progressiveness. In such circumstances, class (or ethnic) dominance is fought for — and against — not simply for its own sake but for the sake of the highest values. A feedback pattern results where power inequalities are internalized in dispositions and identity oppositions, which then serve to reproduce the power inequalities.[23]

This is not all there is to identity, or else there would be only past, no future. Each of us prioritizes the materials of identity, reshuffles them and sometimes watches them collapse, in the process redirecting our own lives and practices and (re)making the materials. To use a philosophy of science metaphor, we rebuild our identity boats while sailing in them. Social psychologists, sociologists and political scientists are beginning to converge on seeing identity as a complexly structured package where particular identity-categories (Irish)

18 Brubaker and Cooper, 'Beyond "Identity"'

19 The point was made by Marx in the *Paris Manuscripts*. More recently, see Alasdair MacIntyre, *After Virtue: A Study in Moral Theory* (London, 1981).

20 Pierre Bourdieu, *Outline of a Theory of Practice*, trans. Richard Nice (Cambridge, 1977); *Distinction: A Social Critique of the Judgement of Taste*, trans. Richard Nice (Cambridge, Mass., 1984); *The Logic of Practice*, trans. Richard Nice (Cambridge, 1990)

21 Bourdieu, *Outline of a Theory of Practice*, 86

22 Béatrix Le Wita, *French Bourgeois Culture*, trans. James A. Underwood (Cambridge, 1994); Bourdieu, *Logic of Practice*, 271–83

23 Bourdieu, *Outline of a Theory of Practice*, 78–79

Willie Doherty
Local Solution II
2006
cibachrome print on
aluminum with plexiglass
edition of 3
121.9 x 152.4 cm
courtesy of the artist and the
Kerlin Gallery

24 Ashmore, Deaux
and McLaughlin-
Volpe, 'Organizing
Framework'; Abdelal
et al., 'Identity as a
Variable'
25 Todd, 'Social
Transformations'
26 Andreas Wimmer, 'The
Making and Unmaking
of Ethnic Boundaries:
Toward a Comparative
Theory', unpublished
manuscript, University
of California, Los
Angeles, 2006; Laitin,
Identity in Formation;
Lamont, *Dignity of
Working Men*

are interrelated with others (Catholic, Gaelic,
working class, European, modern), imbued
with more or less personally meaningful
contents and values.[24] All identity, in this
sense, is an 'identity-package' that can, at a
cost, be remade. Choice points arise, there is
space for reflection, even if our choices do not
always form our identities as we might have
hoped. Choices arise, above all, when social
conditions change, when the power resources
that defined a set of socially dominant
identity-packages are broken. Radical change
in power relations is likely to provoke
cognitive dissonance, which triggers identity
shift. Depending on resources and incentives,
however, the direction of that shift may be
extreme reaffirmation of old binaries, or
movement to new categories and contents.[25]

This broad perspective is informing some
of the most interesting work on ethnic
identity today. It goes beyond the
constructivist–primordialist dichotomy. It
is no longer a question of opposing choice
of identity to imposition of hegemonic
categories, but showing the conditions
under which choice and fluidity is likely, the
conditions under which the lock-in of ethnic
identities takes place, the conditions under
which collective identity shifts may happen
and the sorts of moral and cultural resources
used in such shifts.[26]

Precisely this perspective informed recent
research projects on national identity change
in Ireland. Northern Ireland was a key area,
because there have been radical shifts in

Willie Doherty
Local Solution IV
2006
cibachrome print on
aluminum with plexiglass
edition of 3
121.9 x 152.4 cm
courtesy of the artist and the
Kerlin Gallery

27 Orla Muldoon et
al., 'The Nature and
Meaning of Identity
in Northern Ireland
after the Good Friday
Agreement', *Political
Psychology* 28, 1 (2007),
89–103

28 For discussion, see
Jennifer Todd et al.,
'Fluid or Frozen: Choice
and Change in Ethno-
national Identification in
Contemporary Northern
Ireland', *Nationalism
and Ethnic Politics*, 12,
3–4 (2006), 323–46,
and Jennifer Todd,
'Implementing the Good
Friday Agreement:
Civil Society, the State
and Identity Change',
in Guy Ben Porat, ed.,
*Implementing Peace
Agreements in South
Africa, Northern Ireland
and Israel* (forthcoming,
Houndsmill, 2007).

29 See Todd, 'Social
Transformations' for
a discussion of the
typology, and Todd et
al., 'Fluid or Frozen', for
examples.

30 Guy Ben Porat, *Global
Liberalism, Local
Populism: Peace and
Conflict in Israel/
Palestine and Northern
Ireland* (Syracuse,
NY, 2006); Gladys
Ganiel, 'Emerging
from the Evangelical
Subculture in Northern
Ireland: A Case Study
of the Zero28 and
Ikon Community',
*International Journal
for the Study of the
Christian Church*, 6, 1
(2006), 38–48

the communal power balance, culminating in the 1998 Agreement. Surveys showed that this had not provoked major change in identity-categories: some young Protestants apart, who are moving to a Northern Irish identity, Protestants and Catholics continue to polarize in their choice, respectively, of a British and an Irish identity.[27] Surely the shifts must have provoked change in the oppositional aspects of identity?[28] If they had, why not more political progress? Some eighty in-depth interviews in Northern Ireland helped give answers. Preliminary analysis showed no conversion from one identity package to another, and, surprisingly, relatively little reaffirmation of old dichotomies.[29] It suggested that three types of change are prevalent: assimilation, adaptation and privatization.

Assimilation is where actors reshuffle the elements of identity, retaining the national category of identity but reprioritizing the contents and their relation with other categories, differentiating the substantive cultural meanings of ethnicity from associated oppositions based on status and power hierarchies and retaining the former, while marginalizing or casting out the latter. There is evidence that sections of the business class and of evangelical Protestants in Northern Ireland have done just that.[30] It occurred among a minority of our respondents. Some of the most explicit examples took place through intense, if short-lived, personal crises, where individuals reassessed many of the oppositional contents of their identity-categories and dispensed with them. These

31 Muldoon et al., 'Nature and Meaning of Identity'

32 In an interview with Nathalie Rougier, see Todd et al., 'Fluid or Frozen', 341.

33 Claire Mitchell, 'Protestant Identification and Political Change in Northern Ireland', *Ethnic and Racial Studies*, 26, 4 (2003), 612–31

34 In an interview with Lorenzo Cañás Bottos, see Todd et al., 'Fluid or Frozen', 332–33.

individuals reported a helter-skelter of change, with initial movement (typically within cross-community institutions) leading to new levels of cognitive dissonance — one Protestant woman reported: 'I had been brought up with a stereotype of a Sinn Féin person as an absolute monster, you know, and then on the other hand I had X who was a very friendly, amicable woman and ... I had an awful time trying to reconcile the two ...' Further change results. It is not difficult to explain why this type of identity change is infrequent. The changes are cumulative and radical, involving renegotiation of relations with family and friends. They happen through periods of crisis and involve a number of choice-points, at each of which the process could have stopped. In short, this sort of identity shift requires considerable work, strong incentives and resources (not least safety and space to reassess).

Adaptation is where actors adapt to the practices required in the new social order without changing the oppositional elements of their identity. They keep their own values and self-categorizations distinct from their social conformity. Plausible examples include those mainstream unionists who have given more or less grudging and partial support to the institutions of the 1998 Agreement, while retaining their older conceptual categorizations. It was found to be a common response to change, that could incrementally wear away at the oppositional categories. For example, significant numbers of respondents in a large, predominantly Catholic, border town asserted a discourse of moderation and pluralism, of acceptance of the other, a desire not to offend Protestants, at the same time as asserting uncriticized religious and national categories of identity.[31] This could be interpreted as a 'politically correct' adaptive discourse, covering an oppositional consciousness. However, a similar discourse of moderation and gradualist change was common to respondents who showed

abundant evidence in the interviews that they had opened to radical difference, and had come to relativize the moral contents of their own identity. Some told of journeys from a highly oppositional consciousness to a recognition of the other's viewpoint. Such gradual adaptation, when it relativizes the moral content of national identity and permits a truly liberal nationalism is of major political import. Even when it does not go so far, it can encourage political compromise, although that compromise remains prone to crisis: as one respondent eloquently put it, referring to memories of injustice and repression, 'The ceasefire is very important ... it's the biggest thing you know, it's so important that that's sustained but when wee things happen you know that that memory is still somewhere buried in your brain.'[32]

Privatization rearranges the elements of identity, marginalizing all macro-social elements, making recessive national, political, class and status categorizations, shrinking the core of identity into the private, the familial, perhaps also the religious sphere.[33] It was another common response in the Northern Ireland interviews. On the one hand, there was a significant minority (from both Protestant and Catholic backgrounds) who avoided oppositional identities and wanted above all to live outside of the Protestant/Catholic and unionist/nationalist categories, which they saw as essentially oppositional. One man described himself only as 'a plumber' and tried to steer a way through a sectarian society, while according the least possible recognition to its core categories.[34] Others avoided opposition by seeing all national identities as just official labels, 'something to tick in a box'. It also took the form of detachment from communal norms and practices, while privately espousing new modes of thinking. One woman retained a self-declared identity as British ('It's a number stamped on my passport and that's about it'), even though she would have 'loved there to be an identity of Northern Irish', and also spoke of her liking for Irish culture. It is as if the elements of her identity had changed, while the category of identity remained British, uncomfortably and emptily so.[35] Similar unexpected configurations have appeared in other qualitative research with evangelical Protestants, where Democratic Unionist Party (DUP) voters have, for example, quite radically changed their perspectives on the Irish state.[36] Privatization allows a radicalness of thought, while retaining communal ties. It does not, however, directly translate into politics. The urgent question is what sorts of political opportunity and incentive can translate individual movement into collective politics, what opportunities for public choice will allow 'tipping movements' to occur, where whole populations move to a new perspective?

Revolution Four:
Locking In (and Unlocking)
Ethno-national Identities and Conflict

Two major breakthroughs must be added to those above, which reconnect identity, ethnicity and culture to institutions and social structure. The first, pioneered by Doug McAdam, Sidney Tarrow and Charles Tilly, places identity and identity shift as one part of sequences of mobilization and collective action.[37] For them, the quest is to find common mechanisms and sequences of mechanisms that are combined and recombined differently in different situations to produce more or less intense conflict, more or less oppositional identities, more or less radical mobilization. Ethnic conflict and class conflict thus have much more in common — in the mechanisms by which identities are formed and oppression resisted — than often thought.[38] Similarly, settlement processes are closer to other processes of radical institutional change than usually supposed.[39] The intellectual field is thus opened out to compare different

sorts of mobilization and conflict and transformation.

Second, the notion of lock-in or path-dependence has marked a return of history to the social sciences.[40] The key idea here is that a particular historical moment (the seventeenth-century plantation and its aftermath) can create a configuration of relationships — a concatenation of mechanisms — that generates strong tendencies to self-reproduction. History matters: institutions and relationships that no one would choose may continue for centuries; identities are 'sticky' and once formed do not change. Much of the research involved here is in showing exactly how institutions get regenerated and how they change: the mechanisms by which older repertoires keep their efficacy, and the pressures, choices and incentives that work together to generate at times continuity and at times incremental or radical change.[41]

The implications for the study of ethnic conflict and ethno-national identity are major. In some ethno-national conflicts — and Northern Ireland is a prime example — there are significant continuities over time, the 'dreary steeples' reappear after world wars, and what is required is to show the mechanisms by which seemingly dysfunctional conflict gets reproduced and by which the constant tendencies towards and attempts at change get stalled or stunted. Equally there is the question of the ways in which change occurs: the windows of opportunity given by global developments, the resources that incrementally build up (not least, resources of identity shift), and the ways in which they can be harnessed towards settlement. These perspectives, in short, give us a handle on the question: 'If people's identities are changeable, what then locks in conflict?' The approach, however, involves us in refocusing our attention to the wider communal, institutional and structural-power logics in which identity and identity shift have their place.

35 Interviews by Theresa O'Keefe

36 Gladys Ganiel, 'Ulster Says Maybe: The Restructuring of Evangelical Politics in Northern Ireland', *Irish Political Studies*, 21, 2 (2006), 137–55; Claire Mitchell and Jennifer Todd, 'Between the Devil and the Deep Blue Sea: Nationality, Power and Symbolic Trade-offs among Evangelical Protestants in Northern Ireland', *Nations and Nationalism*, 13, 4 (forthcoming 2007)

37 Doug McAdam, Sidney Tarrow and Charles Tilly, *Dynamics of Contention. Cambridge Studies in Contentious Politics* (Cambridge, Mass., 2000)

38 Michèle Lamont's work, some of which is cited above, shows this clearly.

39 Ruane and Todd, 'Path Dependence in Settlement Processes'

40 James Mahoney, 'Path Dependence in Historical Sociology', *Theory and Society*, 29 (2000), 507–48; Paul Pierson, *Politics in Time: History, Institutions and Social Analysis* (Princeton, 2004); James Mahoney and Dietrich Rueshemeyer, eds., *Comparative Historical Analysis in the Social Sciences* (Cambridge, 2003)

41 Andrew P. Cortell and Susan Peterson, 'Altered States: Explaining Domestic Institutional Change', *British Journal of Political Science*, 29 (1999) 177–200; Wolfgang Streek and Kathleen Thelen, eds., *Beyond Continuity: Institutional Change in Advanced Political Economies* (Oxford, 2005)

42 As well as the two projects discussed here, which produced over 250 in-depth interviews, North and South, other major funded projects were undertaken in University College Cork (on Protestant minorities) and in National University of Ireland, Maynooth (on life histories).

Changing Forms of Irish Identity

For the moment, and it probably is only a momentary phase, paradigmatic constraints appear to have loosened and it is possible to investigate identity change comparatively, cumulatively and empirically, paralleling contemporary discussions on institutional change and learning from interdisciplinary debate. In this context, the beginnings of research funding for the social sciences in Ireland is creating an infrastructure for understanding identity change.[42] Some preliminary findings from the research mentioned in this essay are outlined below to enable further discussion and debate.

- Nationality remains important, even for the young, but how to be national is negotiable and varying.
- Occasions of choice and reflection on national identity are frequent and identity shift is common. Change is seldom radical. It is costly for individuals, socially and personally, and they do not undertake it lightly.
- Individuals combine identity-categories, and in this sense identity-hybridity is very common. Fluidity of movement between different identity packages is rare: one child of a mixed marriage whom we interviewed moved fluidly between Protestant and Catholic repertoires and was uncategorizable in terms of the Northern Ireland binaries, but he was an exception.
- Change is not provoked simply by political events, even major events like the Good Friday Agreement, nor by changing power relations alone. It is only when the events and changed relations impact on interactions and experience in everyday life that they may provoke identity shift.
- What we see is a drama of negotiation and imaginative interaction of nationality, where not only the categories but the modes of being national are in play. As people on the Southern side of the border redefine their nationality in moral terms and in effect cut off Irishness to some from the North, so some Northern Catholics shift to a Northern Irish focus of identity, thus creating a different sort of alienation between North and South: from a moral alienation and definition of difference to a national one.
- This raises a new agenda for analysis of nationalism in Ireland, requiring analysis not simply of the South but of North–South contrasts, challenges and interrelations. This drama of self–other definition takes place in context of radical economic and socio-political changes, which give new incentives for tipping movements, collective change and individual boundary breaching. ∎

The research on which this article is based was made possible by funding from the EU Programme for Peace and Reconciliation, through the Higher Education Authority, North-South Strand Two programme, and from the Higher Education Authority Programme for Research in Third Level Institutions, 3. Research was co-ordinated from the Geary Institute UCD with post-doctoral fellows Lorenzo Cañás Bottos, Nathalie Rougier, Katrina McLoughlin, Theresa O'Keefe, colleagues Orla Muldoon and Karen Trew, and in the Identity, Diversity and Citizenship programme, John Coakley, Alice Feldman, Tom Inglis and Martin Dowling, none of whom is responsible for the arguments here. This analysis draws on work I have published individually and jointly over the last three years.

'That Car'

Modernity, Northern Ireland and the DMC–12

Richard Kirkland

Your eyes skim the sleek, sensuous stainless steel body, and all your senses tell you, 'I've got to have it!'
The counterbalanced gull-wing doors rise effortlessly, beckoning you inside.
The soft leather seat in the cockpit fits you like it was made for your body.
You turn the key. The light alloy V-6 comes to life instantly.
The DeLorean. Surely one of the most awaited automobiles in automotive history.
It all began with one man's vision of the perfect personal luxury car. Built for long-life, it employs the latest space age materials.
Of course, everyone stares at you as you drive by. Sure they're a little envious. That's expected. After all, you're the one Living the Dream. Start living it today at a dealer near you.[1]

1 'Live the Dream', two page colour advertisement for the DeLorean car, *Time Magazine* (January 1982), reproduced in John Lamm, *DeLorean: Stainless Steel Illusion* (Santa Ana, 1983), 100.
2 Douglas Mao, *Solid Objects: Modernism and the Test of Production* (Princeton, 1988), 6; Peter Wagner, *Theorizing Modernity: Inescapability and Attainability in Social Theory* (London, 2001), 4, conceives this 'double connotation' as modernity being 'always both philosophical and empirical, or both substantive and temporal, or … both conceptual and historical'.

The story of the DeLorean Motor Company's venture in Northern Ireland in the early 1980s may be offered as a parable of a state-sponsored policy, there and in Ireland generally, to persuade private capital to assist in the modernization of Ireland. An attempt to build a 120 mph supercar, the DMC–12, for the American market in one of Belfast's most economically deprived areas, the episode proved to be both tragic and farcical. It also became a resonant symbol of the failure of Northern Ireland as a post-industrial economic entity. And this bizarre affair provides a vivid example of the shifting, contested nature of modernity itself. If we can, in Douglas Mao's arresting phrase, 'read through objects to the truth of the social totality that produced them', perhaps a historical understanding of the DMC–12 *affaire* might enable us to

apprehend something of what Peter Wagner has described as modernity's 'double connotation'.[2]

This 'double connotation' has become a central concern in Irish Studies, the focus of an intellectual project through which, in Fredric Jameson's words, '"modernity" is stripped of its semblance of obviousness'.[3] Critics such as Joe Cleary, Luke Gibbons, Colin Graham, David Lloyd, Conor McCarthy and Terry Eagleton have elaborated, for the Irish experience, the dialectical terms of modernity's appeal, and contributed to the development of a critical practice that aims to account for its protean, ultimately ephemeral, nature.[4] The political significance of these interventions derives from the various ways in which critics have addressed a dilemma identified

Lead image: On a tour to impress potential investors in 1978: a prototype DMC–12 in front of the Bonaventure Hotel in Los Angeles. Photograph: Larry Chapman, courtesy of Jerry Williamson.

Left: The DMC plant in Dunmurry, Belfast. Photograph: courtesy of Bill Collins.

by Wagner, namely that 'any attempt at a sociology of modernity risks falling prey to the problematic of its being enmeshed with the social world it tries to understand'.[5] For Graham, this is the 'fundamental question', as any analysis of what he terms 'the utopian and the modernising in relation to Ireland' must be judged in terms of its 'relation to the "progress" it attempts to describe, decry or be thankful for'.[6]

Graham's point is important because it indicates that one of the standard views of the DeLorean project — as the modern declaring itself amidst the wreckage of the old, the atavistic and the uselessly traditional — itself deserves questioning. As Eamonn Hughes has argued, Northern Ireland may be seen, not as a pre-modern location nervously awaiting the modernizing benefits of American corporate finance, but as 'a modern place with the pluralities, discontents, and linkages appropriate to a modern place'.[7] Indeed, the political violence that has occurred in the North since the late 1960s can be understood dialectically as both modern and pre-modern, both of its time and residual.

But we can usefully bypass the worn terms of this account and focus instead on a persistent tendency in the history of Northern Ireland to 'stage the moment of modernity' through a series of discrete events. These would include prestigious cultural projects with an international dimension, public architecture such as the Castlecourt Shopping Centre in Belfast, and exhibitions such as Ulster '71. Their purpose in relation to the state is to act as symbols of invigoration — as enabling myths — that can sustain and advance an idea of Northern Ireland itself as an entity engaged in a productive relationship with the modern. Central to this is fantasy, a mode that Graham has identified as linking both the idea of the nation and that of capitalist modernity.[8] It is in these terms that the British government's investment in DeLorean can be understood — as a fantastical staging of the modern at a time when Northern Ireland was predominantly understood as a site of anachronistic passions.

In this context, the modernity that the DeLorean project embodied came, to use Cleary's terms, 'entirely from "above" and

3   Quoted in Joe Cleary, 'Introduction: Ireland and Modernity', in Joe Cleary and Claire Connolly, eds., *Cambridge Companion to Modern Irish Culture* (Cambridge, 2005), 1–21, 2

4   See Cleary's essay on Ireland and modernity referenced above, Luke Gibbons's *Transformations in Irish Culture* (Cork, 1996), Colin Graham's *Deconstructing Ireland: Identity, Theory, Culture* (Edinburgh, 2001), David Lloyd's *Ireland after History* (Cork, 1999), Conor McCarthy's *Modernisation, Crisis and Culture in Ireland* (Dublin, 2000), and Terry Eagleton's 'The Archaic Avant Garde' in his *Heathcliff and the Great Hunger: Studies in Irish Culture* (London, 1995), 273–319.

5   Peter Wagner, *A Sociology of Modernity: Liberty and Discipline* (London, 1994), ix

6 Graham, *Deconstructing Ireland*, 14
7 Eamonn Hughes, 'Introduction: Northern Ireland — Border Country', in Eamonn Hughes, ed., *Culture and Politics in Northern Ireland* (Milton Keynes, 1991), 3
8 Graham, *Deconstructing Ireland*, 16
9 Cleary, 'Introduction', 3
10 Mao, *Solid Objects*, 6
11 William Haddad, *Hard Driving: My Years with John DeLorean* (New York, 1985), 27
12 Richard Hughes, 'DeLorean: Belfast's Concorde?', *Car* (February 1979), reproduced in R. M. Clarke, *DeLorean 1977–1995 Gold Portfolio* (Cobham, 2005), 22–25, 22
13 Ivan Fallon and James Srodes, *DeLorean: The Rise and Fall of a Dream-maker* (London, 1983), 116
14 Fallon and Srodes, *Rise and Fall of a Dream-maker*, 134

"without", rather than from "within" or "below"', and as such, it can be understood as simply a slightly revised version of the dominant way in which Ireland and modernity have historically been negotiated. For Cleary, this type of modernity is a 'gift of colonial or religious conquest'.[9] The argument here is that it was through the discourses of colonial exchange that the DeLorean company typically came to understand its own particular form of civilizing mission. Central to this mission is, of course, the production of commodities, and it is ultimately the very physicality of the car — corporate finance rendered in startling material form — that carried this message. As a result, the DMC–12 is nothing less than an example of what Douglas Mao calls 'the explosively signifying commodity' — the apprehension of which acts as a marker of modernity itself. This moment of the modern is a disturbance in the midst of the known.[10] It declares itself loudly and unilaterally, but significantly it can never enter the realm of the familiar without a struggle. Instead, the modern is always imagined as being in a conflict with forces it always seeks to supplant. So imagined, it is only identifiable in relation to what it seeks to overcome; in order for it to be visible at all, it must be seen as partially, never wholly, victorious over what it is defined against. Understood as such, modernity is always dialectically dependent on the old.

The basic story of Northern Ireland's DeLorean adventure is well known, but it rewards revisiting. John Zachary DeLorean (1925–2005) was a hugely charismatic, if eccentric, figure who had risen through the corporate hierarchy of General Motors with seemingly effortless momentum. Allegedly on the verge of the presidency of that corporation, he suddenly left, claiming (among other things) that 'the automotive industry has lost its masculinity'.[11] He established his own firm, the DeLorean Motor Company (DMC), in 1973, and acquired investment loans from the Bank of America. With the design and development of the car that would eventually become the DMC–12 in hand, he began his search for a suitable factory site, a place where labour was cheap and state subsidy a likelihood. After talks with government officials from the Republic of Ireland and Puerto Rico — one commentator describing the project as being 'hawked around the world' — a late intervention by the British government in 1978 secured the factory for Northern Ireland.[12] By any measure, the terms of the deal were astonishingly generous. Delorean persuaded the Labour administration to advance £54 million in grants, equity and loans, and this was followed by a further £30 million from Margaret Thatcher's new Conservative administration in 1980. As a result, each of the proposed 2,000 jobs created would cost the taxpayer something close to £25,000 — far more than in any previous government intervention in industrial job creation. The agreement was announced to sceptical journalists on 3 August 1978. In return for his state subsidy, DeLorean undertook to build a 550,000-square-foot factory on a 72-acre site at Dunmurry, six miles to the south-west of the city. With the momentum of free-flowing capital behind him, he 'promised to move from cow pasture to production within eighteen months', a promise that was kept.[13]

But all was not what it seemed. DeLorean's own financial investment in the venture was negligible, bordering on non-existent, almost certainly because he was never entirely convinced that the project would succeed. One month after the deal with the British was signed, he startled DMC executives with the sudden assertion, 'I don't think we'll ever build the car in Northern Ireland; the IRA will blow it up'.[14] More importantly, the heavily subsidized presence of DMC in Dunmurry was, paradoxically, at once confirmation that Northern Ireland's economy was an abnormal failure and part of a governmental effort to represent the society as normal. The economic

situation was certainly grievous. General unemployment in Northern Ireland at the time was, at around 11 per cent, more than twice the UK average; unemployment among Catholics in West Belfast was nearer to 50 per cent, and showing every sign of worsening. But the readiness of an administration as ideologically adverse to state subsidy for industry as Thatcher's Conservatives to follow Labour in the heavy funding and high profile fêting of DeLorean, served only to underline that there was more at stake than mere job creation. Since the mid-1970s, London's Irish policy had essentially been a counter-insurgency strategy of Ulsterization, criminalization and normalization — that is, respectively, the replacement of British troops with locally recruited 'security forces', the representation of insurgents as criminals and gangsters, and the removal of the most overt signs of military conflict. Roy

Mason, the Labour Party secretary of state for Northern Ireland who first championed the project, was a professed believer in the effectiveness of economic intervention as a means of undercutting support for the IRA. Convinced that 'terrorists need unhappiness and hopelessness as fish need water', he assured his Cabinet colleagues in July 1978 that the investment in DeLorean would 'indirectly' save the lives of British soldiers and deal 'a hammer blow to the IRA'.[15]

DeLorean himself was at times ambivalent about Northern Ireland and at others openly dismissive. Still, he was nobody's fool. In the negotiations for financial concessions he had exploited the government's disparate reasons for wanting to bring his factory to the North and he now proclaimed: 'I'm starting to recognise that God stuck me here to be part of the solution to the crisis in Northern Ireland.'[16] Such was the prevailing goodwill for DeLorean that many were prepared to believe him. After all, as the American motoring journalist Tony Swan argued, 'guys with jobs are a lot less likely to enroll in their local extremist bomb factory'.[17] The facile terms of this equivalence effectively reveal the flaws of the argument. By asserting the primacy of economic factors in accounting for IRA support in deprived areas of the North, the government concomitantly underplayed the significance of cultural and historical factors in the IRA's appeal. Rather than a mere misjudgement of priorities, this policy reflected a much more profound misunderstanding of the nature of the conflict, and it was one that would be starkly outlined by the looming H-Block crisis.

As would become increasingly clear, the major instability at the heart of this precarious financial edifice was John DeLorean himself. An inveterate fantasist who would 'sooner be sterilized than go second class', according to Craig Waters, DeLorean was a figure with 'no understanding of his limitations'.[18] Rarely without either a project or a scandal, his

John DeLorean, sitting in the DMC–12, 1981. Photograph: Central Press/ Getty Images.

15 Roy Mason, *Paying the Price* (London, 1999), 21; Paul Dixon, 'British Policy towards Northern Ireland 1969–2000: Continuity, Tactical Adjustment and Consistent "Inconsistencies"', *British Journal of Politics and International Relations*, 3, 3 (2001), 340–68, 362

16 Haddad, *Hard Driving*, 54

17 Tony Swan, 'DeLorean: The American Dream is Alive and Fighting for Survival in Northern Ireland', *Motor Trend* (May 1981), 85–90, 85

18 Craig R. Waters, 'John DeLorean and the Icarus Factor', *Inc.* (April 1983), 35–42, 35, 38

Gloria Hunniford, presenter of Ulster Television's *Good Evening Ulster*, poses with a DMC–12. Photograph: Ken McNally.

19 The complex if entertaining plot of this novel is outlined on Haddad's *Hard Driving*, 13.

20 Tony Scott, 'Jim's Irish Joke?', *Motor* (1 December 1979), reproduced in Clarke, *DeLorean 1977–1995 Gold Portfolio*, 26–29, 26.

21 Swan, 'DeLorean', 39; Peter Martin, 'Supercar that Fuels New Hope for Ulster', *Now* (21 March 1980), 66–67

numerous financial concerns included a potato farm, a stake in two American football teams, a bus-building venture, an avocado farm in California, a plan to import Alfa Romeo, Suzuki, and Daihatsu cars into the US, a replica-car-building firm, investment in an optical laser research company, a snowcat manufacturing business, a stake in a maritime services enterprise, and a (sadly) uncompleted novel about the nuclear arms race.[19] With this record, it is not surprising that the Dunmurry project provoked scepticism from the first: 'Did you hear the one about the flashy America who blarnied £53 million of your money from Jim Callaghan in order to build in Ireland his 120 mph dream car for sale almost solely to the 55 mph-limited Yanks?' joked one car journalist.[20] Others were less cynical. For Swan, DeLorean represented nothing less than 'the last stand of the individual entrepreneur in a business

world populated by faceless conglomerate giants', while Peter Martin, with a faith that would soon appear hopelessly naïve, proclaimed: 'the other partners in this venture are you and me and not least the ragamuffin children who sell newspapers from pub to pub every evening in Belfast's many ghettos of unemployment'.[21] But the most gullible were the ministers and civil servants of the British Government, and it was their opinions that mattered.

Construction of the factory at Dunmurry began on 2 October 1978 with a small tree-planting ceremony conducted by DeLorean, his wife Christine, and one Don Concannon, a minister of state for Northern Ireland. As John Lamm observed, the event 'had a certain air of foreboding'. Appropriately, perhaps, the symbolism of the ceremony was muddled and open to contrasting interpretations. According to Lamm, the three trees planted

Don Concannon, Labour minister of state for Northern Ireland, and John DeLorean at the tree-planting ceremony that marked the commencement of work on the Dunmurry plant, 2 October 1978. Women supporting republican prisoners' campaign for political status can be seen through the wire fence. Photograph: courtesy of Bill Collins.

by DeLorean and various Northern Irish politicians symbolized 'the involvement of DeLorean, England and Northern Ireland'.[22] Conversely, for William Haddad, a DMC executive, they represented 'a trinity marking the joint effort of the Catholics, the Protestants and the British'.[23] Others would mark the event in less convoluted ways. As the *Irish News* reported:

> Throughout the ceremony about 50 women, protesting about conditions in the H-Blocks at Long Kesh, chanted 'Brits Out' and 'Smash H-Block' and sang 'The Soldier's Song'. Mr Gerry Fitt, who was attending the ceremony, described the women's behaviour as 'disgraceful'. The women did not represent the views of the community living in Twinbrook and they were merely involved in a propaganda exercise, he declared. Canon

Padraig Murphy, P.P., St John's, said he hoped DeLorean would not judge the community by extremists on either side.[24]

Despite police protection, the DMC executives were certainly unnerved by their first taste of Northern Irish politics. Jerry Williamson was convinced that 'if they'd had guns they would have shot at us', while John DeLorean recalled with endearing frankness, 'they said they weren't protesting us, they were primarily protesting Don Concannon, who kept taunting them through the fence. I felt like hiding under a car, to be honest with you.'[25]

The presence of the demonstration at the ceremony was appropriate if only because the H-Block campaign and hunger strikes would shadow the fortunes of DMC throughout its short existence. The factory's

22 Lamm, *Stainless Steel Illusion*, 79
23 Haddad, *Hard Driving*, 45
24 'Rush for Jobs at DeLorean', front-page story, *Irish News*, 3 October 1978
25 Lamm, *Stainless Steel Illusion*, 80

26 Fallon and Srodes, *Rise and Fall of a Dream-maker*, 282; the emphasis is DeLorean's.

27 Haddad, *Hard Driving*, 119

28 Martin, 'Supercar that Fuels New Hope for Ulster', 67

29 Haddad, *Hard Driving*, 127

30 Martin, 'Supercar that Fuels New Hope for Ulster', 66

location between Protestant and Catholic enclaves reflected the government's concern that the company be seen to recruit from both sides of the community, but it also made it vulnerable to attack. This fear found material form in the architecture of the site. A separate access road was built from the Lisburn Road to enable Protestants to avoid travelling through the Catholic Twinbrook estate, while the plant itself was surrounded by two fences and split into a number of smaller buildings so that the effects of arson or looting might be minimized. This proved to be a wise precaution. The mother of Bobby Sands, Anti-H-Block MP for Fermanagh–South Tyrone and hunger-strike leader of IRA prisoners in Long Kesh, lived on the Twinbrook estate, and on the night of his death, 5 May 1981, a small group of rioters rammed the outer gates and got close enough to the factory to fire-bomb a small wooden building near the inner perimeter fence. This was the office of DMC's chief engineer, Mike Loasby, and it contained many of the blueprints and engineering drawings for the car. As duplicates of these were held elsewhere, this was an inconvenience rather than a disaster, but DeLorean still used the attack as an excuse to file a massively inflated claim for compensation with the British government. As his confidential memo to Haddad two days later exulted:

> Today DMC is faced with the greatest opportunity of your corporate lifetime. With the troubles in Twinbrook/Belfast for the first time in our tenure there, *no single person in UK begrudges us the $160,000,000 we got from the government!* Most today think we earned it![26]

The fire-bombing of the wooden building, however, was the only significant act of violence that affected the company, and, for the most part, DMC enjoyed good relations with both sides of the community. Notwithstanding the British

army's occasional use of the building as a vantage point for reconnoitring nationalist Twinbrook, republicans were ambivalent about the factory.[27] Its status as a prominent government initiative made it an attractive target, but the fact that DMC was an American company reduced that unwelcome allure. Moreover, the nationalist community generally would have been resistant to any attack on a facility in which working-class Catholics held well-paid jobs. One journalist reported that the 'word is that the people of Twinbrook, which is Catholic through and through, have warned off the Provos: "Don't touch that factory. There's jobs for us in there"'.[28] Whether this was true or not, the IRA took a keen interest in what was happening inside the factory and, according to Haddad, met with him in a flat in Andersonstown in order to discuss the company's employment policy. The IRA was seemingly satisfied with his answers. The company did maintain a fairly equal balance of Catholic and Protestant employees, but Catholics were much more likely to be employed in 'dirty jobs' such as the body-press plant.[29] One euphemism that gained currency at this time was that 'skilled' in actuality meant 'Protestant'.

The most remarkable element of the whole enterprise was, of course, the car itself. Designed by the Italian Giorgetto Giugiaro in the mid-1970s, it was described by one early reviewer as 'a luxurious performance car with brushed stainless steel finish, gull-wing doors and pornographically low Italian styling'.[30] It was certainly an extraordinary creation. With its angular lines, uncompromisingly sharp edges and deeply raked windscreen, the car seemed unwilling to acknowledge its place in traditions of automotive design. It clearly looked nothing like its muscular American competitors, and (despite sharing much of its engineering with the Lotus Esprit) it similarly did not reference any clear European lineage. Car journalists struggled to find a language to describe it:

On first sight, the prototype is just flat stunning. … The image is squat and smooth, like a pumpkin seed, and the stainless-steel skin makes it glow, changing from a metallic grey at midday to ever warmer shades of pink as the sun works towards evening. There is nothing frilly about this car, no flash and filigree for its own sake. Instead there is a kind of purity of form, the same suggestion you get in a well-crafted hand tool.[31]

Starved of origin, the DMC–12 was sold in the US without any acknowledgement that it was built in Ireland — a fact that DeLorean was, if anything, eager to conceal. Indeed, considering the extent to which the history of Irish manufacturing has often been reliant on the production and dissemination of Irishness as a quality inherent to the product, the deliberate concealment of the car's origin in Northern Ireland, perfectly understandable in many respects for a commodity of this kind, is also the more noteworthy. Yet, there is of course an industrial pedigree for heavy engineering products in Northern Ireland, particularly shipbuilding and aircraft, and they too have long histories of public subsidy, readily granted by British governments otherwise hostile to such policies. But these did not conform to the commercial profile of the DeLorean project, nor was their history one he seemed anxious to appropriate. It was not just the stain of Northern Irish origin that had to be erased; it was the stain of *any* origin. This was a dream car, after all. It really belonged to Disneyland. As did its finances. This was a classic case of the fetish commodity, with its labour hidden, the collector's item that came from the Capital utopia of Nowhere — free of the local, the political, the sedimented remains of the historical.

DeLorean's ambitions for the DMC–12 went beyond looks and performance, however. He envisaged the product as an 'ethical car', one that would be light in weight and thus fuel efficient, safer in a collision than its competitors, and with a much extended lifespan, thanks to its striking stainless steel body panels (challenging what DeLorean termed 'this dynamic obsolescence kick').[32] Alongside these innovations, it was intended that each car would require a lot less energy to build than a comparable model constructed in a less advanced factory. In

31 Anonymous, 'The DMC–12', *Car and Driver* (July 1977), reproduced in Clarke, *DeLorean 1977–1995 Gold Portfolio*, 5–12, 9.

32 Anonymous, 'The Gull Wing Snub', *Wheels* (May 1980), reproduced in Clarke, *DeLorean 1977–1995 Gold Portfolio*, 30–32.

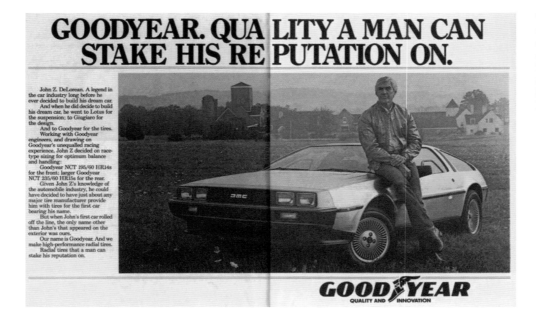

The DMC–12 used Goodyear NCT tyres; a full-colour two-page Goodyear advertisement trades on DeLorean's reputation for rugged individualism. Photograph: courtesy of Robert Lamrock.

33 Hillel Levin, *John DeLorean: The Maverick Mogul* (London, 1983), 206

34 Ed Jacobs, 'Under the Wolf's Clothing Lies a Safety Car for the Real World', *Popular Science* (July 1981), 71–72

35 Don Sherman, 'The DeLorean Dilemma', *Car and Driver* (July 1981), reproduced in Clarke, *DeLorean 1977–1995 Gold Portfolio*, 50–54, 52.

36 Levin, *Maverick Mogul*, 212

37 Sherman, 'The DeLorean Dilemma', 54

truth, however, the car's 'newness' went no further than its immediate visual aspect. Despite DeLorean's claim that it was a 'revolutionary new product', some of its technology was outdated even before it entered production.[33] As design problems with the prototype mounted, DeLorean invited Colin Chapman of Lotus Cars substantially to redesign the vehicle, and while this did achieve the desired outcome of making the DMC–12 production-worthy, the original concept of the ethical car was hugely compromised. Indeed, by the time Chapman had completed his work, in many respects only the external design of the vehicle remained as originally envisaged.

Perhaps because of these compromises the finished car was far from perfect. Even a well-intentioned reviewer from *Popular Science* was forced to acknowledge a high number of peculiar design flaws:

> Above 65 mph all five cars developed a distinct, high-pitched whistle. The markings for the heater and air-conditioner controls were impossible to read in daylight, even though backlit. The digital clock lies nearly flat on the console, and the bottom half is obscured. Some rocker switches are placed on the console under your elbow and frequently bumped during shifting. And none of the heaters was especially effective. Overall, though, the cars were still quite good.[34]

This was not all. As the concept of the ethical car had been gradually compromised, so other design problems asserted themselves. Most obviously, thanks to the replacement of the original advanced plastic frame with a Lotus steel backbone, the production vehicles were excessively heavy. This, in turn, made them too cumbersome for their intended market. Another 'ethical' innovation — the use of stainless steel body panels to combat corrosion — also proved impractical, as their surfaces were marked by the slightest touch. As a result,

the vehicles required constant polishing. Less tangibly, a number of early reviews of the car described the experience of entering it as like being 'entombed'.[35] Instead of embodying a liberating expression of life in capitalist America, as DeLorean had originally intended, the DMC–12 unwittingly reminded its driver of the vanity of mortal desires.

These basic design flaws were compounded by poor construction techniques. While there was general praise for the commitment of the workforce (absenteeism at the factory was a remarkably low 1.2 per cent) and the willingness of the workers to acquire new skills, the lack of any substantial background in manufacturing or engineering created its own difficulties. As one DMC executive observed: 'I was watching one guy putting in water seals around the door, and he was having trouble making it all fit at once, so he was cutting it into pieces, and fitting one little piece at a time. He just had no idea what the seal was for and how it worked.'[36] The first cars constructed by the factory were so poor that they were condemned as 'abysmally short of any standard of commercial acceptability' by *Car and Driver* magazine.[37] Although build quality improved as the workers gained more experience, the car's reputation for unreliability remained. Indeed, according to Dick Brown, vice-president for marketing at DMC, after importation to the US each car had to be 'almost totally reassembled' before it could be shipped on to the dealers — a process that cost a minimum of $1,500 per vehicle. As a result, the one significant advantage of locating the plant in Northern Ireland — the low cost of labour when compared to the US — was almost entirely negated. Common problems that new owners encountered included: malfunctioning doors that would trap the driver inside the vehicle; leaking bodywork; poor panel fittings; radios that did not work; windows that fell out; inoperative fuel gauges; and the fact that the dye from the

DMC–12s being assembled at Dunmurry. Photographs: courtesy of Robert Lamrock.

floor mats would stain the driver's clothing and skin. As if these faults were not enough, some drivers reported a more general problem — the car would not work in cold weather (or if it did work, the throttle had a tendency to freeze jammed open in an alarming manner). The National Highway Safety Administration twice recalled the car in order to rectify serious safety problems, including a potentially faulty fuel pump that in the event of a crash would continue to send fuel to the engine. As Brown noted forthrightly: 'Hey! We can't sell this shit!'[38]

Back in Ireland the project was beginning to encounter other difficulties. For the DMC executives, Belfast was becoming a place of myth and superstition, a city where 'fact and fancy tend to merge', as Haddad put it.[39] In turn they saw themselves as crusaders for modernization, negotiating local sensibilities with a mixture of condescension, timidity, and exasperation. An early episode that illustrates this was the discovery of what was purported to be a faerie tree growing in the middle of the planned factory site. As Dixon Hollinshead, who was in charge of the construction of the plant, recalled:

> we joked about the thorny bush for awhile and then we tried to get one of the crew to cut it down and they wouldn't do it. They'd give us the story about Murphy, who went to cut one down once and cut his leg off. Then I spread a rumour that there was a $100 bill buried under it, but I couldn't get any takers … and then one day it was gone and they all went about their business.

I was accused of cutting it down but I didn't like the publicity, because I figured somebody might blame me for it and get mad about it.[40]

For Haddad the consequences of Hollinshead's act could hardly have been more ominous. As he heard one local construction worker prophesy: 'it's a dark day. You have wrecked everything we're building. The faerie will see to that'.[41]

After DeLorean himself, Haddad is perhaps the most fascinating figure in the DMC story. Haddad had been a journalist, a high-ranking official in the US Peace Corps and a special assistant to Robert F. Kennedy, before pursuing a career in business; according to Mike Knepper, his successor at DMC, he 'had some secretive, undercover-type contacts' and 'was happiest when involved with an intrigue of some kind or another'.[42] In his memoir, *Hard Driving: My Years with John DeLorean*, Haddad describes himself as DeLorean's 'eyes and ears' — the fool to DeLorean's King Lear — informing him of anxieties about the safety of the car and questioning some of the murkier aspects of the financing of the company.[43] Reluctant to listen to these disquieting truths, DeLorean banished Haddad from New York to the factory in Belfast on the day of Sands's funeral. DeLorean believed Haddad was 'scared silly' of the city and, as such, the exile must have seemed like an effective punishment.[44] Scared or not, banishment did not stop Haddad in his self-appointed role as the conscience of DMC. An obsessive memorandum writer, the longer

38 Fallon and Srodes, *Rise and Fall of a Dream-maker*, 288
39 Haddad, *Hard Driving*, 46
40 Lamm, *Stainless Steel Illusion*, 80
41 Haddad, *Hard Driving*, 46
42 Lamm, *Stainless Steel Illusion*, 152
43 Haddad, *Hard Driving*, x
44 www.home.no/delorean/dmcinc.htm

45 Haddad, *Hard Driving*, 52
46 Fallon and Srodes, *Rise and Fall of a Dream-maker*, 134, 283
47 Haddad, *Hard Driving*, 84
48 Fallon and Srodes, *Rise and Fall of a Dream-maker*, 283
49 Haddad, *Hard Driving*, 53
50 Fallon and Srodes, *Rise and Fall of a Dream-maker*, 297
51 Haddad, *Hard Driving*, xi
52 Fallon and Srodes, *Rise and Fall of a Dream-maker*, 379–80

he was in Belfast, the more fantastical his reports back to DeLorean became. Haddad became convinced that the IRA was closely monitoring the movements of DMC executives, recalling that 'British security forces instructed us to book one hotel and stay at another in both London and Belfast; to make several reservations; and not to develop predictable routines'.[45] Although the hybrid discourse of fear and affection that came to characterize his writings about Northern Ireland was typically that of a neo-colonial administrator sent against his will to the empire's furthest reaches, John DeLorean was more one-dimensional in his views. According to Brown, DeLorean characterized the Northern Irish he met as 'dummies, morons, incompetents', while he 'hated and feared' Belfast itself.[46] Little wonder, then, that he investigated purchasing an ankle-length bullet-proof raincoat of a type supposedly pioneered for Henry Kissinger.[47]

Bunkered in Belfast and attempting to keep afloat an increasingly unstable operation, the self-image of the DMC executives began to shift dramatically. Always prone to taking an idealized view of their talents — according to DeLorean, he and his team deserved to 'become the industrial heroes of the UK' — at first they began to think of themselves as war-hardened and somehow invulnerable.[48] Haddad reported with immense pride that the British auditors who oversaw the operation on behalf of the British government compared the DeLorean executives to 'the RAF in 1940: a combination of talent, black humour and suicidal determination'.[49] That many DMC executive memos from Belfast at this time were fantastical in their excesses was perhaps no more than the logical outcome of their attempt to negotiate what they saw as two incompatible world-views. As a memo from Haddad to DeLorean insisted:

John, I have been here when an angry mob (confronted by police firing plastic bullets into a crowd of teenagers) has tried to rip our gate down, and seen them hurl fire and acid bombs within feet of our executives. I have seen our executives retreat to the manufacturing building to keep things going. I have watched them leave in their unprotected individual cars, passing alongside the unpredictable areas. (And we know that steel tipped sniper bullets have ripped into this place.)

Ivan Fallon and James Srodes have pointed out that this was all 'pure fiction'.[50] The factory had only come under significant attack once, on the night of Sands's death, and no executives, including Haddad, were anywhere near the plant at that time. What is of greater interest in Haddad's report, however, is its preoccupation with boundaries, transgressions and penetration (with the executives playing the role of vulnerable maidens); a discourse that can perhaps be described as a form of corporate capitalist gothic. As the gothic is a discursive formation frequently found at the point at which the modern and the pre-modern violently collide, its emergence in Haddad's accounts is certainly symptomatic.

Fearful that the British government — which had been leaked copies of all Haddad's memos by Marian Gibson, a disaffected former DMC secretary — would instigate an inquiry, DeLorean denounced them as forgeries and attempted to destroy Haddad's credibility.[51] By this stage, however, the damage was done. Indeed, DeLorean himself was beginning to exhibit similar symptoms of paranoia, claiming in February 1982 that there had been a total of 140 fire-bombings at the factory, that DeLorean executives had come under sniper attack, and that he had been told to 'stay away from windows when at the facility'. Similarly, he insisted that he could not stay overnight in Belfast, as 'the Brits want me out of here by nightfall — I'm a target!'[52] Although these stories were, as an unnamed DeLorean executive put it, 'unmitigated bullshit', so fearful did

DeLorean become about the possibility of IRA assassination that he began to publicize a previously unknown devotion to the Catholic Church, making a point of stopping at Catholic churches in Belfast whenever he was passing.[53] This was all the more surprising for those who knew him prior to his Northern Irish adventure; when he was at General Motors, he had indicated that he was an Episcopalian.[54]

By the start of 1982, the problems that faced DMC had become so great that the dissolution of the company appeared inevitable. Every part of the business was affected by cash-flow problems, and the failure of a proposed stock issue that would have raised over $27 million meant that the firm could do little to alleviate its situation. DeLorean had alienated most of his original executive team (including Haddad), and the car itself was the subject of increasingly angry customer complaints. Despite DeLorean's appeals, the government was reluctant to provide more funding for the firm unless he was able to raise an equivalent amount; therefore, with no realistic alternative left to him, he invited the government to call in the receivers. The subsequent closure of the factory was prolonged and agonizing. By April 1982, the factory workers were on a one-day week. The unionist *Belfast Telegraph*, which now referred to the DMC–12 as simply 'that car', noted that 'while faith in the car is unshaken', firms supplying parts for the factory were now owed £26 million. Despite this — and surprisingly — it reported that while there was criticism of John DeLorean, 'there is an almost total absence of bitterness'.[55] Instead, a perception developed that the project had been somehow cursed from the start. With the firm in receivership, Loasby left the company bemoaning that 'everything combined against it', while the *Belfast Telegraph* lamented that 'the fates have not been kind'.[56] The nationalist *Irish News* was more forthright in its diagnosis:

The DeLorean tragedy — for that is unmistakably what it is — is seemingly grinding its stark and bitter way towards a not unexpected end. It is difficult to say whether the catastrophe has been made even worse by the tiny flickers of hope kept going from week to week as the official receivers kept interspersing optimistic phrases into the prevailing gloom. … And as usual it is the ordinary man and woman who eventually pick up the tab — in this case the unfortunate 1,500 employees of DeLorean with their families and the local trade they help to maintain — of widening depression, bad housing, high prices and total disillusionment.[57]

Two days after this report, on 27 May, workers from the factory began a sit-in in the canteen, partly in protest at the closure, partly to guard the building from hopeful looters who had begun to circle ominously around the perimeter fencing. It was to no avail and the site closed for the final time on 31 May. Overshadowed by the Falklands conflict and the papal visit to Britain, the final day of the factory was ignored by most of the British news media, but David Beresford in the *Guardian* provided a suitable obituary:

The funeral, such as it was, passed off uneventfully. The obsequies were performed by the 1,500 workers and the Department of Health and Social Security who kept open two social security offices on the Bank Holiday, so the workers could sign on the dole. The factory resembled a well kept graveyard … The presses, huge extractor fans, ovens and jigs were silent; about 1,000 cars sat motionless on the assembly line, vainly waiting for the engineers and fitters to transform them into status symbols for American roads. The tragedy attendant on all funerals was in the pride with which Mr Brendan Mackin, a shop steward and the former DeLorean

53 Levin, *Maverick Mogul*, 234, refers to DeLorean visiting 'St. Patrick's Cathedral'; the Catholic cathedral in Belfast is St. Peter's, and since it is in the republican Lower Falls, it seems unlikely that it would have been on DeLorean's route to and from the factory.

54 Haddad, *Hard Driving*, 82

55 *Belfast Telegraph*, 7 April 1982

56 *Belfast Telegraph*, 12 January and 14 April 1982

57 *Irish News*, 25 May 1982

58 Quoted in Jonathan
Bardon, *A History of
Ulster* (Belfast, 2001),
783

59 http://news.bbc.
co.uk/1/hi/northern_
ireland/3480679.stm

60 See www.dmcnews.
com/cavepaintings.html
for examples of the 'cave
paintings'.

production foreman, guided me through
the factory. As he demonstrated a gull-
wing door, it squeaked and he said:
'Don't be put off by the noise: it's just
the new hinges.'[58]

By this point, DeLorean's affairs were
in meltdown. Desperate (or so he later
told investigating police officers) to save
his floundering company, he attempted
to finance an operation to import 100
kilograms of cocaine into the US from
Colombia. In fact, the operation was an
elaborate FBI sting and on 26 October
1982 he was arrested in Los Angeles. In
1984 a Federal judge ultimately condemned
the operation as a case of entrapment and
acquitted DeLorean, but controversy would
follow him for the rest of his life. Paranoid
to the end, at various times he blamed his
enemies at General Motors, the British
government and even the IRA for setting
him up. He died on 19 March 2005 aged
eighty, still wanted for questioning on fraud
changes in the UK.

The fallout from the DeLorean affair was to
linger until 2004 — twenty-five years after
the first Government investment package had
been agreed — when a report by the
Northern Ireland Audit Office revealed that
the government had spent more than £20
million in its action against Arthur Andersen,
the auditors acting on behalf of DMC. As
John Dallat, of the Social Democratic and
Labour Party, commented, 'everyone did well
out of this project except the taxpayers, the
creditors and the poor workers who were
exploited in a most shameful way'.[59] That
said, and partly because of its central role in
the *Back to the Future* film franchise, the
DMC–12 has had a longer life and has
attracted more affection than might have
been expected. Despite its flawed design and
poor construction, the car has gained a loyal
following of enthusiasts who maintain the
6,500 DMC–12s estimated still to be in
existence. When dismantling their cars for
restoration, some of these devotees have
found brief messages left by the Belfast
construction workers hidden behind
panels.[60] These so-called 'cave paintings'
might be no more than the autographs of the
production team, the date on which the car
was completed, a cartoon, or a cryptic
message about the uncertain future of the
factory, but in each instance they are
recorded, photographed and shared with
something of the veneration one might
associate with a reliquary. It is not difficult to
understand why. Written upon a commodity
that was intended to represent the ultimate
placelessness of corporate capital, they
fleetingly return the object to the moment of
its production, placing the DMC–12 back
into the matrix of Irish history and Belfast
politics. As such, the resonance of the
inscriptions is powerful. Certainly, for the
factory workers who would soon find
themselves once again unemployed and
economically dependent on a state many of
them saw as illegitimate, such writings were
nothing less than a covert assertion of
presence, a refusal to go quietly. ∎

Global Imbalances
The Risks for the World Economy
Alan Ahearne

That which cannot go on forever, won't.

Herbert Stein, chairman of the United States Council
of Economic Advisers under Presidents Nixon and Ford

1   Adam Smith, using
the example of a pin
factory, famously
described the link
between specialization
and productivity in
The Wealth of Nations
(London, 1776).
Today's global supply
chain can be seen as an
international version of
Smith's pin factory.

Increasing globalization since the Second
World War has transformed the global
economic landscape. International trade
in goods and services, migration flows,
and cross-boarder capital flows have all
risen inexorably over the past sixty years.
The closer integration across countries of
markets for goods, labour, and capital has
brought enormous benefits to advanced
and developing countries. In advanced
economies, improvements in information
and communication technologies have
enabled firms to locate separate parts of the
production process in different parts of the
world, allowing them to reap the benefits of
specialization and increasing competition.
The resulting gains in productivity have
boosted employment and standards of
living.[1] In those developing countries,
especially in Asia, that have become part
of the global supply chain for goods and
services, hundreds of millions of people
have been catapulted from poverty into the
middle classes. International capital flows
have steered global savings to their most
productive use, raising the level of world
income. But increased global integration is
not without risks. While international trade
flows have exploded, in some countries
exports and imports have expanded at
very different paces. The result has been a
marked — and in some cases, a worrying
— widening of trade imbalances around
the world. For example, although US
exports to the rest of the world have risen

on average at a double-digit rate over the
past decade, they have been outpaced by
US imports from abroad. As a result, the
US trade deficit — the gap between the
level of imports and exports — has reached
unprecedented levels. Deficits of this size are
not sustainable. Put simply, the US is living
beyond its means. To finance its ongoing
trade deficits — to pay the bills for spending
more on imports than it earns on exports
— the US must borrow from the rest of
the world. At some stage, the amount
that it owes to foreigners will become
unsustainably large.

Contrastingly, in China, booming exports
have helped produce an enormous trade
surplus; Japan has also run large trade
surpluses for many years. Oil-exporting
countries too are registering huge trade
surpluses at present, reflecting the jump
in the world price of oil over recent years.
These trade-surplus countries are currently
happy to lend the revenues generated by
running these surpluses to the US, but there
will almost certainly come a time when they
will no longer want to lend any additional
funds. At that stage, the US deficit will have
to decline. This adjustment may be sudden
and disorderly, involving a sharp fall in the
value of the US dollar and a collapse in the
prices of stocks and other financial assets
in the US and elsewhere. The challenge for
policymakers will be to avoid a disorderly
adjustment process.

Cargo ship. Photograph:
Michael Wells/Getty Images.

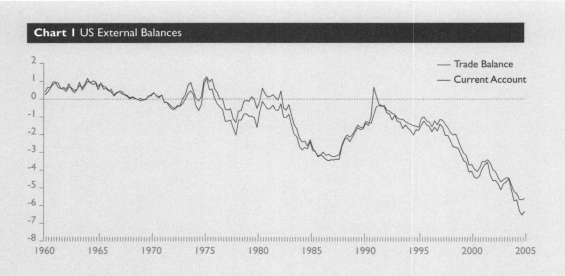

Chart 1 US External Balances

— Trade Balance
— Current Account

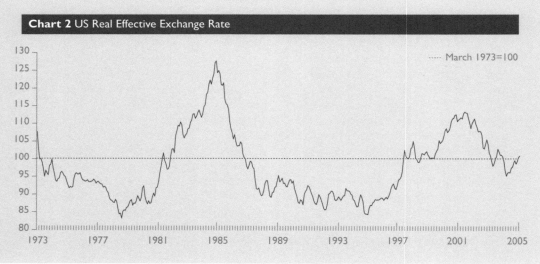

Chart 2 US Real Effective Exchange Rate

------ March 1973=100

Evolution of Global Current Account Imbalances[2]

For several decades after the Second World War, the US recorded balanced trade, roughly speaking, with the rest of the world. The US current account balance — the broadest measure of a country's international balance of trade — fluctuated within a narrow band of +1 to -1 per cent of Gross Domestic Product (GDP) during the 1960s and 1970s (Chart 1). A substantial deficit emerged in the early 1980s, as an overvalued dollar (Chart 2) and robust economic growth in the US relative to the rest of the world boosted its imports and depressed its exports. However, by the end of the decade the US external position had returned to around balance, aided by a sharp fall in the dollar, a pick-up in economic growth in the rest of the world which boosted the demand for US exports, and a drop in oil prices, which lowered the value of US imports of oil. Interestingly, the unwinding of the large current account deficits of the late 1980s was smooth

2　Parts of the discussions below are drawn from Alan Ahearne and Jürgen von Hagen, 'Global Current Account Imbalances: How to Manage the Risk for Europe', Bruegel Policy Brief, December 2005, and Alan Ahearne and Jürgen von Hagen, 'European Perspectives on Global Imbalances', paper prepared for the Asian–Europe Economic Forum conference European and Asian Perspectives on Global Imbalances, Beijing, July 2006.

3   A billion is a thousand
    millions.
4   Yu Yongding, 'Global
    Imbalances: China's
    Perspective', paper
    prepared for the Asian–
    Europe Economic Forum
    conference European
    and Asian Perspectives
    on Global Imbalances,
    Beijing, July 2006.

and caused few problems for the global economy. The first half of the 1990s saw the US run moderate current account deficits. But since 1997 the deficit has ballooned. US imports have outpaced exports in response both to a stronger dollar and to faster growth in income in the US than in the rest of the world. Although the dollar reversed some of its previous gains after 2002, the depreciation was not enough to prevent further widening of the trade deficit. By 2005, the current account deficit had widened to nearly $800 billion, equivalent to about 6.5 per cent of GDP. The deficit increased further to $850 billion in the first half of 2006.[3]

Data on the evolution of global current account balances, shown in Table 1, show that the counterpart of the large and growing US current account deficit are the large and growing current account surpluses in Asia and in the major oil-exporting countries. Over the past decade, the nearly $700 billion increase in the US current account deficit was accompanied by a roughly $330 billion increase in Asia's surplus and a $360 billion increase — most of which happened since 2002 — in the oil-exporters' surplus. For 2005, the US current account deficit of nearly $800 billion is almost entirely accounted for by Asia's roughly $400 billion surplus and the $375 billion surplus of the oil-exporting countries in that year. Europe contributes very little to current global imbalances. Despite some euro-area countries having sizeable current account imbalances, the euro area's current account swung into deficit last year, after three years of moderate surpluses. Germany, for example, has recorded annual surpluses of around $100 billion in recent years. As an aggregate, however, the euro area runs generally balanced trade with the rest of the world. The United Kingdom current account deficit continued to widen, reaching $58 billion (about 2.5 per cent of GDP) in 2005. The fact that trade balances in Europe are not far from zero suggests that the eventual

rebalancing of global current accounts should primarily involve the US, Asia, and the oil-exporting countries.

What explains the very large current account surpluses in Asia? In part, the surpluses reflect deliberate policy measures by governments in Asia to promote exports in order to increase employment in export industries.[4] This policy strategy centres on the use of undervalued currencies to boost exports. In addition, many Asian economies run large surpluses because their demand for imported investment goods remains relatively subdued in the aftermath of the Asian financial crisis in 1997–98. Economies that were hard hit by the financial crisis, such as that of Indonesia, Korea, Malaysia, and Thailand, ran large current account deficits for a long time prior to 1997. Only since then have these economies begun to run current account surpluses. Running current account surpluses has the added benefit of allowing Asian economies to rebuild their foreign exchange reserves in order to protect themselves against future financial turbulences and dependence on International Monetary Fund (IMF) support. One implication of this motive for running current account surpluses is that it is highly unlikely that they will continue to build up their foreign exchange reserves after the reserves have reached a certain level.

Japan has run current account surpluses persistently since the early 1980s, and over the past decade and a half the annual surplus has been above $100 billion. Even when the Japanese economy was booming in the late 1980s, a time when one might have expected Japanese imports to exceed exports, Japan registered a trade surplus. To be sure, part of Japan's chronic surpluses over the past fifteen years reflects the depressed state of the Japanese economy following the bursting of the stock market and property bubble in the early 1990s. Japanese households, and especially Japanese firms, have recorded very high savings rates since 1990, while investment has remained weak. The fact that Japanese households and firms are accumulating large savings instead of spending their incomes and revenues on imported goods has depressed other countries' exports to Japan. In turn, Japan's high propensity to save may reflect demographic factors associated with the ageing of the population. Households are also saving for precautionary reasons, concerned about the weak — albeit evidently improving — condition of the Japanese economy and poor prospects for future income. In addition, the desire to pay off debt and strengthen corporate balance sheets after the damage done by the asset price boom and bust explains some of the savings by firms.

China's trade surplus has expanded markedly over the past decade as it has integrated itself rapidly into the global economy. Its exports have boomed over recent years, especially since it joined the World Trade Organization in December 2001. Exports have far outpaced rapidly growing imports of food and raw materials needed to fuel the country's phenomenal economic growth. China's vast pool of underutilized labour and low labour costs give the country a large comparative advantage in the production of labour-intensive products. In addition, China's government continues to pursue deliberate export-promotion policies, including tax incentives for exporters and its exchange-rate policy. China offers tax incentives to foreign investors who build plants in China that produce goods for export. Many multinational corporations, especially from Japan, Taiwan, and the US, have set up production units in China. These plants operate mainly in labour-intensive assembly activities and the output is mostly exported from China. As a result, China is an increasingly important player in international production networks. China's growing role in the global supply chain is reflected in the rapid growth in processing trade in China. Of total exports of about $750 billion in

2005, more than one-half was accounted for by processing exports and the bulk of those exports was produced by foreign multinationals located in China. In addition, China's exchange-rate policy is favourable to exporters and therefore helps create a trade surplus. China continues to maintain a *de facto* fixed exchange-rate régime aimed at keeping exports competitive in international markets. Until July 2005, the Chinese currency, the renminbi, was firmly pegged to the US dollar. Since then, the renminbi has been allowed to appreciate moderately against the dollar by about 2 per cent but, by most measures, remains significantly undervalued against the US currency.

The very high current account surpluses registered in oil-exporting countries in recent years highlight an important effect of the elevated level of world oil prices on global imbalances. High oil prices have shifted some of the rest of the world's (that is, non-US) current account surplus away from Asia towards net oil exporters. To the extent that the oil-exporting countries have a lower propensitiy to save than economies in Asia, this shift may bring about a faster decline in savings in the rest of the world. That said, Asian economies also have higher investment rates than those in oil-exporting countries. Therefore, it is not clear whether the shift in surpluses from Asia towards oil exporters will slow down or speed up current account adjustment. Moreover, because oil-exporting countries have lower savings and investment rates than economies in Asia, recent developments imply a shift in global demand away from investment goods and towards consumption goods. This might well benefit US exports (which are more heavily concentrated in consumer goods and services) at the expense of German exports (for which capital goods are more important).

Turning to Europe, Table 2 shows the bilateral trade balances that underlay Europe's current account deficit for 2005. Europe's trade surplus of nearly $100

5   The Japanese Ministry
    of Finance reported
    record levels of foreign
    exchange market
    intervention during 2003
    and 2004, with total
    intervention amounting
    to the equivalent of
    $183 billion in 2003
    and $136 billion in the
    first quarter of 2004. No
    official intervention by
    the Japanese authorities
    has been reported since
    the first quarter of 2004.
6   Martin Feldstein, 'Why
    Uncle Sam's Bonanza
    might not be All that it
    Seems', *Financial Times*,
    10 January 2006

billion in 2005 with the US was similar in magnitude to the trade surpluses of Japan and the oil-exporting countries — separately, not combined — against the US, and roughly half the size of China's surplus with the US. Like the US, Europe recorded large bilateral trade deficits *vis-à-vis* China, Japan, and the oil-exporting countries. Although the configuration of bilateral trade positions reflects many factors, one can imagine a global rebalancing scenario in which Europe imports more US-produced goods and services and exports more goods and services to Asia and the oil-exporting countries. This would leave Europe's current account largely unaffected, even as the US current account deficit shrinks, but it presupposes a decline in the Asian current account surplus. The alternative rebalancing scenario is one in which Europe imports more from the US and exports less to Asia, or imports more from Asia, allowing the US current account deficit to decline, while the Asian surpluses remain the same.

To finance a current account deficit — to pay the bills for spending more on imports than it earns on exports — a country must borrow from abroad. Similarly, a country running a current account surplus must lend to deficit countries the excess that it earns on exports over the amount it pays on imports. In other words, there is a financial counterpart to the large current account imbalances that takes the form of large imbalances in net international capital flows — that is, international borrowing and lending. Another perspective on global imbalances can be gained from exploring what role countries have played in generating the observed patterns in financial flows. A striking feature of recent capital flows has been the substantial rise since 2001 in so-called 'official' net capital flows — that is, lending by foreign governments as opposed to lending by foreign private institutions such as private banks and pension funds. These inflows peaked in 2004 at $390 billion as governments and central

banks in Asia intervened heavily in foreign exchange markets by buying dollar assets in an effort to restrain the appreciation of their currencies, before moderating some last year.[5] The step-down in net official inflows in 2005 to $220 billion, as well as the sharp increase in net private inflows, meant that the bulk of the overall net inflows needed to finance the US current account deficit in 2005 was accounted for by net private capital inflows. By contrast, in both 2003 and 2004, net official inflows were the predominant source of financing, accounting for 60 per cent of total net inflows in 2003 and 65 per cent in 2004. Most of these flows came from Asia.

Interestingly, some commentators argue that in reality foreign governments continue to provide overwhelmingly the share of financing for the US current account deficit, and that a substantial chunk of inflows that are classified as 'private' in the balance-of-payment data are purchases of US securities by private institutions acting on behalf of foreign governments.[6] Whatever the truth, there is little doubt that official inflows have become a significant source of financing for the US current account deficit. The sight of the US relying heavily on loans from governments in Asia — and in particular on loans from China — to finance its trade deficit is a source of deep concern. Commentators are worried about a situation in which China exports massive quantities of cheap goods to the US and then lends back to the US the dollars earned from those exports, so that Americans can purchase even more goods from China. To the extent that cheap Chinese exports are destroying jobs in the US manufacturing industry, trade with China on this scale looks to many like a bad deal from a US perspective. Moreover, some are worried that by being essentially a banker to the US, the Chinese government is accumulating leverage over it. Being a large debtor to China puts the US in an uncomfortable political position.

Trading floor, Chicago
Options Exchange.
Photograph: Paul Chesley/
Getty Images.

The rise in net private inflows in 2005 in part reflected the continued recovery in the demand for claims on the US private sector from their recent lows in 2003. Private foreign purchases of US securities (excluding US Treasury securities) jumped last year, largely reflecting a marked increase in private foreign purchases of US corporate bonds, though purchases of US equities and US agency bonds also rose. Foreign purchases of US debt (including corporate bonds, agency bonds, and Treasury securities), relative to purchases of portfolio equities and direct investments, have become an increasingly important source of financing of the US current account deficit in recent years. Private foreign purchases of US Treasury securities also rose in 2005. The increase in purchases in that year was broad-based across foreign regions. The largest private purchasers of US Treasury securities in 2005 were from Europe, followed by the Caribbean financial centres

and Asia; the large purchases by Caribbean financial institutions partly reflects their use by some oil-exporting states to channel funds. In addition, although private foreign direct investment in the US declined by $23 billion in 2005 relative to 2004, US direct investment abroad plummeted from $244 billion to $9 billion, as foreign subsidiaries of US multinational corporations repatriated large amounts of funds back to the US in response to incentives associated with the American Jobs Creation Act of 2004. These incentives expired for most companies at year-end 2005.

Current Account Adjustment

Thus, to finance ongoing current account deficits, the US must borrow from the rest of the world. This adds to its net external borrowings, which have risen from less than 3 per cent of GDP in 1990 to an estimated

Interior of the Hong Kong Stock Exchange. Photograph: Gary Cralle/ Getty Images.

7   A trillion is a million millions.

8   Alan Greenspan, 'Stability and Economic Growth: The Role of the Central Bank'; speech at the Banco de Mexico's 80th Anniversary International Conference, Mexico City, 14 November 2005

22 per cent of GDP today. This trend of rising US net external borrowings relative to GDP cannot continue for ever. Like any debtor, the US must service its liabilities, for example by paying interest on loans from other countries. The US currently owes a net amount of $2.5 trillion to the rest of the world.[7] Given the low level of interest rates at present, the US can easily service this debt. However, a continuously rising stock of external borrowings would eventually see the burden of servicing these borrowings become unbearably large. Anticipating this, foreign investors will grow increasingly reluctant to continue to lend to the US, even before this happens. The US can live beyond its means only so long as foreigners are willing to bankroll this overconsumption. At some stage, foreigners presumably will decide that they have extended enough credit to the US — as the former chairman of the Federal Reserve, Alan Greenspan, puts it: 'at some point foreign investors will baulk at

further financing'.[8] When this occurs, global current account adjustment will commence and the US deficit will begin to shrink to a more sustainable level.

Importantly, global current account adjustment will almost certainly involve a drop in the value of the dollar. Given the fact that the responsiveness of US exports and imports to changes in the exchange rate is relatively small, substantial dollar depreciation, perhaps in the range of 20–40 per cent, will be required to shrink the US trade deficit. Moreover, with US imports now twice as large as exports, exports need to grow at a rate nearly twice as fast as imports to prevent the trade deficit from widening further. In other words, the gap between imports and exports has grown so large that a dramatic acceleration in exports is necessary if they are to catch up. Worryingly, the longer current account adjustment is delayed, the more pronounced the depreciation of the dollar will be. Perhaps, ironically, a weakening dollar is likely to have relatively benign effects on the US economy, at least if the correction is orderly. US exports will increase and the Federal Reserve will respond to contain any effects on inflation. The consequences of adjustment for the rest of the world, however, will be much more problematic. As one US official said to a foreign visitor: 'It's our currency, and your problem.'

For starters, if the adjustment started today, a narrowing of the US trade deficit to about zero would imply a contraction of US net imports of roughly $850 billion at an annual rate. The flip side of this adjustment is that the rest of the world's trade surplus with the US would necessarily shrink by $850 billion. It is not clear if many countries are growing robustly enough to be able to withstand such a sizeable decline in exports. For example, let's assume that the burden of adjustment is shared equally among Asia, Europe, and the major oil-exporting countries. This would imply a decline in European net exports of $280 billion, equivalent to about 2.25 per cent of EU-15 GDP.[9] For the currently anaemic European economy, this decline in exports would represent a significant blow, even if it were spread over several years. Current account adjustment will also affect the global economy through financial channels. When adjustment eventually occurs, holders of dollar assets in the rest of the world (that is, outside of the US) will suffer negative wealth effects. The rest of the world held about $9,300 billion of gross dollar assets at the end of 2004. The euro area's holdings amounted to nearly $3,000 billion, equivalent to about one-third of its GDP. If adjustment started today, depreciation in the dollar of 30 per cent would imply a loss of wealth for the rest of the world equal to nearly 10 per cent of rest of the world GDP. The hit to euro-area wealth would be of a similar order, relative to GDP. These numbers assume an orderly adjustment. The wealth effect of a disorderly

adjustment would be even greater. Such a scenario would not only involve an abrupt drop in the dollar, but would also see surging US interest rates, falling US stock prices, and weaker economic activity in the US. The effects would probably spill over into financial markets in other countries, dragging down asset prices in Europe and elsewhere.

What Should Policymakers Do?

What should policymakers around the world do to prepare for global current account adjustment? For policymakers in the US, the challenge is to reduce overconsumption by raising the savings rate. The proportion of national income that is saved in the US has fallen sharply over recent years and is low compared with savings rates in the rest of the world. In part, US households save very little because soaring house prices have made them feel considerably wealthier and many homeowners have withdrawn equity from the value of their houses to increase consumption spending. Recent interest rate increases by the Federal Reserve have put an end to the US housing boom and may slow consumption spending. However, additional interest rate increase would likely push the economy into recession. From the US perspective, this would not be an acceptable solution to the problem of current account imbalances. Total US national savings also include savings — or dissavings — by the US government. Over the past five years, the US fiscal balance has swung from a surplus of 2.5 per cent of GDP to a deficit of 3.5 per cent of GDP. By running such a deficit, the US government is reducing national savings by an amount equivalent to 3.5 per cent of GDP. Much of the swing in the fiscal balance from surplus to deficit over recent years reflected the tax cuts introduced by the George W. Bush administration. As a result, tax revenues raised by the Federal government as a share of GDP have fallen to post-Second World War lows, while government spending as a share of GDP has

9   The EU-15 are Austria, Belgium, Denmark, Finland, France, Germany, Greece, Ireland, Italy, Luxembourg, the Netherlands, Portugal, Sweden, Spain and the United Kingdom.

remained largely unchanged. One course of action that US policymakers could take to facilitate an orderly reduction in the US current account balance would be to increase taxes and thus increase national savings. That said, the very large tax hike that would be needed to eliminate the US trade deficit altogether would risk plunging the US economy into a deep recession. Therefore, fiscal consolidation in the US should be seen as a complement to a depreciation of the dollar, not as a substitute for it.

The exchange-rate adjustment will require the reallocation of resources. In Europe, policies that increase the flexibility of its unusually rigid labour markets will be of crucial importance. Drawing on the example presented earlier, adjustment that would cause European net exports to contract by €280 billion, would result in more than three million job losses in Europe's export industries. If these displaced workers were not able to find new jobs in other industries, such as services, European unemployment would jump considerably. To keep unemployment from rising, significant resources would need to shift from the traded goods sector to the non-traded sector. In order to promote a smooth reallocation of resources, policymakers in Europe and elsewhere need to do more to liberalize credit and labour markets. These reforms would also help to boost potential growth in Europe. A lasting correction of global current account imbalances is likely to require an improvement in European potential growth, not just a cyclical pick-up of European growth above potential, and an associated temporary boost to imports from the US. Stronger domestic demand in the form of business investment should also contribute to higher potential growth. Rising net financial inflows into Europe, as net inflows to the US decline, would provide financing for this additional investment. Moreover, higher real consumption in Europe would have positive effects on European consumers.

Fiscal policy in Europe can cushion some of the shock to aggregate demand that will accompany adjustment. When adjustment begins and European exporters come under pressure from a falling dollar, governments in Europe should cut taxes and increase government spending to boost the economy and make up for the decline in exports. To facilitate this reaction, European governments should now be striving to improve fiscal positions by cutting fiscal deficits. Also, the European Central Bank (ECB) should make it clear that it would respond to the deflationary pressures that will stem from adjustment by easing monetary policy significantly, thus avoiding the risk of deflationary expectations that might raise the cost of adjustment even further.

When adjustment starts and the dollar begins to drop, investors and central banks around the world may view the euro as a safer currency in which to hold assets. Should Europe welcome the euro becoming an international reserve currency? A significant and lasting increase in the euro's share in the currency baskets that China and other Asian countries peg to, and in their asset portfolios, would certainly give a boost to the euro's position as a global reserve currency. A key question is whether Europeans are willing to let that happen, given that it would imply large and lasting current account deficits for the euro area in relation to Asia, as it absorbs the excess savings coming from that region. European reactions to a decline in Europe's current account balance will influence the attractiveness of euro assets for Asian investors. In the past, European governments have been quick to call for exchange-rate depreciations in the face of current account deficits, fearing that such deficits might result in the loss of jobs in Europe. Reserve currency status promises revenues resulting from the global use of a currency, but it would also expose the euro to potentially large and volatile shifts in the international demand for liquidity, which would result in higher exchange-rate volatility. In the past, some national central banks in Europe were reluctant to accept that possibility. It is not clear whether the ECB will be more inclined to tolerate more volatility.

Perhaps the greatest fear for policymakers in Europe regarding global adjustment is that the dollar may depreciate excessively against European currencies. There are two reasons why an excessive appreciation of European currencies against the dollar would be a serious cause for concern in Europe. First, notwithstanding recent indicators that suggest an incipient recovery in the euro area may be under way, economic growth remains sluggish. Economic growth in the euro area has been very disappointing for a long time, dragged down by dismal real GDP growth in some of the larger European Monetary Union (EMU) countries such as Germany and Italy. Recent indicators on activity have been more positive, but it is not clear whether the recent pick-up in growth in domestic demand can be sustained. As a result, a sharp appreciation in the real exchange-value of the euro that would depress net exports carries with it the risk of deflationary pressures and of a severe recession.

In addition, an excessive appreciation of the euro would be a serious concern for Europeans because it could exacerbate the problem of economic divergences in growth and inflation between existing EMU members. A sharp appreciation in the euro would represent a common shock to countries in the euro area, but one that would probably have asymmetric effects on individual euro-area members. These asymmetric effects would complicate the response of policy to the rise in the euro, especially the response of the euro area's one-size-fits-all monetary policy. These effects could be alleviated, however, by a shift in demand towards the oil-exporting countries, if these countries buy primarily investment goods in Europe. In that case, a large share of the extra demand would fall on Germany and help the adjustment.

Appreciation in the euro would probably have asymmetric effects on individual countries in the euro area for several reasons. First, the importance of trade with the US varies considerably across euro-area countries. Exports to the US in 2005 represented less than 1 per cent of GDP in Greece and Spain. At the opposite end of the scale is Ireland, where exports to the US accounted for a whopping 10 per cent of GDP in 2005. Ireland also imported a relative large share from the US, along with other countries such as Belgium and the Netherlands. In contrast, imports from the US were relatively small for Finland, Spain and Portugal. As a result, the size of the effect of movements in the euro on individual countries' real effective (trade-weighted) exchange varies considerably. In addition, some industries would be affected more than others by euro appreciation, so differences in industrial structure and the composition of trade with the US will cause asymmetric effects. More generally, in the context of a Chinese currency pegged to the dollar, the relevant trading partner is not just the US, but the wider 'dollar zone' of countries whose currencies would depreciate along with the dollar. All euro-area members have seen their imports from China rise markedly since the launch of EMU, with Belgium and the Netherlands importing the most from China. As well as different trading patterns, asymmetric effects of a sharp appreciation may arise because of differences across euro-area members in trade elasticities, initial conditions, investment patterns, and flexibility.

What role will China play in global adjustment? Given the size of China's trade surplus with the US, it is clear that an orderly unwinding of global imbalances will require a significant reduction in China's surplus. For Chinese imports to grow faster than Chinese exports over the next few

10 Jaime Marquez and John Schindler, *Exchange-Rate Effects on China's Trade: An Interim Report*, International Finance Discussion Papers 861, Federal Reserve Board, Washington DC (2006)

years, a substantial appreciation of the renminbi against the dollar will be required. Chinese policymakers have so far been very reluctant to allow a large rise in the value of their currency because they are fearful that the damage to international competitiveness could hurt export growth and lead to a politically destabilizing increase in unemployment. While the problem in the US is insufficient savings, China's difficulties arise because Chinese households are saving too much. Given rapid changes in the structure of the Chinese economy over the past few decades, it is not surprising that Chinese households are putting money away for a rainy day. In the past, state-owned enterprises (SOEs) provided secure employment for workers and guaranteed pension benefits to retirees. In addition, SOEs paid for the education of workers' children and took care of medical expenses for workers' families. The ongoing reforms of the SOE sector have done away with these guaranteed entitlements and prompted an increase in precautionary spending. Moreover, since markets for mortgages are still underdeveloped in China, prospective homebuyers must save the bulk of the purchase price of a new house. Financial sector reforms will eventually eliminate the need for such savings, although considerable time will be required for the effects of these reforms to be felt.

In the near term, the key to reducing national savings in China will be a cut in government savings through tax cuts and increases in government spending. It is clear that the economic well-being of Chinese citizens would benefit from higher government expenditures directed at improving China's infrastructure, health and education systems, social safety net, and public housing. One concern is that greater government spending would cause the already rapidly expanding Chinese economy to overheat. The answer, therefore, is for the Chinese government to let the renminbi appreciate. The resulting loss of

competitiveness will slow the growth of exports and thus will offset the expansion in domestic demand and prevent overheating and a pick-up in inflation. China's economy will come to depend more on domestic demand as a source of growth and less on exports. In the end, China's economy is simply too large relative to the rest of the world for China to rely indefinitely on export-led growth. How much China's currency will have to appreciate will depend on the sensitivity of China's exports and imports to changes in the exchange rate. Recent estimates suggest that a 10 per cent appreciation of the renminbi lowers the share of aggregate Chinese exports by half a percentage point — in other words, China's exports are not particularly sensitive to exchange-rate changes.[10] The same appreciation lowers the share of aggregate imports by about one-tenth of a percentage point. The upshot is that a large appreciation in the value of China's currency may be needed to put a dent in China's massive trade surplus.

Elsewhere in Asia, Japan has also been running large current account surpluses. Like China, Japan also records very high household savings rates. To a large extent, high savings rates in Japan reflect the depressed level of household confidence about future employment and income prospects. In turn, consumers' anxiety about the future reflects the country's fifteen-year-long economic slump that followed the bursting of the asset price bubble in the early 1990s. Weak investment has also contributed to the poor performance of Japan's economy. To facilitate smooth global adjustment, Japan, like China, faces the challenge of boosting domestic demand to compensate for the drag on economic growth that will come from slowing exports. Unlike China, there is little room in Japan for additional government spending. Japan's fiscal deficit is already large at 6 per cent of GDP and its national debt has reached 150 per cent of GDP, the highest level among industrial countries. Demands on government spending, stemming from the ageing of the population, will put further burdens on the country's fiscal position as expenditures on pensions and health care rise. With the option of a large fiscal expansion off the table, much of the heavy lifting will have to be done by monetary policy. The Bank of Japan, the country's central bank, recently ended its five-year-old policy of zero interest rates by raising interest rates to a still low 0.25 per cent amid signs that the economy may be recovering and a decade-long period of deflation (that is, falling prices) may be coming to an end. The trick for the Bank of Japan will be to make sure than in its efforts to gradually return Japanese interest rates to more normal levels it does not inadvertently snuff out the economy's nascent recovery. Global adjustment will require that the Bank of Japan displays patience and keeps interest rates low for the foreseeable future.

As in the case of China, global adjustment calls for an appreciation in Japan's currency. The yen has recently weakened considerably against both the dollar and the euro. After adjusting for price developments, the drop in the yen is even larger, as prices have been falling in Japan. The resolution of global imbalances will require that this depreciation be reversed. In addition, Japanese policymakers can take steps to increase domestic demand by accelerating the pace of structural reforms. In particular, measures to strengthen the still-troubled banking system and further liberalize product markets should improve the economy's potential rate of growth and eventually boost consumer and business investment spending.

How will the Burden of Adjustment be Shared?

When the dollar depreciates sharply, as it will have to do to boost US exports and contain US imports, the key factor determining how the burden of adjustment is shared across countries will be movements in bilateral exchange rates. From a European perspective, policymakers in Europe are fearful of an unfair distribution of the adjustment burden, because, unlike some other major players, their exchange rates are flexible and are determined by market forces. In contrast, China has a pegged currency régime and limits the amount by which the renminbi moves. Tellingly, the bilateral dollar–euro and dollar–sterling nominal exchange rates have moved much more over recent years than the US trade-weighted exchange rate, suggesting that a large amount of the effective dollar depreciation since 2002 has been borne by Europe. Unless something changes, Europeans are fearful that this unequal distribution of adjustment will continue. Taking a longer-term perspective on current account balances in the major regions, the EU has been largely a self-financing region over the past twenty-five years. Current account imbalances have never been very large. For Europe to shoulder a major part of the new adjustment would be an unprecedented experience. To put it differently: Europeans have never accepted large changes in Europe's current account position to allow global adjustment. The only exception is the brief period between 1986 and 1988, when Europe tolerated a moderate shrinking in its current account surplus, coinciding with the period in which international co-ordination was effectively in place (that is, over the period from the Plaza Accord of September 1985 to the Louvre Accord of February 1987). A second, interesting observation is the stark difference between the 1980s imbalances and today's. In the 1980s, Japan contributed most of the adjustment and acquired most of the dollar assets. In recent years, the adjustment has been shared more equally among the Asian economies. In contrast to the 1980s, there is now a co-ordination problem on the Asian side. In other words, in the 1980s, any externality from the adjustment (the fact

Aerial view of Monfort Beef's cattle feedlot near Greeley, Colorado; it is the world's largest cattle feed-lot (120,000 head). Photograph: Glowimages/Gettyimages.

that stopping support for the dollar would have consequences for the home-currency value of the previously accumulated dollar assets) was internalized by Japan. This is no longer the case. This may be one reason why developing Asia and Japan seem to have gone in different directions since 2004, with an increasing share of the action being official interventions: as Japan slows its support for the dollar, developing Asia increases its support, in fear of a falling value of the dollar.

This is significant from a European perspective. In the 1980s, the Europeans were dragged into the Plaza Accord (against opposition, especially from the Bundesbank) because the US and Japan were able to reach an agreement. Now the situation is different. It would take co-ordination between the US and many Asian economies before Europe could be coerced into a similar exercise. The same logic suggests that Europe has little interest in promoting international co-ordination with the Asian economies and the US. Europe would prefer to hide behind

the argument that the ECB is independent and cannot be forced to co-operate. The key point is that there are profound implications for Europe of exchange-rate régime change in Asia. Currency régimes in Asia continue to receive a great deal of attention from policymakers and the press around the world. The US, for example, has been a strong advocate for a more flexible exchange-rate system in China. Obviously, European policymakers, fearful that Europe may have to bear a disproportionately large share of the adjustment of the US external position, have a keen interest in this debate. So far, the response of euro-area policymakers has been to make the sensible suggestion that other countries, whose bilateral dollar and effective exchange rates have not appreciated over the past few years, and in many cases have depreciated in effective terms, should allow their currencies to adjust.

Since adjustment will involve depreciation in the US exchange rate, the question arises: to what extent will governments in

Asia allow their currencies to appreciate? Especially important in this regard is China's exchange-rate régime. As we have seen, China, in particular, has pegged its currency firmly to the US dollar for many years. In July 2005, the renminbi was allowed to appreciate about 2 per cent, and has been stable since. China's government announced that, in the future, it would peg to a basket of currencies, but the exact composition of this basket remains unspecified. Future adjustments in China's exchange-rate policy have two dimensions that are relevant for Europe. One is the level of the exchange rate. The more the renminbi is allowed to appreciate against the dollar, the larger the part of the US current account adjustment that falls on the trade flows between China and the US and the less need there is for adjustment between the US and Europe. The other dimension is the exchange-rate régime. The more the Chinese peg shifts from the dollar to the euro, the more China will become a net buyer of euro assets. This is likely to result in a euro-area current account deficit *vis-à-vis* China, and an appreciation of the euro's real exchange rate, thereby weakening euro-area exports. Europe therefore has a clear interest in a significant appreciation of the renminbi against the dollar, but not in an increase in the euro's share in the currency basket to which the Chinese peg their currency.

From a European perspective, a key consideration revolves around what might happen to the foreign exchange value of the euro *vis-à-vis* the dollar, should China move to a floating exchange-rate régime, as some observers are advocating. On the one hand, if China moves to a floating system, its demand for dollar assets will drop, eliminating a major source of demand for dollars. As a result, the dollar might be expected to drop against the euro. On the other hand, to the extent that the renminbi appreciates against the dollar under a Chinese float (as most observers would expect), then the euro may not have to

play as large a role in bringing about the necessary drop in the real effective dollar to close the US trade deficit.

Can Europe Cope?

Given that the single European currency has been in existence for only a short period of time, there are legitimate questions about the ability of European institutions to cope effectively with an exchange-rate shock. Whether or not these institutions can deliver in the face of a sharp exchange-rate adjustment obviously matters enormously for Europe, but it also has important implications for Asia. If EU institutions do not deliver, Europe's responses could be more erratic, with an increased risk of a more protectionist response. What role will EU institutions play during global current account adjustment and what are the main open questions concerning the likely effectiveness of the current arrangements in Europe? If a sharp adjustment in exchange rates were to occur that threatened to result in deflationary pressures in the euro area, the ECB would be expected to loosen monetary policy promptly and aggressively. One issue is the extent to which a rise in the value of the euro passes through into imported prices. If exporting firms practise a price-to-market policy, then an appreciation of the euro will squeeze the profit margins (after being converted into euros) of European firms exporting to the US, but the (euro) price of imports from the US will not be affected. As a result, the dampening effect on inflation of lower import prices will be absent, possibly ruling out aggressive ECB actions.[11]

Moreover, the experience of 2001 when the ECB showed a pretty subdued reaction to the risk of deflation — at least compared with the Federal Reserve — raises questions about how quickly and forcefully the ECB would respond to a large exchange-rate shock. For example, by the time of the first ECB interest rate cut in mid-2001, when the policy rate

11 Thomas Warmedinger, 'Import Prices and Pricing-to-Market Effects in the Euro Area', ECB Working Paper 299 (January 2004)

12 ECB President Jean-Claude Trichet recently offered a different point of view, arguing that central bank 'activism' cannot be quantified by simple statistics such as the frequency and size of policy moves, and that the 'ECB's strategy is as active as it needs to be to fulfil our mandate'. See his 'Activism and Alertness in Monetary Policy', a lecture at the Conference of Central Banks, Madrid, 8 June 2006.

13 C. Randall Henning, 'The External Policy of the Euro Area: Organizing for Foreign Exchange Intervention,' Institute for International Economics Working Paper 4, June 2006

14 Article 111, paragraph 1 of the Treaty of Amsterdam states that 'By way of derogation from Article 300, the Council may, acting unanimously on a recommendation from the ECB or from the Commission, and after consulting the ECB in an endeavour to reach a consensus consistent with the objective of price stability, after consulting the European Parliament, in accordance with the procedure in paragraph 3 for determining the arrangements, conclude formal agreements on an exchange rate system for the ECU in relation to non-Community currencies'.

15 Article 111, paragraph 2, states that 'In the absence of an exchange rate system in relation to one or more non-Community currencies as referred to in paragraph 1, the Council, acting by a qualified majority either on a recommendation from the Commission and after consulting the ECB or on a recommendation from the ECB, may formulate general orientations for exchange rate policy in relation to these currencies. These general orientations shall be without prejudice to the primary objective of the ESCB [European System of Central Banks] to maintain price stability'.

16 See, for example, ECB President Willem F. Duisenberg's comments reported in 'Careful Planning behind Banks' Euro Surprise', *Financial Times*, 24 September 2000.

17 Wolfgang Munchau, 'Eurozone Pettiness is Preventing Policymaking', *Financial Times*, 26 June 2006

was trimmed 25 basis points to 4.5 percent, the Federal Reserve had already carried out 250 basis points of easing. As a result, real interest rates in the euro area at that time, at about 2 per cent, were almost double the level in the US.[12] National governments would also play a part in responding to adjustment. A fiscal expansion in Europe can mitigate the effects of the decline in aggregate demand that would follow upon the US current account adjustment. To facilitate this response without endangering the sustainability of public finances in the EU countries, governments should move their budgets to balance or to small surpluses now. An additional benefit of these sound policies would be to make European assets more attractive to Asian investors. But the story here is more complicated. The Stability and Growth Pact (SGP) might hinder a sufficiently strong fiscal reaction, especially one that would be forward-looking in the sense that it could act quickly when the dollar declines fast. Furthermore, if the ensuing recession is asymmetric across countries within the euro area, there may be more tension in the European Council between the strongly affected countries, which desire a large fiscal response, and those less affected, which will insist on staying within the SGB limits. Some commentators have argued that the European Commission might be slow to provide the leadership necessary in such situations. Again, this may result in delayed responses.

Another possible policy response in Europe to a perceived excessive appreciation in the euro would be intervention in the foreign exchange market.[13] According to the Treaty of Amsterdam which revised the Maastricht Treaty, responsibility for exchange-rate policy is divided between the Council of Ministers and the ECB.[14] The council chooses the exchange-rate régime under certain provisions and subsequently the national central banks in the euro area carry out the interventions. Since a formal agreement to peg the euro to the dollar is unlikely, this division of responsibilities is

not of major relevance. That said, the treaty does give the council power to 'formulate general orientations for exchange rate policy'.[15] It is unclear at this stage how the council might use this power in the event of an excessive exchange-rate shock. Although the ECB decides on all details of intervention, in the only episode of ECB intervention to date — the intervention in 2000 to support the euro — the ECB chose to consult with the Eurogroup of euro-area Finance ministers. ECB officials stressed at the time, however, that the ECB does not need Finance ministers' permission to intervene in foreign exchange markets.[16] Nevertheless, intervention is unlikely to be successful if Finance ministers were publicly to oppose it. However, in the case of global adjustment, the situation is likely to be the reverse of that in 2000: the Finance ministers may want intervention (to stem the appreciation of the euro), but the central bankers may be opposed to such a move.

The relationship between European institutions and the effectiveness of arrangements in the euro area also comes into focus in the context of the new IMF multilateral consultations on global imbalances. The consultations began in summer 2006 (initially on a bilateral basis with IMF staff) and involve China, the euro area, Japan, Saudi Arabia, and the US. Reportedly, the euro area's representation consists of the Eurogroup, the ECB, and the European Commission. However, recent squabbling between the ECB president, Jean-Claude Trichet, and the Eurogroup president, Jean-Claude Juncker, augurs badly for effective co-ordination between European policymakers.[17] In sum, an orderly unwinding of global imbalances is by no means guaranteed. Appropriate policy actions in all of the major economies will be needed to reduce the risks of a disorderly and painful adjustment. And given the magnitude of the imbalances, these actions need to be taken immediately. ∎

124

Rethinking Civil Liberties in a Counter-Terrorism World

Conor Gearty

The most exasperating misuse of language in our political culture is also the most dangerous. This is when we are told that we are living in an 'age of terrorism' or that we are partisans in a 'war on terror'. Such terms have no meaning that can be located in the representative work done by these words in the past.

An 'age of' something suggests the occurrence of the thing concerned on such a regular basis that it can be said to characterize the times in a way that is different from all those other 'times' through which we have lived or which our culture has experienced. But 'terrorism' is an uncertain term with no shared meaning. The moment we agree on what it involves — let's say the killing/harming of civilians or doing great physical damage (or both) to communicate a political message — is the point at which we can see immediately that there is no age of terrorism in the conventional sense at all, that in fact such bouts of violence are few and far between — hardly ever occurring in North America and practically absent from a Western European society that has endured far more frequent episodes of subversive political violence in the past.

It is the same with 'war on terror'. The word 'war' prepares us for mass mobilization, for casualties on a large scale, for attacks on our political liberties and on our state's geographic integrity. Above all, it suggests some structured group of persons — a community, a nation, a state — on which we are waging our war. It is not conventionally possible to make war on a state of mind,

or even on a technique of violence: we would not feel able to declare 'a war on anxiety' or one 'on kidnapping' or 'on aerial bombardment.' It is true that these warrior metaphors had begun to infiltrate our language even before the attacks of 11 September 2001 — in the 1990s we had the 'war on drugs' and the 'war on serious crime' and to this day we are occasionally mustered to play bit parts in the 'war on obesity'. But the current war on terror is of a different order altogether, connoting an all-consuming series of battles with an evil and malignant Other that is intent upon our destruction.

There are many things that could be said about the reasons behind the deployment of the language of war and terror in these new ways: the genuine trauma of 9/11 as far as most Americans are concerned; the translation of the emotional response to that event into a policy of world-wide aggression, which was strengthened by the fact that it happened to suit powerful forces within the United States for reasons unconnected with the attacks themselves; the desire of many of the allies of this most powerful nation in the world to express solidarity at what the leaders of these various, smaller states judged to be a critical time; the self-fulfilling effect of the war on terror, in that

Paddy McCann
The Window
1995
oil on canvas
162 x 130 cm
courtesy of the artist

it has greatly exacerbated the campaign of terrorism (in occupied and formerly occupied territories at least), which it was supposedly initiated to suppress; and much else besides. These are not the focus of this essay. Instead, our concern here is with how the war on terror has exposed levels of hostility, unprecedented in the democratic era, to the protection and promotion of civil liberties, and with what can be done to counter this hostility. The point can be made about the US, the UK, Ireland — indeed, about large numbers of liberal societies. It is true that in many of these places during the Cold War the civil liberties of left-wing radical activists, politicized labour leaders and members of indigenous communist parties were on occasion greatly restricted. It is also the case that terrorism laws in at least some of these countries in the 1970s and 1980s had a chilling effect that went well beyond the violent subversives at whom they were primarily aimed. But the repression of these past decades did not threaten to reconfigure liberal democracy's whole relationship with freedom in the way that the generality, pervasive effect, unendability and international cohesiveness of the current war on terror threaten to do.

Those who care about civil liberties need to take this danger seriously and organize properly in order to fight back. This must involve some serious reflection on what is meant by civil liberties, how far the term extends, what it encompasses and how best to deal with the tensions that are inherent in it, tensions that have been exposed by the pressure that the concept of terrorism has put on the term. This essay is offered as a contribution to such a discussion. It argues that the subject of civil liberties has got where it is today by creative exploitation of the pressures that result from three paradoxes that lie at its heart. These relate to national security, to democracy and to political violence. Terrorism law threatens to expose these paradoxes and, in so doing, to tear apart the structures that hold the

concept of civil liberties together, leading — if we are not careful — to a reconstitution of these same liberties in an altogether more reactionary, more authoritarian form. And yet despite this, it is clear that progressive vigour can be restored to civil liberties so that their emancipatory and radical dimensions can be sustained even in the face of this antagonistic anti-terrorism narrative.

National Security

The first paradox can be simply put: to be effective, civil liberties protection must provide a mechanism for its own failure. Or to put it another way, an absolutist civil liberties culture is not one in which civil liberties are afforded unqualified protection. The point here is not just the obvious one that every guarantee of the right to vote and to the freedoms of expression, assembly, association, and so on, necessarily have to contain exceptions on account of the fact that these concepts are simply too wide to be of use without further modification. This is of course true: even the entitlement to vote is predicated on a minimal level of mental capacity and, as the public law cliché puts it, no one has the right falsely to shout fire in a crowded cinema. But the point is deeper than this. Democratic freedom sometimes requires the truncation of these rights even in their political, civil libertarian manifestation.

It is not inherently contradictory for a democratic culture to prohibit certain kinds of political expression, whether in the form of speech, membership of an organization or public protest. Most democratic states ban many substantive communications that could broadly be described as forms of political expression. How wide or narrow such censorious actions are depends on the history and politics of the state concerned and in particular on how fragile and/or vulnerable its institutions are to the sentiments being banned: the Germans today are understandably more anxious about

Rowan Gillespie
Victims of Hate (front)
34 x 33 x 19 cm
courtesy of the artist

Nazis than are the Americans, the British keener to crack down on racially motivated hate speech than other countries that do not share its colonial past and diverse population. The European Convention on Human Rights contains a number of clues as to what is going on with these apparent subversions of civil liberties. Many of the key civil liberties set out in that document are capable of being overridden when certain legitimate goals come into play and when this derogation is prescribed by law, but, crucially, this can be done only when it is considered 'necessary in a democratic society'. Article 17 declares that 'Nothing in this Convention may be interpreted as implying for any State, group or person any right to engage in any activity or perform

any act aimed at the destruction of any of the rights and freedoms set forth herein or at their limitation to a greater extent than is provided for in the Convention.' If things get really rough, this paradigmatic political rights charter permits states to derogate from their obligations under it in 'time of war or other public emergency threatening the life of the nation' (albeit only 'to the extent strictly required by the exigencies of the situation').

Most democratic constitutions have clauses along similar lines. If they do not, the responsible authorities tend to read them as implied in the document (if they are judges) or to assert them (if they are elected leaders). The important civil libertarian point to make is that this should not surprise us or disturb us as a matter of principle. The test of a successful democratic culture is not its willingness to implode when faced with illiberal forces inclined to misconstrue the freedoms offered by such a society as invitations to destroy it. This is the case whether the threat comes from the Left, the Right, or from some pre-modern brand of politicized religion. The willingness of representative democracy to equip itself to fight against forces that would destroy it must entail an openness to the curtailment of civil liberties, where this is judged essential to survival. Those who reject this premise as an unwarranted invitation to authoritarianism are likely to be closet libertarians, verging on anarchists, rather than civil libertarians in the political sense in which the term is being used here.

If there can be no serious argument against the need for such a democratic override button, however, there is great controversy over who should have the right to push it. The difficult question is not one of principle but of practice. This is where the pressure arises. The issues were simpler before mass suffrage. Power was then in the hands of élites whose invariable tendency was to confuse the threat they individually (or as a class) faced with a danger to the country as a whole. In such situations, the claims of national security were often a mere camouflage for the vested interests that lay behind them. In 1688, King James II no doubt thought he was putting England first even while parliament put him to flight for, among other misdeeds, 'endeavour[ing] to subvert and extirpate ... the lawes and liberties of this kingdome'. Two generations later, the justly celebrated civil liberties case of Entick v. Carrington (1765) established that the British executive branch's version of state necessity did not necessarily accord with that of the law of the land. The importance of this case lay in the way it established on behalf of the judges a claim to have a shared responsibility for the

assessment of what kinds of abridgement of civil liberties were required in the name of national survival. Many of the advances in civil liberties in eighteenth-century Britain were made in the courtroom, by brave judges, courageous counsel and unintimidated juries.

With the growth of the democratic movement at the end of that century and its revival after a period of repression inspired by anxiety about the possible contagiousness of the French Revolution, advocates of civil liberties found themselves facing the hostility not only of a propertied class used to parliamentary power but also of their allies on the bench, now increasingly unsettled by the prospect of sharing power with the merchants and other beneficiaries of the Industrial Revolution. During the first half of the nineteenth century, the national interest, in Britain and in other countries, was wheeled out to provide a rhetorical veneer for class partisanship, but once again it was unsuccessful. Resistance to a widened franchise involved savage repression, military attacks on protesters and, when the modest reform measure of 1832 came up for debate in Britain, warnings of imminent national doom in both Houses of Parliament. The same cycle was then played out in the course of the late nineteenth and early twentieth century as a truly democratic culture secured its niche in the industrialized West with the support of the socialist and trade-union movements and via a strong commitment to a universal right to vote. Ireland's anti-imperialist struggles of the nineteenth and early twentieth century fit a similar pattern, with the dispute in its case being about the composition of the national entity as well as the supposed threat to national survival.

So much for the past, when resistance to the democratic goals of civil libertarians turned the assertion of even the basic freedoms of expression, assembly and association into highly dangerous acts, potentially

Rowan Gillespie
Victims of Hate (back)
34 x 33 x 19 cm
courtesy of the artist

treasonable or seditious if the authorities chose to see things that way. With an elected parliament to which the executive is accountable and upon which it depends for support, the entitlement of those who decide what can be done in the name of national security has become less of a subject of controversy. The ministers asserting the need to constrain civil liberties for these reasons have been able to invoke their democratic mandate as a moral basis for their action. In Britain, the US and elsewhere, this made the crackdowns on radical political speech during the Cold War both possible and, broadly speaking, tolerated by the general public. During the period 1945-89, there

was a general acceptance that the challenge to the legitimacy of the state was real enough to warrant defensive action. The courts as well as the legislative and executive branches in most liberal democracies accepted this assumption, as did important regional tribunals like the European Court of Human Rights. Certainly, this meant that there were allegations of partisanship in the protection of civil liberties, with certain categories of persons being quite unable to actualize their rights, while others (less subversive of authority) were free to protest as they wished. But allegations of double standards were thought a price worth paying for the preservation of democratic structures. The same was broadly true of the terrorism laws prior to 9/11: these were sharply focused and usually applied with the kind of restraint that could only flow from a culture whose commitment to freedom and democracy did not feel challenged by the sporadic acts of relatively weak — albeit occasionally very violent — subversives.

The change since 9/11 has been in the way in which terrorism laws have become generalized and in the flimsiness of the national security claims that have underpinned their expansion. We see this in the extraordinary attempt by the current president of the United States to establish himself as commander-in-chief in a never-ending war on terror that places him above his country's own constitution, able, in his view, to disregard legislative and legal constraints on his actions. It has been evident as well, though as yet to a much lesser degree, in the British reaction to 9/11; this initially involved detention without charge for suspected international terrorists and has now led to a scheme of 'anti-terrorism control orders', restrictions that can be imposed on suspects without proof of any criminal activity (albeit subject to judicial oversight). Large numbers of countries have followed in the repressive paths blazed by these supposedly model democracies. Even the United Nations, depressingly, has joined in the action, with Security Council resolutions having led to a return to blacklists of banned persons and groups, resolutions which, when challenged, have been held by many judges (including the important Court of First Instance of the European Court of Justice) to be beyond the reach of human rights inquiry. Much of this activity is predicated on a definition of terrorism so vague that it permits action against persons whose only offence is that of radical political activity. It is this potentially broad field of attack on civil liberties that anti-terrorism law has opened up, which, allied to a ratcheting up of the anti-terrorist rhetoric and the resulting chill that affects the whole democratic culture, has rendered the changes of the recent past potentially so dangerous as compared with the anti-communism and anti-terrorism of the more distant past.

The civil libertarian must answer these developments. The first point is to acknowledge that civil liberties are not absolute: to claim otherwise is to fly in the face of history. But having acknowledged this, the defender of civil liberties must insist that no elected leader can have a blank cheque to act as he or she wishes in the name of national security, that the fact of democratic legitimacy is not sufficient to warrant the seizure of such a power. Judgements as to what is required to ensure national survival must be shared, with the legislative, but especially with the judicial, branch. Civil libertarians must swallow whatever suspicions they might have had of the judges ('right-wing', 'reactionary', 'illiberal', etcetera) and recognize that because the authoritarian tendency has made such advances recently, judges have found themselves in the front line of the defence of freedom. This is an odd place to see them, it is true, but they must be cheered on nonetheless. This is the case when the British House of Lords rules that detention of suspected international terrorists is a breach of human rights, when the US Supreme Court, largely composed of Republican appointees, decides that President George W. Bush has gone too far even for them, and when the International Court of Justice bravely castigates the Israeli Wall. There are many other examples as well — the news on the judicial front is not at all as bad as is sometimes supposed by those of us who are dyed-in-the-wool critics of judicial conservatism. But the 'war on terror' has made liberals of us all. When the executive and legislative branches have been won back to the civil libertarian side, we can go back to arguments about how judges are holding up social progress, but now is not the time for such luxurious disputes.

Democracy

If the first paradox is concerned with the subject of civil liberties' requirement to contain within itself the seeds of its own destruction, the second is likewise taken up with absorbing another contrary impulse within its deep structure. The historic purpose of civil liberties as the law and practice of political freedom has been to secure a representative system of government; in its classic form this is what all the protesting and speech-making and associating has been about. The achievement of this form of rule does not, however, bring an end to the subject of civil liberties or even a restriction of it to the legislative arena; rather the reverse. In fact, one of the tests of the success of a democratic culture is its willingness to accept political expression that is not focused on the duly elected representatives of the community, but that lies well outside the parliamentary mainstream. This continued appreciation of the need for popular protest in a country with plenty of formal democratic channels open to it is another historical legacy of civil liberties, which fortunately we have been unable — so far at least — to shake off. During the democratic revolution of the seventeenth century through to the mid-twentieth century, civil liberties had to exist separately from the legislature because (albeit to a progressively lesser extent as time went on) that body was not representative in a truly democratic sense. But the Suffragettes were the last civil libertarian movement in the West that was able to say with perfect clarity that the elected persons making decisions about their future were in no way their representatives, having achieved their positions on the basis of votes cast by one gender only.

If the democratic developments of the twentieth century did not render the subject of civil liberties redundant, they did affect it in important ways. With universal franchise having been largely achieved by the late 1920s, civil libertarian energy found itself caught up in a new field of battle. The main arena of dispute has not been about winning power to change the system but about exercising the rights to freedoms of expression, assembly and association in order to influence legislators in favour of particular points of view. Highly relevant at this juncture is the fact that so many of the world's people are now, formally at any rate, citizens of states organized entirely on democratic principles. In such places governments have a new way of rebutting public protest — pointing not to the substantive error of the policy change that is sought, but rather to the inadmissibility of the mode of bringing it to the legislators' attention. The country is a democratic one, the relevant decision-maker tells the crowd: go and write to your MP/TD/Senator, run for office or seek to inform opinion in more orthodox/less invasive ways. This democratically rooted counter-attack on civil liberties was first in evidence during the Red Scare in the US in the 1920s and the General Strike in Britain in 1926. In both cases, government ministers justified their actions — draconian emergency regulation, strong police action, tough prosecution policies — with a new authority based on their democratic legitimacy and the existence of alternative mechanisms for calling executive decision-making to account. More recent protests that have similarly been on the margins of political debate have been equally vulnerable to control on the basis that such forms of protest are unnecessary in today's free society: examples in Britain include CND activism in the early 1980s, Stop-the-City protests, eco-demonstrations, and other forms of direct action.

Of course, the political leadership did not in the 1920s and 1930s, and does not today, regard an operative democratic system of government as a sufficient basis for the removal of political freedom altogether:

Brian Maguire
Strange Fruit
2003
lithograph A/P 1
(edition of 20)
courtesy of the artist

the paradox lies precisely in the need to continue to allow those earlier hard-won civil liberties. The men and women who run Britain or Ireland today recognize the need for civil liberties as a matter of principle, and concede the legitimacy of this or that particular public protest as a social fact, but it by no means follows that they welcome the practice of public protest with open arms. These democratically elected officials cannot help but see themselves as the current winners in an impeccably fair electoral race and with a consequent monopoly of wisdom, which public protesters are seeking by the short cut of direct action to undermine. From time to time ministers are emboldened to take a tougher line with protest than might otherwise have been expected; on such occasions, their negative energy suggests an underlying sense of grievance about the need for public protest in general. The frustration of Tony Blair's administration at the anti-war protest mounted over many years in Parliament Square by Brian Haw, that led to legislation specifically designed to remove him, is one example; the same prime minister's whipping up of national anger about a proposed May Day demonstration in central London in 2001 was another. What we see in each case is a playing out of the tension between democracy and civil liberties, which is, in turn, a direct result of this paradoxical necessity for continuing the protection afforded by civil liberties in a country where civil liberties appear to have achieved their goal.

The new climate of anti-terrorism places fresh pressure on this ambiguous approach to extra-parliamentary activity. The breadth of the definition of terrorism in most legal frameworks, already noted as usually going beyond acts of violence, makes it possible for the police and security services to be deployed not only against violent subversives but against those involved in direct action and public protest as well. These expansive readings of the law are not resisted by a political leadership that in its heart of hearts is not clear why, in these truly democratic days, any public protest is really required. So, when the police use their anti-terrorism stop-and-search powers to harass protesters on their way to a demonstration outside an arms fair, as happened recently in the UK, the authorities feel no embarrassment and continue to authorize the laws that have permitted such abuses to occur. Only when publicity becomes really intense, as when the terrorism laws were invoked in 2005 to prevent a member of the Labour Party, who

had been ejected from the party conference for heckling the foreign secretary, from returning to his seat, is there enough anger generated to secure an official apology. The civil libertarian needs to meet this official antipathy to public protest by explaining afresh why the forms of democracy do not mean the end of civil liberties, why public protest is a vital part of good government and why the laws on terrorism should be restricted to the core of serious criminal acts, to which they ought exclusively to refer: murder, manslaughter, causing explosions, and the like — not general destabilizing behaviour, as is often the case today. The civil libertarian needs to be unafraid to argue that instability, inconvenience, disconcerting direct action, and the like, are routes to a better democratic future, not evidence of terrorist subversion.

Political Violence

The final paradox can be more briefly stated than our first two. It flows from both, and its central relevance to contemporary discussion of political freedom will be immediately grasped. The subject of civil liberties presents itself as necessarily involving a rejection of political violence as a matter of principle, but in fact it has in the past depended on exactly this sort of violence, or the threat of it, for its success. This is not only a point about the way in which parliamentary government was established in England, Ireland and the US by means of a successful usurpation of power, backed by the force of arms. It is a reference as well to the political ferment that built up for mass suffrage across the industrialized world in the nineteenth century. It encompasses the politically inspired subversion of the Chartists and the famous willingness of the Suffragettes to engage in subversive violence to achieve their ends. Just as the English parliament of the 'Glorious Revolution' spoke of the need for rights to secure the nation from the disorder

A security man removes
82-year-old Walter Wolfgang
after he heckled Britain's
Foreign Secretary Jack Straw
as he delivered a key note
speech during the annual
Labour Party Conference
on 28 September 2005
in Brighton, England.
Photograph: Scott
Barbour/Getty Images.

of a failed royal despotism, so, generations later, the Universal Declaration of Human Rights in 1948 asserted in its preamble that it was 'essential, if man is not to be compelled to have recourse, as a last resort, to rebellion against tyranny and oppression, that human rights should be protected by the rule of law'.

The civil libertarian needs to be unafraid of remarking that the achievement of political freedom has depended on violence in most countries, and that there are situations of imperial domination or domestic tyranny where even today this is the only progressive option. The language of terrorism needs to be tackled head-on so that it ceases to be the overarching prohibition on political violence, regardless of context, that it has recently become. Such tackling of fundamentals will make the position of the civil libertarian easier because less defensive. The legacy of the successful subversion upon which the subject of civil liberties is built produces an ambiguous relationship between it and political violence: generally condemning the latter but being quick to ensure that those accused of it receive a fair trial; deploring criminal acts but being ready to accept and defend conduct that is well into the zone of the lawless; complaining about the abuse of police discretion rather than the undeniable fact that a law has been broken; agreeing that inflicting injuries to persons is wrong but being a bit uncertain about property; and being more than willing to describe as merely robust direct action what others would call a criminal mob.

This edge to the subject of civil liberties is what keeps it honest, stops it becoming the handmaiden of power, makes it serve rather than challenge the established (democratic) order. But it does leave civil liberties vulnerable to being tarred with the wrongs of others. The answer is a dual commitment to democracy and the criminal law, with the former being a *sine qua non* for the ruling out of subversive violence and the latter being the best way in which to protect the rights of the majority without destroying individuals and whole communities in the process. The civil libertarian should argue unashamedly for the replacement of the language of terrorism with the language of the criminal law, for a return to policing rather than military metaphors to describe this branch of serious crime. In order to ensure the continued survival of civil liberties as a subject, it needs to be shown successfully that all the threats posed by terrorism can be catered to by the criminal process, invigorated by reform and by a stronger international cohesiveness if needs

be, but criminal (rather than administrative or emergency-based) nevertheless.

Conclusion

It is in the state's recent and growing preoccupation with terrorism that civil liberties as a subject has faced its greatest challenge in the democratic era, with the exposure of all the three paradoxes discussed above combining to impose immense pressure on it. The alleged necessities of counter-terrorism have already compromised the right to life and the prohibition of torture and inhuman or degrading treatment or punishment. Its demands have also impacted severely on other basic freedoms, such as those of liberty, speech, assembly and association. It would be absurd to claim that civil liberties are dead or dying in the liberal democratic world. But they are certainly under severe attack from a variety of sources; chief amongst these is the idea that the West is engaged in some kind of global 'war on terror' or 'clash of civilizations', which threatens the integrity of the nation in such exceptional and unprecedented ways that exceptional and unprecedented actions are needed to defend it, that (to quote Tony Blair, who has driven so much of the reorientation in this area) 'the rules of the game are changing'.

The health of civil liberties as a subject depends on its being able to balance the tensions that flow from its paradoxical need to provide exceptions to itself, its continued insistence on the legitimacy of extra-parliamentary opposition, and its determination — rooted in its violent history — not to regard all disturbances of public order as inherently wrong. The danger of the counter-terrorism discourse is that it leads to a collapse of all these tensions in the direction of security and away from civil liberties. A tranquil state that is rooted in fear is not a free society. ∎

Sister Patrice, 2005

Jackie Nickerson's 'Faith'

In a convent or monastery, prayer and contemplation are magnified by ritual, so much so that the sense of a spiritual presence within the buildings becomes pervasive, and this most potently takes the form of light. Photography, itself founded on light, is an art form that saturates the world of objects and people in that medium.

The source of light in a painting is usually traceable to a source or an area, and from there the structure and geometry of the painting is illuminated in ways that we are accustomed to read as being a blend of inner and outer light, always establishing for us a ratio between the physical and the spiritual worlds. In these photographs, that painterly inheritance is palpable, but in them the intimacy between the technology of the camera and the use of light is especially strong. The blaze of light through a window, the gloss of polish on a floor, the echo of light down a corridor, the pressure of light within a face, all bespeak the spirituality and discipline which together create the beauty of silence and community we witness here.

A statue, a saucepan, a table or a chair are not merely dead objects; they are mute, but alive. The photographs create silence as a dimension, although they also allow for conversation and cheerfulness. These are communities steeped in an interiority which they have discovered is not their own but something wider and deeper than themselves of which they are a part. The purity of line in these shots — verticals, horizontals, deepening perspectives — indicates a certain completeness, a spiritual integrity that belongs to and is part of the goal as well as the effect of the monastic spirit. Yet too

there is the implication of the historical time of these institutions. The iconography has that unmistakable combination of catholic revivalism and kitsch of the nineteenth century, of the Virgin and the Sacred Heart, the anti-secular devotions of that era that stand out here like insignia of time in a world otherwise concerned to register its timeless dailiness. We are looking here at an eternal present and at a historical past. Jackie Nickerson's achievement is to embed one within the other with such gentle skill that their contrast with one another produces little more than an eddy of conflict that perhaps deepens their meditative calm.

'Faith' is the result of three years photographing the interior and exterior spaces of religious communities throughout Ireland. Nickerson had uncommon access to the private worlds of the religious in their places of work and prayer. The series was exhibited in the Paul Kane Gallery, Dublin in 2006 and is going to be on display in the Jack Shainman Gallery, New York, in October 2007, and will be published by SteidlMack in September 2007. Now resident in County Louth, Nickerson's other recent work includes 'Farm' based on several years spent travelling around Southern Africa, photographing farm labourers and their environment.

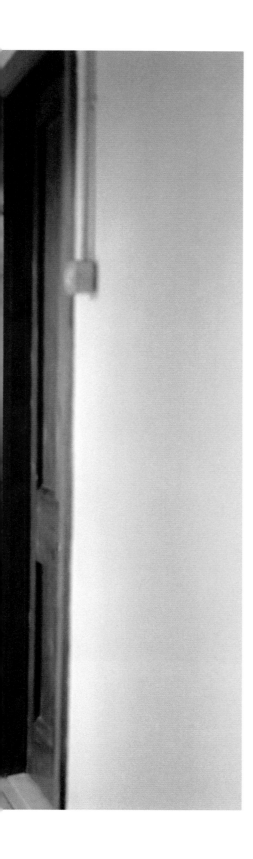

Blue corridor, 2005

Drying cupboard, 2005

Confession, 2006

Sister Damian, 2005

Hallway, 2005

Sister Peter, 2004

Brother Michael, 2005

Seminarian I, 2006

Seminarian II, 2006

Green room, 2005

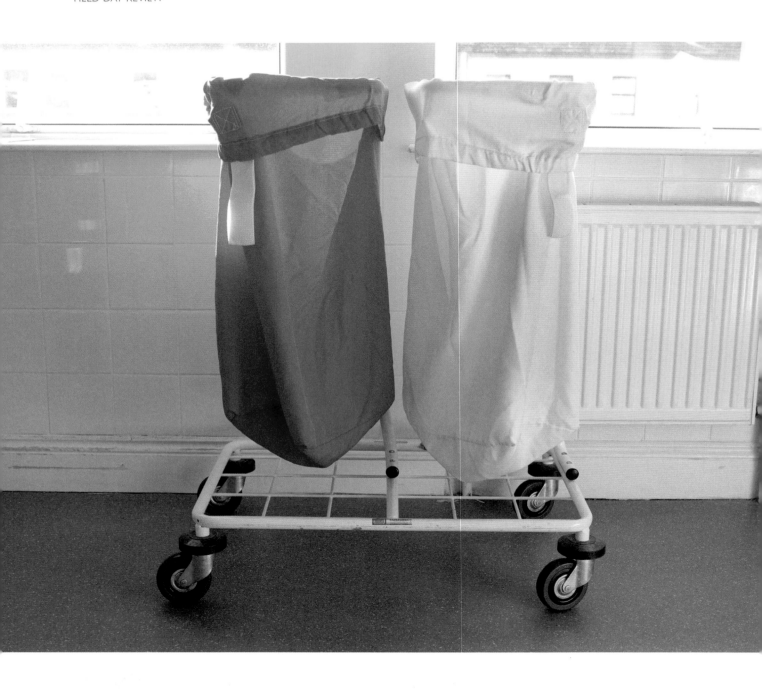

Laundry bags, 2005

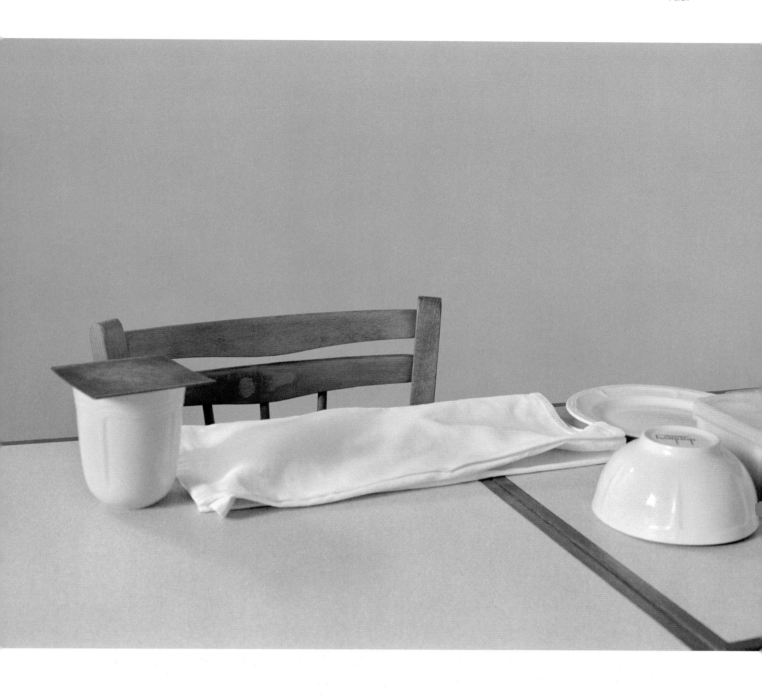

Place setting, 2005

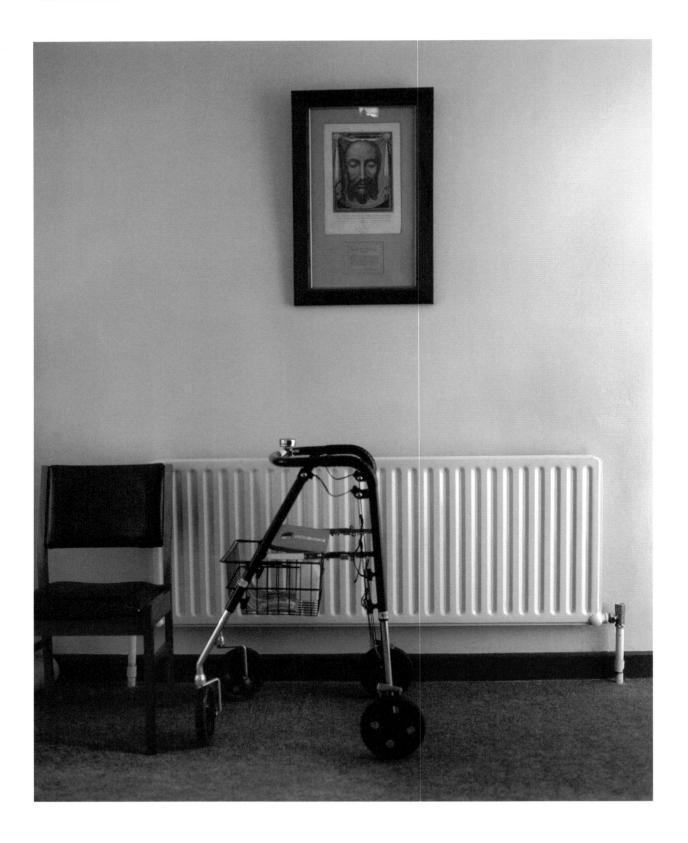

Choir, 2005

Stairway, 2004

Sister Faustina, 2005

Sister Louis, 2005

Cloaks, 2005

Yellow corridor, 2005

Aga, 2005

Review Essays

Bodies Once Again

Terry Eagleton

Novel Relations: The Transformation of Kinship in English Literature and Culture, 1748–1818
Ruth Perry
Cambridge: Cambridge University Press, 2004. x + 466 pages. IBSN 0-521-83694-8

The Body Economic: Life, Death and Sensation in Political Economy and the Victorian Novel
Catherine Gallagher
Princeton: Princeton University Press, 2005. 240 pages. ISBN 0-691-12358-6

If you open a history of the world at random, you will find it making three claims about whatever period you happen upon: it was a time of rapid change; it was essentially an age of transition; and the middle classes went on rising. Like the sun, or the cost of housing in Dublin, rising is what the middle classes are eternally destined to do. It is as natural to them as falling is to American TV evangelists.

It is true that in today's late bourgeois society, with its jobbers, media moguls, computer nerds and open-neck-shirted CEOs, the traditional *bürgerlich* class — the kind of solid, cultivated, eminently reputable types who populate the pages of Thomas Mann — have risen without trace. By the mid-eighteenth century in England, however, they had entrenched an aggressively new culture of individualism; and the effects of this on domestic life are what Ruth Perry's superbly erudite *Novel Relations* is mostly about.

What Perry has in her critical sights is the Whiggish, dewy-eyed fable of historians like Lawrence Stone, for whom the eighteenth century witnessed a new form of cosy, intimate, 'companionate' marriage, a deepened affectivity that elevated the status of women. The narrative Perry herself has to deliver is rather grimmer. As far as the role of women goes, there was indeed a tectonic shift in the age of Enlightenment; but it was one from father patriarchy to husband patriarchy — from kinship defined as consanguinity to kinship defined by conjugality. If marriage moves centre stage in social and literary thought, it is not because men and women have finally learned how to love their spouses (least of all from reading romantic novels), but because there were social forces abroad that ensured that you could rely less and less on the family into which you were born.

In earlier historical periods, it is by no means clear that marriage was seen as the most important kin connection, even (when compared with sisterhood or daughterhood) in the case of women; now, however, women were mostly to be defined in relation to their husbands and children. In the seventeenth century, Perry argues, individual desire was rarely distinguished from the good of the community; you might resist the spouse your parents tried to foist on you, but only with the support of local public opinion. An adult female was defined at least as much by work, property and motherhood as by sex or marriage. Later, however, a husband's love — a fragile enough commodity, to be sure — came to be a woman's only law and protection. As daughters were redefined as strangers-in-the-house or potential émigrés, fathers took less responsibility for them and mothers began to feel more competitive with them. As Michel Foucault argues in *The History of Sexuality*, a work that prefigures Perry's case but which she acknowledges, glancingly, only once, the 'deployment of alliance' gave way to the 'deployment of sexuality' in kinship systems.

This bold, essentially simple, thesis, one which should be distinguished from the banal claim that the period saw the growth of the 'nuclear' family, is the fulcrum on which *Novel Relations* turns; and it manages to hold a vast array of disparate materials deftly together. If the book is capacious in scope, it is agreeably tight in conceptual focus. In eighteenth-century England, so Perry argues, the meaning of the term 'family' was undergoing a seismic change. An axis of kinship based on consanguineal ties or blood lineage was gradually yielding ground to one centred on the conjugal couple; and the chief battleground between consanguinity and conjugality was the figure of the daughter. Women were forced to sacrifice what power and status they derived from their family of origin to the narrower, more unstable, less protected status of loving spouse; and the conflicts between these antithetical roles form much of the stuff of eighteenth-century fiction. There is, Perry considers, an 'intense anxiety about family membership' in this troubled condition, one which Jane Austen (who creates the *locus classicus* of sister–wife conflict in *Sense and Sensibility*) cannily avoided herself by the simple device of never marrying. As often, the function of the novel here is essentially strategic or therapeutic: it provides a vital way of working through painful social contradictions, in what Perry sees as a world being rapidly transformed by market

forces, urban anonymity and the spread of literacy. In the course of her book, then, all three history-of-the-world axioms are triumphantly confirmed (it was, she informs us in addition, 'an age of great social mobility and class instability'), which is no more than one might expect.

There is a broader background to this change in family fortunes, which it is no part of Perry's brief to investigate. With the emergence of what was only fairly recently dubbed 'modernity', the symbolic dimension of human affairs (religion, art and sexuality) is increasingly divorced from the socio-economic, shifted from the public sphere to some more private, peripheral status. This, like most aspects of modernity, represents both loss and gain — a Janus-faced view of modernity that only Marxism, for which the great epoch of the rising bourgeoisie is simultaneously a story of breathtaking liberation and an unspeakable nightmare, has managed to sustain in our own dismally undialectical times. It is a view as inimical to nostalgic anti-modernists as it is to those post-modernists who leap to their state-of-the-art computers to denounce the very notion of progress. It is distasteful alike to the callow avant-gardists for which the past is merely a tale of oppression to be transcended, and the cultural mandarins for whom the present is one long, lamentable degeneration from it.

Both camps abandon the notion of the past as a potentially revolutionary force. It is not dreams of liberated grandchildren that drive men and women to revolt, Walter Benjamin wisely observed, but memories of enslaved ancestors. Nationalists are more likely to be mindful of this truth than most; it is just that their problem is finding a way of utilizing the past that does not fetishize it. Modernity is likely to appear equivocal in their eyes, since if it signifies the forces that oppress them, it also furnishes them with some of the instruments for resisting it. Eighteenth-century individualism, *Novel Relations* argues, was similarly doubled-edged. If it

William Hogarth
Marriage à-la-Mode: 1.
The Marriage Settlement
c. 1743
oil on canvas
90.8 x 69.9 cm
National Gallery, London

allowed every man to be king of his castle, it curtailed the autonomy of women. Market capitalism liberated men, but deprived women of community support.

Because of its colonial status, Ireland lived through the divorce between the symbolic and socio-economic fairly belatedly. Religion was hardly a private option: it remained a formidable public institution well into the twentieth century, second in power only to the state and considerably more authoritative. The narrative of the metropolitan nation, in which religion evolves from Protestant inwardness to private pastime, did not apply so forcibly here. While art in Britain was an affair of market forces, in nineteenth-century Ireland it remained locked firmly into the political sphere, as it is in most nationalist cultures. As for sexuality and the family, we are dealing less with the erotic or affective than with a pre-modern world of dowries and matchmakers. It is less a question of Jamesian intricacies or

Lawrentian intensities than of birth rates, labour requirements, emigration, impartible inheritance, welfare provision, clerical regulation, enforced celibacy and the like.

In the directness of relation between cultural forms and material forces, colonial societies lend themselves admirably to vulgar Marxism. One has only to consider the historical coincidence of the United Irishmen with Thomas Moore, the rise of the first Catholic novelists alongside Daniel O'Connell, the conveniently synchronous deaths of James Clarence Mangan and a million famine victims, the co-existence of the Literary Revival with the decline and fall of the Anglo-Irish Ascendancy, the near-miraculous simultaneity of James Joyce's *Portrait* with the Easter Rising and of *Ulysses* with the birth of the Free State, the emergence of the first major Catholic dramatists after political independence (the Protestantism of Sean O'Casey was a historical oversight), and the legendary twinning of the Northern poets and the

Troubles, to recognize that nothing of this could be other than providential.

Privatization, of course, can be progressive. With the consummation of modernity, the church pew, marital bedroom and artist's studio are absolved from the more brutal sort of state invigilation. Art can become critique, while religion and sexuality are nobody's business but your own. But this, needless to say, is just what is so anaemic and impoverished about them. The symbolic domain can give power the slip only at the price of progressive irrelevance.

Novel Relations, by contrast, examines an aspect of the transition from traditional to modern that remains firmly within the political sphere. We are not speaking here of any simple-minded shift from public to private. If 'love' increasingly conquers 'money' when it comes to marriage, it does so in ways which express an individualistic drive for economic independence. Affection and economy are not yet the polarities they will come to appear in some major currents of Romanticism. The family is one of those curious institutions (Fox TV and the Church of England are others) that in classical Marxist terms belong simultaneously to base and superstructure, reproducing labour power and ideological values at the same time.

Women, so Perry's thesis runs, lost power in their natal families; and though they might retrieve some social clout in their conjugal set-ups, the net result was a disinheritance of daughters. It is a compulsively repeated plot line in the fiction of the period. A woman born into a powerful family might shed the benefits of that status when she married. Inhabiting two domestic systems simultaneously, poised on the thresholds of both, daughters were the chief units of exchange between the consanguineal kin group and the conjugal economy. Women's autonomy as wives and mothers may have been more limited than it had been as sisters and daughters. Samuel Richardson's Clarissa

Harlowe, for example, enjoys considerable independence in her natal family (she has a dairy-house of her own), before being thrown in the path of the villainous Lovelace. The novels of the day, Perry considers, were obsessed by father–daughter relationships, in a surge of literary nostalgia for the time when young women, now at the mercy of their husbands, could turn to their progenitors for guidance and solace. The relationship of sisters, another constant literary focus, represents the claims of blood kin in its purest form, 'uncomplicated by the seductions of wealth, power, or the right of succession'. Fictional images of sibling intimacy, Perry argues, are symptomatic responses to its declining significance in society at large.

Brothers are key figures too, since only they could compete with husbands for the love of a woman. Indeed, the profoundly conservative *Mansfield Park* privileges the brother–sister bond above all other affinities. Elder brothers in eighteenth-century novels are often spoiled, arrogant, profligate types, just as older sisters tend to be vain and younger ones giddy; but an idealized version of the chastity-protecting good brother stages its appearance in scores of eighteenth-century tales, as what is decreasingly possible in life is still viable in art. As men came to think of themselves as at their best in the role of brothers, brotherhood became idealized as the kin position *par excellence*, and was accordingly ripe for conversion at a later historical point to a revolutionary political concept.

The theoretical birth of children, generally known as the 'invention of childhood', accompanied the new focus on conjugality; and this in turn necessitated the invention of a new kind of motherhood, desexualized and sentimentalized, to feed and clothe these emergent cultural constructs. Previously, English culture had not particularly venerated the notion of maternity. Yet the actual power of mothers dwindled throughout the century, which may be one reason for their notorious absence in the fiction of the period. Aunts and other maternal substitutes act instead as counsellors to anxious, isolated young married women. Meanwhile, sexuality was redefined as a cardinal sin, a special weakness requiring special vigilance, while the commodification of women as sexual objects grew to the point where it became well-nigh impossible for anyone reflecting on the condition of women to mention wives without mentioning prostitutes, or vice versa. Commodified social relations were replacing older kin and communal obligations.

Novel Relations, as that last sentence might suggest, is something of a Fall narrative. It is hard to close the book without feeling a faint twinge of nostalgia for the good old days of consanguineal patriarchy, when woman had more male oppressors and not just one male to protect them. Since deteriorationist fables, however, are almost always truer than ameliorative ones, the human animal being what it is, the account rings a good deal more plausibly than Lawrence Stone's, whose study of the family, sex and marriage in early modern England had the distinction of being discredited almost as soon as it fell from the press. Perry has done her historical spadework, and provides us with plausible reasons for the transition in question. These changes in the family were for the most part functions of economic individualism, which repositioned women with respect to their families of origin. If lineal kinship gradually ousted the collateral variety in law, it is because patrilineal inheritance reinforced the accumulation of property within families and undercut its wider distribution. Legal changes funnelled more domestic resources to the elder son to supply him with a stake in the new competitive economy, diminishing the portions of the other siblings and leaving women in particular at a disastrous disadvantage. Marriage as an alliance of kin groups provided a means to class mobility and the amassing of property. State policies

tended to recognize the rights of marital kin over natural kin. Primogeniture and patrimony turn out to be the villains of the piece. Alarmingly enough, it begins to sound as though the Marxists may have been right after all.

This steady material preoccupation is one of *Novel Relation*'s signal strengths — not least in a United States where even the Left is coy of the word 'capitalism', and one current of feminism sniffily regards any talk of production as 'economistic'. (Curiously, however, they do not regard their own culturalism as equally reductive.) The study is not of that dispiriting school of North American feminist criticism that treats gender in stark isolation from other social factors, a partiality that has much to do with the dearth of a socialist culture in such societies. It is not in the least unusual to stumble across American feminists today who support the despicably opportunistic warmonger Hillary Clinton, just as the Irish feminist who can see no more in republicanism than a tiresome virility complex and whose politics on everything but the issue of gender are impeccably Dublin 4, is a drearily familiar figure. One of the most splendid consequences of the global decline of Marxism is that we can no longer be accused by feminists of 'appropriating' their concerns, since we are scarcely any longer thick enough on the ground to do so. They, instead, are most welcome to appropriate ours, if they have a mind to. Ruth Perry is not exactly a Marxist; but she is not in the least shy of discerning the destructive impetus of early modern capitalism at the root of the dislocating and demoting of the eighteenth-century heroine.

A publisher's note to this vastly learned, strikingly original study describes the book as using social history to examine literary texts. In fact, it does more or less the opposite. Its author is remarkably well versed in the kind of utterly obscure eighteenth-century novels that one devoutly

Andrés de Santa Maria
El lavadero sobre el Sena
c. 1887
oil on screen
200 x 302 cm
The Art Archive/Museo
Nacional de Colombia en
Bogota/Dagli Orti

hopes one will never have to read oneself; but she treats them almost exclusively as historical documentation, not as literary artefacts. This is the kind of method that gets us materialists a bad name. Perry speaks of trying to read the 'unconscious' of literary texts, but she actually gets up to nothing so sophisticated. Aside from a comment or two on genre, her approach throughout is to stare resolutely through literary form in order to plunder novels of their social content. The closest she comes to any more intricate approach is to point out that the fictions she deals with are not always a direct reflection of real life — a point she rather spoils by surrendering to the post-modern neurosis of placing the phrase 'real life' in scare quotes.

There are a few microscopic flaws. 'Duel' is not a transitive verb, at least not in English-English, and one is envious of someone else's eminence, not jealous of it. Perry should not confirm the stereotype of the nation as an irony-free zone by overlooking a blatant

example of the figure in a quotation from *A Sentimental Journey*, though she does compensate somewhat for this fault by entitling a chapter on incest 'Family Feeling'. Nor should she give comfort to trendy epistemological sceptics by placing the word 'true' in scare quotes. Such miniscule blemishes apart, *Novel Relations* will surely prove a seminal, immensely authoritative text for any future discussion of eighteenth-century letters and social history; though more — much more — with regard to the latter than the former.

⁂

In the 1970s and 1980s, it was advisable to include the word 'Dialectics' or 'Dynamics' in your title if you wished to get your book published. These days, the requisite buzz word is 'Body'. In fact, there will soon be more bodies in contemporary criticism than on the fields of Waterloo. Mangled members, tormented torsos, bodies emblazoned or incarcerated, disciplined or desirous: all this, no doubt, can be laid at the door of Michel Foucault, for whom bodies were a way of talking about human subjects without going all soggily subjective. With his well-nigh pathological aversion to subjectivity, which, obtusely, he could see as nothing but self-repression, the later Foucault discovered in the notion of the body, a discourse of the self which could remain resolutely external to anything as messily humanistic as psychology or emotion. It is ironic in this respect that the cult of the body was then hijacked by feminist critics whose interest, quite properly, lay precisely in this marshy terrain, far removed from the virile, self-grooming gymnastics of the French philosopher himself.

There are, however, more bodies than one. On the whole, it has proved acceptable to speak of the sexual or reproductive body, but not of the labouring one. Disciplined, monstrous or imprisoned bodies have been granted the Foucaultean imprimatur, but not for the most part sick or suffering ones. Such partisanship is one reason among many to applaud the appearance of Catherine Gallagher's *The Body Economic*, with its refreshing reminder that there is a zone of production as well as a realm of reproduction.

In a stunningly innovative gesture, Gallagher points out that the thin-blooded political economists and the warm-hearted Romantic organicists of early nineteenth-century Britain had a good deal more in common than is generally supposed. Both, after all, dealt in life, energy, sensation, nature and corporeality. Utilitarian political economy is a eudemonic doctrine, all about pains and pleasures, appetencies and aversions, desire and depletion, life and death. Nations must store up great reserves of vigour and sensation, which is really just another name for wealth, and sluice these energies out again in production or consumption; but sufficient reserves could only be stored up if expenditure was restricted, which meant

withholding present enjoyment and releasing more pain than pleasure into the system. It is not a doctrine the citizens of advanced capitalism, as opposed to the industrial variety, would greet with much enthusiasm.

In this sense, political economy shares a vitalistic basis with the discourse that contests it most hotly from Samuel Taylor Coleridge to I. A. Richards: the aesthetic, which (as Gallagher might have pointed out) begins life in a work of 1750 by Alexander Baumgarten as a discourse of the body — of perception and sensation — not of art. Since there are few keener sensations than starvation, and since it is not hard to see the nation's economy as an organic system of vital energy, aesthetics and political economy share a naturalistic source. Behind the book's preoccupation with the circulation of energies, one can dimly hear the dying strains of the new historicism.

Gallagher even manages the improbable feat of rescuing Thomas Malthus from the enormous condescension of the literati. In fact, the critic of copulation begins to sound positively sexy. She shows just what a sensual materialist he was, and how this scandalized his more loftily idealist critics. Malthus, like the work of some of his high-minded Romantic castigators, is all about feeling — but in his case, about the miseries and fleshly enjoyments of the poor, pleasure and happiness, energies and aversions, the productivity or sterility of bodily life. The moral perfectionists, he considered, were hostile to the just claims of the body, and David Ricardo's preoccupation with exchange-value discounts, in his view, the fact that political economy is rooted in the collective material needs of labouring bodies. Economic actors strive in the end for the maximizing of their pleasurable sensations. Malthus, Gallagher observes, was the originator of the very sentiments that John Ruskin thought of as *anti-*Malthusian in his reflections on economic and bodily health. Like Ruskin, he valued above all those commodities that are most easily reconverted into flesh, and deplored Adam Smith's failure to distinguish among commodities on the basis of their biological value. Much of this somatic theorizing flows from the labour theory of value; and the notion of labour as coercive or unpleasant work provides Gallagher with a link between the aesthetician Edmund Burke, for whom the pain of labour is a form of sublimity, and the political economist's conclusion that pain, in the sense of disagreeable work, is the source of value. Burke's aesthetics, Gallagher remarks, rest on the same groundwork of vitalist physiology as Smith's economics.

It is not hard to see novels as stored up energy and sensation, awaiting their release by the act of reading; and where Gallagher's book has the edge over Perry's is in this attention to the forms and performances of fiction themselves, rather than simply to their content. Even so, she does a scintillating job on that as well. In an eye-opening account of Charles Dickens's *Hard Times*, she asks why a novel that protests against the industrial grind should have been dedicated to Thomas Carlyle, champion of hard labour (and even of slavery), while lambasting the Benthamites, who shared Dickens's view that labour is disagreeable and denied it any divine glory. 'Aversion', Jeremy Bentham wrote, 'is the emotion, the only emotion, which *labour*, taken by itself, is qualified to produce' — a sentiment in which many of us would heartily concur. The only good reason for welcoming communism, for example, is that it means not having to do any work. Marxism is for the indolent, not the strenuous. If Ruskin, William Morris and their honourable progeny sought to humanize labour, Marx sought to abolish it. In this sense, he is closer to Oscar Wilde than to Morris. It was Wilde who believed that one could lie around all day in loose-fitting purple garments and be one's own communist society.

If *Hard Times* is about fruitless labour, this is also in Gallagher's view a fair description of the act of reading it. The novel 'cranks out life stories with deadening regularity and utter indifference … powerless to produce or even anticipate enjoyment at the end of its own process'. It is the novel's notorious 'lack of play' that catches Gallagher's astute critical eye. Even the famous circus, Dickens's only apparent alternative to the oppressive factories of Coketown, is a soulless kind of factory in itself, as the performers are portrayed as well-disciplined workers and the narrative consequently undercuts the work/play antithesis it has so simple-mindedly set up.

The highpoint of the book, however, is a chapter on the bioeconomics of *Our Mutual Friend*, a novel that might have been written especially to confirm Gallagher's thesis. In its portrayal of the trade in corpses in the Thames and garbage recycled into wealth, it is all about the circulation of bodies, organic and inorganic processes, life plucked from death, Nature as both regenerating and laying waste. There is also a chapter which boldly illuminates George Eliot's debt to W. Stanley Jevons and marginal utility theory in, of all things, *Daniel Deronda*, and a Malthusian reading of her *Scenes of Clerical Life*. No doubt a revisionist Malthus international summer school will soon be in full swing. Ireland, home of both famine and revisionism, might offer a particularly appropriate home for it.

Dublin, however, would be appropriate for another reason as well. For it was home in the nineteenth century to a school of political economy that does not figure in this study, yet which is mightily relevant to it. Political economy in Ireland, given the state of the nation, was from the outset interwoven with ethical, cultural and political motifs, just as what E. P. Thompson used to call a 'moral economy', with its infrastructure of tacit rights and unwritten obligations, still exerted some authority in the Irish countryside. It proved impossible to distinguish the study of economic institutions from the cultural and political question of British colonialism. Political economy in Ireland worked within a general humanistic context, in which discussions of rent or land tenure could scarcely be dissociated from matters of custom, value and sentiment. It was also clear to the Irish, as it was not by and large to the British, just how culturally specific the so-called universal economic laws of Smith, Ricardo and John Stuart Mill actually were. Their own culturally different situation thus allowed them to put some intellectual daylight between themselves and the Ricardians.

Issac Butt, lawyer, novelist and politician, was spurred into economic discourse as a nationalist by the Whig *laissez-faire* response to the Famine. The great John Elliot Cairnes, economic counsellor to Mill, saw political economy as the science of well-being, rejected grand teleological narratives in typically colonial fashion, and insisted on the role of cultural pecularities in economic life. A critic of *laissez-faire*, he was outraged by the wretched condition of the small farmers, and spoke up for so-called peasant proprietorship long before it became a nationalist mantra. He is best known outside Ireland for his *The Slave Power*, a passionate indictment of American slavery that made him illustrious in his own time. Thomas Cliffe Leslie, a neglected figure ripe for retrieval, also returned political economy to its moral and historical context, and argued what we might now call a culturalist case against the naturalism and universalism of economic orthodoxy. He also drew attention to the overlooked role of the family in his discipline and, like Cairnes, stressed the epistemological opacities and instabilities of any discourse that sought to determine human needs and desires. John

Kells Ingram, a card carrying Comtean, considered that his subject should be as much a study of historical *mentalités* as of the history of production, and to illustrate the point, he wrote a historicizing account of the rise and fall of economic theories. Economy must not be treated in isolation from culture and morality. He also saw ancient slavery as progressive and spoke out against secondary education for the working class, but nobody's work is perfect.

It was Sigmund Freud who remarked in his customarily cynical way that economic necessity was the only reason we were not permanently indolent. Without the goad of economic coercion, we would simply lie around the place all day in various interesting postures of *jouissance*. Freud was deeply wary of Marxism; but he, like Marx, believed that the economic was the ultimately determinant force in human affairs. Were it not for the need to labour, the pleasure principle could have its own sweet way. Freud is an economist of the psyche, whose work is all about labour and expenditure, storage and release, repression and circulation, investment and disinvestment, pain and pleasure, desire and death. He is, then, the obvious inheritor of the lineage this book traces, even though the book seems to be unaware of it. Gallagher might also have looked more closely than she does at Marx's *Economic and Philosophical Manuscripts*, in which (at an outrageously early age) the young former Hegelian seeks with breathtaking ambitiousness to argue his way up from the sensuous body to an ethics and politics. If communism is essential for Marx — if the sensuous particularity of use-value must be liberated from the abstract prison-house of exchange-value — it is, among other things, so that we might begin to experience our bodies once again. ∎

India, Identity and Globalization

Deana Heath

The Argumentative Indian
Amartya Sen
London: Allen Lane, 2005. 409 pages. ISBN 0-7139-9687-0

The 'nation' may not have been as significant as once thought in the making of modern India. While nationalism played a key role in securing India's freedom from colonial rule, other identities, beliefs and ideologies continued to exist, and arguably to predominate. As the historian Partha Chatterjee has argued, the nationalist imaginary in India was posited not on *identity* but on *difference*, and was thus distinct from the purportedly 'universal' modular form supplied by Europe (regarded in the West as one of its greatest 'gifts' to the world).[1]

1 Partha Chatterjee, *The Nation and Its Fragments: Colonial and Postcolonial Histories* (Princeton, 1994)

2 Ashis Nandy, *The Illegitimacy of Nationalism: Rabindranath Tagore and the Politics of Self* (New Delhi, 1983)

3 V. D. Savarkar, *Hindutva* (Nagpur, 1928)

Indian Congress Party activists stage a silent protest in Calcutta to demand the return of the Nobel prize medal awarded to poet Rabindranath Tagore (1861–1941) in 1913. At least 30 items, including the medal belonging to Tagore, disappeared from the museum at Visva Bharati University on 26 March 2004. Photograph: Deshakalyan Chowdhury/ AFP/Getty Images.

For the Indian humanist Rabindranath Tagore, nationalism, patriotism and anti-imperialism had come to be regarded as synonymous in India by the early twentieth century. The problem with this, for Tagore and other Indian critics of nationalism such as Mahatma Gandhi, was that in a colonial condition such as India's, nationalism produced a fundamental contradiction. Nationalist ideology served culturally to consolidate the West in India while at the same time nurturing rebellion against the West politically. As the scholar and critic of Indian nationalism Ashis Nandy has argued, nationalism for Tagore and Gandhi was thus an imposition, an attempt to internationalize an alien history (as well as to exteriorize the internal conflicts that had been wrought in India by colonialism) in order to mould the Indian concept of the public realm to the requirement of standardized Western categories.[2]

Tagore and Gandhi were not the only ones to critique the ideology of nationalism or to question the internal dissonances of the emergent Indian nationalist movement in the second half of the nineteenth century. Some of the most prominent critics of Indian nationalism were Muslim intellectuals and clerics, individuals such as Sayyid Ahmed Khan, Maulana Mohamed Ali, and Maulana Husaain Ahmad Madani. They feared for the status of India's Muslims in an independent nation-state in the face of a growing Hindu nationalist movement (which sought to exclude Muslims from the Indian nation-state on the basis, as averred by the prominent Hindu nationalist V. D. Savarkar, that India may have been the *pitribhumi*, or fatherland, of Indian Muslims but was not their *punyabhumi*, or holyland).[3] The attitude of Indian Muslims was not, however, simply reactionary. For Indian Muslims, 'difference' (namely their distinct religious identity) did not automatically translate into a communal consciousness. For most Indian Muslims there was, in fact, no tension or contradiction in feeling a love for India (their *watan*, or motherland) and pride in being Muslim.[4] In a remarkable treatise written in 1938, at a time of severe (largely nationalist-induced) tensions between Hindus and Muslims in India, Madani issued a call for what he termed 'composite nationalism', in which he argued forcefully for the formation of a secular nation-state.[5] Such secularism did not, however, reject the role of religion in framing an Indian polity. As Maulana Mohamed Ali famously declared in a speech in 1930:

> I have a culture, a polity, an outlook on life — a complete synthesis which is Islam. Where God commands I am a Muslim first, a Muslim second, and a Muslim last, and nothing but a Muslim … But where India is concerned, where India's freedom is concerned, where the welfare of India is concerned, I am an Indian first, an Indian second, an Indian last, and nothing but an Indian.[6]

Rather than removing religion from the realm of the state, as has generally been the case in the West, Indian Muslims such as Ali and Madani sought to construct a particularly Indian variant of secularism, in which all religions were accorded an equal place within the state. While such an understanding of the relationship between religion and state was undermined during the course of the Indian independence movement, most notably — and ironically — by individuals such as the atheist, rationalist and 'modernist' Mohammad Ali Jinnah, who deployed religion to achieve specifically political ends, and more recently by a resurgent Hindu nationalism — it still exists in India today.

Amartya Sen is one of the few individuals who has entered into that debate and sought to make it accessible to a non-academic audience, not only in India, but in the West as well. Moreover, his central argument — that Indian identity is multifarious and cannot simply be subsumed within either religion or the history of the nation-state

— merits serious consideration in the West, where the writing and teaching of history remains wedded to the nation-state, and where non-Western societies continue to be conceptualized largely in terms of religion.[7] The sixteen essays in this collection range from diegeses on Indian history, culture and thought to economic critiques of problems, such as inequality in India, to more intimate studies of individual authors or artists (such as Rabindranath Tagore or the Indian film-maker and writer Satyajit Ray). For Sen, what binds these diverse themes together is their elucidation of the long history of what he terms the 'argumentative tradition' in India, one that embraces, moreover, 'heterodoxy and dialogue'.[8] Such a tradition, Sen argues, is under threat in contemporary India, thanks primarily to the resurgence in the past two decades of Hindutva, or Hindu nationalism, which seeks to reconstruct India's past and promote a narrow view of Indian civilization. The ideology of Hindutva has been subject to scathing critique by defenders of India's secular tradition, particularly following the destruction, by Hindu nationalists, of a mosque in the Indian pilgrimage city of Ayodhya in 1992 (because, according to Hindu nationalists, it was built on the birthplace of the Hindu god king Lord Ram, the protagonist of the *Ramayana*). Sen seeks, however, to tread a more nuanced path than most critics of Hindu nationalism between the cultural tenets of Hindutva (in which the history of 'Hindu' India has been pushed back a millennium to the third millennium BCE and the key texts of Hinduism, most notably the Vedas and the *Ramayana*, are deployed for political ends) and the ideology of secularism. While he lauds the 'integrationist approach' to Indian history and society by advocates of Indian secularism, and is understanding as to why such advocates regard 'the harking back to ancient India with the greatest of suspicion', he nonetheless critiques them for seeking to challenge Hindutva through disregarding

4 See, for example, Aysha Jalal, *Self and Sovereignty: Individual and Community in South Asian Islam since 1850* (New Delhi, 2001).

5 Maulana Madani, *Composite Nationalism* (New Delhi, 2005 [1938])

6 Mohamed Ali, speech at the fourth plenary session of the Round Table Conference in London, 19 November 1930

7 See Dipesh Chakrabarty, *Provincializing Europe: Postcolonial Thought and Historical Difference* (Princeton, 2000); Arjun Appadurai, *Modernity at Large: Cultural Dimensions of Globalization* (Minneapolis and London, 1996).

8 Amartya Sen, *The Argumentative Indian* (London, 2005), ix; hereafter cited as *AI*.

Rabindranath Tagore,
poet and philosopher.
Photograph: Photo by E.
O. Hoppe/Hulton Archive/
Getty Images.

the importance of the 'Hindu classics'
— namely India's literary and philosophical
writings, as well as folk traditions — in
India's history and culture. Thus, for Sen, 'It
would be as difficult to ignore [the] general
importance' of the Vedas or the *Ramayana*
on some allegedly 'secular' ground, 'as it
would be to insist on viewing them through

the narrow prism of a particularly raw
version of Hindu religiosity'.[9] Not only,
he believes, do the 'Hindu classics', as well
as many other pre-modern Indian texts,
reveal the *longevity* of the secular tradition
in India, but they also serve to 'Indianize'
it and, in the process, afford the basis for a
more inclusive Indian identity.

A critique of the undermining of the argumentative tradition by both Hindutva and advocates of Indian secularism are two of the strands that tie the essays in this volume together. A third is Western perceptions of India, particularly of understandings of India as a land constructed and defined by religion. The liberalization of the Indian economy in the 1990s and the IT boom have, undoubtedly, served to alter perceptions of India in the West. So too has the globalization of Indian culture, as transformations in India's political economy have effected major changes in Indian film and literature, which have made Indian culture more accessible to Western audiences (although Indian cinema has always been popular throughout much of the non-Western world). Transformations in the political economy of the West have in turn opened it to what we might term the globalization of Indian affect, or 'structures of feeling'. Such changes offer strong evidence that globalization is not a one-way process, and that it is not synonymous with 'Westernization'. They have done little, however, to alter Western perceptions of India. While Sen seeks to challenge Edward Said's analysis of Western perceptions of the 'Orient' by arguing that there are in fact three intellectual traditions through which India has been understood in the West (which he terms 'exoticist', 'magisterial' and 'curatorial'), they all, he is forced to admit, privilege the 'exotic', 'spiritual' India over the 'rationalist' one. The framing of India in religious terms emerged during the colonial era as a means of justifying and validating British rule: Indians, according to the ideology of colonialism, were irrational, backward, incapable of self-control, effeminate, and slaves to 'tradition', while the British were rational, progressive, manly, and 'modern'. But the British do not bear full responsibility for the longevity of these perceptions, since such Orientalist myths were in turn embraced by Indians during the course of the nationalist movement as a means of fashioning an Indian identity

outside the domain of Western power. They are in turn fostered today through such means as didactic films, which circulate widely at international film festivals and which offer up India's 'truth' to the West and serve to reinforce its perceptions — including their understanding of the causes of India's problems. As Sen notes in his critique of Mira Nair's film *Salaam Bombay!*, 'The exploitative form draws at once on the knowledge — common in the West — that India has much poverty and suffering, and also on the comfort — for which there is some demand — of seeing the faces of the "baddies" who are causing all the trouble'.[10] They thus serve to undermine, once again, the complexity of Indian society.

A final strand that unites these essays is the undermining of India's argumentative tradition by post-colonial scholars. In contrast to the other three strands, Sen's debate in this case is not about the role of religion in shaping Indian identity, but about the universalism of particular socio-political norms. This is the ground, ultimately, on which Sen's battle line is drawn. One of the tenets of post-colonial studies is a denial of Enlightenment values as universal and a rejection of their legacies as the historical path that all peoples were destined to follow. This has provoked debates about the nature of global modernity. Until relatively recently, modernity was envisioned as a process that originated in, and was then 'disseminated' by, the West, primarily under the aegis of colonialism. Modernity was thus viewed as being both homogenous and 'Western'. Scholars working on colonial contexts such as India, however, have argued that this view of modernity is flawed, for while modernity introduces a radical rupture in colonized societies, aspects of the new modernity may have already existed in them. Furthermore, since modernity is constituted by a plurality of processes and an unfolding set of relationships that are constantly being made and unmade, contested and reconfigured,

10 *AI*, 128

11 See, for example, Sudipta Kaviraj, 'Modernity and Politics in India,' *Daedalus*, Special issue on Multiple Modernities, 129, 1 (2000), 137–62; Gyan Prakash, *Another Reason: Science and the Imagination of Modern India* (Princeton, 1999).
12 *AI*, xii
13 *AI*, 16

the sequence in which these occur and the manner in which they are interconnected in each context means that the conditions of modernity differ in each society. Western modernity cannot, therefore, simply be 'imposed' on colonized societies, it needs to be translated and adapted. For proponents of 'alternative' or 'multiple' modernities, what was therefore produced in contexts such as India was a hybrid — and therefore decidedly distinct — modernity.[11]

This is, ultimately, an argument about Indian 'difference', although one that seeks to reverse the binaries of Orientalist discourse. It therefore rejects universalist frameworks — there is no *singular* mode of socio-political development that all societies are destined to follow. For post-colonial scholars India will never, therefore, become a carbon copy of the West. But while Sen shares the enthusiasm of post-colonial scholars to celebrate India's diversity and difference within *India*, he largely denies the existence of diversity and difference within *history*. While he refutes the perception predominant in the West that its modernity is purely 'Western', believing instead that it is a blend of Western and non-Western cultures, there is thus no such thing, for Sen, as alternative modernities.

What, then, is the argumentative tradition that Sen is so keen to define and defend? He outlines the nature of this tradition in the first two parts of the book, 'Voice and Heterodoxy' and 'Culture and Consumption', which explore the nature of the argumentative tradition and its contemporary relevance in supporting democracy, secularism, social justice, and scientific inquiry within India, as well as India's ability to communicate with and understand other cultures. The first essay, from which the title of the book derives, is superb, and outlines the basic arguments that he elaborates throughout the succeeding chapters. The argumentative tradition is, however, a relatively amorphous concept; rather than

stemming from a particular philosophical or religious discourse or tradition in India, Sen seems to imply that it is, instead, more of a state of mind endemic to Indian culture brought about through the constant negotiation of its peoples with cultural and religious 'difference'. Sen makes much, for example, of the diversity of faiths in India and the longevity of this diversity. Hinduism, Buddhism, Jainism, and Judaism were already co-existing by the first millennium BCE, which in turn, Sen implies, made India receptive to other faiths — namely Christianity, Islam and Zoroastrianism, which arrived in India in the first millennium CE, and Sikhism and Baha'ism, which followed in the second millennium.

The argumentative tradition, for Sen, is evident among all these faiths. In the third century BCE, the Buddhist Emperor Ashoka, Sen argues, 'not only outlined the need for toleration and richness of heterodoxy, but also laid down what are perhaps the oldest rules for conducting debates and disputations'.[12] He claims that the key texts of Hinduism, most notably the *Bhagavad Gita* (also dated to the third century BCE) — essentially a dialogue about the rationality of contending moral positions — likewise encouraged disputation, as did the medieval mystical poets such as Kabir and Mira Bai and the Muslim Emperor Akbar in the sixteenth century CE. Indeed, Akbar's 'overarching thesis that "the pursuit of reason" rather than "reliance on tradition" is the way to address difficult problems of social harmony included a robust celebration of reasoned dialogues', which he did through staging public debates between members of different faiths (including atheists) and laying the foundations for a non-denominational secular state.[13] At the root of Sen's argumentative tradition, therefore, is a belief in the necessity of toleration and the value of dissent. Akbar is a figure whom Sen returns to again and again, since he embodied, for Sen, India's principles of toleration, and he enunciated them at a time, moreover, when 'the Inquisition was in full swing in Europe' — a useful reminder at a time when Western perceptions of Islam are at one of their lowest ebbs since the Crusades.[14]

India not only has a long and vibrant history of toleration and heterodoxy, according to Sen — it also has arguably the longest history of scepticism, a key component of the argumentative tradition, which dates back 3,500 years. The 'Song of Creation' in the *Rigveda*, for example, questions the existence of god, while the Sanskrit literature of which it is a part 'has a larger volume of agnostic or atheistic writings' than exists in any other classical language. This history of scepticism in India is another point that Sen turns to repeatedly, in part to undermine Western perceptions of India's 'religiosity' (in particular of religion as constituting the primary, or even the only, form of identity in India). Such a focus on religiosity has contributed to 'an underestimation of the reach of public reasoning' and of the 'long tradition of rational assessment' in India.[15] It has also led to an underestimation of Indian science and mathematics. In two of the finest chapters, Sen examines some of the achievements of Indian mathematicians and astronomers such as Aryabhata — whose work on the diurnal motion of the earth and his elucidation of the force of gravity pre-dated their 'discovery' by Galileo and Newton by over a thousand years — while mocking colonial British conceptions of Indian science, as embodied most famously in James Mill's *The History of British India* (which declared that Indians could not have made such discoveries themselves since they had 'a general disposition to deceit and perfidy' and had taken only 'a few of the earliest steps in the progress to civilization').[16]

The significance of India's scientific traditions or its history of scepticism, or the larger history of the argumentative tradition of which they are a part, is the role they have played in facilitating the development — and successful maintenance — of democracy in India. The transition from colonialism to the formation of a democratic nation-state was achieved, Sen argues, because India was able to merge alien institutions (the apparatus of the nation-state) with its own traditions of reasoning, toleration, and heterodoxy. Discussions and arguments according to Sen, 'are critically important for democracy and public reasoning.' They are central, furthermore, both to the practice of secularism and to challenging poverty and social inequality, since 'Voice', as he forcefully contends, 'is a crucial component of the pursuit of social justice'.[17]

But while India's democracy has managed to survive, glaring problems nonetheless remain. Some of these, such as the resurgence of Hindu nationalism, are of notably recent origin, and are in fact a product, in part, of the democratic process (although Sen does not acknowledge this). The root of many of these problems is the contemporary obsession with 'see[ing] people mainly, or even entirely, in terms of their religion' rather than in the multifariousness of their identities (such as class, language, literature, or political beliefs), an understanding that undermines both India's argumentative tradition and the secular democracy that it has served to foster.[18] Hindu nationalism, with its emphasis on constructing and enforcing a single, dominant identity, is clearly the chief target here. In part four, 'Reason and Identity', Sen rehashes many of the familiar arguments against it, including its ignorance of the nature and implications of India's long history of religious diversity, and makes much of the fact that India currently has a Muslim president, a Sikh prime minister, and a Christian head of the ruling party (and one who is, moreover, a woman of foreign origin). But while he protests that the ideology of Hindutva forces Indians to '"go through" their religious identity first,

14 *AI*, xiii
15 *AI*, 23, 25
16 *AI*, 79
17 *AI*, xiii
18 *AI*, 165

19 *AI*, 307
20 *AI*, 164
21 *AI*, 54
22 *AI*, 69
23 *AI*, 285

before asserting their Indianness' (which it does in order to 'build up' Indian identity 'on the constitutive basis of the different religious identities') and argues, rightly, that 'religious identity has to be separated from its relevance in the political context', he offers few insights as to how this can be achieved.[19] One of the reasons he is unable to do so is because he does not explore *why* Hindu nationalists seek to assert the primacy of religion in constructing Indianness, or the *meaning* of concepts such as 'nation' and 'democracy' in contemporary India.

Sen is much stronger in critiquing the 'religious reductionism' of Indian identity in the West, which, he contends, completely ignores the argumentative tradition in India (or rather is completely ignorant of it) and continues to regard Indian society as unchanging and 'eternal'.[20] Such perceptions have been reinforced in the past decade by 'the contemporary obsession with classifying the world population into distinct "civilizations" defined principally by religion', as illustrated notably in Samuel Huntington's conservative and highly provocative best-seller *The Clash of Civilizations and the Remaking of the World Order*. The world, for Huntington and his followers, is divided into discrete civilizations, and India, in spite of the fact that it has more Muslims than the population of Britain and France put together (and more Muslims, moreover, than every other country barring Indonesia and Pakistan, which Huntington labels as part of 'Islamic' civilization), is relegated to the status of a 'Hindu civilization'. They ignore the fact that 'There is a difference between a constitutionally secular nation with a majority Hindu population and a theocratic Hindu state that might see Hinduism as its official religion.'[21] What makes India differ from nation-states such as Pakistan or Bangladesh is therefore that it is a secular democracy, which accords an equal place to every citizen regardless of their religious background. Moreover,

in spite of the importance of religion in India, Sen also rightly notes that 'there is a resilient undercurrent of conviction across the country that religious beliefs, while personally significant, are socially unimportant and should be politically inconsequential'.[22] This is a claim substantiated in India by the fall from power in 2004 of the Hindu right-wing Bharatiya Janata Party (a party that, notably, had only been able to form a government in coalition with almost two dozen other political parties), and more broadly in the subcontinent by the separation of East from West Pakistan in 1971 (brought about by divergences in secular ties, such as language and literature). Such a claim once again raises questions, however, about the nature and meaning of 'democracy' in contemporary India.

The implications of such 'religious reductionism' are significant, since such a perception fosters important misconceptions in the West about the nature of Western culture and power. In an excellent essay on 'The Reach of Reason', Sen explores the impact that Western ignorance of India's argumentative tradition (as well as that of other non-Western cultures) has had in constructing conceptions of Western 'uniqueness' and superiority. The role that reason plays in this sense of uniqueness and superiority cannot be overestimated. Ever since the Enlightenment (which shaped the ideologies through which Western culture continues to define itself), the West, Sen argues, has come to see itself as 'having exclusive access to the values that lie at the foundation of rationality and reasoning, science and evidence, liberty and tolerance, and of course rights and justice'.[23] Yet while 'it is by no means clear that, historically, greater importance has been systematically attached to freedom and tolerance in the West than in Asia', these continue to be viewed as specifically 'Western' values (essentially a product, for Sen, of poor and biased scholarship which '[attaches] significance to particular components of Western thought without looking adequately for similar components in non-Western intellectual traditions').[24] Western faith in the irrationality of non-Western peoples has served to justify conquest, colonization, and exploitation from the birth of the modern era to the present. In an essay on 'India and the Bomb', Sen demonstrates that such a belief also serves to rationalize the continued inequities in global power, resentments against which, in turn, have played an important role in fostering the nuclearization of the subcontinent (beliefs about the irrationality of non-Western peoples have also led to efforts by countries such as the United States and United Kingdom to prevent non-Western states from obtaining nuclear technology).

The emphasis on reason is yet another example of defining identity 'by contrast', although Sen's focus here is on the ways in which 'divergence with the West' is central to such constructions. His underlying concern with identity and difference serves to explain the apparent anomaly of the essays in the third part of the book, 'Politics and Protest'. Focusing on issues such as globalization, class, and gender, they examine the nature of inequality in India, and propose possible means to erase such internal differences. For Sen, multivalency and difference cease to be socially beneficial when they serve to undermine individual freedom and human rights. Notable here is Sen's elaboration of how factors such as gender, caste, class, globalization, and regional differences have to be taken into account to understand problems such as female infanticide and foeticide in India. In an essay entitled 'Women and Men', which generated considerable controversy when it was originally published, Sen argues that in 1986 (the year for which he seems to have the most recent statistics) there were 100 million 'missing women', not simply in India but in Asia as a whole (an estimate he produces by an analysis of male–female

ratios in India and China). Contrary to popular perception in the West (as well as, to some extent, in India), the problem of missing women cannot be explained by resorting to the old binary between 'modernity' and 'tradition' — in fact, not only are there notable differences in male–female ratios between the north and west of India and the east and south (the latter of which have higher ratios than the former), but India's temples of modernity, its great metros, have lower male–female ratios than its hinterlands. Culture, class, and education clearly, therefore, play an important role in shaping the gender balance in India, although it is notably the *higher* classes rather than the lower who are availing of foetal sex screening and the abortion of female foetuses. Since the opening of the Indian economy in the early 1990s and the ensuing expansion of the Indian middle classes, clinics offering foetal sex screening have mushroomed in India (although the practice was made illegal in 1994) which has fostered fears, as embodied in Manish Jha's 2003 film *Matrubhumi,* that India will become 'a world without women'. The only way to prevent this, according to Sen, is to focus on improving women's agency rather than simply their well-being.

Sen does not regard globalization, therefore, as a panacea for all of India's ills, either for the nation or the individual — he argues, in fact, that 'even a hundred Bangalores and Hyderabads [India's globalization hot spots] will not, on their own, solve India's tenacious poverty and deep-seated inequality'.[25] The only way to do so is to change what he terms 'global arrangements' (by which he seems to mean the institutional frameworks through which global economic policy is shaped) and domestic policies, although central to both is finding the means to increase individual agency. He makes it clear that such changes need to be made not just in India but in the West as well — as he notes in the case of women, for example, there are different forms of gender

24 *AI*, 135
25 *AI*, 197

inequality, and while female infanticide and foeticide remain a problem in South Asia, all the major countries in South Asia, namely India, Bangladesh, Pakistan and Sri Lanka, have or have had female heads of state, and a third of all seats are now reserved for women in the Indian parliament. Few political systems in the West have, in fact, incorporated women to the degree that India's has. As Sen demonstrates in the most delightful essay in the book, 'India through its Calendars', the world may now follow the same calendrical system (namely the Gregorian calendar), but dozens of other calendars are still in use throughout the globe, including thirty in India alone. Not only have those other calendars not been erased, but the predominance of one calendar over all the others is not a result of its superiority as a system of marking time, but is a result, rather, of imperialism, colonialism, and globalization. And globalization, furthermore, is an ancient phenomenon, one in which the East has played as vital a role in transforming the West as the West has in transforming the East — and the West still has much to learn from the East.

Sen's emphasis on India's argumentative tradition is thus valuable in raising questions about identity and understanding in both India and the West that processes of globalization are making ever more pressing. His analysis is not, however, entirely convincing, due largely to his understanding — or misunderstanding — of history, particularly of the relationship between colonialism, nationalism, and the nation-state in South Asia. Apart from a reference to Indian Defence Minister Krishna Menon's historic nine-hour speech at the United Nations in 1957, all his examples of the argumentative tradition date from pre-modern or early modern India. What, then, happened to the tradition after that? The glaring absence in Sen's text is, in short, colonialism, and its impact on Indian culture and identity in the post-colonial era. Modern Indian conceptions of difference were, to a considerable extent, shaped by colonialism, since delineating and fostering differences between colonizers and colonized, and among the colonizers, served to facilitate colonial rule. The Indian nationalist movement was also shaped, therefore, by colonial conceptions of difference, although the struggle for independence from colonial rule also unleashed and mobilized alternative understandings of identity — as well as, significantly, conceptions of what constituted 'freedom' and how to achieve it (in which heterodoxy and dialogue did play an important role) — to those based on colonial categories. Hence, the ultimate flaw in Sen's argument is his understanding of the 'nation' in India — for him it is, like 'democracy', a universal category with a modular form of historical development. But how can the 'nation' in India, in which it is a recent and imposed concept, mean the same thing that it does in places where it has a longer history, and where the concept emerged organically? These are questions that need to be addressed in order to understand the nature of contemporary Indian identity, and of contestations over it. ■

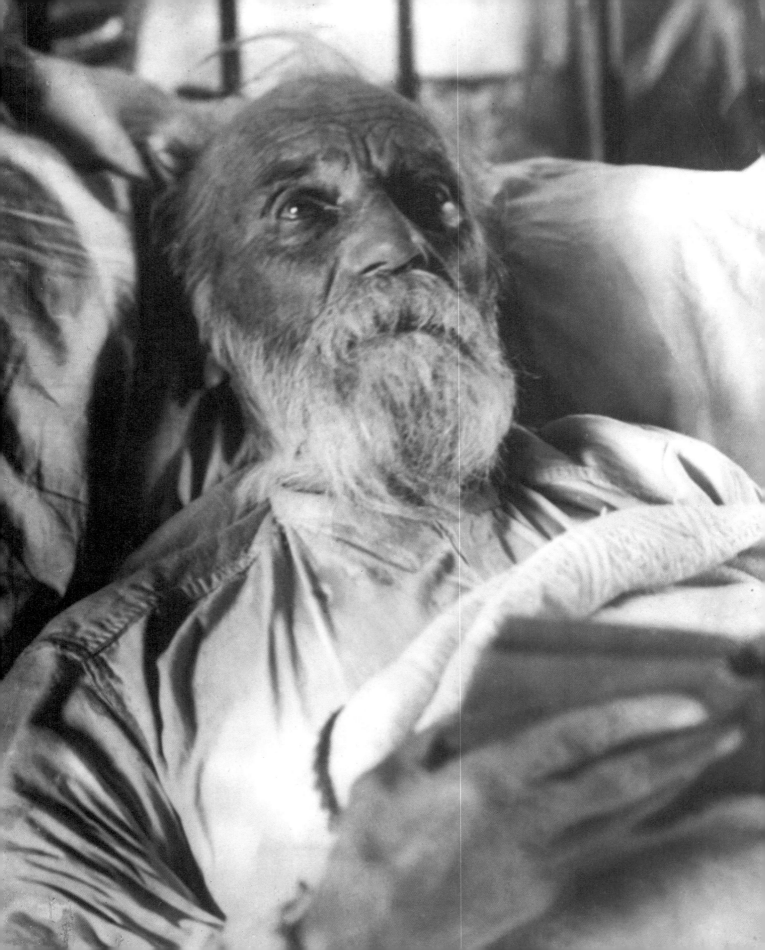

Cuttlefish, Cholesterol and *Saoirse*

Brendan O'Leary

Irish Freedom: The History of Nationalism in Ireland
Richard English
London: Macmillan, 2006. 625 pages. ISBN 978-1-4050-4189-8

> He that uses many words for explaining any subject, doth, like the cuttlefish, hide himself for the most part in his own ink.
>
> John Ray, seventeenth-century naturalist

> In sum, rather like cholesterol, there is good and bad revisionism, and we have had too much of the latter in recent years.
>
> L. Perry Curtis Jr.[1]

Richard English, by his own account, has tried to do three things in a quarter of a million words: write the story of Irish nationalist history for the general reader, provide 'an authoritative but accessible up-to-date, single volume account of what scholars now think and know (or think that they know) about Irish nationalism', and, more ambitiously, 'explain' Irish nationalism.[2] *Irish Freedom* is partially successful in its first goal, and much more partisan than it presents itself. For that reason it is much less successful in achieving its second goal. It fails in its last goal.

1 L. Perry Curtis Jr., 'Comment: The Return of Revisionism', *Journal of British Studies*, 44 (2005), 134–45, 145

2 Richard English, *Irish Freedom: The History of Nationalism in Ireland* (London, 2006), 4–5

Jeremiah O'Donovan Rossa, prominent Fenian, in New York, 1911. Photograph: Topical Press Agency/Hulton Archive/Getty Images.

Professor English recently wrote a highly regarded history of the IRA.[3] Here his tone is often conciliatory but displays the high-handed conciliation that exasperates. He is widely read, cultured (especially in music), eclectic, and presents as generous and fair-minded in his readings. But he has blind spots. The most significant are linguistic, methodological, and ideological. He has also become garrulous. He, like others who imagine themselves to be radical, swims with the present tide of imperial historiography, which cleanses, and even celebrates, the British Empire, or at least accentuates its

positive dimensions.[4] Yet Ireland's colonial treatment by Great Britain, before and after the Act of Union of 1801, remains a salutary reminder of negative entries in the ledger of Empire. In accounting for some present nationalist passions and arguments, the 'catastrophic dimension' of the Irish historical experience in what we may call the 'far past' needs to be emphasized — violent conquest, expropriation, religious oppression, famine, immiseration and demographic collapse.[5] In the 'near past', what demands focus is the long denial of democratic autonomy, followed by an unjust partition, and the renewal of domination in one political unit by the historic beneficiaries of the colonial settlements. Such emphases are warranted not as a brief for present courtrooms, not for the joy of savouring past horrors, and not for wallowing in ancient grievances to the neglect of our ancestors' past pleasures and achievements. Quite simply, the catastrophic components of the past significantly explain Ireland's present, both its institutional outcomes and the present mentalities of its principal agents, collective and individual. Richard English's book fails fully to appreciate these matters, but his failure is instructive.

Of course, neither Ireland's nor Northern Ireland's histories are unrelieved catalogues of disaster, and only the last stranded platoons of the Thirty-Two County Sovereignty Movement might argue otherwise. In fact, the island's current circumstances stem, in part, from catastrophes that did not happen. The Nazis or Stalinists, who homogenized Central and Eastern Europe under the cover of 'Nacht und Nebel', never conquered Ireland. In the seventeenth century Ireland was not comprehensively 'cleansed' of its natives, nor was it religiously homogenized, though both enterprises were conceived and embarked upon before being abandoned for less spectacular forms of subordination. In a comparative perspective, it is the catastrophic past, with its long-term repercussions, that explains the emotional and intellectual wellsprings of Irish nationalism. And it is the current resolution of these repercussions that explains the diminution of hostility toward the British state and the peaceful accommodations that now prevail in both of Ireland's political entities.

Whose ancestral voices?

Nowhere in Part One, 'Ireland before 1800', does English admit incompetence in the Irish, Latin or French languages. This would seem a necessary acknowledgement by someone

who has taken upon himself the task of appraising the existence (or non-existence) of national consciousness in Ireland's pre-modern past. Since no works in Irish, Latin or French are cited in the bibliography the reader may assume that English lacks these languages. This observation is not advanced in a spirit of ethnic or linguistic trumping — I have mostly forgotten Latin and French, and have but a few words of Irish. Nor does the observation imply that only those with the relevant linguistic skills can have worthwhile opinions. Solid historical judgements can emerge from reading secondary interpretations of primary sources, provided there is a scholarly consensus that is not contested as partisan by reasonable persons.[6] But English's notes and bibliography convey no mastery of those historians, past or present, who have a full command of Irish, and who differ from their 'angloglot' colleagues — and among themselves — on questions pertinent to Irish national consciousness before the nineteenth century. So we must be sceptical that English can achieve his goal of assessing Gaelic Ireland's self-consciousness.

Like most of us, he is heavily dependent on anglophone secondary sources for readings of Ireland's Gaelic past. So it is incumbent upon him to show why we should take *his* word, rather than the word of others, for any reading of that past, where there is no consensus. This criticism, moreover, does not apply only to his treatment of the consciousness of the pre-modern Gaelic Irish. Consider the issue of how to name those who invaded Ireland in 1169, or, in the account English prefers, who were invited in by a locally dethroned pretender. He says there was no '"English" invasion at all'. Rather, Ireland was colonized 'by an international group', 'Anglo-Norman lords … and their hybrid followers'.[7] But at least one study of how the Normans became English, not cited, maintains that 'the Celtic Other served not only to draw Normans and English together [for security reasons],

3 Richard English, *Armed Struggle: The History of the IRA* (London, 2003). I wrote a favourable review of this book, 'Lethal Mixture of Armalite and the Ballot Box', *Times Higher Education Supplement*, 1609 (2003), 27–28, with some reservations, recently re-expressed in 'Mission Accomplished? Looking Back at the IRA', *Field Day Review*, 1 (2005), 216–46.

4 Niall Ferguson, *Empire: The Rise and Fall of the British World Order and the Lessons for Global Power* (New York, 2003); Stephen Howe, *Ireland and Empire: Colonial Legacies in Irish History and Culture* (Oxford, 2000)

5 Brendan Bradshaw, 'Nationalism and Historical Scholarship in Modern Ireland', *Irish Historical Studies*, 26, 104 (1989), 329–51

6 Ian Lustick has written of the difficulties political scientists (and historians) have in dealing scientifically with rival secondary readings of primary sources, and the resulting types of 'selection bias'; see his 'History, Historiography, and Political Science: Multiple Historical Records and the Problem of Selection Bias', *American Political Science Review*, 90 (1996), 605–18.

7 *Irish Freedom*, 38

8 Hugh M. Thomas, *The English and the Normans: Ethnic Hostility, Assimilation and Identity 1066–c. 1220* (Oxford, 2003), 315

9 Brendan O'Leary and John McGarry, *The Politics of Antagonism: Understanding Northern Ireland*, 2nd expanded edn. (London and Atlantic Heights, 1996)

10 See John Gillingham's 'The Beginnings of English Imperialism', *Journal of Historical Sociology*, 5, 4 (1992), 392–409; 'The English Invasion of Ireland', in Brendan Bradshaw, Andrew Hadfield and Willy Maley, eds., *Representing Ireland: Literature and the Origins of Conflict, 1534–1660* (Cambridge, 1992), 24–42; and *The English in the Twelfth Century: Imperialism, National Identity and Political Values* (Woodbridge, 2003).

11 *Irish Historical Studies*, the professional journal for someone in English's field, contains an elegantly written article, which he does not cite, by a master of French, Latin, Irish and English sources, which shows that the Irish described the said 'Anglo-Normans' as 'English', and nicely suggests parallels between twentieth-century Ulster's divided peoples and those of late medieval Ireland; see Art Cosgrove, 'The Writing of Irish Medieval History', *Irish Historical Studies*, 27, 106 (1990), 97–111.

12 *Irish Freedom*, 43

13 *Irish Freedom*, 26; my emphases

14 Some of the more egregious errors in Professor Elliott's book are a matter of record, see my review 'History of North's Catholics Riddled with Inaccuracies', *Sunday Business Post*, 22 October 2000.

15 Brian Sykes, *Saxons, Vikings and Celts: The Genetic Roots of Britain and Ireland* (New York, 2006)

and to reinforce Englishness where it already existed, but ... also helped to make the former [the Normans] adopt the identity of the latter [the English]'.[8] Hugh Thomas argues that the Normans acculturated very quickly into an English identity. Similarly, John Gillingham has persuaded me that John McGarry and I were wrong to write in one of our books of 'Anglo-Normans' invading Ireland, even though that label has been standard in Irish and British historiography.[9] Rather, Gillingham insists, the native Irish were right to describe the relevant events, then and later, as the coming of the English. Gillingham has demonstrated that the 'incomers' had no such expression as 'Anglo-Norman' for themselves. This absence is supplementary evidence for a very fast assimilation of Normans into English identity between the 1120s and 1140s.[10] We might call this the *Nous sommes les anglais* Thesis. So the (French-speaking) English, not the Normans, or Anglo-Normans, invaded Ireland, or, as English prefers, were invited in — and, of course, it was both.[11]

The expertise to adjudicate the interpretations of medieval documents is not among my accomplishments but I am able immediately to observe as the book begins that English has missed an important controversy in the ethnic history of these islands, and has instead replicated the old historiography. Has he done so through ignorance? Perhaps; no one can read everything, even on the scholarship relevant to a small country. Has he preferred the old historiography on empirically defensible grounds? Perhaps; but if so, he does not supply them. The suspicion arises that the old historiography is in this instance comforting: it enables him to emphasize 'hybridity' in Irish history, and to disparage traditional nationalist accounts of long-standing English and Irish animosity rooted in colonial relations. That is perhaps why he can later refer to 'the English in Ireland and the Irish in Ireland (as they might respectively be called)', without acknowledging that is what the respective groups called themselves,

according to extant sources in each of their respective languages.[12]

On politically correct cosmopolitanism

Independent Ireland, thanks to prosperity and immigration, is now multi-ethnic, multi-religious and multi-lingual in novel ways. Northern Ireland, thanks to the peace process, is also increasingly attractive to immigrants. Excellent. But it is an anachronism to read and celebrate this present back into the mists of time, whether the mists be deemed Celtic or otherwise. We are confidently told by English, without sources, that

> Different civilizations and peoples and groups were, from the earliest history of old Ireland, written into the story of its inhabitants; *so notions of a monochrome race, of any supposed racial 'purity' or homogeneity, are deeply misplaced. Since ancient times the Irish gene pool has been profoundly mixed* ... There was no single, original Gaelic or Irish race, just as there were no discernible natives in the sense of an original people than whom all others and their descendants are less truly Irish [*sic!*] ... Even in the Iron Age, the people of Ireland were *genetically very mixed* ...[13]

Readers may then expect to be told that there really were 'black Irish', or at least 'black and tan Irish', and anticipate tales of the skeletal remains of persons whose reconstructed phenotypes are not Caucasian. Instead, we get a quotation, and a citation. The quotation reads 'Prehistoric Ireland was a considerable racial mix.' The citation is to Marianne Elliott's *The Catholics of Ulster*. Now, whatever merits Professor Elliott may have as an historian, she is not notably distinguished as a geneticist.[14]

By contrast, Brian Sykes, professor of Human Genetics at Oxford University, arguably is.[15]

In his recently published *Saxons, Vikings and Celts* (yes, he uses the 'C' word), he argues that the DNA evidence shows that the 'matrilineal history of the Isles is both ancient and continuous', and the strong evidence of 'exact and close matches between the maternal and western clans of western and northern Iberia and the western half of the Isles is very impressive, much more so than the poorer matches with continental Europe … On our maternal side, almost all of us [British and Irish] are Celts'. Sykes confirms that the genetic data falsify the old notion that the Celts of Ireland originate from middle Europe. We Hibernians are Iberians: 'The Irish myths of the Milesians were right in one respect. The genetic evidence shows that a large proportion of Irish Celts, on both the male and the female side, did arrive from Iberia, at or about the same time as farming reached the Isles'.[16] The paternal Y-chromosome data also suggest Iberian origins for the males of the Isles, especially in Ireland. The recent discussion of the 'Uí Néill chromosome' enables Sykes to have some fun; it is said to be an example of the 'Genghis effect', that is, very large numbers of men are descended from only a few genetically successful ancestors: 'the longer a clan has been in place like the Isles, the more similar the Y-chromosomes become'.[17] The Hibernian Genghis in question is Niall of the Nine Hostages.[18]

Before political panic sets in among readers of *Field Day Review* let me emphasize that Sykes's use of DNA data is not being deployed to confirm some primordial conception of the Irish nation, but merely to show that English's anti-primordialism is poorly founded. I lack the competence to adjudicate the validity of inferences from technical genetic research, and would want a lot of assurances about the representativeness of the relevant DNA samples from which major historical conclusions are being drawn, but what can be said without fear of rebuttal is that neither Professors Elliott nor English have

the authority to pronounce confidently on pre-modern Ireland's genetic make-up. And, to the extent that we can rely on current scientific evaluations, pre-modern Ireland was rather ethnically (and genetically) homogeneous. We may suspect that for English the assertion, and it is no more than that, of a profoundly multi-cultural and multi-people 'far past' is intended to hide the largely dichotomous recent past or to sermonize for the present.

In the case of 'the Celts', English also strays from careful appraisal of the historical evidence, because of a keen determination to debunk Irish nationalist myths. He thereby misleads the general reader. The idea of a unified Celtic people — with a heartland in the former forests and mountains of Mitteleuropa — is indeed a recent construction, as certain archaeologists have loudly complained.[19] But English errs when he declares that 'If no racial or ethnic group in Ireland in the ancient or medieval period, was known, or identified itself as Celtic, then we should not pretend that they did so, and "the Celts" is a title which therefore should be rejected for Irish people from these centuries'.[20] Geoffrey of Monmouth's influential — if largely fictive — *The History of the Kings of Britain* has the Celts as one of the five nations of the larger island. So some labelling of people as Celts did occur in the twelfth century. More importantly, we can and should use the word 'Celtic', in agreement with the canonical classifications of linguistic branches, to refer to Gaelic speakers, and writers. Such speakers, and writers, preceded English speakers, in history and in residence, on the island of Ireland, and on the neighbouring island. One can neither explain the past accurately, nor improve the political temper of the present, by seeking to deny homogeneity in pre-English Ireland, or by trying to efface the cultural and linguistic distinctiveness of Ireland from eastern and southern Britain before the twelfth, and indeed before the seventeenth, century.

16   Sykes, *Saxons, Vikings and Celts*, 279, 280, 281, 282

17   Sykes, *Saxons, Vikings and Celts*, 285

18   Research conducted in the Smurfit Institute of Genetics at Trinity College suggests that 8 per cent of Irish men possess a particular Y-chromosome: see Laoise T. Moore, Brian McEvoy, Eleanor Cape, Katharine Simms, and Daniel G. Bradley, 'A Y-Chromosome Signature of Hegemony in Gaelic Ireland', *American Journal of Human Genetics*, 78, 2 (2006), 334–38. This Y-chromosome has a cluster of concentration in the north-west running from Roscommon to Strabane, where 23 per cent of local males possess it. Genealogical evidence has subsequently suggested that Niall of the Nine Hostages is also Father Niall of near numberless descendants. The Uí Néill (and their affiliated families) really do have a common ancestor, though they may not yet have mixed their blood or DNA with Richard English or Marianne Elliott.

19   Simon James, *The Atlantic Celts: Ancient People or Modern Invention?* (London, 1999)

20   *Irish Freedom*, 28

'Erin's Valentines', colour supplement with *United Ireland*, 16 February 1884. National Library of Ireland

ERIN'S VALENTINES.
Compliments of the Season from Ireland's old loves and new.

What is your methodological poison?

Two classes of canines roam in the social science jungle. They gather in packs which rarely mix. One growls, 'So what? What's the story? What does it tell us theoretically?' The other tends to bark, 'What's the method? How do you know what you know? Given that we know how difficult it is to know, why should we accept your conclusions?' It is far easier to answer the growler than the barker. The barkers, like theologians, have many monists among them, and want to

know whether an argument survives their tests. Methodologically, *Irish Freedom* is a disappointing mess, no matter how pluralist or lax one is on these matters. English deserves credit as a historian in a political science department for engaging in interdisciplinary reading. Such trespassing is still uncommon among Ireland's cohorts of political historians, who have remained until recently somewhat dismissive of the social sciences, especially if educated in Cambridge or Dublin. But on anyone's sensible starting premises, explaining Irish nationalism requires a social-science-influenced

Republican women protesting against Britain's execution of political prisoners in Mountjoy Jail, 1921. Photograph: Topical Press Agency/Hulton Archive/ Getty Images.

21 The expression 'revisionist' is unfortunate because it stems from the Second International's debate between 'orthodox' and 'revisionist' Marxists (led by Karl Kautsky and Eduard Bernstein respectively). It suggests a contrast between a calcified orthodoxy of Irish nationalism, and a freethinking adaptation of doctrine to reality. All historians should, of course, be open to the revision of their arguments — for example, upon the discovery of fresh data, or the demonstration that their interpretations have been unrepresentative of archival materials, or if they are shown to have contradicted themselves, or to have overlooked critical materials, to list a few reasons for which revision is the appropriate response. Revisionist historians, so-called in Ireland, are, in the main, either opposed to most streams of Irish nationalism, or regretful of the successes, political or cultural, of Irish nationalists. Their intelligent critics are not anti-revisionist *per se* — that would be to embrace having a closed mind. Rather, they are either supportive of at least one stream of Irish nationalism, or happy to demonstrate that the revisionists have misinterpreted or misrepresented the Irish past.

historian to generate explicit hypotheses from the general theoretical literature, and to use these to account for the origins and development of Irish nationalism, its expression, and mobilization, and successes and failures. Secondary materials — and sometimes appropriate primary materials — should be used to appraise the merits or otherwise of these hypotheses. Such case-materials must be carefully selected to test the relevant hypotheses fairly — and are more compelling if treated through comparative analysis. A long romp through the history of Ireland, mildly touched over as a history of Irish nationalism, with a selection bias toward intellectuals, followed by a general survey of the large social science literature devoted to explaining nationalism, with asides on Irish materials, and polite unionist homilies, does not meet the standards of either social science or of rigorous evaluative historiography.

In short, one cannot sensibly present an apparently detached 'story' of Irish nationalism first, and then follow up with a general literature survey of the social science of nationalism, and leave it at that. Either the 'story' is profoundly influenced by the literature survey, in which case it is theoretically 'saturated', as the epistemologists say. Or it is not, in which case the survey must be defended according to some other clear principles of selection. No such clear principles are proffered. In fact, the story of Irish nationalist history presented here is far from a detached account; it is an account of Irish history according to the currently conventional wisdom of those who unfortunately are called 'revisionists', married to a series of rebuttals of extremist or foolish Irish nationalist claims that are too often undocumented.[21]

22 *Irish Freedom*, 95, 104
23 *Irish Freedom*, 526, 529, 530, 519 n. 20
24 David George Boyce and Alan O'Day, eds., *The Making of Modern Irish History: Revisionism and the Revisionist Controversy* (London, 1996); Ciaran Brady, ed., *Interpreting Irish History: The Debate on Historical Revisionism 1938–1994* (Dublin, 1994)
25 I have written detailed appraisals of Gellner and Kedourie's explanations of nationalism ('Gellner's Diagnoses of Nationalism: A Critical Overview *or* What is Living and What is Dead in Gellner's Philosophy of Nationalism?', in J. A. Hall, ed., *The State of the Nation: Ernest Gellner and the Theory of Nationalism* [Cambridge, 1998], 40–90; and 'In Praise of Empires Past: Myths and Method of Kedourie's *Nationalism*', *New Left Review*, 2nd series, 18 [2002], 106–30), and plan to do the same with Anthony Smith's work; the first was my doctoral examiner and friend, the second a former colleague and chair of my former department, and I co-taught an interdisciplinary seminar with the third for many years.

Let me submit some adjectival evidence on the 'revisionist' bias. We are told that Ian MacBride is 'the most authoritative historian of eighteenth century Presbyterian radicalism', and that Marianne Elliott is Tone's 'most accomplished biographer'.[22] We are informed of Paul Bew's 'important series of books', of Roy Foster's 'magnificent two-volume biography', of Senia Pašeta's 'fascinating article' and 'fine treatment', and of Stephen Howe's 'judicious' discussion of whether Ireland had a colonial experience.[23] No similar authoritativeness, accomplishment, importance, magnificence, fascination, fineness or judiciousness appear to attach to the works of Irish nationalists, their sympathizers, or empathizers, or those academics critical of revisionists. Now let me submit some bibliographical evidence. The collection on the revisionist controversy edited by George Boyce and Alan O'Day is frequently cited, whereas that edited by Ciaran Brady is not, period.[24] Would it be unjust to conclude that is because anti-revisionists are more vigorously present in one of these works?

As noted, English hoped to provide 'an authoritative but accessible up-to-date, single volume account of what scholars now think and know (or think that they know) about Irish nationalism'. That would lead one to expect regular passages, if only in his notes, that would be of the following type, 'historians A, B, and C once argued proposition x, but historians D, E and F have discredited these arguments *because* of the following considerations, a1, a2, and a3'. That style of argumentation happens fairly rarely. Instead, we are typically and presumptuously expected to believe that each professional historian drawn in support of English's story is an impartial expert, and, by inference, that those whom they criticize are mission-committed, blinkered, or old-fashioned nationalists. Rival views are simply dismissed, and where a controversy is noted, English has a consistent habit of selecting the position of the reasonable

unionist in the relevant quarrel. That would be fine were it to be admitted, but instead the author presents himself as an objective a-nationalist rather than an anti-nationalist, let alone a British nationalist, that is, a unionist.

Explanations are answers to questions or puzzles. Surveys of explanations, what the psychologists call meta-reviews, can be extremely valuable. The puzzle in *Irish Freedom* is to know what exactly is being explained.

1. Are the questions or puzzles being answered or resolved in English's book set by the general explanatory literature in the works of major theorists of nationalism, for example the London School of Economics' Elie Kedourie, Ernest Gellner and Anthony D. Smith?[25] Or Cornell's Benedict Anderson — or Benedict O'Gorman Anderson, to give him his fully hybrid Irish names? Apparently not, because these theorists are surveyed at the end. They are not used to marshal the story, or stories, or to resolve controversies. At best the survey tells us how important thinkers have explained the salience of nationalism in the modern world.

2. Are the questions being answered set by the political claims made by Irish nationalist historians about Ireland's past, for example Eoin MacNeill, whose books are not cited in the bibliography? Again, apparently not, though 'easy pickings' are sought against popular historians such as Alice Stopford Green, rather than engagements with tougher professional specimens such as J. J. Lee, L. Perry Curtis Jr., Emmet Larkin, or Eunan O'Halpin.

3. Are the questions being set by the claims of mobilized Irish nationalist activists, past and present, about their island's past, such as those of Irish Labour's James Connolly, Fianna Fáil's Frank Gallagher (some of whose books are cited), Sinn Féin's Gerry Adams, or the

Social Democratic and Labour Party's John Hume? Yes, in part. (Indeed English manages to be generous toward Hume).

4. Lastly, do the questions flow from the political opponents of Irish nationalism, past and present, whether unionists, cosmopolitans or self-styled post-nationalists?

In fact, one can find elements of all four interrogative agendas in *Irish Freedom* — the social scientific, those of the (actual and presumed) nationalist historians, the beliefs of popular politicians, and those we may deem the Hibernophobes. But they are scattered rather than gathered and considered in sequence, and the general reader will be as perplexed as me. English never explicitly presents his explanatory agenda. Is the question, 'Why do Irish nationalists hold the beliefs that they do?', or 'How valid are the beliefs of Irish nationalists?', or 'Why do these typical nationalist beliefs resonate among some Irish people?'? Had these separate puzzles been distinguished and evaluated one might feel that some worthwhile explanation had been accomplished.

Instead, the book reads like a first draft, or a transcript of lectures. Not in the sense that the prose is uniformly weak; though it is careless, and wordy. Here is an example of carelessness. 'From earliest times the inhabitants of Ireland were racially mixed rather than joined by ties of blood ...'[26] Now, *either*, the mixture resulted in interbreeding, in which case the inhabitants *were* joined by ties of blood, *or*, the mixture did not result in interbreeding — in which case, in what sense were they 'mixed', other than by residency of the same island? It is good to be against racism, an ideology, but it is not wise to confuse blood ties and kinship with racism. Here is an example of the need for pruning:

> Frequently, nationalism involves the enforcing of attempted reversal of power imbalances (imposing a national empire, liberating a colony from imperial control), *by means of the use of power as leverage. Much of the practical definition of nationalism — what it does, day to day; how it affects people's lives; why it appeals so much to people — involves questions of the deployment of power as attempted leverage.*[27]

Everything italicized could have been profitably cut.

The book, in short, has not been edited down to produce a fully coherent argument. The commendable aiming of the text at the general reader has a price: a lot of basic sociology, anthropology and indeed evolutionary psychology are presented clearly, but laboriously, and occasionally misleadingly. Parts Two and Three, the general history of the nineteenth and twentieth century, do not work, despite their length, because too much is taken for granted, and more care is devoted to treating famous leaders' personalities than narrating the political history of nationalist organizations. Part Four, the explanation of Irish nationalism, turns out to be an eighty-page guide to the general reader on recent anglophone literature on nationalism, in which accessibility leads to the sacrifice of rigour and depth. Instead of isolating a range of testable propositions on nationalism, and evaluating them against Irish case-materials, we are treated to an unobjectionable account of why nationalism has been so persistently dominant in many modern lives.

What might have been done?

Let me provide examples to illustrate methodological underachievement, lest my complaints seem peevish. In each of the five paragraphs that follow I take an agenda from one or more thinkers, whose works English has read, or might reasonably be expected to know. The exercise provides a synopsis of testable propositions and questions that could have been the focus of a

26 *Irish Freedom*, 495
27 *Irish Freedom*, 479

Eamon de Valera working under a plaque of Michael Collins, 1954. Photograph: Carl Mydans/Time Life Pictures/Getty Images.

28 Ernest Gellner, *Thought and Change* (London, 1964), and *Nations and Nationalism* (Oxford, 1983)

proper evaluative historiographical survey of Irish nationalism.

Ernest Gellner's theory of nationalism has at least two testable implications: it predicts nationalism arising in conditions of unevenly developed industrialization; and it predicts nationalist conflict over state-management of modern (generic) primary, secondary and university educational systems.[28] It also has a typology of 'nationalism-inducing' and 'nationalism-thwarting' situations, using three independent variables across two groups (access to political power, access to modern education, and access to a modern high culture). These testable implications, and the typology, could be explicitly evaluated, modified or falsified to appraise their merits in confrontation with Irish historiography. That would involve grappling with difficult questions, notably the meaning of 'high culture' (which is not a reference to atonal music and opera). It would suggest, in particular, a detailed appraisal of research on the development of schooling and tertiary education systems, and the controversies to which they gave rise. That is not attempted. It is simply not enough to reject Gellner's approach by saying that Irish nationalism developed before industrialization developed in Great Britain — one needs to understand what Gellner meant by 'industrialization', which was more than smelting furnaces and smoking factories, and to consider Gellner's own responses to alleged cases of nationalism before industrialization, for example in the Balkans. It is also essential to consider what uneven development might mean, and to use census, demographic and economic data to evaluate matters. But not one table graces English's book, even though he has read many books with the relevant data on these matters.

Elie Kedourie's theory of nationalism claims — wrongly — that nationalism was 'invented' at the beginning of the nineteenth century, a claim refuted by any dispassionate reading of the later writings of Wolfe Tone and other members of the United Irishmen before 1798.[29] Kedourie's more interesting claim, elaborated in a later work on *Nationalism in Asia and Africa* and not directly considered by English, suggests that nationalism is spearheaded by 'marginal men', those situated between native and imperial cultures, at home in neither, and blocked from attaining the social mobility to which they think their education entitles them.[30] The 'blocked social mobility' thesis is partly investigated for late nineteenth- and early twentieth-century Ireland, notably in a quick survey of John Hutchinson's subsequently published doctoral thesis, some of which is cited by English, but not the

census data.[31] Moreover, no consideration is given to applying these insights explicitly and rigorously to the situation of Northern Catholics after 1921.

Michael Hechter's recent work, *Containing Nationalism*, is more innovative than his better-known earlier work on *Internal Colonialism* — the latter is not considered by English, though it produced some interesting debates.[32] *Containing Nationalism* is cited, but simply among those numerous books that treat nationalism as a modern belief system. *Containing Nationalism* is more original than that, and could have been a fertile source of testable hypotheses, which seem to fit well with some of the materials that English presents. Part of Hechter's problematic is to explain attempted secession (the departure of an existing territory and its respective persons from a state to create a new sovereign nation-state), *and* the containment of secession. Secession is political, and has to be explained politically, he argues. His key idea is that secessionism is a strategic response to 'direct rule', that is, to a political centre's displacement of traditional élites who have enjoyed some degree of provincial autonomy. 'Indirect rule' or 'autonomy', especially if applied early, and maintained with flexibility, staunches secessionist dispositions through the incorporation of key political élites. An obvious agenda suggests itself: a comparative assessment of the Welsh, Scottish and Irish disposition to secede from the United Kingdom. The successful 'containing of nationalism' was in fact the norm in agrarian empires in which systems of indirect rule or 'dual polities' were technological necessities. By contrast, the modern centralized and penetrative state, facilitated by the resources of industrialization and modern militarism, disrupts older modes of autonomy and is therefore more likely to provoke nationalist responses in the periphery. This theoretical lens is suggestive for Irish history. It treats nationalism as a dependent variable, and central state activity as the independent

29 Elie Kedourie, *Nationalism* (London, 1960); O'Leary, 'Myths and Method of Kedourie's *Nationalism*'

30 Elie Kedourie, ed., *Nationalism in Asia and Africa* (London, 1971)

31 John Hutchinson, 'Cultural Nationalism, Elite Mobility and Nation-Building: Communitarian Politics in Modern Ireland', *British Journal of Sociology*, 38, 4 (1987), 482–501; *The Dynamics of Cultural Nationalism: The Gaelic Revival and the Creation of the Irish Nation State* (London, 1987); 'Moral Innovators and the Politics of Regeneration: The Distinctive Role of Cultural Nationalists in Nation-Building', *International Journal of Comparative Sociology*, 23, 1–2 (1992), 101–17

32 Michael Hechter, *Internal Colonialism: The Celtic Fringe in British National Development, 1536–1966* (London, 1975)

33 Ian S. Lustick, *State-Building Failure in British Ireland and French Algeria*, Research Series, Number 63 (Berkeley, 1985); *Unsettled States, Disputed Lands: Britain and Ireland, France and Algeria, Israel and the West Bank-Gaza* (Ithaca, 1993)

variable. Its key hypotheses are that attempts to conquer Ireland and to accompany them with direct rule from London provoke nationalist responses — whether in the reactions of Gaelic lords unhappy with metropolitan efforts to monopolize political patronage, or those of eighteenth-century Anglo-Irish Protestant Patriots seeking to govern Ireland without reference to London. Hechter's lens suggests that accompanying centralization with novel settler élites (and the importing of massively disruptive whole settler societies) is even more likely to provoke nationalist responses. The approach suggests that the break-up of the Union was the predictable consequence of refusing a home rule settlement early and flexibly. It suggests that we should read the Act of Union as an act of centralization; and the Government of Ireland Act of 1920 as a belated effort to 'contain nationalism' by creating two local Irish forms of home rule. Explaining the failure to deliver a home rule settlement before 1920 in turn requires a focus on Irish Protestants (especially Ulster Protestants), not as Protestants *per se*, but rather in their historic formation as privileged settlers. Hechter, like Gellner and Kedourie, in short, is not mined for explanation in the way he could be. Even though English has read all three authors, and summarized part of what they say, he has not used them for explanatory purposes.

Secession may also be conceived as the end-point of a régime's failure to render a territory's status 'hegemonic', that is, unquestionably part of the 'natural' order. Political scientist Ian Lustick's *Unsettled States, Disputed Lands*, not cited, is a major effort to explain why Britain, France and Israel respectively failed to render the incorporation of Ireland, Algeria and the West Bank and Gaza as 'hegemonic'.[33] His answer lies in régime actions, in particular the fateful decision in each case to build settlements displacing native élites and some native populations but without entirely expelling or exterminating the

natives. The existence of colonial entities within parliamentary régimes posed a simple dilemma: democratization and the expansion of full citizenship would unwind the respective conquests and damage the interests of the descendants of settlers. Variations on this thesis lie at the heart of many recent accounts of conflict in Northern Ireland. English does not explore this thesis directly, perhaps because he has not read Lustick's version, or perhaps because he has made his mind up that settler colonialism has no role to play in explaining the blockage of home rule, partition or the development and mobilization of (Northern) Irish nationalism.

A fifth source of explanatory review could have arisen from considering why Irish nationalist secessionist movements have failed (most have), and why only one has (partly) succeeded. In the wider world the number of failed secessions always exceeds the number of successful secessions, and we need to explore both failures and successes. That secessions frequently fail testifies to the strength of states, and the difficulties faced by secessionists. Should we seek uniform explanations of all attempted secessions (or successful secessions, or the failures?). Is geopolitics what matters? — that is, whether the relevant territory is controlled or contested by great powers. Are geography and topography important? Is the potentially secessionist territory mountainous, insular, contiguous? Is it the military strategy of the nationalists that is decisive for their chances? Or the régime's counter-insurgency strategy? Does democratization — through the formation of new élites and followings — precipitate the conditions for secessionist success? Do material factors matter? Is the region backward or advanced? The analytical questions continue without pause. When are secessions contested? When are they accepted? In contested cases, secessionists are called 'separatists' or 'traitorous', by 'unionists' (or 'federalists'). The language suggests betrayal within the family. Are such unionist claims 'nationalist'?

Ivan Cooper, chairman of the Derry Citizens' Action Committee, outside the House of Commons, 23 January 1969. Cooper led about 70 Irish civil rights campaigners in a march to Downing Street to hand in a petition demanding an inquiry into alleged police terrorism in the Bogside area of Derry on 10 January. Photograph: Central Press/ Getty Images.

Materialist theories of secession emphasize exploitation. The secessionists may claim they are being taxed without representation. They may claim the land system is exploitative, that it benefits settlers, or that the tariff system benefits the metropolis. The secessionists may argue that secession is in their collective material self-interest. There is an abundance of Irish historiography to test such claims. Materialist explanations have problems: How do we judge their comparative importance, as motivations, or as causes? 'Group pride' and 'group self-esteem' may relate to economic variables in non-linear ways — that is, groups may seek self-government even when it is neither objectively nor subjectively in their material

self-interest. 'Ethno-nationalism' may matter more than 'eco-nationalism', as Walker Connor has crisply put it.[34] The Irish data, properly evaluated, may sustain Connor's thesis. Cultural theories of secession, by contrast, emphasize cultural differences. These theories conform with nationalists' self-conceptions of their mobilizations; and they are what English tends to accept. Yet secessionists may have significantly acculturated into the culture of the dominant group before they secede. Irish nationalists had become more like the English before the War of Independence; Northern Irish nationalists, it is widely agreed, had become more like the British before the civil rights movement and the launch of the Provisional

34 Walker Connor, 'Eco- or Ethno-Nationalism?', *Ethnic and Racial Studies*, 7 (1984), 342–59

35 *Irish Freedom*, 62–63

IRA. The disposition to secede within a state may *not* be strongly related to cultural differences between potential secessionists and the dominant culture: Welsh speakers are far more culturally differentiated from Westminster than working-class Belfast Catholics. Political theories of secession, by contrast, generally suggest that three variables matter in explaining nationalist support among (prospective) citizens of a secessionist state. They are *fear* (for their nation/group — which may include cultural fears, but may also be a response to past or anticipated repression); expectations of prospects for *prosperity*; and, lastly, *recognition* (of identity or status), that is, is the group in question respected as an equal, or not? The 'strong democracy thesis' suggests that democracies stop secessions because they reduce fear, enhance prosperity and settle recognition disputes (as optimistic Castilian unionists say of modern Spain). The converse implication is that Irish nationalism became secessionist because the United Kingdom was not democratic in the right ways. Explaining Irish nationalism therefore requires a rigorous appraisal of the British state and its public policies since at least 1798. That is not provided in this book.

On building bridges between one's eyes

Having suggested the linguistic and methodological blind spots of *Irish Freedom*, let me turn to the ideological failings, where objective appraisal is necessarily more difficult. English criticizes Gerald of Wales for seeing 'history writing as involving a moral dimension', but he has morals of his own which he regularly imparts. He wishes to emphasize the permanently hybrid character of Ireland's population. He prefers to emphasize interaction, exchange and diffusion in British–Irish relations rather than conquest, colonization and control. He isolates and mocks weak points in Irish nationalist hagiography and political propaganda rather than properly

addressing the catastrophic dimensions in Irish history that provided Irish nationalists with their well-documented and non-mythical resentments against British rule. He perhaps concentrates too much on politically radical Irish nationalists — the United Irishmen, the Fenians, the IRA — and not enough on moderate Irish nationalist organizations — the Repeal movement, the Irish Parliamentary Party, the parties of independent Ireland and of Northern nationalists. The ideas of Irish liberals and non-socialist republicans are treated with less scrutiny than those of leftists, socialists, and fascists — whose tastes have always been those of demographic minorities; and Ireland's nationalist feminists, as always, are rather neglected. Data on clerics per person among Protestants compared with clerics per person among Catholics are not provided. Personal jibes are occasionally odd: Erskine Childers's use of cocaine is remarked on; it is not remarked that it did not stop him from being a first-class analyst of legal materials. And so on.

Rather than engage in tedious questioning of every normative judgement of the work, it is better to assess its ideological content by considering what it deals with brusquely — or ignores. It treats Oliver Cromwell's conquest of Ireland over one page.[35] No estimates are provided of the total death tolls this deeply unpleasant man and his henchmen produced, both in war and through laying waste fields. William Petty, a pioneering demographer, suggested one-third of Ireland's population died as a result of massacre, disease and deliberately induced famine in Cromwell's reconquest of Ireland. No reference is made to Cromwell's partially implemented expulsion programmes, offering Hell as an alternative condominium to residency in Connaught. A statue of this man — whom Irish nationalists typically consider a genocidal murderer or an ethnic cleanser, or both — stands outside the House of Commons of the Westminster parliament. No contrast better represents the rival narratives of English and Irish nation-building. Perhaps we can put matters in a different comparative perspective. What would one think of a 625-page history of Zionism that minimally referenced expulsions and mass slaughter of Jews at the hands of European rulers? Or a 625-page history of Palestinian nationalism that dealt with the suppression of the Arab Revolt and the expulsion of the Palestinians over one long paragraph, without data? The Cromwellian massacres are locally and internationally 'contextualized' by English. He observes that they occurred after the 1641 massacres of Protestant settlers in Ulster, for which a figure of 4,000 dead is provided (but with no citation); and, more obscurely, after the slaughter of Protestants in Magdeburg in 1631. English does not believe that to explain all is to excuse all, but this type of 'contextualization' veers toward apologetics.

The neglect of major colonial settlements and moments of conquest and their long-term repercussions is consistent. There is method here. The Statutes of Kilkenny (which are not quoted), we are told, 'said much more than just that the Englishness of the English in Ireland should be preserved from corrupting Gaelic influences, but it is for this that they tend to be remembered'.[36] The Penal Laws are treated over a page and half, with most words deployed there to suggest their non-implementation.[37] One can only expect some two centuries hence that an Afrikaner historian will emphasize that the apartheid laws were often not applied, and fell into desuetude. I say this in response to English's unexplained and unjustified aside that 'comparisons between the Irish Penal Laws and the twentieth century South African apartheid system are *utterly misconceived*'.[38]

He wants to emphasize the centrality of religion in the eighteenth century, and here the method reveals itself. If religion rather than colonialism is analytically primary, then Irish nationalism can be presented as collective — he prefers 'communal'

— sectarianism, rather than as movements to reverse the conquest(s). The argument is this: Protestants fought and displaced Catholics from power in the seventeenth century; the Catholic population was not ethnically homogeneous, because it was a fusion of the Old English and the Irish; ergo, it was not — then — an ethnic conflict, but a religious conflict. Yet the very fact that we can talk of the New English, the Old English and the Irish, and that English himself does so, shows the fact of ethnic differentiation, and conflict. That new settlers displaced previous settlers from power does not mean there was no distinction drawn between colonizer and colonized. Rather, the new conquest and settlement meant that the Old English who had acculturated with the Irish were reclassified as Irish Catholics, and as political inferiors. Geoffrey Keating's work, not cited, foundational for Irish nationalism, deliberately sought to incorporate the Old English into a shared Gaelic national past in opposition to the imperial New English.[39]

The allegation that religion was the great divide — rather than the major marker of the distinction between colonizer and the colonized — is said by English to demolish 'any neat sense that Irish nationalism-versus-unionism involved a native-settler division: not only were many modern Irish unionists not descended from the Plantation [*sic!*], but many of the supposed nationalist "natives" were themselves drawn from comparatively recent waves of immigration'.[40] This statement is most revealing. Settlers accompanying conquests are conflated with voluntary economic immigrants. English assumes, without citation, that 'many' modern Irish unionists are not descended from the Plantation settlers. Such statements are typical, but I have never seen them statistically verified, or documented, either by demographers or geneticists. They may be true, depending on what we mean by 'many'. If they are true, that means there must either be extensive evidence of conversion, intermarriage or illicit sex

36 *Irish Freedom*, 44–45
37 *Irish Freedom*, 84–86
38 *Irish Freedom*, 83; my emphases
39 There are old and new guides to Keating: Geoffrey Keating, *Foras Feasa ar Éirinn: The History of Ireland*, 4 vols., ed. D. Comyn and P. S. Dineen (London, 1902–14); Bernadette Cunningham, *The World of Geoffrey Keating: History, Myth and Religion in Seventeenth Century Ireland* (Dublin, 2000). 'Foundation of Knowledge of Ireland' is a better translation of *Foras Feasa ar Éirinn* than 'History of Ireland', say those who know.
40 *Irish Freedom*, 64–65

Jim Fitzpatrick
Bernadette
from *Hibernia Fortnightly
Review*, 25 April 1969
courtesy of the artist

across the religious boundary, or extensive evidence of immigration of Protestants into Ireland since the eighteenth century, or some conjunction of such phenomena, which, peculiarly, escaped the attention of contemporaries and subsequent historians.

As for the assimilation of the Old English and the Gaelic Irish, this is well attested,

and denied by none, and was celebrated by Geoffrey Keating (*c.* 1569–1644), but this assimilation occurred outside of Ulster, because the latter was conquered late.

English's ideological perspective is plain: let us not code the recent conflict as a settler–native conflict. As he puts it, 'can people born in a country, and possessing ancestors there who date back very many years, really be delegitimized as inauthentic settlers? Would this be an argument to deploy against Americans with Irish, or Polish, or German, or Italian ancestry, or against Pakistanis or West Indians in contemporary England?'[41] The rhetoric is revealing, but the moral heat leads to loss of intellectual control. If there is any 'delegitimizing' going on, it is presumably because people are alleged to be authentic rather than inauthentic settlers — or descendants of such settlers. The argument conflates voluntary immigrants (the Irish and Poles in America and the Pakistanis and West Indians in England) with settler colonialists who dispossessed natives. Most importantly, the slippage reveals how politically important it is for him to code the key conflicts of recent times as religious rather than as rooted in a past settler–native confrontation. The former coding suggests that the Catholics of Ireland become the historical problem; the latter coding suggests that the British state and its settlers become the historical focus. These respective ways of framing Irish history are not likely to be resolved by empirical evidence, as English's cavalier approach to evidence on this crucial matter suggests. But both framings should be evaluated properly in any large scale explanatory evaluation.[42] It does not occur to English that to use settler colonialism as a key factor in explaining Irish nationalism's strength has no necessary consequence for political prescription. It does not follow that any settlers' descendants should be expelled. It does not follow that their presence in Ireland is now politically illegitimate, even if some say so. Explanation and prescription are not always tightly coupled.

For English, the key question of modern Irish history is 'Why did the Reformation fail in Ireland?' The assumption is that had it not failed, there would have been almost no Irish Catholics, and ergo, no Irish nationalism. He reviews a range of explanations for this failure, including: the lack of royal will (including closet Catholic kings); the lack of state capacity; the strength of reformed Catholic institutions; and 'the lack of guile, craft and subtlety involved in the attempted Protestant implementation'. He says that 'Numerous mistakes were made. Rather than dealing with the relevant Irish elites … as allies, the Tudor régime increasingly relied instead on the policy of plantation or settlement'.[43] And they preached Protestantism in English rather than Gaelic. These 'mistakes', as we are to call them, made Protestantism seem foreign, and 'the Reformation came to be seen as an English, foreign imposition … In contrast … Catholicism came to be seen as native and indigenous' — even though, as he has spent time trying to establish, Irish Catholicism (via St. Patrick) was a British import.[44] The Tudors, like any other policymakers, were capable of errors, but they embarked upon colonial settlements for a reason. They wanted to secure Ireland. The failure of the new Protestants to preach extensively in Irish may also have been no mistake: seeking conversion across the linguistic boundary would have removed the barriers between the new colonists and the Irish.

A last reflection. No history of Irish nationalism can avoid evaluation of violence, including insurgent violence, state repression and paramilitary brutality. English has an entirely commendable distaste for violence. But he is not impartial between his state and Irish nationalists. He cites Michael Davitt for the view that 'England's rule of Ireland is government by physical force, and not by constitutional methods', and observes that such views could legitimate 'cruel and awful acts'.[45] Yet he does not directly engage Davitt's thesis with arguments. There is a consistent underemphasis in his book on the repressive and illiberal nature of British rule in Ireland — a judgement that is not intended to justify a single killing by any Irish nationalist, past or present. General Lake's coercion of Ulster before the 1798 uprising, the police surveillance of nineteenth-century republicans, the

41 *Irish Freedom*, 65
42 John McGarry and Brendan O'Leary, *Explaining Northern Ireland: Broken Images* (Oxford, 1995)
43 *Irish Freedom*, 52
44 *Irish Freedom*, 53
45 *Irish Freedom*, 213

46 *Irish Freedom*, 123

undemocratic nature of the Union in Ireland, internment without trial in 1971, to name but a few examples, are not given their appropriate historical weight and impact.

He writes of Robert Emmet that 'in truth the notion that Irish freedom could be won and Irish differences resolved through violence remains as questionable now as it was in 1803'.[46] Independent Ireland obtained its freedom through both democratic and violent means. Its independence was resisted both by coercion and undemocratic means. After a very long period of violence, Northern Ireland now has an admirable political settlement. It would be pleasant to conclude that both of Ireland's current political régimes could have materialized without violence by Irish nationalists, but, regrettably, nothing in English's book compels this conclusion.

Spinoza, the first modern secular democratic republican, declared that the purpose of the state is political freedom. The typical mobilizing purpose of political nationalism is freedom from an empire or from a state that blocks collective self-government or otherwise maltreats a nation. Ireland's nationalists did not win self-government from the British state by exclusively peaceful means. It is unclear that they could have done so. Ireland's history within the Union of Great Britain and Ireland, and Northern Ireland's subsequent history within the Union of Great Britain and Northern Ireland, is a reproach to those who favour regulating national, ethnic and religious differences through integrationist and unitary government. Integration has its place with immigrant minorities; but it cannot settle national minorities. The prospective resolution of the Northern Ireland conflict shows the merits of consociational and federal philosophies, institutions, policies and norms. A more flexible British state might have been able to deliver a federal reconstruction of the Isles in the nineteenth century, which would have left Ireland associated with but not subordinated to the British state. It did not do so partly because it was in the grip of an imperialist unionism — a British nationalism. Yet Robert Emmet's epitaph may be written because his country has taken its place among the free nations of the earth. ∎

Ireland's History Troubles

Ian McBride

Trials of Irish History: Genesis and Evolution of a Reappraisal 1938–2000
Evi Gkotzaridis
Abingdon: Routledge, 2006. 272 pages. ISBN 0-203-39125-X

The writing of Irish history, as a professional or academic enterprise, has a complex history of its own, the subject of recurrent and sometimes rancorous controversy since the late 1980s. Although popular usage of the label 'revisionist' (generally as a term of opprobrium) dates from that decade, the origins of the 'new' history are usually traced back a further fifty years to the founding of the journal *Irish Historical Studies* (1938) by T. W. Moody and R. Dudley Edwards.

1   T. W. Moody, 'A New History of Ireland', reprinted in Ciaran Brady, ed., *Interpreting Irish History: The Debate on Historical Revisionism 1938–1994* (Dublin, 1994), 38
2   T. W. Moody, 'Irish History and Irish Mythology' (1978), reprinted in Brady, ed., *Interpreting Irish History*, 71

19 April 1976: British troops storming through the gates of Milltown Cemetery, Belfast, to disperse republicans who had gathered to commemorate the 60th anniversary of the Easter Rising. Photograph: Keystone/Getty Images.

Drawing primarily upon English models — both men had been trained in the seminars of the Institute of Historical Research in London — the editors encouraged articles based on 'scientific' research methods, selections of annotated documents, guides to published and manuscript sources and 'Historical Revisions', or essays devoted to the reinterpretation of received wisdom in the light of new evidence. Over the next three or four decades Moody and Edwards presided over an exponential boom in historical research, centred on the expanding history departments of the Irish universities and, to a lesser extent, their British and North American counterparts. It was, as Moody boasted in 1967, 'an era of remarkable advances in specialist research [and] in professional technique'.[1] From the beginning, moreover, the revolution in method was associated with a higher intellectual or even moral purpose. Faith in scientific research, for Moody in particular, was bound up with a 'mental war of liberation from servitude to myth'.[2] As a visit to any of the major bookshops in

Dublin or Belfast will quickly demonstrate, the history boom still shows no sign of faltering. Yet the self-assurance and sense of purpose that characterized its architects have been so severely shaken that they already seem to belong to a different world. The optimism with which Moody, Edwards and their students once defined their goals and measured their achievements has largely evaporated, along with the broad currents of liberal humanism that underpinned their approach to the past.

In de Valera's Ireland, of course, received wisdom meant the crude nationalism that underpinned the state. In itself this was not an unusual predicament. What else, after all, was the Whig interpretation of England's past if not nationalist complacency? In the later nineteenth century the English Civil War, for so long the test of party politics, was losing its divisive energy as the relationship between crown and parliament and the conflict between Church and Dissent were displaced by social concerns. Only the Irish question, which still shaped party alignments at Westminster, continued to supply seventeenth-century conflicts with a contemporary edge: to write of Ireland, Thomas Macaulay warned, was to tread on a volcano on which the lava was still glowing. The success story celebrated by English Whigs, centred on the gradual achievement of moderated liberty and parliamentary government, was no longer marked by partisanship or sectarianism — unless it was, in John Burrow's matchless phrase, 'the sectarianism of English respectability'.[3] Its force was still felt in Oxford and Cambridge, even as scholarship diversified; reading G. M. Trevelyan, for one recent critic, was rather like taking 'a tour of a beautiful country house conducted by one of the last surviving members of the family'.[4] It was in this context that the brilliant young Cambridge historian Herbert Butterfield achieved widespread recognition with his iconoclastic tract, *The Whig Interpretation of History* (1931), an attack not only on the story of English constitutional development, but all national teleologies, and all present-centred history.

In Ireland, still feeling the tremors of yet more volcanic activity, the new historians found themselves in a peculiar situation. Both in public commemorations and in popular historical texts, the Southern state commemorated its revolutionary origins in the Easter Rising, launched by a militant vanguard without (or in advance of) what we would now call a democratic mandate. This rhetoric sat oddly with the Free State's very pragmatic acceptance both of the realities of Anglo-Irish relations and of the inequalities of traditional social hierarchies. Subsequently, of course, the revolution had received popular endorsement by a majority of voters, 'awakened' to national consciousness by the exemplary violence of Patrick Pearse or alienated by British repression. Either way, the democratic credentials of the Easter Rising were, to put it no more strongly, contestable. Free State governments fought hard to establish a monopoly on the graves of the patriot

dead at Glasnevin and Bodenstown, but neither W. T. Cosgrave nor Eamon de Valera succeeded in appropriating nationalist remembrance for themselves. They could not ignore the survival of revolutionary nationalism among the irreconcilable IRA in the South and, even more obviously, the continuity of republican sentiment in the North. In 1957 de Valera himself introduced internment, in parallel with the Stormont government, during the IRA border campaign. Although the path was far from smooth, intergovernmental co-operation would eventually triumph in the 1980s, also the highpoint of historical revisionism.

It was not until the late 1970s, following a decade of instability in Northern Ireland, that the antithesis between the new history and the old mythology was articulated with explicit force. In his well-known and much derided farewell to the Trinity College History Society, Moody contrasted the knowledge the historian acquired through 'the application of scientific methods to his evidence' with popular tradition. The opposition between history and mythology quickly became a standard trope as the historian's duty to address the causes of communal division in Ireland received greater prominence. By 1986, in his presidential address to the Irish History Society, Ronan Fanning was calling for the extension of the historiographical revolution into the twentieth century, where myth, defined as 'any historical narrative which is either imaginary or fictitious or both', could be found holed up in its final bastion.[5] With their heads down in their archives, most of the professionals were too busy to notice the juggernaut heading towards them. Outside Ireland, Hayden White's argument that *all* historical narratives were essentially fictitious was making converts; at home, meanwhile, discontent with the sceptical assault upon the 'apostolic succession' of national heroes was escalating. Over the next decade these two trends would slowly become soldered together.

3   J. W. Burrow, *A Liberal Descent: Victorian Historians and the English Past* (Cambridge, 1981), 92–93
4   Stefan Collini, *English Pasts* (Oxford, 1999), 24
5   Ronan Fanning, '"The Great Enchantment": Uses and Abuses of Modern Irish History', reprinted in Brady, *Interpreting Irish History*, 147

R. D. Edwards and T. W. Moody outside the Four Courts, Dublin, during the Foyle Fisheries case, *c*. 1947.

6   Desmond Fennell, 'Against Revisionism', reprinted in Brady, *Interpreting Irish History*, 183–90

The accusation that professional historians operated as the propagandist adjunct of a series of reactionary governments was first made by journalists and political commentators like Desmond Fennell. It was an 'objective fact', he asserted, that the revisionist trend was 'the historiography of the counter-revolution' — a narrative capable of legitimizing the state's deviation from the nationalist doctrine of its founders and, in particular, the increasing co-operation with Britain in joint security measures against republican insurgency in the North. Academics were mocked as the 'servants' of the establishment.[6] Within the academy, Brendan Bradshaw's unexpected assault on the value-free principle of the Moody/Edwards school, although it dominated the early debate, was something of a red herring. Bradshaw and his opponents, after all, were basically agreed on what was happening — revisionism had rinsed the heroism out of the Irish past, dismissed the concept of the aboriginal, all-absorbing Gael, and replaced the central dynamic of nationhood with an emphasis on complexity, ambiguity, and contingency — they merely differed on whether or not this was a good thing. Critics gleefully seized on Bradshaw's suggestion that the

'received version' of Irish history might after all constitute 'a beneficent legacy — its wrongness notwithstanding', and got back to their index cards and folders. It seemed that 'myth', after fifty years of giving ground to 'history', had the temerity to attempt a late, no doubt futile, comeback. The really subversive challenge, however, was the growing post-colonial direction of Irish literary criticism. Drawing eclectically on Michel Foucault, Edward Said, or Hayden White, a number of scholars associated with the Field Day enterprise had adopted positions that tended to dissolve the boundaries between historical narratives and literary fiction altogether. The distinction between scrupulous scholarship and self-conscious propaganda, between 'history' and 'mythology', was beginning to crumble.

One important straw in the wind, in this connection, was the eighteenth-century historical geographer Kevin Whelan, whose superb *annaliste* studies of Wexford had established his reputation as one of the most innovative and thought-provoking scholars of his generation. In 1992 Whelan had issued a manifesto for what he called post-revisionism, in which he appeared to endorse Bradshaw's objections to the portrayal of the Irish nation as an 'ethnic mongrel cocktail'. Like Bradshaw, he complained that revisionists had soft-pedalled on landlords, unionists, the Orange Order, and successive British governments. Worst of all, he objected to the close links between revisionist historians, the media, and the political establishment. 'Caesar and Clio should not cohabit,' he counselled in a notably infelicitous phrase, 'otherwise, the muse could quickly become a prostitute.'[7] So far, however, the *constructive* aspects of Whelan's post-revisionist agenda — an openness to French historiographical models, more attention to popular *mentalités*, and greater use of Irish-language sources — were relatively uncontroversial; not very different, in fact, from Tom Dunne's proposals for post-revisionism announced in the *Irish Review* around the same time.[8] Equally uncontentious was Whelan's prediction that more comparative scholarship, by setting Irish experiences against a wider European frame, would reveal them to be 'normative' rather than exceptional.

Four years later, Whelan's sparkling collection of essays, *The Tree of Liberty*, was published, deservedly the most influential of the bicentenary crop of '98 books. Like historians of France such as Lynn Hunt and Keith Baker, new research on the United Irishmen was now turning to the role of language, symbols and rituals in politicization, and Whelan was no exception. Both his distinctive take on the United Irish movement and his distinctive phraseology soon acquired semi-official status. Whelan provided the text panels and exhibition guide for the Fellowship of Freedom exhibition held at the National Museum of Ireland in Collins Barracks; he helped organize the 1798 Bicentenary Conference, whose published proceedings were subsequently structured around his own interpretative think-pieces; and he became adviser to the Government Commemoration Committee, in which capacity he supplied speeches for

ministers attending bicentenary occasions. Throughout 1998, Clio and Caesar flaunted their on–off affair with unprecedented openness — though we must assume that Whelan emerged with his scholarly virtue intact. Significantly, however, *The Tree of Liberty* and its spin-offs contained little about the *Annales* school (or, indeed, about Irish-language research); Whelan's earlier theoretical co-ordinates had been succeeded by the citation of post-colonial critics, especially Seamus Deane, Luke Gibbons and David Lloyd. The difference could be felt less in the *substance* of the essays — on the social and cultural role of middlemen and the 'underground gentry', or on the United Irish propaganda machine — than in the intensely politicized critique of revisionism that now provided his interpretative frame.

What is most depressing about Ireland's recent history wars is the frequency with which the historical scholarship of several generations is explained primarily — sometimes solely — in terms of the crude ideological function imputed to it. Recent accounts of the new history school, to paraphrase W. E. H. Lecky on James Froude, singularly lack *gradation*. For Whelan, revisionism was 'a specific ideological response to the needs of the Southern state in coming to terms with the major political crisis'.[9] This is undeniable. Disagreements between scholars are partly political disagreements; and that is partly why they remain interesting and relevant. No one really believes, for example, that the quarrel between those who see the Protestant Ascendancy as a species of colonialism and those who stress eighteenth-century Ireland's fundamental similarities with *ancien régime* Europe is ever going to be resolved by more archival discoveries. The business of verifying and weighing up evidence does matter, of course, as David Irving discovered in the 'Holocaust Denial' libel case brought against Deborah Lipstadt and Penguin Books in 1999. Anthony Julius's victorious defence team chose as their historical expert the bullish Richard Evans, whose popular primer

7 Kevin Whelan, 'Come All You Staunch Revisionists: Towards a Post-Revisionist Agenda for Irish History', *Irish Reporter*, 2 (1991), 23–26

8 Tom Dunne, 'New Histories: Beyond "Revisionism"', *Irish Review*, 12 (1992), 1–12

9 Whelan, 'Towards a Post-Revisionist Agenda', 26. See more recently, Kevin Whelan, 'The Revisionist Debate in Ireland', *boundary 2*, 31, 1 (2004), 179–206.

10 D. D. Guttenplan, *The Holocaust on Trial: History, Justice and the David Irving Libel Case* (London, 2001), 218

11 Mary Fulbrook, *Historical Theory* (London, 2002); Georg G. Iggers, *Historiography in the Twentieth Century: From Scientific Objectivity to the Postmodern Challenge* (Middletown, 1997)

In Defence of History (1997) claims that the reconstruction of the past is, after all, a matter of sifting the empirical evidence and evaluating sources. In court, Evans succeeded in establishing that Irving's books were a 'knotted web of distortions, suppressions and manipulations' of the primary material.[10] In the academy, however, Evans's rather sneering attempts to meet the challenge of post-modernist theory with reassertions of disciplinary practice have had a mixed reception. Statements can be falsified, documents can be misread or wrenched out of context, but the larger scale narratives, as we all know, rarely stand or fall on the basis of the evidence. Is it possible, then, for the professionals to distinguish historical knowledge from ideology without falling back on the old 'common sense' position that so often replicates, whether consciously or not, contemporary presuppositions and prejudices?

One aspect of historical writing notably missing from our recent historiographical skirmishes is something like the concept of the paradigm, as defined by the historian of science Thomas Kuhn. In his classic book, *The Structure of Scientific Revolutions* (1962), Kuhn presented an iconoclastic account of the ways in which scientific knowledge is produced. According to the traditional view, scientific progress depended upon the duplication of experimental knowledge by individual researchers whose task it was to isolate themselves from the social forces and political interests that otherwise produced distorted judgements or bias. Kuhn was intrigued by the cultural practices of scientific communities, which, like other cultural practices, were transmitted from one generation to the next through apprenticeship, processes of socialization, and established mechanisms of social control. Typical research, he argued, does not occur in a vacuum, but builds upon a specific, concrete, scientific achievement, an authoritative model — or 'paradigm' — which subsequent scholars are committed to elaborating and extending. The key point

for Kuhn was that scientific paradigms never establish themselves for logical reasons alone, nor are they abandoned simply because of the accumulation of anomalies (evidence that cannot be assimilated). Paradigm shifts occur when the community finds a new scientific achievement that can both assimilate anomalies and serve as a concrete model for future work, a realignment that Kuhn relates to the social psychology of the scientific community rather than logical justification. Historians, who generally aim to cultivate scepticism, originality and controversy, are not as dogmatic as Kuhn's scientists, nor do they engage primarily in collaborative research. But Kuhn's position has recently been adapted in Mary Fulbrook's *Historical Theory* (2002), and it is close in spirit to the widely admired work of Georg Iggers on twentieth-century historiography.[11] For Fulbrook in particular, it offers a middle way between the post-modernist view that historical accounts can really only be evaluated according to ethical or political criteria, and the traditional response of the historian that the documents, ultimately, speak for themselves. In some ways Evi Gkotzaridis pitches her *Trials of Irish History: Genesis and Evolution of a Reappraisal 1938–2000* (2006) towards this middle ground, though her central concerns are quite different.

Moody and Edwards, as they appear in *Trials of Irish History*, were human beings as well as historians. As such, they shared a whole series of assumptions about the nature of the individual and society, the nation and the state, Ireland and Europe, with their educated (and uneducated) contemporaries. Part of the Gkotzaridis's achievement is to bring to light new correspondence and occasional pieces that enable her to flesh out the intellectual careers of the new historians. One result is that their dissatisfaction with nationalism is presented not as an insular Irish concern but a broader European one. In 'History,

Politics and Partition', written for the *Leader* in March 1955, Edwards appears as an enthusiast for the Council of Europe, which had passed the European Convention on Human Rights in 1951 and which he hoped would some day be underpinned by a greater sense of a shared European identity. His warning that 'good propaganda can be bad history' sounds exactly like the sort of statement that gets us historians a bad reputation among the denouncers of naïve empiricism. But the statement was made in the same year that West Germany was admitted to NATO and the formation of the Warsaw Pact was announced. For most Europeans the memory of the Second World War was very fresh, and the possibility of a third was very real. Statesmen and historians were then more intimately connected (in 1940, just after the Finest Hour speech, G. M. Trevelyan had written to thank Winston Churchill for the mastership of Trinity College Cambridge, reminiscing about their schooldays together at Harrow).[12] In the years after the Nuremberg trials, both the gentlemen scholars and the gentlemen statesmen would ponder the failure of the Versailles settlement of 1919. Butterfield's first substantial book, *The Peace Tactics of Napoleon* (1929), which emphasized the role of accident and incompetence in the shaping of the Treaty of Tilsit rather than imperialist ambitions of Napoleon, should be viewed in this context.

As Gkotzaridis reminds us in one of her most interesting sections, T. Desmond Williams, a close associate of Edwards, had studied diplomatic history at Peterhouse (Butterfield's Cambridge college) before his appointment by the Foreign Office to a team of British, French and American historians to edit German Foreign Ministry papers from 1919 to 1945. Recommended by Butterfield as the most promising historian *ever* — 'no other contemporary historian was so aware of the traps and dangers in contemporary history' — Williams went on to dispute Lewis Namier's deterministic view of German nationalism in a brilliant essay on the historiography of the Second World War, demonstrated that Neville Chamberlain's rejection of appeasement was a mixture of misinformation and miscalculation, and criticized the conduct of the Allied powers at the Nuremberg trials on the grounds that they had not permitted access to their own archives. In 1961, Geoffrey Barraclough's paper, 'German Unification: An Essay in Revisionism', a critique of present-centred history read to the Conference of Irish Historians, was enthusiastically welcomed by J. C. Beckett: 'Perhaps in the long run,' Beckett concluded, 'one of the strongest justifications for the serious study of history is the need for protecting the public from policies based on a false interpretation of the past.' Value-freedom, now so much derided, appears here in a rather different light.

Edwards and Williams both believed that Ireland's neutrality permitted them greater detachment on European matters than English historians could muster. At the same time, they believed that a comparative perspective gave them greater insight into the Irish past. In 1960, depressed by the poor performance of his students in a matriculation examination, Edwards deplored the faith-and-fatherland history taught in the schools, which, he thought, tended to drive young men into either the Church or the IRA: 'What is needed is a history of Ireland in its relations with civilisation in which the unity of Europe gets more influence and can be balanced against English aggression and Protestant bigotry.' The distinction between the true historian and the amateur, for Edwards, turned on the latter's identification with his subjects, which led to celebration rather than critical evaluation. It is worth recalling that the sort of books he had in mind were Frank Gallagher's polemic *The Indivisible Island* (1957), which began with a chapter entitled 'A Nation through the Centuries', or P. S. O'Hegarty's *Ireland*

12 David Cannadine, *G. M. Trevelyan: A Life in History* (London, 1992), 135

13 *Trials of Irish History*, ix

14 *Trials of Irish History*, 1, 7, 11, 22

15 Tom Dunne, *Rebellions: Memoir, Memory, and 1798* (Dublin, 2004), 48

under the Union (1952), with its 'story of Ireland in the last phase of her captivity'. Such transparent invitations to anachronism and emotive idealism had already become embarrassing. But professionalism was also, crucially, defined by source criticism. The amateur was merely 'a commentator on commentaries', whereas, for the genuine historical critic, contemporary documents were the 'real quarry' of research work. Once again, we have to remember that the distinction between historical scholarship and propaganda was formulated at a time when political history was largely based on memoirs and speeches.

Unfortunately, *Trials of Irish History* is structured around the author's 'ever-imposing' revelation that Irish revisionism and post-modern theory present 'an astonishing twin-ship in sensibility, spirit and method'. Gkotzaridis, a Greek scholar based at the European University Institute in Florence, charts this journey of discovery in a disarming, off-key kind of europrose: 'I mused it was like having a cryptic intelligence message in front of my eyes and feeling frustrated at not having found the means to break the code yet.'[13] Her writing, sometimes baroque, sometimes almost spoof-Joycean, is marred by grammatical errors, half-sentences, and cumbersome locutions that a more attentive editor (or just *an* editor) might have corrected. There is of course little evidence, as she concedes with some understatement, that the new historians were acquainted with Foucault, Roland Barthes, Jean-François Lyotard or Jacques Derrida. Since the chronology is all wrong, Gkotzaridis argues instead on the basis of affinities. But can we really believe that the 'primeval rift in the entrails of Irish society' produced a generation of historians who were, as she puts it, 'stupendously precocious in divining the serious obstacle created by the intrusion of power in knowledge?' Her new historians appear as iconoclastic, sceptical and, above all, courageous, as a 'harried

minority', as 'champions of freedom' who empowered future generations with the ability 'to think for themselves'. Their opponents, meanwhile, are viewed as facile, opportunistic and mean; they are engaged in a kind of priestcraft; their 'righteous' and 'sermonising' polemics are designed to perpetuate 'the old naive infatuation' with the story of Ireland. This value-laden account, the sort of historical writing that Moody and Edwards deplored, does little to advance her case. 'From the perches of posterity's condescension,' she remarks, in another dizzying metaphorical flight, 'glib accusations of archaism in method and intention were vituperatively thrown at the faces of those trailblazer historians who dared to imagine the empowerment of the Irish intellect inside two regimes, which had instead thrived on its emasculation.'[14]

Connections between revisionism and post-modernism are repeatedly asserted but never demonstrated in any detail. We are told that the new historians resembled Foucault's method because they questioned the notion of the Irish nation expressed in de Valera's 1937 Constitution, or that, like Derrida, they were anti-dogmatic; in one chapter Conor Cruise O'Brien metamorphoses into a French post-modernist philosopher, while Seamus Deane appears briefly as the French counter-revolutionary and monarchist Joseph de Maistre. Even by Anglo-American standards, however, Irish historians have been relatively averse to theoretical reflection on their trade. One suspects that Theo Moody's admission to Marnie Hughes-Warrington's crammer, *Fifty Key Thinkers on History*, is a testament to national inclusiveness rather than his originality. Tom Dunne, who was taught by Edwards at University College Dublin in the 1960s, recalls simply an emphasis on independence, critical thought, and the importance of deploying evidence. What stayed in the mind was the idea 'that history mattered, and each one of us was entitled, indeed expected, to have an opinion'.[15] The new historians have far more in common with the twentieth-century English scholars surveyed in John Kenyon's *The History Men* (1983) — where, incidentally, Butterfield is damned for his 'modest and rather random output' — or indeed with the emphasis on accident and contingency in Alan Bennett's play *The History Boys* (2004).[16]

That 'propaganda' was something that infected 'knowledge', but with the careful forensic skills of the historian might be surgically removed, was a basic assumption of the Anglo-American world in the decades after the Second World War. At the Conference of Irish Historians in 1945 Butterfield preached against xenophobia, national vanity and, above all, the failure 'to put ourselves in another's place'. In 1957 the English conservative philosopher Michael Oakeshott presented a paper entitled 'The Activity of Being an Historian', warning that the common preoccupation with 'origins' produced a restricted history in which the past was read backwards and assimilated to subsequent events. In his conclusion, which would have warmed the heart of any Irish revisionist, he contrasted the detached writing of the historian with the 'obscene necromancy' of the journalist, who sought to resuscitate the dead and to dress them up in modern clothes so that they could be 'made to gesticulate again'.[17] Academic historians everywhere justifed their existence by separating scholarly history from communal memory. While the former was used to sanctify political institutions, social hierarchies or religious beliefs, the progress of the latter, according to the Cambridge historian Jack Plumb, would purge the human story of such 'deceiving visions'. Plumb's simplistic injunction to analyse what happened on its own terms, rather than in the service of religion or national destiny, was intended to facilitate 'a more extended, a more rational, a more detached sense of human destiny'.[18] The common hope that historical research might contribute to the dismantling of prejudices

between neighbouring communities was shared by both Moody and Edwards — primarily, of course, preoccupied with the divisions on the island of Ireland. It is hard, however, to see this mission as part of a state-sponsored project. Certainly, Edwards's experience of collaboration with politicians and civil servants over the Bureau of Military History, an interesting episode reconstructed for the first time by Gkotzaridis, was not encouraging. In a *Sunday Independent* article entitled 'Fianna Fáil and Frankenstein', Edwards accused the government of treating its archives with the same defensiveness as Soviet Russia.

The other striking feature of the new history school, not properly addressed by Gkotzaridis, is related to the deep Christian convictions shared by its central practitioners. Moody, as one of his colleagues wrote, 'had a view of history as at once moral, rational and in a deep non-technical sense religious'.[19] The major lesson of history, according to Williams, was 'the simple Christian truth of original sin and the simple Christian admonition not to cast the first stone'. In this respect, too, they resembled Butterfield, a Methodist lay preacher from Yorkshire who published widely on Christianity, history and science. In 1954, when Butterfield gave the first series of Wiles Lectures at Queen's University, Belfast, he chose 'Man on his Past' as the theme, evidence of his continuing preoccupation with historical scholarship; but he concluded with a summary of his own approach entitled 'The Idea of Providence' — almost unimaginable today. *Trials of Irish History* reinforces Alvin Jackson's study of J. C. Beckett's professional and private writings, which reveal him as moderate, liberal and, above all, Anglican in outlook.[20] Both Beckett and Moody were from a Northern Protestant background, as indeed was R. B. McDowell, the most influential eighteenth-century scholar of the period. Yet their strong sense of Irishness — inclusive, rather

16 John Kenyon, *The History Men* (London, 1983), 261

17 Michael Oakeshott, 'The Activity of Being an Historian', in T. Desmond Williams, ed., *Historical Studies*, 1 (London, 1958), 17–18

18 J. H. Plumb, *The Death of the Past* (Basingstoke, 1969), 13, 17, 144

19 F. S. L. Lyons, quoted in Thomas Bartlett, 'Review Article: A New History of Ireland', *Past and Present*, 116 (1987), 207.

20 Alvin Jackson, 'J. C. Beckett: Politics, Faith, Scholarship', *Irish Historical Studies*, 33, 130 (2002), 129–50

21 Fanning, 'Uses and Abuses of Modern Irish History', 156

22 John M. Regan, 'Southern Irish Nationalism as a Historical Problem', *Historical Journal*, 50, 1 (2007), 1–27. I am grateful to the author for an advance copy of the article.

patrician, 32-county Irishness — precluded any genuine identification with the Stormont régime, or indeed its Southern counterpart. It also helps to explain their faith in the integrative, conciliatory potential of the historian, and their optimistic belief that a scientific approach to the evidence would gradually erode dangerous popular traditions, whether Orange or Green. Beckett's political ruminations, recorded in his diaries, were often interesting, but never profound or systematic. His central conviction, that the Anglo-Irish tradition (or an idealized version of it) offered a *via media* between the sectarian excesses of Gaelic nationalism and Ulster loyalism, is easily mocked. Yet the greatest testament to the 32-county nationalism of the new historians is the survival — in the face of some hostility at Stormont — of the journal *Irish Historical Studies* itself. The unity they achieved was not the unity of the 1916 Republic, or even the second Republic of 1937, but of the 1920 Government of Ireland Act: two distinct historical societies for North and South, united by the journal and by the umbrella organization, the Irish Committee for Historical Sciences (and, their critics might add, ultimately dependent on London).

Almost a decade into the third Republic — the one ratified on 23 May 1998 — the partition of Ireland seems paradoxically more stubbornly entrenched and yet more futile than ever. It is becoming clear, however, that the intellectual climate in which historians conduct their research has been rapidly transformed. 'Nowhere else in the European, North American or Antipodean democracies,' Ronan Fanning declared in 1986, 'does the writing of twentieth-century history demand so constant a confrontation with mythologies designed to legitimise

violence as a political weapon in a bid to overthrow the state.'[21] Future undergraduates are unlikely to feel the pressures of unfinished business in the same way as recent generations. As the polarizing issues presented by the Troubles begin to fade, what remains of the Moody/Edwards project? Professionalization, if anything, has intensified, and nowhere more so than among the highly specialized circles of literary critics who have laid siege to traditional historiography. The historians, though somewhat chastened, seem set to maintain their traditional vigilance against propaganda, however complex and problematic their commitment to objectivity may be. In the current issue of the *Historical Journal*, John Regan develops a detailed critique of revisionist accounts of the Civil War (1922–23), which, he contends, have been structured around the implicit assumptions of a hidden Southern or 26-county nationalism.[22] Once again, the renewal of communal violence and republican insurrection after 1969, which Regan emphatically calls the Northern 'war', provides the essential backdrop. Since Regan confesses that his earlier research was restricted by a kind of self-censorship, his argument that revisionism was a 'conscious, or perhaps unconscious, enterprise between intellectuals and the state' has the unusual distinction of being a conspiracy theory in which the theorist himself was formerly complicit. Ultimately, however, his critique of revisionist historiography is tied to a closely argued reinterpretation of state formation in 1922, recovering the 'uncomfortable, challenging, or inexpedient' aspects occluded, he contends, by the pervasive assumptions of Southern nationalism. Surely Moody and Edwards would have approved? ■

Varieties of Irish Evangelicalism

David W. Miller

Much of what happened in nineteenth-century Irish Protestantism is described as 'evangelicalism', and over the past generation evangelicalism has become a major focus of research by students of religious history throughout the North Atlantic world. To the (considerable) extent that that literature is written by scholars who are committed evangelicals themselves, it is part of a process of social construction. David Bebbington's typology of 'evangelical characteristics' — conversionism, activism, biblicism and crucicentrism — is a British example of such a construction.[1] The work of social construction takes on a more contentious character in the United States, in which 'the evangelicals' are major participants in what have come to be called the Culture Wars.

1 David Bebbington, *Evangelicalism in Modern Britain: A History from the 1730s to the 1980s* (London, 1989), 2–17

2 John Wesley, *The Journal of the Rev. John Wesley*, 8 vols., std. edn., ed. Nehemiah Curnock (New York, 1909–16), vol. 1, 475–76

3 Grayson Carter, *Anglican Evangelicals: Protestant Secessions from the Via Media, c. 1800–1850* (Oxford, 2001), 64–65

Detail:
Nathaniel Grogan
The Itinerant Preacher
1783
oil on panel
44 x 61 cm
private collection, courtesy of Sotheby's

The origins of evangelicalism are usually traced to the conjunction around 1740 of *pietismus* in central Europe, the 'great awakening' in New England, and the career of John Wesley in England. Wesley recorded his own conversion experience on 14 May 1738 with the words 'I felt my heart strangely warmed', and he brought evangelicalism to Ireland in numerous visits between 1747 and 1789.[2] The 'religion of the heart', 'vital religion' or 'serious religion' that he preached seemed the very converse of the religion practised in the contemporary Church of Ireland, many of whose clergy were preoccupied with enhancing their own careers and whose leading laymen (like their counterparts in England) abhorred any religious initiative that smacked of 'enthusiasm'. Wesley and other Wesleyan preachers were most successful in converting ordinary lay people belonging, at least nominally, to the Church of Ireland, and around the end of the eighteenth century this religion of the heart also became very attractive to a generation of candidates for the Anglican ministry as well as a number of élite laymen and laywomen.

In his study of Anglican evangelicals throughout the British Isles, Grayson Carter argues that Irish landlords who had 'previously opposed methodistical "enthusiasm" … welcomed travelling preachers' in the wake of the 1798 rebellion as a way to deal with Catholic insurgency: 'it was hoped that the conversion of the peasantry to "vital religion" might bring about the social stability which force of arms could not achieve'.[3] The standard means in the evangelical armoury for promoting vital religion was a style of preaching calculated to focus the mind upon the rewards and punishments of the afterlife and to evoke a highly emotional response understood to mark the sinner's conversion. But, as Irene Whelan points out:

Itinerant open-air preaching modelled on the system that had proved so successful in England was totally unsuited to conditions in Ireland, certainly in areas where the population was predominantly Catholic. Designed to revive religious consciousness rather than to bring about formal adhesion to a church, it was virtually useless unless reinforced by a network of scripture schools and the active involvement of local organizers.[4]

Indeed, apart from a claim by John MacHale (then Catholic coadjutor bishop of Killala) that '"fanatic females" fell into trances and prophesied' during the celebrated 1826–27 commotions over alleged Catholic converts in Cavan, very little, if any, evidence has come to light that Catholics were induced to have the sort of experience understood to be conversion by evangelicals of the English, methodistical, type.[5] Presbyterian evangelicals, who were more concerned that converts have the right answers than that they have the right ecstatic experience, were subject to similar disappointments. Two decades later, at the height of the Famine, a Presbyterian missionary in Kerry, his candour perhaps enhanced by his fear that the many souls dying around him were, in his words, 'going down to hell', wrote: 'We may have erred … in going to Roman Catholics as we would have done to careless Protestants, who had some knowledge of Scripture terms and duties, and we may have wondered why the Gospel was not the power of God to their salvation.'[6]

To place the Second Reformation in context, we should remember that in the nineteenth century, the idea of converting Irish Catholics to Protestantism was not new; the Penal Laws of the preceding century had provided material incentives for propertied Catholics to conform to the Established Church, and about 5,800 did so simply by subscribing to certain oaths and a declaration. Nothing in the process was intended to warm the subscriber's heart or

to elicit evidence that such warming had occurred. Several contributors to *Converts and Conversion in Ireland, 1650–1850*, have examined conversion 'narratives' by Catholics (mainly priests) who conformed. In some cases these documents do suggest that the subjects were acting on 'conviction', rather than mere self-interest, but it seems to be *intellectual* conviction that Protestant doctrines constitute a more rational system than Catholic teachings, not a deep, heartfelt conviction of their own sinfulness accompanied or followed by a sense of assurance of their salvation.[7] The evidence suggests that the Second Reformation also sought not *conversion* in the sense that that word is used by evangelical historians, but *conformity* — albeit on the part of ordinary Catholics rather than the Catholic élite. For the unpropertied, a suitable inducement was not security of the family estate or admission to a profession, but might be a new suit of clothes suitable for wearing to church or even something as tenuous as the good favour of the landlord's agent.

If the Second Reformation was not primarily a conversionist effort, as evangelicals generally understand the term 'conversion', perhaps its evangelical character derives from what the evangelical historians call 'biblicism', for 'scripture schools' were central to the movement's efforts. A deeply affective devotion to the Bible is certainly another aspect of vital religion that the movement might have tried to instil in Catholics. Once again Whelan cautions us not to jump to conclusions. The movement, she writes, 'was supported by many who were not evangelical in the sense of basing all spiritual authority on a personal interpretation of the Bible'.[8] Indeed, the scripture schools associated with the Second Reformation of the 1820s were only part of a much larger movement on the part of élites in various parts of the North Atlantic world in the early nineteenth century to provide accessible education as a means of gaining some control over

4 Irene Whelan, *The Bible War in Ireland: The 'Second Reformation' and the Polarization of Protestant–Catholic Relations, 1800–1840* (Madison, 2005), 89

5 Stewart J. Brown, *The National Churches of England, Ireland, and Scotland, 1801–1846* (Oxford, 2001), 124

6 *Missionary Herald* (May 1847), 431

7 Thomas P. Power, '"A Weighty, Serious Business": The Conversion of Catholic Clergy to Anglicanism'; James Kelly, 'The Conversion Experience: The Case of Fr James O'Farrell, OP, 1785–7'; Michael Brown, 'Conversion Narratives in Eighteenth-Century Ireland', in Michael Brown, Charles Ivar McGrath, and T. P. Power, eds., *Converts and Conversion in Ireland, 1650–1850* (Dublin, 2005)

8 Whelan, *The Bible War in Ireland*, 139

9 George Browne, *The History of the British and Foreign Bible Society: From Its Institution in 1804, to the Close of Its Jubilee in 1854: Compiled at the Request of the Jubilee Committee*, 2 vols. (London, 1859), vol. 1, 3. Edward Kilsdonk, 'Religious Groups, Benevolent Organizations, and American Pluralism', at 'The American Religious Experience', http://are.as.wvu.edu/

10 M., 'The True Method of Studying the Bible', *Orthodox Presbyterian*, 3, 33 (1832), 320–22

The Society for Irish Church Missions to Roman Catholics was founded by the Rev. Alexander Dallas (1791–1869) in March 1849. Its purpose was 'The great work of the enlightenment of large bodies of Roman Catholics in Ireland, by the affectionate preaching of an outspoken Gospel in antagonism to Roman Dogma ...'. The map (detail shown) and large (89.9 x 117.1 cm) hand-coloured illustrations reproduced here were designed by the ICM for an exhibition on its activities *c.* 1858; two additional illustrations in this series are not reproduced here. National Library of Ireland.

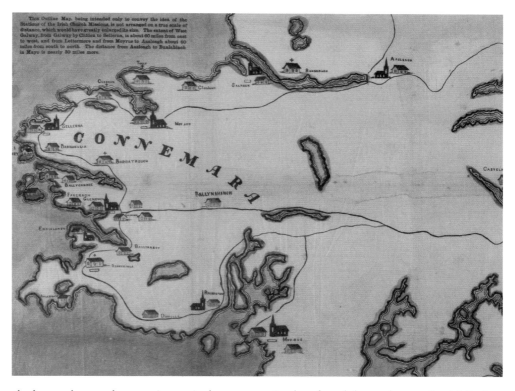

11 John Brown and H. Cooke, *The Self-Interpreting Bible, Containing the Old and New Testaments According to the Authorized Version; with an Introduction, Marginal References and Illustrations; a Summary of the Several Books; an Analysis of Each Chapter; a Paraphrase and Evangelical Reflections Upon the Most Important Passages; and Numerous Explanatory Notes. A New Edition in which the Text is More Fully Elucidated by Upwards of Eight Thousand Explanatory and Critical Notes, and Concluding Observations on Each Book, by the Rev. Henry Cooke* (New York, 1876)

the lower classes who were increasingly being empowered by the rise of democracy. Few advocates of such education could imagine it succeeding without a religious curricular component, and for Protestants, including Irish advocates of the Second Reformation, the usual formula for that component was 'the Bible without note or comment'. That shibboleth was not a basic principle of evangelicalism, or indeed of any other religious party. It originated as a convenient device to avoid contention among different Protestant denominations, and turned out to be especially unacceptable to Catholic clergy.[9] In 1832, the *Orthodox Presbyterian*, the semi-official voice of Irish Presbyterian evangelicalism led by Henry Cooke, ran a letter praising an edition of the Bible with 'marginal references' to parallel passages elsewhere in the Bible as an alternative to the use of commentaries.[10] At that moment in the political conflicts over the new national education system it was convenient to promote Bible helps that

simply referred the reader to other biblical material and could be represented as neither 'notes' nor 'comments'. However, later in his career, after the education issues of the 1820s and 1830s had been largely resolved, Cooke himself devoted considerable effort to producing a new edition of *Brown's Self-Interpreting Bible*, whose subtitle promised readers 'a Paraphrase and Evangelical Reflections Upon the Most Important Passages', which, upon inspection, look suspiciously like notes and comments.[11] 'Without note or comment' was a rhetorical weapon in the education wars, not a piece of pastoral advice intended for any evangelical minister's own flock.

Of course we have long known that the Second Reformation had at most a miniscule effect on the ratio between Catholics and Protestants in the Irish population. However, its effect on the *relations* between the Catholic and Protestant communities is more contested. The issue arises because

Irish Church Mission street preachers in an Irish town, *c.* 1858. National Library of Ireland.

in the first two decades of the century, the Catholic bishops and respectable Catholic laymen shared the view of many Protestants that the poor should be educated, and they co-operated in the efforts of government-subsidized philanthropic associations like the Kildare Place Society to establish primary schools. Whelan takes strong exception to Desmond Bowen's suggestion that there was a 'religious peace' in Ireland between 1800 and 1822, and perhaps Bowen was a bit too ready to read accommodation between élites as an indicator of wider reconciliation.[12] Nigel Yates is closer to the mark when he writes of 'a decision on the part of the *leadership* of the three main religious groups in Ireland, the Church of Ireland, the Roman Catholics, and the Presbyterians to develop a strategy of mutual toleration and cooperation'.[13] We should understand such developments as part of the quest by respectable Catholics to prove their *bona fides* and gain full membership within the new polity created in 1801. That process was cut short during

the 1820s when very different contenders for membership in the polity — the Catholic peasantry — were mobilized and then, in 1829, won for their respectable co-religionists the very prize that the Catholic élite had hoped to win for themselves. This sudden democratization of constitutional politics not only made the education question more urgent, but also terminated the polite interaction between Catholic and Protestant leaders that had developed in the first two decades of the century.

Yates overreaches, however, when he argues that inter-Church reconciliation was continuous for the period from 1770 to 1820 (though he does concede that the events of the 1790s 'threatened to destabilize this fragile framework of relative ecumenism'). Perhaps if he had studied the mountain of pamphlets generated by the so-called Dublin paper war of the 1780s, he would have understood that, prior to the focusing of élite minds by the events of 1798, any ecumenism was even more

12 Whelan, *The Bible War in Ireland*, 132 n. 27, 270. Desmond Bowen, *The Protestant Crusade in Ireland, 1800–70: A Study of Protestant-Catholic Relations between the Act of Union and Disestablishment* (Dublin, 1978), x

13 Nigel Yates, *The Religious Condition of Ireland, 1770–1850* (Oxford, 2006), xx; emphasis added

A confrontation between a Protestant preacher and a Catholic priest, *c.* 1858. National Library of Ireland.

14 Yates, *The Religious Condition of Ireland*, 62, 270–71

15 Alan Acheson, *A History of the Church of Ireland, 1691–2001* (Blackrock, 2002), 156–57

16 Whelan, *The Bible War in Ireland*, 157

17 Brown, *The National Churches of England, Ireland, and Scotland*, 98

18 Brown, *The National Churches of England, Ireland, and Scotland*, 93–167

fragile than he supposes. In any event, he apportions much of the blame for the tensions from 1820 to 1850 to 'the growth of Evangelical extremism within both the Church of Ireland and Irish Presbyterianism' and the 'proselytizing tendencies of the Irish Evangelicals' which, he argues, brought about the Second Reformation.[14] The launching of the Second Reformation is usually attributed to the charge that the new archbishop of Dublin, William Magee, delivered to his clergy in 1822. Magee was a high-churchman in an episcopate that had only one evangelical prelate (Archbishop Trench of Tuam) until the 1840s. Naturally evangelicals were prominent in trying to convert poverty-stricken Catholics in the 1820s and 1830s; the opulent livings in attractive locales were no doubt being awarded to clergymen whose theological leanings were more consistent with those of the bishops.[15] Whelan is reading the evangelical dominance of the Church of Ireland a generation later back into the 1820s when she describes Magee's initiative

as 'jumping on board and taking over the reins'.[16] Stewart J. Brown offers a more accurate formulation when he describes the Second Reformation as 'a movement that united the Irish Evangelical and High Church parties in a common cause'.[17]

Brown considers the movement within the framework of power relationships in the whole United Kingdom polity during the first half of the nineteenth century.[18] In that context, the primary dynamic was the growing willingness within the British governing classes to reconsider the confessional character of the state, not the growing evangelical component of the Irish state Church. Of the three Established Churches in the UK, the Church of Ireland was the most vulnerable to attacks on its constitutional status, and Magee's initiative is seen as an effort to protect the Church from such attacks by, at long last, making Protestants of the native Irish. For about a year, starting in the autumn of 1826, a spate of apparent conversions in Cavan and

Rev. Alexander Dallas preaches in Sellerna, Co Galway; hostile crowds in both foreground and background, *c.* 1858. National Library of Ireland

a few other localities allowed supporters of the movement to believe that they had made the strategic breakthrough that would vindicate the state Church's claim to be a national Church. By the end of 1827, however, reported conversions dwindled, and whatever opportunity there may have been to dispel British doubts of the Church of Ireland's ability to play its appointed Erastian role had been lost. The Irish Protestant confessional state soon suffered two vital blows: Catholic Emancipation in 1829, at the hands of a Tory government, and the Church Temporalities Act in 1833, at the hands of its Whig successors. So the Second Reformation can reasonably be seen as a sort of epiphenomenon resulting from the high politics of reform among the British governing classes. It was carried out on the ground mostly by individuals who called themselves 'evangelicals', but at the bidding of others who definitely were not evangelicals.

At one point Whelan very discerningly observes that Catholics came to define the term 'evangelicals' as 'all those who espoused converting Irish Catholics to the Protestant faith'.[19] Such a perception on the Catholics' part was understandable, but unfortunate, given that most evangelicals subsequently lost interest in converting the Catholics. For example, in the 1850s the Presbyterian General Assembly undertook a summertime programme of open-air preaching by Presbyterian ministers for the purpose of reaching lapsed members of their own communion. In 1857 a series of such open-air sermons provoked sectarian rioting in Belfast. Janice Holmes has convincingly maintained that to regard these events as merely an episode in the continuing battles over territorial dominance in Belfast is too simplistic.[20] As I have argued elsewhere, the assembly's larger open-air preaching campaign was not an effort either to convert or to annoy Catholics, even if that

19 Whelan, *The Bible War in Ireland*, 140
20 Janice Holmes, 'The Role of Open-Air Preaching in the Belfast Riots of 1857', *Proceedings of the Royal Irish Academy*, 102C (2002), 47–66

21 David W. Miller, 'Did Ulster Presbyterians have a Devotional Revolution?', in James H. Murphy, ed., *Evangelicals and Catholics in Nineteenth-Century Ireland* (Dublin, 2005), 47–50

22 David Hempton and Myrtle Hill, *Evangelical Protestantism in Ulster Society, 1740–1890* (London, 1992)

23 Andrew R. Holmes, *The Shaping of Ulster Presbyterian Belief and Practice, 1770–1840* (Oxford, 2006)

24 Holmes, *The Shaping of Ulster Presbyterian Belief and Practice*, 36–39

25 *Oxford English Dictionary*, sub 'revival' 3.b. David W. Miller, 'Religious Commotions in the Scottish Diaspora: A Transatlantic Perspective on "Evangelicalism" in a Mainline Denomination', in David A. Wilson and Mark G. Spencer, eds., *Ulster Presbyterians in the Atlantic World: Religion, Politics and Identity* (Dublin, 2006), 22–38

is how it was perceived; its priorities were reflected in the fact that the preaching occurred primarily in areas where there was a substantial Protestant, especially Presbyterian, population.[21]

Most of the insights offered by recent treatments of the Second Reformation fit tidily into the framework provided in David Hempton and Myrtle Hill's 1992 study of Ulster evangelicalism.[22] Unfortunately, Hempton and Hill failed to take sufficient account of the divergence between evangelicalisms of English and Scottish origin. The authors do acknowledge a difference between the religious experience of Presbyterians (53 per cent of Ulster Protestants in 1861) and that of Protestants of English descent, but their model of evangelicalism is resolutely English and methodistical. Happily, Andrew Holmes has now very ably addressed these shortcomings.[23] He traces the eighteenth-century origins of two strains of Presbyterian evangelicalism. The first of these strains, developed in the Popular Party of the Church of Scotland and the 'Old Light' party in the Synod of Ulster, sought 'to promote correct views of the person and work of Christ rather than a certain conversion experience'. The second, fashioned by the Seceders in both Scotland and Ulster, was more open to a 'gospel of grace' for 'everyone as individuals and without distinction' but only in the context of 'an orthodox understanding of preaching as a means of grace animated by the Holy Spirit rather than a rejection of the Reformed understanding of limited atonement'.[24] These two strains both contribute to the emergence in mainstream Irish Presbyterianism of a clear evangelical identity during the period between the 1829 schism, in which ministers opposed to subscription to the Calvinistic Westminster Confession of Faith were forced out of the General Synod, and the 1840 merger of the General and Seceding synods to form the General Assembly of the Presbyterian

Church in Ireland. The result was a variety of evangelicals who valued vital religion as much as did their Anglican counterparts, but for whom confessionalism — adherence to the Westminster standards — was as central as conversionism. By clarifying the distinctiveness of what Presbyterians meant by 'evangelical', Holmes has shed a flood of light on Irish Protestant history.

By the 1820s many Presbyterian clergy had reconciled in their own minds the tensions between vital religion and Calvinist orthodoxy. However, they were far from reconciled with the particular mechanism developed in America for making conversion happen: a meeting or series of meetings, often outdoors, in which one or more preachers used homiletic techniques calculated to induce highly emotional responses understood as symptoms of conversion and frequently accompanied by physical manifestations on the part of some converts. Contemporaries used various terms to describe such events — 'display of God's grace', 'surprising work of God', 'outpouring of the Holy Ghost' — but apparently the term revival was never used until the very end of the eighteenth century, except in phrases like 'revival of religion' (to distinguish it from, say, the revival of a stage play). However, around 1800 'revival' as an elliptical noun entered the language to describe such events on the American frontier; from that time forward it was possible to say, 'we need a revival', without any modifier and be understood to be making a statement about religion. It took a bit longer for the new usage to catch on in the British Isles; as late as 1818 an English traveller could write: 'The Methodists of Cincinnati are very zealous, and have what they call "a revival" in the country.'[25] But the next wave of American revivals, from 1824 to 1835, was widely enough reported that religious professionals in Ireland knew exactly what 'a revival' was.

During the 1820s and 1830s, Holmes finds evangelical ministers redefining 'revival' to denote the very process of 'reform and renewal of the church' that they themselves were promoting in those decades; especially the 1829 purging of ministers with Unitarian tendencies, growing interest in home and foreign mission initiatives, and the 1840 merger of the two synods.[26] During the next two decades, Holmes finds some clergy cautiously revising their concept of 'revival' to correspond more closely to the word's actual usage in general discourse. In 1859, however, ministers found themselves suddenly facing exactly such a revival as many of them had tried to define out of existence, complete with trances, convulsions and even stigmata. In the wake of that event, Holmes argues, the earlier clerical redefinition of 'revival', in terms of Church renewal and reform, became 'fragmented'. Ulster Presbyterianism came to rely on outside professional revivalists, such as Dwight Moody, to provide well-orchestrated events consistent with middle-class respectability. In the long run the Presbyterian Church, failing to engage effectively the populist revivalism of 1859, would confront a serious threat from 'non-denominational and lay evangelicalism' in the twentieth century.

Holmes's ability to convey the implications of these very important findings is constrained by his vague conceptualization of the relationship between official and popular religion. Throughout his book he refers to a 'symbiotic relationship' between clergy and laity without giving that metaphor analytic power. Yet he seems to view contemporary lay people and later scholars as simply wrong if they fail to toe the party line advocated by the clergy. For example, he disparages 'the *mistaken* assumption' by three different scholars 'that the basic characteristics of revival … are enthusiasm and an unrestrained populism, aptly expressed in sudden conversions and physical manifestations'.[27] Perhaps it would make more sense to recognize that in this instance the clergy had a new product called

Church reform and renewal. They tried to sell it to working-class lay people by labelling it 'revival', a very different product widely available and quite popular in America. Their potential customers — many of them from the poorest stratum of the Presbyterian population — simply insisted on the real thing. Faced with the sudden and massive import of a real American-style revival in 1859, the clergy moved quickly, and with some short-term success, to represent themselves as vendors of that product. In the long run, however, there was considerable leakage from Presbyterianism to Methodism and smaller evangelical sects.[28] The clergy chose to meet the demand by their middle-class clientele for respectable religion and thereby forfeit a significant market share of working-class customers.

Holmes illustrates this choice in a recent article demonstrating that although Irish Presbyterian clergy were slower than their Scottish counterparts to accept the findings of the higher critics, by the 1920s this new approach to scripture was no longer scandalous to most of them.[29] During that decade, the Irish Presbyterian Church experienced a 'fundamentalist-modernist conflict' comparable to the one that was causing turmoil in the (northern) Presbyterian Church, USA, and in both cases the 'modernist' side won (though perhaps not as decisively as appeared to be the case a generation ago). The relevance of this comparison is highlighted by the work of David Livingstone and Ronald Wells on 'Ulster-American religion'. Between about 1860 and 1940, they persuasively argue, Irish Presbyterianism had reoriented its relationships within the Presbyterian world; Princeton Theological Seminary replaced the Scottish universities as the lodestar of Irish Presbyterian theology.[30] That reorientation is important because the rise of fundamentalism in the United States has created a popular evangelical culture quite different from that of Britain and arguably not found in such strength in

26 Holmes, *The Shaping of Ulster Presbyterian Belief and Practice*, 49–50. Andrew R. Holmes, 'The Experience and Understanding of Religious Revival in Ulster Presbyterianism, *c.* 1800–1930', *Irish Historical Studies*, 34, 136 (2005), 361–85

27 Holmes, 'The Experience and Understanding of Religious Revival in Ulster Presbyterianism', 375; emphasis added

28 David W. Miller, 'Did Ulster Presbyterians have a Devotional Revolution?', in Murphy, *Evangelicals and Catholics*, 38–54

29 Andrew Holmes, 'Biblical Authority and the Impact of Higher Criticism in Irish Presbyterianism, *ca.* 1850–1930', *Church History*, 75, 2 (2006), 343–73

30 David N. Livingstone and Ronald A. Wells, *Ulster-American Religion: Episodes in the History of a Cultural Connection* (Notre Dame, 1999)

31 George Marsden, 'Fundamentalism as an American Phenomenon: A Comparison with English Evangelicalism', *Church History*, 46, 2 (1977), 215–32

any other Protestant society today, *except*, as the distinguished historian of American evangelicalism George Marsden has observed, in Northern Ireland.[31]

Over the past generation, historians of Irish Catholicism have had the good fortune to be able to pose and offer answers to a question prompted by a striking contemporary development: If the Catholic Ireland remembered by Irish adults is saying 'Goodbye,' when did it say 'Hello'? The discovery that less than 50 per cent of Irish Catholics ordinarily attended mass on Sunday during the 1830s, together with research on various devotional innovations, have made it plain that that 'Hello' occurred sometime in the latter half of the nineteenth century. The implications of such research were resisted for a time by Catholic denominational historians with a stake in the social construction of a timeless isle of saints, forever models of piety, but the historical profession now works with a fundamentally new paradigm for understanding Irish Catholicism. Holmes, Livingstone and Wells are dancing around a problem that has similar potential to recast our thinking on the history of Irish Protestantism. That problem is how and why the popular religious culture that has sustained the career of Ian Paisley came into being. To solve that problem, historians must adopt a trans-Atlantic perspective. They must also move beyond the theological and institutional history that dominates both of these books and, for example, treat 'non-denominational and lay evangelicalism' (that is, gospel halls and similar phenomena) not as mistakes, but as serious objects of study. ■

Books considered in this essay:

Converts and Conversion in Ireland, 1650–1850
Edited by Michael Brown, Charles Ivar McGrath, and T. P. Power
Dublin: Four Courts Press, 2005
Pages 320. ISBN 1-85182-810-9

The National Churches of England, Ireland, and Scotland, 1801–1846
Stewart J. Brown
Oxford: Oxford University Press, 2001
xi + 459 pages. ISBN 0-19-924235-6

Anglican Evangelicals: Protestant Secessions from the Via Media, c. 1800–1850
Grayson Carter
Oxford: Oxford University Press, 2001
xv + 470 pages. ISBN 0-19-827008-9

The Shaping of Ulster Presbyterian Belief and Practice, 1770–1840
Andrew R. Holmes
Oxford: Oxford University Press, 2006
xv + 374 pages. ISBN 0-19-928865-8

Ulster-American Religion: Episodes in the History of a Cultural Connection
David N. Livingstone and Ronald A. Wells
Notre Dame: University of Notre Dame Press, 1999
x + 201 pages. ISBN 0-268-04304-3

The Bible War in Ireland: The 'Second Reformation' and the Polarization of Protestant–Catholic Relations, 1800–1840
Irene Whelan
Madison: University of Wisconsin Press, 2005
xx + 347 pages. ISBN 0-299-21550-4

The Religious Condition of Ireland, 1770–1850
Nigel Yates
Oxford: Oxford University Press, 2006
xxiv + 401 pages. ISBN 0-19-924238-0

Revisiting the City, Revising Nationalism

Michael Rubenstein

Postcolonial Dublin: Imperial Legacies and the Built Environment
Andrew Kincaid
Minneapolis: University of Minnesota Press, 2006. 296 pages. ISBN 0-8166-4345-8

There's a famous joke in the 'Aeolus' episode in *Ulysses*, where Professor MacHugh cracks wise at the plebeian pragmatism of the old Roman Empire: 'It is meet to be here,' he has his Romans announce upon planting their flag in their newly conquered territory, 'let us construct a watercloset.'

Let's pass over for the moment the comical reduction of monumental Roman aqueducts and baths to a humble toilet. This is not what we imagine the Celt might announce in a similar situation. The Celts might very likely announce the having of a few drinks to fête their arrival before they ever thought of building a toilet, a project whose urgency might, *might*, finally be felt only after the having of a few drinks. Assbackwards, this is, from the Roman point of view: *the* Arnoldian difference between the races, the conquerors and the conquered. It is, in any case, hard to envisage a toilet designed and constructed by Matthew Arnold's Celtic Imagination, except to say abstractly that it would probably be less functional than it would be funny (or witty, if a toilet can be called witty), a romantic whimsy of a toilet, not built to last except in the music of its scatological poetry, in the memory of the people, in folktale and ballad all across the land, etcetera. But as it happens, MacHugh makes his joke neither from the public house nor the watercloset, but from a printer's office. And this is his point: the Roman Empire, and by extension the British Empire, are stupidly interested in infrastructure at the expense of culture, in the pragmatics of building everyday life instead of the transcendent experience of literature and the arts. The latter are the domain of the Celt, his relegated sphere of excellence, and though the entire distinction may be born of the colonial relationship — an arbitrary division of labour imposed by British cultural élites through the work of the stereotype — MacHugh comically turns it into a point of Irish pride.

MacHugh's author might laugh along with him, but he would not agree at all with the joke's import. Joyce's well-known boast, that if Dublin were ever destroyed, it could be rebuilt from the pages of his works, shows how little he respected the division between fact and fancy. He was interested in the built environment, in itself and as a crucial aspect of his own literary vision. *Ulysses* did not so much attempt to transcend Dublin as it attempted to transcribe it, to remember it, memorialize it, memorize it, mesmerize it, all at once. Joyce's literary map of Dublin makes a mockery of Arnold's binary between the industrious Saxon and the poetic Celt, because it collapses the distinction between textual building and the built environment, a kind of Borgesian conundrum that de-emphasizes the boundary between reality and representation: an attempted three-

O'Connell Street, Dublin, *c.* 1950. Photograph: George Pickow/Three Lions/Getty Images.

dimensional, one-to-one scaled map of the city, which, trying to represent it wholly, instead swallows it whole. In 1916 large parts of Dublin were destroyed, mostly by British bombardment. Joyce's Dublin had already outlasted parts of 'real' Dublin even before *Ulysses* was published. And soon after, even more of the city was destroyed in the Civil War. But the point is that in *Ulysses* Joyce revalued the built environment of the city, placed it at the very centre of his literary work. I say this because Andrew Kincaid claims that so much of the critical energy of Irish Studies goes into Irish literature that, say, urban planning and the built environment go criminally understudied:

> The field of Irish Studies has long been dominated by a literary paradigm … one of the pitfalls that literary approaches to Dublin has led us into is that the textual city has come to take on a greater degree of reality and importance than the physical city … A city is more than language, more than the pages of a book. My work seeks to bring the material city back into focus.[1]

Kincaid goes on to show that literary critics provided the basic paradigm for Irish Studies. He is also a professor of English, so to read him arguing against a literary paradigm is startling. His position is difficult, it seems to me, but it is backed up by other critics outside literary studies. Patrick Carroll-Burke, a sociologist at the University of California, Davis, has made a similar plea. 'Books have been written,' he charges, 'on "Representing Ireland", "Writing Ireland", and "Inventing Ireland", but in every case the focus has been literary.' From an interdisciplinary perspective, book titles like these seem to beg the question of whether their authors think 'Ireland' as such is wholly a literary 'invention', like, say, Wilde's 'Japan' in *The Decay of Lying* — 'In fact the whole of Japan is a pure invention'. It leaves practically untouched the question of 'invention' as a techno-

scientific domain of building, architecture, law, the state, public services, and all that physically and institutionally constructs the fabric of everyday life. The reasons for this neglect of what Carroll-Burke calls the 'engineering cultures' of the state have partly to do with Irish shame, since so much of Ireland's architecture was built by Ireland's erstwhile British masters, and because so much of it simply passed over into the Free State's jurisdiction in 1922 without — or with only symbolic — modification. As a matter of fact, there is at least one example of an Irish toilet — not so much a toilet of Irish design as one designed for the Irish, though whether it was ever constructed or not is unclear. In 1855 John Grey presented the Royal Dublin Society with a design for a more efficient, less private version of the standard apparatus for use in Irish workhouses. Grey designed his toilet to seat four people at a time, and integrated a 'self-acting flusher', because he did not believe 'that domestics could be trusted to operate the device.' That shame would last a long time. 'Only in the past couple of decades,' says Carroll-Burke, 'has Ireland forgotten the past sufficiently to rediscover and to embrace its engineering culture.'[2]

Kincaid wants, now, to account for some aspects of Ireland's engineering culture through a focus on Irish architecture in Dublin from the late nineteenth century to the present. Beginning from the premise that British colonialism in Ireland was characterized by a general tendency to urbanization, Kincaid concentrates on Ireland's capital city to observe how the nation's architectural projects embodied the social ideas and ideals of the empowered. In the mid-nineteenth century, a paradigm shifted in civic planning. The city stopped being a fortress, and became a modern metropolis. Instead of thinking about how to protect themselves by force, urban élites began to think about the 'public good' — both as a form of social control and of social improvement — as the most important consideration in urban planning, and

1 Andrew Kincaid, *Postcolonial Dublin: Imperial Legacies and the Built Environment* (Minneapolis, 2006), xiv–xv

2 Patrick Carroll-Burke, 'Material Designs: Engineering Cultures and Engineering States — Ireland 1650–1900', *Theory and Society*, 31 (2002), 25–114, 97, 103, 106

Beat Klein and Hendrikje
Kühne
Property
1998
newsprint on card,
dimensions vary
Irish Museum of Modern Art

3   Kincaid, *Postcolonial Dublin*, xxix
4   Kincaid, *Postcolonial Dublin*, 80, 83

began to form 'trusts' to implement their schemes and improvements. 'Public Health' and 'Town Planning' became the new buzzwords. In 1890 the Guinness Trust was formed and started on the building of six hundred dwellings for the poor in the centre of Dublin, in order, as the trust's founder put it, to ameliorate 'the condition of the poorer of the working classes'.[3] But the new discourses of town planning and public health could not quell the revolutionary feeling in Ireland, and in the early twentieth century the very buildings that represented improvement, progress and rationality — the General Post Office, the Custom House, and the Four Courts, among them — were occupied, razed, or burned, and generally heavily contested as power changed hands.

This is the preamble to Kincaid's main argument, which is a revision of the revisionists' disdain for Irish nationalism. We get a very different picture of the Free State when we look at town planning instead of, say, censorship. The first decade of the Free State's existence saw the construction of four thousand new dwellings. Kincaid points out: 'This number is not as insignificant as contemporary commentators would have us believe; it represents a quarter of all the buildings that had ever before been built by Dublin Corporation.' Slum clearance in Dublin was one of the state's main priorities, both to improve the lives of the slums' inhabitants and to guard against social unrest. In 1924 W. T. Cosgrave made the stakes clear: 'no populace housed as so many of the people of Dublin are, can be good citizens, or loyal and devoted subjects of the State, no matter what the State may be'.[4] The solution was suburbanization, which in those years was carried out on a small scale. Cosgrave's government initiated the Shannon Scheme in 1925, which dammed the country's largest river to create a hydro-electric power station. When the station opened in 1929 it produced — though only for a short time, until demand caught up with supply — three times the amount of electricity then consumed in all of Ireland. The scheme effectively relocated the sources of electrical power in Dublin from local coal-fired plants to the mythical West, nationalizing Dublin's power, reducing the dependence on British coal, and setting the stage for wholesale rural electrification in the decades to follow. In 1932 Eamon de Valera's Housing Act attempted to raise the standard of accommodation. The Newfoundland Street Scheme was particularly 'ambitious in its reach and hopeful in its aims ... providing each new apartment with hot and cold water and electric light'. House-building stepped up considerably after Fianna Fáil's victory in 1932, from 2,000 a year between 1923 and 1931 to 12,000 a year during de Valera's tenure.

All these facts add up to a real revelation about the Free State: it did more, much more, to win consent and to service the population than has been previously asserted by most critics. As Kincaid puts it: 'The vast majority of contemporary commentators on postcolonial Ireland have got it wrong. Fresh, creative, and energetic discussions about the legacy and future of urbanism were taking place in Ireland during the 1920s and 30s.'[5] His point is well taken; the stereotype of the censorious, protectionist, narrowly nationalist Free State has prevented the acknowledgement, and therefore the critical analysis, of its substantial achievements in town planning — achievements that effectively spatialized a curious mixture of nationalist ideology, international architectural theories, and technological transformation.

In the 1950s, 1960s, and 1970s, the Republic slowly awoke from its pipe dream of economic self-sufficiency; nationalism lost some of its grip and Keynesian common sense won the day. Or so the revisionist story goes. Kincaid shows a confluence between the discourse of urban planning, the new architectural projects that emerged from it, and the emergent popularity of historical revisionism amongst the Irish intelligentsia. In 1961 Ireland applied for membership in the European community; in 1962 'television became nationally available'; and in 1966, fifty years after the revolution, Ireland built its first truly modern residential housing project in Dublin. Ballymun was made up of seven fifteen-storey buildings and, like most such projects in cities like London and New York, was a massive social failure. That version of the modernist experiment proved untenable, and the country, with Sean Lemass at the helm, veered away from 'social investment' in things like housing and hospitals towards 'productive investment' in things like factories and offices. Housing, once the single most salient issue for the Free State — in so far as it made a population of 'devoted subjects of the state' possible — was given up as an urban planning priority, shoved aside by new mandates for office parks, financial complexes, and malls, all designed to encourage industry and lure foreign investment:

> In 1960, Ireland had only one large modern office block — Michael Scott's Busáras. By the mid-1970s, there were over three hundred, providing over ten million square feet of bureaucratic space to a still shabby and quite provincial city, a city still in the process of constructing its own middle class.[6]

Among these new urban monoliths was the Electricity Supply Board's new headquarters in Fitzwilliam Street, whose construction in 1963 required razing 'the longest complete Georgian streetscape in Europe'. Ireland's first glass-façaded skyscraper, the rebuilt Liberty Hall headquarters of the Irish Transport and General Workers' Union, signified 'the arrival of labor as a neo-corporate player willing to compromise with the free-trade tendencies of the state'.[7] All this — and Kincaid offers many more examples — signified, in the realm of the built environment, a shift from cultural nationalism to economic nationalism, from an identification with the colonial world to an identification with the European economic core: an ideological shift — almost on the order of a reversal — in which the contours of historical revisionism were manifest in the streets, just as they were gaining popular momentum in scholarship.

In his fourth and final chapter, Kincaid examines the Dublin cityscape in the era of the Celtic Tiger. If in the Lemass years Ireland renounced nationalism in favour of modernization, in the 1990s nationalism was declawed, repackaged and auctioned off to the tourists. Meanwhile, Dublin was becoming a financial hub and a world city. Kincaid focuses on a few central sites and their transformations: the gentrification of Temple Bar, the construction in 1991

5 Kincaid, *Postcolonial Dublin*, 77, 93
6 Kincaid, *Postcolonial Dublin*, 119, 145
7 Kincaid, *Postcolonial Dublin*, 152, 156

8   Kincaid, *Postcolonial Dublin*, 224

of the International Financial Services Centre, and Rowan Gillespie's bronze sculptural monument to the Great Famine, which has stood since 1997 at the entry to the above-mentioned IFSC. He observes Dublin's built environment embroiled in a furious dialectic of remembering and forgetting. The IFSC has to install netting to protect its façade from the rocks thrown by denizens of the surrounding working-class neighbourhood, and so we come full circle: from the pre-'urban planning' fortress Dublin of the nineteenth century to the high-tech securitized cities of the twenty-first. The Famine monument is a bad sign that forgetting is winning the day, as corporate interests pose as custodians of collective memory. And so finally, Kincaid turns to literary analysis of a burgeoning genre, the Dublin memoir, to make a provocative claim: 'an altered and altering landscape necessitates its own literary form, the urban memoir', a form that is 'rooted in the physical environment'.[8]

Despite that, strange to say, Kincaid's readings of the memoirs — very brief, in any case — are perhaps the least compelling aspect of his book. And I worry about the loose ends left in the last chapter concerning the 'disappearance' of nationalism. While Kincaid cites the 1998 revision of the Irish Constitution — which renounces the Republic's absolute claim to the six counties of the North — as evidence of nationalism's retreat, the more recent debates over whether to revoke the constitutional guarantee to Irish citizenship — granted to any child born on Irish soil — make it clear that nationalism may not stay down much longer. Of course these debates may not have occurred by the time Kincaid's book went to press, but it is also true that Ireland's recent waves of immigration are conspicuously absent from the Celtic Tiger chapter. The recent popularity of the Dublin memoir may be as much about a growing Irish xenophobia — about a nostalgic, racialized geography — as it is about the new built environment. And there is evidence from all over the globe that nationalism can and does come back from the dead, often in its ugliest incarnations.

The real argumentative strength of Kincaid's work lies in the emphasis on the built environment. The book is a goldmine of research into some of the more important and controversial construction projects undertaken since Ireland became a nation-state in 1922. Deliberately discarding the literary paradigm allows him to speculate on what Irish history would look like if we took urban planning and state planning to be the measure of the state's success or failure. And it does look different; the state comes out looking a little better than it did before. Further, *Postcolonial Dublin* demonstrates that the cultural phenomenon calling itself 'revisionism' was anticipated, if only minutely and only in its popular manifestation, by urban planning discourse and by urban development projects. We are left with a rare vantage point from which to see how Dublin's urban environment impressed the ideas it embodied on the intellectual climate of the time. It becomes possible, that is, to see revisionism as an effect of urban planning projects, rather than seeing it as the cause of reforms in urban planning. Although such a reversal of perspective is probably no more accurate that its mirror image, it is a perspective that would be very hard to see from within the literary paradigm. Kincaid's thesis makes for an interesting and timely corrective to the dominant paradigm in Irish Studies. He launches a promising beginning to the pressing work of investigating the multiple aspects of Ireland's engineering cultures, too long neglected. ■

Nothin' to do but walk up and down?

Matthew Kelly

The Irish Policeman, 1822–1922: A Life
Elizabeth Malcolm
Dublin: Four Courts Press, 2006. 272 pages. ISBN 1-85182-920-2

'Nothin' to do but walk up and down,' continued Joe Sproul, recalling his early dreams. 'Your boots shinin' an' the heels soundin' on the curb-stone. Pintin' your baton to a dung-heap an' saying "Take that out o' that," and findin' it gone when you'd come again. Comin' to a row when 'twould be over, an' runnin' the fellow in that you'd know 'ud go quiet. Keepin' your cap on in the courthouse, and calling "Silence" whenever you'd like. Standin' at the corner with a little varnished cane in your hand admired by the young women, gentle an' simple; goin' occasionally to a dance in colored clothes, an' givin' sixpence to the fiddler.'

So complained Constable Sproul in the Fenian Charles Kickham's novel *For the Old Land: A Tale of Twenty Years Ago …* (1886). Sproul had expected much more. His mother's cousin, the head constable, had promised his father that if his son joined the Royal Irish Constabulary he would lead a 'gentleman's' life. Instead, we come upon him driving three pigs out of a ploughed field, his partner on the beat, Acting-Constable Finucane, looking down 'at his high-heeled stylish boots, plastered all over with clay and mud'. Sproul's predicament, gently lampooned by Kickham, parallels many of the themes of Elizabeth Malcolm's elegantly written collective biography of RIC men over their force's century-long existence.

Malcolm's portrait makes clear that chasing pigs out of a field was at odds with the social aspirations that propelled young Irish men into the force, but as Sproul's complaints suggest, the constable's social status was unstable. One moment an admired figure in the neighbourhood, the next the orderly in the courtroom, or chasing pigs. Numerically Catholics dominated the force, comprising some 69 per cent of the total in the 1840s and 79 per cent in the 1900s, and for a healthy, well-built, intelligent son of an Irish farmer, a career in the RIC was an attractive proposition. It guaranteed accommodation, a reliable income and, increasingly, a decent pension, a very valuable commodity. Joining the RIC also kept these men and their families in Ireland, though service did demand a form of internal migration. With the exception of Belfast, County Antrim, where different rules pertained, no man was allowed to serve in his home county, and on marriage, he, along with his wife, was liable to be transferred again. Marriage itself was judged a privilege rather than a right, and the restrictions imposed on their right to marry, besides pension rights and questions regarding pay, were among the Irish policeman's perennial complaints.

Dublin Metropolitan Police constable, Eden Quay, Dublin, *c.* 1900. Photograph: J. J. Clarke/National Library of Ireland.

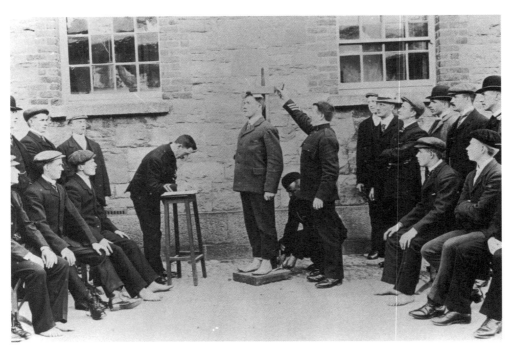

Measuring recruits, the Depot, Phoenix Park, Dublin, *c.* 1900. Photograph: courtesy of Jim Herlihy.

Protestants, however, dominated the officer class, accounting for around two-thirds of the cohort, and they were fiercely protective of the privileges associated with their status. In particular, they resisted promotion from the ranks and Malcolm has found in the social politics of the RIC a further example of the way class sensibilities and religious identities often overlapped in nineteenth-century Ireland. Officers, whose world was that of the Big House and the hunt, did not wish to be demeaned by the idea that their position could be achieved through hard work and long service; for them, their professional rank was a mark of gentility. And though promotion from the rank and file became more common as the professional expectations of high-flying career policemen advanced and as the culture of the force became less military and more civilian, entry into the officer class did not see former constables welcomed into the county sets. Instead, they found themselves socially isolated, ostracized by their professional equals but social superiors, and newly distanced from their old comrades.

Sproul's complaint that the duties of the policeman were dull, largely confined to the beat, contained a great deal of truth. Rural police duties were monotonous and often arduous, sometimes severely affecting the policeman's health. Tramping across fields in all weathers hoping to catch illegal distillers at work or lying in ditches to keep watch for local ne'er-do-wells, added little to the appeal of the beat. In effect, policemen were always on duty and, if not physically incapacitated, they were expected to remain available for emergency service even after retirement. During their professional lives, they generally lived in cramped conditions in barracks, which were usually converted townhouses, and their families had to adhere to strict rules of behaviour, which wives found highly intrusive. To marry an RIC man was to accept the institutionalization of much of your family life. Though policemen were rarely permitted to dress other than in their dark and sombre uniforms, during their occasional moments of levity, such as at a dance, there were social obligations — tipping the fiddler, perhaps — which many policemen could ill-afford.

RIC recruits in class, the Depot, Phoenix Park, Dublin, *c.* 1900. Photograph: courtesy of Jim Herlihy.

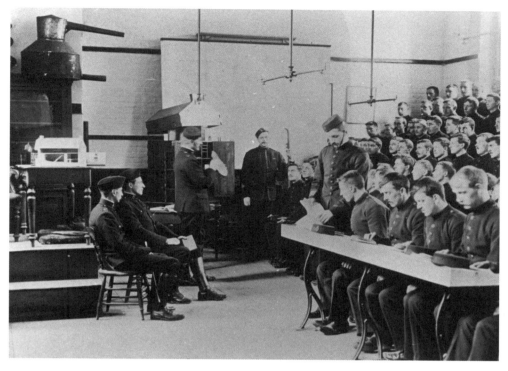

When not in the company of his colleagues, levity did not always come easily to the RIC man. The constables and their officers were put through a rigorous — though separate — training régime that moulded, as one policeman put it, 'the country boy into a stern, suspicious policeman'. This demeanour was an essential part of the RIC man's armour, distancing him from the members of the community in his care. It was the product of the military-style atmosphere and regulations that governed his compulsory six months' training at the Depot in the Phoenix Park, Dublin. The men slept in barracks, sixteen to a room; attended lessons in reading, writing and accounting, improving what was in theory already good literacy and numeracy; and, above all, they were instructed in drill, a constant feature of life at the Depot. Malcolm points out the significance of the patent leather stock, the first piece of uniform all new recruits were expected to acquire: 3.5 inches wide, this very stiff and hard leather collar was fastened round the

neck with a buckle and strap. The RIC man's head was always to be held aloft, a symbol of his physical, mental and moral superiority. Significant as this Foucauldian disciplining of the body was, also important was the social whirl of the Depot. As Malcolm notes, the Depot was a 'total institution', and in providing the recruits their every need (except, perhaps, sex), it came to determine what those needs were.

The camaraderie and caste loyalty the Depot nurtured sustained many policemen through their years of service and into retirement. This powerful sense of loyalty to their comrades and the force as a whole, Malcolm persuasively argues, did not necessarily coincide with shared political identities. Holding moderate unionist or nationalist views was thought compatible with service in the RIC, though, with the predictable exception of the Freemasons, membership of any political organization was strictly forbidden. In marked contrast to its successor organization in Northern

Ireland (the Royal Ulster Constabulary), the RIC regarded the Orange Order with particular suspicion. Conversely, Malcolm observes that unionists viewed the RIC with suspicion, regarding it as a Trojan horse for the advancement of Irish Catholics at the behest of an increasingly green Dublin Castle: for northern Unionists in particular, it intimated what a Home Rule Ireland would be like, a place in which Dublin's tentacles would increasingly penetrate society and culture.

As Sproul implied, there were times when the exercise of state power seemed superfluous, the exercise of bureaucratic niceties of little practical value. Few of the certainties of the Dublin parade ground were to be found in provincial Ireland and the real tasks of policing were learnt on the job. Moreover, attempts to exercise that authority often

ran the danger of revealing the RIC's vulnerability. Although there was one policeman for every 791 people in Ireland in 1842, as opposed to only one for every 1,611 in England, when faced with faction fights or mass protests, the few police officers stationed in any single country district were often little more than bystanders dependent on army reinforcements, if and when they were deployed.

Day-to-day, the RIC's tasks rarely concerned the political events familiar from the histories of nationalist, agrarian, or Orange agitations, and when not upholding the law and endeavouring to maintain order, they functioned more generally as an 'all-purpose government agency', arguably becoming the most significant state institution in nineteenth-century Ireland. With a command structure centralized at Dublin Castle and

Police attending at the eviction of Michael Connell, Moyasta, Co. Clare, 1888. Photograph: National Library of Ireland, Lawrence Collection (Royal).

EVICTION SCENE. 1767. W.L.

Items from the Museum of Crime in the Depot, Phoenix Park, Dublin, *c.* 1900. Photograph: courtesy of Jim Herlihy.

under the control of the chief secretary and the lord lieutenant, Irish policing was of a different hue to that of England and Wales, where it came under the control of partially democratic local government. As Malcolm observes, these differences are often seen as evidence of the colonial nature of the Irish government and many historians of British policing throughout the Empire have argued that the RIC provided a pioneering model. Following Friedrich Engels, Malcolm suggests another model, noting that, as an armed force controlled by central government, the RIC might be more helpfully compared to continental police forces. Rather than showing evidence of a British genius for oppressive innovation, the government, in creating the RIC, was aping continental practices long held to be necessary by centralizing states that could not rely on the loyalty of their citizens. Indeed, in the early 1880s when the awkwardly named Crime Branch Special was established within the RIC to combat advanced nationalist conspiracies like the Invincibles, British critics feared it would open the doors to 'continental abuses', creating an unaccountable,

invisible force that would do the bidding of unscrupulous political masters. Similar arguments were made at the time of the Dublin Police Act (1786) and when Robert Peel guided his Peace Preservation (Ireland) Act (1814), and the Constabulary (Ireland) Act (1822) through parliament: such forces were thought to be at odds with English ideas of liberty.

Nonetheless, the development of the RIC highlighted the extent to which the cultural and social ties, the systems of deference, which sustained the peculiar British system of government elsewhere in the Union, were too weak to be a source of stability in Ireland. The Irish élites did not have the authority to maintain peace and stability along the localized lines that pertained in England, Wales and Scotland, a system that, according to an idealized Tory discourse, had created a Britain that did not need to be governed. Irish differences, according to the same discourse, required a statist solution — that is, centralized policing under the direct control of the government. The command structures of the RIC — and

Dublin Castle more generally — reflected the lack of faith Westminster had in the Irish gentry as much as it did the strength of Irish Catholic disaffection.

Conscious of the failings of the Irish élite, Dublin Castle developed an almost paranoid appetite for information about what was going on in provincial Ireland. The RIC came to be depended upon as the government's eyes and ears, providing, county by county, monthly reports on local events, the economy and agricultural prospects. These reports were highly repetitive and formulaic, and although they contain valuable information on political activity of all hues, the bulk of this vast corpus of material is distinctly mundane, as any government official would have been pleased to note. It seems likely that these police reports had a sobering effect on government, often counteracting, for example, the impression of frenetic nationalist activity conveyed by the nationalist press. Indeed, successive chief secretaries, when facing tough questioning in the House of Commons, relied on the RIC to provide the evidence needed to combat lurid questions regarding the state of Ireland, questions that were often of an anti-Irish or sectarian bent. Like any evidence, police records need careful handling, but it should be borne in mind, when faced with the uneventfulness of much Irish policing, that no government agency, chasing finite resources, would intentionally play down the significance of its role.

Under the Union, Ireland's lot was not a happy one and Malcolm's analysis of moments of tension within the force provide a new lens on the difficulties faced by those attempting to govern Ireland. In each of the flashpoints she identifies, RIC discontent coincided with political unrest. The late 1860s saw a falling off in rates of recruitment, increased resignations, and a detectable restlessness in the force. 'Fenian fever' had placed added burdens on the police and constables felt they were not being adequately rewarded for their work during this period of rising prosperity and prices. Similar grievances led to the Limerick 'mutiny' of 1882, which Malcolm rightly prefers to call an 'agitation'. Again, discontent followed a period of sustained political unrest, which had seen policemen form the front line in the conflict between landlord and tenant, forcing them into the unenviable position as the 'body-servants of privilege and property'. Petitioning-RIC men attracted a great deal of sympathy, not least because their demands primarily concerned working conditions and pensions, revealing their desire for a lifestyle less confined by the regulations and routine of the barracks. The chief secretary's insistence that 'submission should precede redress' was met and the 1880s saw a gradual liberalization of the RIC régime and improvement in pay and pension rights. Similar unrest surfaced in Belfast in early 1907, where the cost of living was high and the job particularly tough. Although Belfast RIC men enjoyed certain privileges, they were aggrieved that their working conditions did not meet the higher standards that were the norm for the men of the Dublin Metropolitan Police, a separate force. Although they couched their demands in the language of loyalty, their claims were dismissed, the ringleaders sacked, and many men were transferred out of the city. Each of these flashpoints, Malcolm argues, was remarkable less for its rebellious character than for the loyalty to the service that it revealed. Profoundly discontented policemen often chose to leave both the force and the country, choosing emigration over a sustained conflict with their superiors or the government.

How, then, can the RIC man be classified? Was he the servant of the government, of the people, or of an oppressive colonial régime? In Malcolm's sympathetic collective portrait he was something of all three. Malcolm appears neither to subscribe to Albert Memmi's view, which is quoted, that policemen in colonial situations form a category of the colonized which attempts to escape from its political and social oppression by adopting the ideology of the colonizer, nor to wholly accept the pertinence of Franz Fanon's view, also quoted, that in 'colonial countries the agents of the government speak the language of pure force'. What is clear is that Malcolm rejects P. S. O'Hegarty's demonization of the RIC as a 'Janissary force' comprised of men who 'bullied, terrorized, and when ordered, murdered their own people without compunction for nearly a hundred years'.

The notion that the men of the force were unchanging agents of government tyranny, the quislings of the British state in Ireland, must be modified. Naturally enough, many Catholics were grateful for the protection the force, as an agent of the law, accorded, and it is not difficult to imagine, had the Home Rule campaign succeeded, the RIC evolving into a force broadly acceptable to the majority of Irish Catholics. By contrast, to take but one example, during the 1890s when Protestant evangelists took to preaching in southern Irish towns, unionist opinion was highly critical of the RIC for moving the preachers on, rather than protecting their freedom of speech as British subjects. At such moments the RIC were caught between two highly vocal populations, each acutely conscious of their rights and dignity: a place differently liminal to that between the British state and the Irish people. For although nationalist polemic identified Dublin Castle as the quintessential symbol of oppressive government in Ireland, the RIC only featured in such discourse during periods of agrarian agitation or distress. That is, of course, until the force became a target during the Irish War of Independence (1919–21), a watershed in the force's history. And although the RIC's record before the revolution should not be sanitized, popular nationalist perceptions

of the force were transformed by the logic of the revolutionary war waged by the IRA, which identified the agents of the British state as their enemy; 600 RIC men died as a direct result of the conflict.

This logic has become a mainstay of cinematic portrayals of the conflict, as in Ken Loach's highly problematic *The Wind that Shakes the Barley* (2006). Loach has RIC men warned that continued service in the pay of the British will make them a legitimate target. With equal polemical effect, Peter Hart set the tone of his brilliant but contentious *The IRA and Its Enemies* (1998) by opening with a detailed description of the IRA's assassination of an RIC man, Sergeant O'Donoghue. Sympathetically portrayed by Hart as a family man and pillar of his community, O'Donoghue's fate demonstrates how revolutionary logic transformed the RIC man from being a person who could be judged by the community on the basis of his individual merit, to a symbol. The same shift in the categorization of the RIC is traced in Sebastian Barry's novel *The Whereabouts of Eneas McNulty* (1998). Barry tells of the fate of the innocent fool of the novel's title who returns from service in the British army in 1918 and in exchanging his army uniform for an RIC uniform fails to recognize the transformation that has taken place in Ireland. The Sligo IRA forbids him from setting foot in Ireland ever again, an injunction they sustain throughout McNulty's life, and so his wanderings begin. Few RIC men suffered so severely, but as Malcolm shows in this fine study, for the great majority of RIC men who did survive the revolutionary conflict, service in the RIC left a very mixed legacy. For Catholic families, often with a cross-generational history of service in various police forces, having had a brother, a father or a grandfather in the RIC could be at once a dirty secret and a source of pride. ∎

Consumption and Identity

Mary P. Corcoran

The Irish in Us: Irishness, Performativity, and Popular Culture
Edited by Diane Negra
Durham and London: Duke University Press, 2006. 392 pages. ISBN 0-8223-3728-2

1   For a more sociologically grounded account of how a changing Ireland brings with it new risks but also new opportunities, see M. P. Corcoran and M. Peillon, eds., *Uncertain Ireland* (Dublin, 2006).

2   David McWilliams, *The Pope's Children: Ireland's New Elite* (Dublin, 2005). See also *In Search of the Pope's Children*, a three-part series made by RTÉ Television, broadcast in November 2006.

There are at least two explanations that can be advanced for the current preoccupation with Irishness. Since the turn of the twenty-first century, the Irish demographic landscape has changed beyond recognition. Ten per cent of the Irish population is now foreign-born, and new immigrant communities are making not just the cities but also country towns and villages their home. The integration of these groups into Irish society has moved issues of identity centre stage. In 2004, the question of who is Irish (and more crucially, who is not) lay at the heart of the referendum on citizenship and the subsequent amendment of the Irish Constitution. Second, there is a widespread feeling that economic gains have come at the expense of a 'traditional' Irish value system. This has engendered a kind of existential anxiety among social and cultural commentators. For example, the ombudsman, Emily O'Reilly, received extensive coverage in November 2004 when she pronounced that the materialism of modern Ireland should be recognized for its faults and that we should 'begin tiptoeing back to the Church'. Self-absorption and the pursuit of the material, O'Reilly argued, had hardened Irish hearts. John Boorman has taken up this theme in his recent film, *The Tiger's Tail* (2006), proffering an excoriating analysis of the materialism, vacuity and downright greed unleashed by the Celtic Tiger.[1]

Workers dye the Chicago River green to begin the city's St. Patrick's Day celebration, 11 March 2006. The tradition of dyeing the river dates back over 40 years. Photograph: Scott Olson/ Getty Images.

The vogue for self-examination was evidenced by the success of David McWilliams's book, *The Pope's Children*, published in 2005, and the follow-up TV series in late 2006.[2] The book enjoyed a wide readership and the TV series drew a large audience. McWilliams identified a plethora of new types that inhabit modern Ireland. 'RoboPaddy', for example, borrows against properties at home to accumulate a property portfolio abroad. The 'Decklanders' of suburbia engage in conspicuous consumption, literally decking out their back gardens to create the ambience of the south of Spain. 'HibernianCosmopolitans', or HiCos, blend aspects of Irishness (such as love for the Irish language and a predilection for organically grown Irish food) with more cosmopolitan outlooks and tastes. In doing so, they simultaneously distinguish themselves from the middle mass of suburbia, and identify with the global transnational élite. 'I shop, therefore, I am' appears to be the new gospel. Irishness is performed, not through saintliness or scholarship, but through conspicuous consumption. The Irish, McWilliams tells us, relentlessly buy decking, botox, plastic surgery, handbags, fast food, slow food, spa hotel breaks, alcohol, exotic holidays, and so on. Mostly, though, the Irish buy houses — ranches in the countryside, penthouses in the city, seaside properties in Sunny Beach, Bulgaria, and Daytona Beach, Florida. McWilliams sketches a post-modern vision of Ireland and the Irish, as a people increasingly defined not by what they produce, but by what they consume.

Diane Negra's edited collection speaks to both of these quintessentially post-modern themes — identity and consumption — and their attendant enchantments and disenchantments. The formation of identity is the outcome of a constant negotiation with those around us, and a parallel process of internal negotiation.[3] In *The Irish in Us* contributors wrestle with the theme of Irish identity, how it is constructed and deployed, and how identity politics are played out in popular culture. As a corollary, the book explores how new patterns of consumption of material culture provide the means for shaping, reshaping and appropriating Irish ethnicity. Not surprisingly, most of the analyses in this book take as their starting point the phenomenon of the Celtic Tiger and the particular transformations it has occasioned. The Celtic Tiger economy

is itself a product of globalization, so its impact reverberates far beyond the island of Ireland. The contributors to *The Irish in Us* are concerned with the manifold ways in which Irishness and Irish identity have become inscribed in popular culture texts and have migrated from the ethnic margins into the American mainstream. Audiences beyond Irish America now play with notions of Irishness, and, in the process, contribute to its further hybridization and commodification.

In considering identity, several contributors allude to the palpable tensions inherent in our understanding of how Irishness has come to be defined, particularly within popular culture. A number of the essays are predicated on a view of Irish performativity as fundamentally a process of 'becoming, not being, white'.[4] Indeed, the notion of Irishness as a form of liminal whiteness resonates throughout the book. Lauren Onkey, for example, quotes Van Morrison's refreshingly candid comment on his lowly status as a Paddy in England in the 1960s: 'To be in London and to be Irish, you were fucked.'[5] On the other hand, several essayists suggest that the success of Irishness lies in its capacity to function as a differentiating device, without risking classification as 'the other'. In this sense, the Irish fit Georg Simmel's classic characterization of 'the Stranger' — they occupy the ambiguous position of being outside of society while also being a part of it.[6] The Irish are both the same and different, or as Stephanie Rains suggests, 'the extent to which Irishness now constitutes a relatively comfortable version of whiteness, may well be an important consideration in its popularity among those of mixed white ethnicity'.[7] In a similar vein, Catherine M. Eagan suggests that Irish Americans' renewed interest in ethnic identity is part of an effort to reassert lost innocence and still benefit from the privileges of whiteness.[8] The issue of identity therefore, crystallizes around the issue of whether Irishness, as

3 Ian Craib, *Experiencing Identity* (London, 1998), 4

4 Maria Pramaggiore, '"Papa Don't Preach": Pregnancy and Performance in Contemporary Irish Cinema', 117

5 Lauren Onkey, 'Ray Charles on Hyndford Street: Van Morrison's Caledonian Soul', 174

6 Georg Simmel, 'The Stranger', in Kurt H. Wolff, ed., *The Sociology of Georg Simmel* (New York, 1950), 402–08

7 Stephanie Rains, 'Irish Roots: Genealogy and the Performance of Irishness', 155

8 Catherine M. Eagan, '"Still 'Black' and 'Proud'": Irish America and the Racial Politics of Hibernophilia', 50

9 Diane Negra, 'The Irish in Us: Irishness, Performativity and Popular Culture', 3

10 See Mary P. Corcoran, *Irish Illegals: Transients between Two Societies* (Westport, 1993).

11 Onkey, 'Ray Charles on Hyndford Street', 174

12 Michael Malouf, 'Feeling Eire(y): On Irish-Caribbean Popular Culture', 318–53

13 Onkey, 'Ray Charles on Hyndford Street', 178

14 Maeve Connolly, '"A Bit of a Traveller in Everybody": Traveller Identities in Irish and American Culture', 282–317

we understand it today, is fundamentally determined by an oppressed past, or a privileged present. Neither position proves ultimately satisfactory and most of the contributors appear to subscribe to the view that 'Irishness seems to move between a quasi-blackness and a politically-insulated ethnic whiteness'.[9]

Here, issues of identity are primarily explored in the context of popular culture. But they are, of course, always alive in political discourse. For instance, illegal Irish immigrants in New York city in the 1980s invoked their 'minority' status as exploited, undocumented workers at the same time as they used their platform as members of a privileged white ethnic group to lobby for immigration reform.[10] The new Irish in the United States in the 1980s benefited greatly from their perceived status as white English-speaking ethnics, rather than as members of the more prosaic lumpen-proletariat of illegal aliens. This conferred on them an almost quasi-legal status, which smoothed the way for a programme of regularization.

In the early 1990s *Bringing It All Back Home*, an acclaimed TV series, demonstrated the process of musical osmosis that lay at the foundation of the canon of Irish traditional music. Irish music is the outcome of many disparate influences and is constituted simultaneously through the local and the global. This theme is revisited in an extended essay by Lauren Onkey, in which she argues that the profound and ambiguous impact of African-American music on Irish culture is embodied in the life and work of Van Morrison. She claims that in sharp contrast to more tendentious equivalences that have been drawn by others between black and Irish experiences, Morrison's *œuvre* suggests 'that the relationship between blackness and Irishness can be a modern, transatlantic and creative one that provides alternatives to fixed identity rather than one that re-inscribes colonial, racial stereotypes'.[11] Morrison is perceived here

as a troubadour version of globalization, adapting and reworking soul music and diaspora experiences through his own locally grounded experience. Morrison's work is also informed by his own lived experience of being Irish in London in the 1960s, and the years that he spent in the United States experimenting with black music. Onkey returns repeatedly to the issue of authenticity, a theme that resonates through the whole book, most notably in Michael Malouf's essay on Afro-Caribbean interpenetration of Irish culture.[12] Morrison's ability to weave R & B and Irish musical styles meant that for Irish-American audiences 'Morrison could be a conduit, to an authentic, mysterious, ethnic Irishness that had guilt-free connections to African Americans'.[13] While other forms of Irish popular culture such as *Riverdance* are critiqued for ignoring the racial, gendered and class divisions that stratify ethnic groups, Morrison is lauded for his reflexive interpretation of his own Irish identity through black music. Morrison can keep us guessing or, as Onkey puts it, he 'trades in an authenticity of interdeterminate' — we cannot disentangle the various cultural, social and ethnic filaments that, woven together, produce his particular version of soul music. Morrison, of course, is not the only exponent of this kind of post-modern reflexivity. The music of the Pogues is also embedded in a kind of migratory narrative that links the particular (individual stories of emigration) with the universal (the diasporic sense of dislocation) in a *mélange* of musical traditions and styles.

Onkey's exploration of how identity is formed in and through a range of disparate influences is highly relevant to present-day Ireland, where issues of ethnicity and difference, race and tolerance have become ever more significant. The challenge of interculturalism remains acute and is brought into sharp relief in any examination of the fate of the Irish Traveller community whose self-identification as a distinct ethnic

Wall mural representing
rural Ireland, Yonkers,
New York, December 2005.
Photograph: Stan Honda/
AFP/Getty Images.

group remains controversial. In the film
Into the West (1992) the discrimination
experienced by the Traveller community as
an indigenous, yet racialized, ethnic minority
in Ireland is foregrounded. As a result,
Maeve Connolly suggests, the film may
also be seen as offering a starting point for
a more self-conscious examination of Irish
identity.[14] While the analysis of the films
presented here — *Into the West*, *This is My
Father* (1998) and *Traveller* (1997) — is
compelling, an opportunity was lost by not
considering the recent *Pavee Lacken* (2005).
Into the West self-consciously locates itself
within a heritage dreamscape and stars
Hollywood actors, but the grittier *Pavee
Lacken* uses child actors drawn from the
Traveller community itself to explore one
family's day-to-day struggle with poverty,
bureaucracy and prejudice in contemporary
Ireland. Directed by Perry Ogden, it has
as its pivotal focus a spirited and resilient
young Traveller girl. This sets the film apart
from *Traveller*, *This is My Father* and *Into
the West*, all of which, Connolly says, fail

to engage with the actual experiences of
women. Connolly concludes that patterns
of suspicion and intolerance, developed in
relation to Travellers, are readily extended
to encompass other racialized minorities,
even when they too are classed as 'white'.
Recent research carried out among the
Polish and Chinese communities in Dublin
appears to bear out this assessment. Both
groups provide evidence of being subjected
to prejudicial attitudes, as well as individual
and institutional discrimination. Given their
virtual exclusion from economic, social and
political power in Ireland, it remains to be
seen how these new Irish communities will
be represented and will begin to represent
themselves in the Irish cultural domain.

A second theme that animates *The Irish in
Us* is that of the valorization of Irishness
within American consumer culture.
Irishness, it seems, is a commodity that
can be invented, imagined and ultimately
consumed. Several of the essays in this
volume seek to interrogate theoretically the

Wall mural representing
Irish culture, Yonkers, New
York, December 2005.
Photograph: Stan Honda/
AFP/Getty Images.

15 Negra, 'The Irish in Us', 14
16 Seamus Heaney,
    'Correspondences:
    Emigrants and Inner
    Exiles', in Richard
    Kearney, ed., *The Irish
    at Home and Abroad*
    (Dublin, 1990), 23
17 Alas, when they return,
    many are disenchanted
    by the changes that have
    occurred in Ireland. See
    Mary P. Corcoran, 'Global
    Cosmopolites: Issues of
    Self-identity and Collective
    Identity among the
    Transnational Irish Elite',
    Études Irlandaises, Special
    Issue on Ireland/America
    in the twentieth century,
    28, 2, (2003).
18 Natasha Casey, '"The Best
    Kept Secret in Retail":
    Selling Irishness in
    Contemporary America',
    84–109

Hibernophilia 'that drives the consumption
of Irish themed plays, dance performances,
film, and television and the economies of
tourism, genealogy and kitsch'.[15] Despite
all the transformations that have occurred
in Ireland since the 1990s, romantic
Ireland is not dead and gone. Negra points
out, for example, that the phenomenally
successful painter Thomas Kinkade,
who specializes in nostalgic landscapes,
interprets Ireland through the lens of
rurality, tradition and stability. This is not
simply a projection of Irish Americans,
but is also common among returned Irish
emigrants. For returners, place is treated as
having particular existential significance.
During their sojourns abroad, whether or
not they eschewed an ethnic persona, they
nevertheless clung to a particular imaginary
of the country and the community they had
left behind. There is nothing new about
this, of course, as all emigrants over the
generations have been sustained by drawing
on an imagined Ireland, what Seamus
Heaney has described as 'a mythologically

grounded and emotionally contoured island
that belongs in art time, in story time, in
the continuous presence of a common,
unthinking memory life'.[16]

Frequently the decision of returning Irish
emigrants to leave the cities of New York
and London is bound up with a sense of
existential isolation. They feel disconnected
from their past, and disconnected from their
present. The moral resources necessary to
counter isolation are to be found in webs
of familial, friendship and communal
affiliations, which returners believe to be
more readily accessible in Ireland than in the
United States.[17]

According to Natasha Casey, the
primary associations that Irish-American
consumers have with Ireland, remain highly
romanticized and sentimentalized.[18] Her
contribution speaks to the currency of
Irishness among discerning (and not so
discerning) consumers. She demonstrates
how new markets can be constituted

through repackaging ethnic products and symbols. In turn, these are appropriated by consumers who seek ethnic authenticity. George Ritzer, in his classic study of the new means of consumption, has pointed out the myriad ways in which the means of consumption have diversified in recent years and how globally recognizable brand identities have assumed such importance in people's everyday lives.[19] The Irish are as implicated in this headlong rush to consume as is everyone else. While upper middle-class Americans appropriate Irish goods and products to 'add value' to their weddings, in Ireland upper middle-class teenagers (colloquially known as D4s) dispatch their parents on shopping expeditions to New York to purchase clothing from Abercrombie and Fitch. Irish shoppers have become the best kept retail secret in America. 'Just Nipping Across to the Shops' was the headline of a recent newspaper article, which argued that 'as mass movements go, the pre-Christmas exodus to the Big Apple hardly matches the dramas of the Wild Geese or the Famine ships, but it surely says as much about the wealthy of twenty-first century Ireland as those earlier events were markers of more difficult times'.[20] An estimated 25 million was spent last year on pre-Christmas shopping trips abroad. While Casey focuses on the appeal of Irishness to those America shoppers seeking to distinguish themselves from the masses, Irish shoppers are embracing Americanization and the global brand culture.

Casey distinguishes between three disparate groups that consume Irish-themed material culture. The first are self-designated Irish Americans who have a strong attachment to Ireland. The second group is made up of deviant consumers of Irishness — for example, extreme right-wing groups who have appropriated Celtic iconography to elaborate their white supremacist views. Irishness, in essence, is used as 'a white identity marker'.[21] The third group identified is the ancillary consumers of Irishness, mainly white suburban middle- and upper middle-class Americans who lay no claim to Irish ancestry but covet all things Irish. This is suggestive of post-modern flexible identities, wherein people chose their own signifiers and avatars, projecting onto them their desires, aspirations and alter egos. Irishness for them becomes something that is performed in the backyard, much as McWilliams's 'Decklanders' perform 'the Mediterranean' in theirs. These consumers seek to demonstrate their quirkiness, individuality and taste, thereby marking themselves out from others but, as David Harvey has observed, this ultimately leads to the serial reproduction of homogeneous culture.[22]

In the era of consumerism, ethnicity is increasingly seen as a form of tradable currency — a cultural palette from which Americans (and indeed the Irish) can pick and choose symbols and signifiers to form their own bespoke identities. This is not to deny the continued political significance of ethnicity. Indeed, Negra argues that in post-9/11 America Irishness has become a crucial discursive platform for articulating white working-class legitimacy and innocence. In the realm of popular culture, received notions about the primordial elements of Irish ethnicity continue to be questioned and subverted as Maria Pramaggiore and Gerardine Meaney demonstrate in *The Irish in Us*.[23] Irishness as an identity marker or as a means of consumption cannot be taken for granted. Its meaning can change from the poetic to the political to the polemical and back again.

The Irish diaspora, in common with other national and ethnic collectivities, 'construct[s], and continually reconstruct[s], a sense of themselves by reference to the signs provided by cultures'.[24] In his challenging work on the multicultural project in the United States, Schlesinger delineates the key features of collective identities: first, the making of identities is an active process. We are what we are because of how we

19 George Ritzer, *Enchanting a Disenchanted World* (Thousand Oaks, 1999)

20 *Irish Times*, 25 November 2006

21 Casey, '"The Best Kept Secret in Retail"', 96

22 David Harvey, *The Condition of Postmodernity* (Cambridge, Mass., 1989)

23 Pramaggiore, '"Papa Don't Preach"', 110–29, and Gerardine Meaney, 'Dead, White, Male: Irishness in *Buffy the Vampire Slayer* and *Angel*', 254–81

24 Arthur Schlesinger Jr., *The Disuniting of America: Reflections on a Multicultural Society* (New York, 1991), 44

25 Kevin Morley and David Robins, *Spaces of Identity* (London, 1995), 5

as a group have evolved and interrelate to other groups. Second, the complex process of creating traditions and of activating collective memories occurs in a temporal dimension — our version of history, or mythology. Third, there is a spatial dimension to our understanding of the collectivity. The primordial attachment of a collectivity is often to a particular land or territory. In a world where the constraints of time and space are rapidly being obliterated, it has been argued that 'places are no longer the clear supports of our identity'.[25] In this context, more and more of us inhabit a liminal space in which we must master the various contradictions and ambivalences associated with identity formation in late modernity. Increasingly we do this through symbolic means.

Several decades ago, Herbert Gans coined the term 'symbolic ethnicity' to give expression to *à la carte* ethnic identification. *The Irish in Us* provides striking examples of this in relation to Irishness and sheds new light on the central issues surrounding ethnicity, performativity and popular culture. The book succeeds in exploring the multifaceted ways that the trope of Irishness has suffused American popular culture, and it lays bare the ideological implications of the heightened performative and mobile qualities of Irishness. ■

Returns, Regrets and Reprints

Timothy W. Guinnane

Family and Community in Ireland
Conrad M. Arensberg and Solon T. Kimball
3rd edn., with a new Introduction by Anne Byrne, Ricca Edmundson and Tony Varley
Ennis: CLASP Press, 2001. 560 pages. ISBN 1-900545-13-6

Saints, Scholars, and Schizophrenics: Mental Illness in Rural Ireland
Nancy Scheper-Hughes
20th anniversary edn., expanded and updated
Berkeley: University of California Press, 2001. 417 pages. ISBN 978-0-520-22480-3

1   Conrad M. Arensberg,
*The Irish Countryman:
An Anthropological
Study* (London, 1937)

Daniel O'Neill
The Kitchen Dresser
c. 1955
oil on board
46.3 x 61.6 cm
private collection;
Christie's Images

A long tradition of writing on rural Ireland has produced its share of classics. *Family and Community in Ireland*, the product of fieldwork in County Clare in the 1930s, is one of these. Conrad M. Arensberg and Solon T. Kimball presented a comprehensive account of the life of two rural communities and the town of Ennis, including customs and practices related to marriage and sexuality, the transmission of property, the treatment of the young and the aged, etcetera. Their account, although not entirely admiring, reflects a generous sympathy and an effort to understand these Clare people on their own terms. Nancy Scheper-Hughes's *Saints, Scholars, and Schizophrenics* is famous (or perhaps infamous), not least because of its self-consciously diagnostic and critical perspective. She takes as her point of departure rural Ireland's allegedly extreme incidence of schizophrenia, and sets out to uncover the features of one Kerry community that would account for this epidemic. The book made an immediate splash upon publication, and much discussion of it ever since has centred on whether she betrayed confidences, made her informants too easy to identify, or was too harsh in her judgements. These matters warrant discussion and reflection (and she provides a good starting point in the new material here), but this consideration has almost entirely crowded out discussion of the book on more narrow, scholarly grounds.

This CLASP press edition of *Family and Community in Ireland* is most welcome. The new edition contains a facsimile of the 1968 (or second) edition of the book, along with a new Introduction by Anne Byrne, Ricca Edmundson and Tony Varley and a bibliography of works about Arensberg and Kimball and their impact on anthropology in Ireland and elsewhere. Just keeping Arensberg and Kimball in print is justification enough for a new edition. Byrne, Edmundson and Varley's Introduction is a nice bonus: they provide a useful history of the research and some broader context about its reception. Many readers will be aware of Arensberg's earlier volume, *The Irish Countryman*.[1] But even those familiar with the larger project will learn much from the Introduction. Byrne, Edmundson and Valey consulted unpublished papers and sought out Arensberg and Kimball's friends and acquaintances. They also were lucky enough to have the support of Vivian Garrison Arensberg, Conrad Arensberg's widow.

Under the direction of Professor Earnest Hooton of the Harvard Anthropology Department, three teams from three different disciplines began fieldwork in Ireland. In addition to the social anthropology project that resulted in *Family and Community in Ireland*, the Harvard project sent teams of archaeologists and physical anthropologists. Hooton apparently never visited Ireland during the project, but was overall director and closely involved with the physical anthropology component. Started with a $25,000 grant from the Rockefeller Foundation, the project intended to 'attempt a scientific interpretation of a modern nation, the country of origin of more than one-fifth of the population of the United States'.[2] The original plan had been to use all three disciplinary approaches to write an integrated account, but that never took place. The Second World War placed other demands on the researchers (Arensberg, for example, worked for US Army Intelligence during the war) and developments in the

social sciences made the original plan seem less compelling. The archaeological findings were published in Irish journals, and the physical anthropology appeared in a separate volume.

From the start the Harvard teams displayed a keen awareness of the problems they might encounter if they did not cultivate Irish public opinion and tread lightly on Irish sensitivities. The archaeologists sought the blessing and assistance of the keeper of the Irish Antiquities Division of the National Museum of Ireland, Adolf Mahr, and his support remained important to fending off criticism from those who either opposed excavations in general or feared the objects discovered would not remain in Ireland. The physical anthropologists' task was perhaps more delicate. They sought to gather evidence on the 'racial' characteristics of the Irish population, and thus needed, in addition to measures such as height and weight, the full array of cranial and other measures familiar to these studies. The team responsible for taking these measures relied on local authority figures, including priests, doctors and the police, to encourage others to volunteer. One can only guess what the participants would have thought had they known that their measurements would be used to detect the presence of a 'tall, dark, long-headed strain surviving from the Old Stone Age' alongside a 'shorter, dark haired, round-headed element which may have come in during the Bronze Age'.[3] Some declined to participate for more practical reasons; a few apparently assumed the Harvard researchers were working for the Irish government, and would use their data to take away old age pensions.[4]

A second central figure in the Irish project was William Lloyd Warner, another Harvard anthropology professor who was directly responsible for Arensberg and Kimball's research. Warner had studied aboriginal peoples in Australia, but he is most famous for the 'Yankee City' studies, which used the methods of social anthropology to study

2 Conrad M. Arensberg and Solon T. Kimball, *Family and Community in Ireland*, 3rd edn., ed. Anne Byrne, Ricca Edmundson and Tony Varley (Ennis, 2001), xix. In 1931, $25,000 had about the same purchasing power as $330,000 in 2006. At later stages in the project Harvard University, private individuals, Cosgrave's Cumann na nGaedheal government and de Valera's Fianna Fáil government also made financial contributions.
3 *Family and Community in Ireland*, xxvi
4 *Family and Community in Ireland*, xxv

Zita Reihill
Emotional Weight
2006
oil on board
46 x 46 cm
courtesy of the artist and
the Paul Kane Gallery

5   From an unpublished
manuscript by Kimball,
quoted in *Family and
Community in Ireland*,
xli

the people of Newburyport, Massachusetts. Both Arensberg and Kimball had worked on the Yankee City project; as Byrne, Edmundson and Varley remark, Warner's influence can be seen in both the effort to extend the methods of the Yankee City study to another context, and in the selection of the two researchers who would carry out the Irish research. *Family and Community in Ireland* has little explicitly comparative discussion, but, given its origins, one can understand that it was firmly grounded in a comparative sensibility.

Warner took great care to negotiate the reception of the project in Ireland. Perhaps a more important step was Warner's interview with Eamon de Valera in July of 1932,

which resulted in a letter of endorsement for the project. Warner had the tact not to use de Valera's name where it would not help, such as when he met with the bishop of Killaloe, no admirer of de Valera. Kimball later recounted the project's method: '... it was standard procedure to acquaint local religious and political authorities with the objectives of the research and to enlist their support. In no instance was such a request ever denied and there were many among the Irish whose assistance was invaluable.'[5] This is not to say that the Harvard team did not encounter opposition or create ill will. Even in 1992, when Varley interviewed people in the two rural communities Arensberg and Kimball studied, there were bad feelings among the descendants of some of those whom the Harvard team had described less than positively.

⁂

Most research monographs enjoy a hardcover edition and, if lucky, appear also in paperback. Only a book that has achieved classic status deserves to be reprinted more than sixty years after its first publication. *Family and Community in Ireland* certainly qualifies as a full-blown classic. No account of rural Ireland can ignore it, and it stands as a landmark in rural ethnography more generally. Yet this classic status poses some problems for readers today.

The first problem reflects not so much what Arensberg and Kimball wrote, as how others have used what they wrote. Arensberg and Kimball dealt with a particular part of Ireland at a particular historical juncture. The Harvard project went to some lengths to decide which area of Ireland was most 'typical', and the selection of Clare on those grounds was deliberate. Subsequent discussion of *Family and Community in Ireland* has challenged this characterization, and at some level it is both fatuous and harmless.[6] The greater problem is that others have pulled the work out of its historical context, and tried to view it as applicable to some 'long-ago' rural Ireland that could just as well be the 1860s, the 1930s, or the 1960s. There is a serious danger in this, at two levels. First, many social scientists cannot escape the temptation to split human history into a before and an after, a 'pre-modern' and 'modern', and to assume tacitly or explicitly that 'pre-modern' societies do not change. Arensberg and Kimball clearly thought rural Clare was pre-modern, and if we follow their claim and the assumptions about modernization, then we have a slippery but convenient line of thought that allows us to assert that their fieldwork could just as well have taken place in the 1860s. This just won't do, but we cannot blame it on Arensberg and Kimball.

The second problem reflects the assumption that Arensberg and Kimball's Clare is a sort of rural Irish 'benchmark' and that later studies can deduce change over time from how their communities differ from the picture given in *Family and Community in Ireland*. Byrne, Edmundson and Varley's discussion of this point is especially useful. Hugh Brody, although at points very critical of what he saw as the a-historicism in *Family and Community in Ireland*, also compared his 'Inishkillane' to the Harvard study as a way of deducing change over time.[7] The temptation is there; we have a classic text about a rural community in the 1930s, and if we want to document 'change and decline' in the same region, we can compare life in our period to life in the 1930s. The problem with this is that, even setting aside any reservations about Arensberg and Kimball, it pulls their Clare study out of its geographic context. What Brody saw as change over time could just as well reflect differences at a given point in time.

In describing the impact of *Family and Community in Ireland*, Byrne, Edmundson and Varley neglect another literature in which Arensberg and Kimball have figured heavily. Many historians, including myself, have tried to understand Ireland's unusual demographic patterns, especially in the period between the Famine and the 1950s.[8] Probably starting before the Famine, the proportions that ever married rose to very high levels, and emigration became a central feature of the demographic system. By the First World War the Irish were relatively unlikely to marry if they remained in Ireland, but had large families if they did marry. The net result was an Irish birth rate too low to offset all the emigration, and the Irish population shrank continuously even after the Famine's direct impact was long past, a decline that was reversed for good only in the 1990s. Efforts to understand these patterns have often turned to the institutions of marriage and family-transmission, and tried to understand

6   Chris Curtin and Peter Gibbon argue that Arensberg and Kimball were taken in by a Fianna Fáil-inspired romanticism about the Irish countryside, and that much of what they say is simply ideological. The possible danger is clear. As the Introduction notes, the Harvard researchers were at times concerned about being in the middle of a renewed civil war. But it seems to me that the real test of whether Arensberg and Kimball were fooled by nationalist propaganda is whether we can verify aspects of their account from other sources. This is what Gibbon and Curtin attempted to do, as I outline below.

7   Hugh Brody, *Inishkillane: Change and Decline in the West of Ireland* (London, 1973)

8   Timothy W. Guinnane, *The Vanishing Irish: Households, Migration, and the Rural Economy in Ireland, 1850–1914* (Princeton, 1997)

9 Frédéric Le Play, *L'Organisation de la famille, selon le vrai modèle signalé par l'histoire de toutes les races et de tous les temps* (Paris, 1874)

10 The best account of the Cambridge view can be gleaned from the chapters collected in Peter Laslett and Richard Wall, eds., *Household and Family in Past Time* (Cambridge, 1972).

11 Peter Gibbon and Chris Curtin, 'The Stem Family in Ireland', *Comparative Studies in Society and History*, 20, 3 (1978), 429–53; David Fitzpatrick, 'Irish Farming Families before the First World War', *Comparative Studies in Society and History*, 25, 2 (1983), 339–74. Gibbon and Curtin's parting shot was 'Irish Farm Families: Facts and Fantasies', *Comparative Studies in Society and History*, 25, 2 (1983), 375–80.

12 My own interest in the 1911 census manuscripts was kindled by reading the debate between Gibbon and Curtin, and Fitzpatrick. They were of course not the first to use them for demographic history, but they more fully appreciated what could be done with a source like this.

what role they could play in the restriction of marriage to relatively few. The first systematic such efforts were due to Kenneth H. Connell, who relied heavily on folklore records and all but ignored Arensberg and Kimball's work. Later demographic historians, including David Fitzpatrick, Cormac Ó Gráda, and myself, have tried harder to extract lessons from the Harvard studies. This latter effort risks the a-historicism criticized above, of course, but the coherent account at the centre of *Family and Community in Ireland* has probably done more harm than good in coming to grips with Ireland's demographic patterns.

Family and Community in Ireland first appeared in 1940. The editors provide a lengthy if necessarily incomplete bibliography of works about the study, and just perusing that list gives some sense of how much fruitful research it has generated. We can best convey that sense of debate here by briefly describing one way in which it encouraged a new line of research. Arensberg and Kimball's account of the structure and dynamics of rural Clare households is nearly identical to the famous 'stem' family described by Frédéric Le Play.[9] In contrast to a 'nuclear' family, in a stem family system one son brings his bride into his parents' home, and the resulting offspring live in that household with their parents and grandparents. The result was, supposedly, a three-generational household that might also include other extended kinsfolk. The stem family played a particular role in the attack Peter Laslett and his colleagues in the Cambridge Group mounted against romantic conceptions of a lost 'extended' family in European history.[10] Arensberg and Kimball's account pre-dated Laslett's work, and its status made the Irish stem family a credible exception to the generalization the Cambridge historians were pushing.

Peter Gibbon and Chris Curtin turned to the manuscript census of Ireland for 1911 to ask whether the type of rural family Arensberg and Kimball described was as common as they thought. This effort is precisely what historians and others should have done all along; rather than debate the ideological or other influences on the Harvard researchers, one could simply check other sources for the veracity of the claims made in *Family and Community in Ireland*. Gibbon and Curtin conclude that the stem family was no myth, but that Arensberg and Kimball had mistakenly over-generalized; the extended family system was most common among a middle range of farmers, and was not typical of either the poorest or the wealthiest. David Fitzpatrick later used more of the 1911 census manuscripts, as well as records of landholding, to mount a defence of the account in Arensberg and Kimball.[11] The reader can turn to their publications to make up his or her own mind on the matter; I think Fitzpatrick got it right, but we owe Gibbon and Curtin for raising the question in the first place. More perhaps than they realized, these authors demonstrated what could be done with the 1911 manuscript census schedules, which constitute a rare and valuable historical source.[12] And this debate in Ireland formed an important warning to scholars interested in the history of family structure that the stem family was not the simple myth that Laslett at first claimed it was.

Family and Community in Ireland enjoys a rare place in Irish history and social science. Byrne, Edmundson and Varley have done the world the added service of researching the project's background and helping us to understand how it came about and how it has been received since. For that, they and the press are owed an additional debt of gratitude.

⁂

Saints, Scholars, and Schizophrenics is also a very well-known work, although its fame is of a sort very different from *Family and Community in Ireland*. Most discussions

Gerard Dillon
Island People
c. 1950
oil on board
58.4 x 67.8 cm
Crawford Municipal Art
Gallery

of Arensberg and Kimball have been about the quality of the research. Nancy Scheper-Hughes's book, on the other hand, has been famous as much (or even more) for the offence it caused her informants as for any scholarly merits, and this part of the story motivates much of the new material in the 2001 edition. Scheper-Hughes and her family lived in the parish of An Clochán, on the Dingle peninsula, during the period 1974–75, and she returned to the community for the first time in 1999. The account she first published in 1979 deeply offended many she had come to know during her fieldwork. In the new edition she acknowledges as inadequate her efforts to conceal both the place (which she calls 'Ballybran') and the identity of specific people among her informants. An *Irish Times* correspondent (Michael Viney) figured out the real name of 'Ballybran' soon after the book was published, and in reading her accounts of specific individuals in that very small community, it is no wonder they recognized themselves and each other.

But there is a second reason for the anger: she not only humiliated the people of An Clochán, she did so in writing a book that was, at best, not very good. In a curious way both the original controversy over the book and her reflections on it in this new edition have obscured the book's real weakness. *Saints, Scholars, and Schizophrenics* argues — to put the matter only a little too baldly — that the way these rural Irish people were socialized made them unable to have normal sexual relationships; that some parents crippled their sons psychologically, to make sure they remained at home to 'care for the old people'; and that an inability to deal with this stress accounted for what Scheper-Hughes then thought was the unusually high incidence of mental illness and even schizophrenia in rural Ireland. Setting aside the understandable feelings of those who

13 Laslett and his colleagues put the study of family history on more firm quantitative footing, but these basic facts about European marriage patterns had been known since at least Thomas Malthus.

thought themselves betrayed by a young scholar they had welcomed and befriended, the real question is not whether Scheper-Hughes violated confidences so much as whether her harsh conclusions are true.

This twentieth anniversary edition contains a new prologue and epilogue. The new material has two aims. One is to explain how her thinking has evolved since she first wrote *Saints, Scholars, and Schizophrenics*. The second purpose is to tell something about her relations with the people of An Clochán since she first published the book in 1979, and about an abbreviated and clearly painful return trip in 1999. The new material is interesting, and it is much to her credit that she is willing in effect to apologize in print in this way. (She even concedes that her title, while cute, was not a good idea.) That said, the new material is frustrating in its own way. Many of the original reviews of her book were positive, but several also raised, in a critical way, the problems I summarize here. A few of these problems she more or less concedes, but in the new edition she is vague, almost evasive, about the central intellectual issue in the original work, which is the aetiology of schizophrenia and her explanation of its prevalence in rural Ireland. And as much as she was clearly saddened by her reception in 1999, one can hardly escape the sense that she still did not quite understand why the people of An Clochán were so angry.

Three general weaknesses of *Saints, Scholars, and Schizophrenics* stood out at first reading, and do even more so today. The first is a puzzling lack of interest in how communities such as An Clochán were or were not unusual either in Ireland, or in Europe, at that time, and, more especially, in the longer sweep of European history. This weakness is part of a broader lack of comparative context. The second is a cavalier approach to facts, quantitative or otherwise. And the third is perhaps the most important: at no point did Scheper-Hughes try to situate An Clochán in the

context of its own history, or in the context of the adjustments it was trying (and in her judgement, failing) to make in the 1970s.

The challenge and opportunity of comparative social analysis is simple and, at the risk of a bad joke, maddening. An Clochán is not quite like any other place on earth; An Clochán is very much like many other places on earth. Understanding how it is different enables us to learn more about variations in the human condition. Understanding how it is similar would yield several benefits, not the least of which is not believing that we are looking at some new and exotic variant on the human condition. Much of what Scheper-Hughes thought was shocking or pathological about An Clochán was in fact typical of much of Ireland throughout the nineteenth and early twentieth centuries. More generally (and importantly), these same features had long roots in European history. The most glaring example is the marriage patterns that so amazed her. Historical demographers have long noted that Western European societies usually had household-formation systems that required some adults to live out their entire lives without marrying.[13] The numbers of Irish adults who never married had, by the early twentieth century, reached extreme levels, and by mid-century were at levels hardly known anywhere else before or since. By the 1970s on the Dingle peninsula marriage was indeed rare. But the basic role she finds so appalling — young people who know they will never marry — was the fate of millions of Europeans for centuries before she wrote on this small community in the West of Ireland.

There are many places in the text where she points out something about the people of An Clochán with the confident assumption that the reader will understand it to be bizarre, even pathological. But the implicit assumption can be baffling. For example, her discussion of Irish attitudes toward food, which is part of a larger argument about the denial of physical gratification, says '… it is not considered odd for children to develop strong aversions to certain categories of food, this within an already restricted diet'.[14] What child has not decided, at one point or another, that a specific food (raisins in oatmeal, Brussel sprouts, and that all-time killer, peas) is poisonous to those under the age of fifteen? In another example, Scheper-Hughes makes much of the rarity of breastfeeding in An Clochán. Again, demographic historians have documented that breastfeeding was rare in several apparently mentally healthy European societies and, as Scheper-Hughes should know, it went out of fashion for a long time in the United States.

Not thinking through how An Clochán really differed from other places led to some very strange conclusions.[15] She blames a specific 'Jansenist' Catholicism for producing these patterns, yet other parts of Europe with similar demographic patterns were not Catholic at all. One could wonder, in addition, how arrangements that led to mental illness in Ireland would not have the same effect elsewhere. She thanks Robert E. Kennedy, a professor at Berkeley where she did her graduate work. Kennedy authored a very fine account of Irish demographic behaviour that displays a keen understanding of how the Irish demographic system fits into the more general European pattern. But she neither accepted its message nor explained why she disagreed.[16] And while she cites some of Connell's work on marriage and households, she missed his insistence that permanent celibacy had been common in Ireland for over a century by the time she wrote.

Saints, Scholars, and Schizophrenics also bears a strange relationship to *Family and Community in Ireland*. She calls Arensberg and Kimball's research 'definitive'.[17] But Arensberg and Kimball explicitly deny one of her central claims. She says:

> Marriage in Ireland is, I suggest, inhibited by anomie, expressed in a lack

of sexual vitality; familistic loyalties that exaggerate latent brother-sister incestuous inclinations; an emotional climate fearful of intimacy and mistrustful of love; and an excessive preoccupation with sexual purity and pollution, fostered by an ascetic Catholic tradition.[18]

Arensberg and Kimball were fully aware that the marriage and inheritance system they described required some adult siblings to remain unmarried all their lives. They saw nothing sinister or damaging about this. The Harvard authors were aware that some claimed the Irish were repressed about sexual matters, and they explicitly deny this. The passage is worth quoting:

> Yet these [puritanical] attitudes [about sex] coexist together with other very hearty, casual, and sometimes ribald attitudes which make their appearance in banter, joke, and repartee even between speakers of different sex. These even take the form of taunts about prowess and mild ridicule for the possession of a greater relish than is meet, or fanciful recitation of past magnificent misdeeds. This is particularly true in the recitations of stories and adventures of persons in the ken of the community, where details of amorous desire and accomplishment are given with considerable gusto, and greeted and reiterated again and again amid hearty laughter.[19]

We should not simply assume that Arensberg and Kimball were right, so Scheper-Hughes must be wrong. But no scholar can proclaim an earlier work 'definitive' and then ignore how its message contradicts her own.

A second weakness in *Saints, Scholars, and Schizophrenics* is a cavalier attitude toward factual statements. Some of the original reviews noted that Scheper-Hughes was fuzzy about quantitative matters (which is true) but, given that she has backed off some of her original views about the

14 *Saints, Scholars, and Schizophrenics: Mental Illness in Rural Ireland*, 20th anniversary edn. (Berkeley, 2001), 245

15 I summarize the argument in *The Vanishing Irish*, 220–23, but I cannot take credit for the basics. I recall hearing a hysterically funny outline of this criticism from David Fitzpatrick, and I am sure it has been raised many times.

16 Robert E. Kennedy, *The Irish: Emigration, Marriage, and Fertility* (Berkeley, 1973)

17 *Saints, Scholars, and Schizophrenics*, 177

18 *Saints, Scholars, and Schizophrenics*, 195

19 *Family and Community in Ireland*, 199

20 *Saints, Scholars, and Schizophrenics*, 240
21 *Saints, Scholars, and Schizophrenics*, 147
22 *Saints, Scholars, and Schizophrenics*, 256

incidence of mental illness in Ireland, these specifics do not merit discussion here. There are many assertions, however, that lack any documentation whatsoever. Other statements are just hard to credit. For example, '... breast-feeding appears to have disappeared in the first decades of this [the twentieth] century with the introduction of the bottle (if the midwife is correct) by the English'.[20] Setting aside the ritual blaming of the English, this is a thin evidentiary reed on which to hang a claim about the lack of breastfeeding, which she sees as verging on child neglect. Clarity on when breastfeeding supposedly died out might lead her to better understanding of long-term changes in child-rearing practices, which should be central to the argument. In another passage she claims that 'The social services in Ireland — including orphanages, old age homes, and hospitals — are exceptionally prolific, well staffed, and heavily endowed.'[21] There is no source given, and she does not elaborate; does she mean more than other countries with similar incomes? Does she mean more than any mentally healthy society would require? The claim matters: she wants to argue that these institutions were used as a refuge from intolerable stress and as a way of removing from the community those viewed as in any way deviant. So it matters whether Ireland was in fact 'prolific' in this regard. There are many statements just like this, and while no single example is devastating, in the end their accumulation makes one wonder just how seriously to take any claim.

Historians who read *Saints, Scholars, and Schizophrenics* complained of a different problem. Her argument is at one level historical: a culture and demographic system that might have functioned tolerably well in the past was producing intolerable strains on the generations she observed in the 1970s. But her placement of the community in that history is at best sketchy. There are a lot of references to the 'ancient Irish', the Famine, and so forth, but almost nothing more recent. In particular, the reader would be at

a loss to understand the long-term changes in the Irish economy between the Famine and the 1970s, and how those changes had depopulated the countryside but left those who remained in much better economic conditions. She could have used the work of Connell, or Kennedy, or Brendan Walsh to place Ireland's marriage patterns in historical context. These omissions are puzzling at several different levels. Her argument matches a particular understanding of Irish culture and Irish Catholicism to the dwindling economic possibilities of this small Kerry community. Given the argument, it would be important to have a clear understanding of both of these and, specifically, to understand why that particular Irish culture had not produced the same effects in Kerry in the 1890s.

The central problem with the book, however, is the aetiology of schizophrenia. This is the core of her discussion of An Clochán: all of her accounts of social life, sexuality, and child-rearing are an effort to understand why so many rural Irish people ended up hospitalized for schizophrenia. And it is here that she makes claims that are understandably offensive to many. At one time psychiatrists thought of schizophrenia and other psychoses as rooted in early childhood experience. Yet the standard medical textbooks in print when she wrote in 1979 dismissed virtually any role for socialization in the aetiology of the disease; it is difficult to understand why she was still making it the centrepiece of her account. In the original text of *Saints, Scholars, and Schizophrenics*, Scheper-Hughes at several points acknowledges the medical view, but then in effect ignores it. This is both baffling and frustrating. She takes great pains to discuss and dismiss the old theory of the 'schizophrenogenic mother', an 'unfortunate term' that 'conjures up the image of hysterical, possessed women imbued with discriminating pathogenic powers that destroy the lives of one or more of their children...'[22] But then, to explain mental illness in rural Ireland, she makes an argument that self-consciously evokes the theory of the 'schizophrenogenic mother'.[23]

Here the new material included in the 2001 edition does not go nearly far enough. In the new edition Scheper-Hughes concedes, in effect, the medical view, but in an evasive way. Regardless of her understanding with the good people of An Clochán about their privacy, this seems to be well-founded grounds for anger. She did not just criticize the way people raised their children, in effect saying that the parish was populated by 'schizophrenogenic' parents, she did it in the cause of an explanation she should not have taken seriously. The new prologue discusses the difficulties of doing ethnographic work in Ireland, and gives the reader to believe that some Irish proclivity for 'book burning' makes it nearly impossible to do so without provoking strong reactions. The only example she mentions here is Eric Cross's 1942 book *The Tailor and Ansty*, which was indeed banned by a Fianna Fáil government. But this is argument by selective example. Scheper-Hughes is not the first anthropologist to write a provocative account of a West of Ireland community. Enough copies of those books escaped the bonfires to remain reliably available on bookshelves in Dublin and elsewhere. And there are ethnographic works from rural Irish communities that have contributed to a fuller, if not always appreciated, understanding of Irish society. The most telling example is one she relegates to a footnote mention. Rosemary Harris's *Prejudice and Tolerance in Ulster: A Study of Neighbors and Strangers in a Border Community*, which is based on fieldwork in 'Ballybeg' in the 1950s, deals clearly and sensitively with that deepest of Irish sensitivities, the sectarian divide. Her findings — that Protestant and Catholic farmers treated each other with respect, and that the local Orange Order was as much about class resentment among Protestants as sectarian identity — were unwelcome to extreme nationalist and unionist alike. But scholars have treated Harris's work with the

respect it deserves.[24] Others have followed in Arensberg and Kimball's footsteps without provoking the reaction that greeted Scheper-Hughes.

Saints, Scholars, and Schizophrenics was puzzling when first published, and the appearance of this new edition only deepens the puzzle:

> So, in the end, I regard *Saints, Scholars, and Schizophrenics* as falling into that large and forgiving category I have called good enough ethnography, a book that captured *something* true about the country people of County Kerry in the mid-1970s while it obviously missed a great deal as well.[25]

We could debate the precise threshold of 'good enough', but for a scholar as celebrated as Scheper-Hughes, even this is an enormous concession. The original text gave the impression of a harsh and judgemental author, one who wanted to improve people's lives without having any apparent warmth for them. The new material in this edition, as well as her subsequent work in other contexts, belies that impression. In the years since writing *Saints, Scholars, and Schizophrenics*, Nancy Scheper-Hughes has laboured long and hard on behalf of several groups of people who deserve any help they can get. One wonders if the good people of this small Kerry parish can claim some credit for that.

These projects both started as fieldwork in rural Ireland. The difference in their receptions reflects, among other things, their authors' very different aims. Arensberg and Kimball thought they were participating in the writing of an 'objective' 'science of man'. Claims such as this invite giggles today, even when placed in inverted commas, but we should at least try to give them credit. Arensberg and Kimball were trying to understand the people of Clare

23 *Saints, Scholars, and Schizophrenics*, 258
24 John Messenger's *Inis Beag: Isle of Ireland* (New York, 1969) also provoked strong reactions.
25 *Saints, Scholars, and Schizophrenics*, 56

26 *Saints, Scholars, and
    Schizophrenics*, 311
27 http://ls.berkeley.edu/
    dept/anth/nsh.html
28 *Saints, Scholars, and
    Schizophrenics*, 325

on their own terms. They were not trying
to improve the people of Clare, and not
horrified when their family and sex lives
diverged from those of Harvard graduate
students. It has to be easier to observe when
one is not also trying to judge.

Nancy Scheper-Hughes was after something
else when she lived in An Clochán. There
is an old joke about the post-modern
anthropologist that has the 'native' informant
interrupting the logorrhoeic ethnographer
with an exasperated 'Can't we talk about
me?' There are more than a few passages in
Saints, Scholars, and Schizophrenics where
the reader thinks he is learning more about
Scheper-Hughes than about the people of
An Clochán. That was certainly one taunt
thrown in her face when she returned in
1999. She quotes an ex-friend as saying,
'Who made *you* such an authority? You
weren't such a grand person when you and
your family came to live in our bungalow.
You could hardly control your own
children.'[26] Scheper-Hughes disapproved of
the way the locals raised their children. It
turns out the feeling was mutual.

Her intentions in writing *Saints, Scholars,
and Schizophrenics* seemed to be less a
characterization of human communities
than a self-conscious effort to improve them.
Today Scheper-Hughes's website at Berkeley
says that her

> lifework concerns the violence of
> everyday life examined from a radical
> existentialist and politically engaged
> perspective. Her examination of
> structural and political violence, of
> what she calls 'small wars and invisible
> genocides', has allowed her to develop a
> so-called 'militant' anthropology, which
> has been broadly applied to medicine,
> psychiatry, and to the practice of
> anthropology.[27]

When she returned to An Clochán in
1999, she was essentially run out of town,

presumably by militants who had had quite
enough of anthropology. The anecdote, as
she recounts it, is itself quite revealing. Her
hosts turned against her because they found,
in her room, discarded pages from a journal
she was keeping about the return trip. The
original offence was to publish people's
secrets, and here she was at it again, in
their view, collecting material with which to
humiliate them some more.

But Scheper-Hughes was 'no novice at the
art of quick getaways'. She compares her
experience in An Clochán in 1999 to her
detention after the military coup in Brazil in
1965, and to close calls with both militants
and police in Selma, Alabama, 'during a
period of transition to Black power'.[28] The
reissue of this work fits into a broader
pattern. If she had wanted to respond to the
many serious academic criticisms of the
book, or update her thinking on the issues
she raised in the original edition, the
appropriate forum would have been an
article in a professional journal. If she had
truly understood the damage done to the
people of An Clochán, she would not have
consented to a reissue of the book and the
reopening of old wounds. The book sold
many copies in the original hardback and
softcover editions, and remains widely
available in used book outlets. The only
legitimate reason for a new edition would be
a thorough reconsideration of her original
arguments. Yet she declines to provide that
here. This new edition of *Saints, Scholars,
and Schizophrenics* represents its own kind
of 'quick getaway'. ∎

The Big CHIL

Joep Leerssen

The Cambridge History of Irish Literature
Edited by Margaret Kelleher and Philip O'Leary
Cambridge: Cambridge University Press, 2006. 2 vols., 1,400 pages. ISBN 0-521-82224-6

'There they are.' I made a sweeping gesture to include the whole library. 'They look still and silent but they talk amongst themselves, even though they seem to ignore each other. They communicate through their authors, just as the egg uses the hen to produce another egg.'

Arturo Pérez-Reverte, *The Club Dumas*, trans. Sonia Soto (1996 [1993])

Let's agree, at the outset, that the *Cambridge History of Irish Literature* (CHIL) is a useful book. It is, by its nature, a compendium, aimed not at the specialist in need of probing analysis but at the general reader in need of context, offering as it does the vantage point of a *survey*. That reader is admirably served by this collection, which brings together specialists in the various languages, fields, genres and centuries, and which consolidates the critical debates and insights of the past two decades into a magisterial, canonical overview of two volumes containing 28 articles covering 1,400 pages. The specialist reader can, unavoidably of course, see flaws (I personally find it unforgivable that not a single mention is made of one of the giants of Irish letters, Scotus Eriugena), and future critics will use this survey as a kicking-off point rather than as a Final Word. But on the whole, the two-tome *CHIL* does achieve its ambitious aim to provide a comprehensive description of the developments of Irish literature over the last ten centuries or so.

Rather than list the various articles, their various merits and shortcomings, it may be useful to address two underlying questions that meet and overlap in this book: What

is Irish literature? and, How do we write literary history? Neither of these questions has been really grappled with within *CHIL*, but each of them is hugely complex, and the interference between them causes conceptual turbulences of great interest and importance.

To begin with the latter: how do we write literary history? The definition of 'literature' is a tired semantic chestnut that we need not rehearse extensively here, beyond noting that the term vacillates uneasily between two meanings. Literature means either 'any textual form of culture' (in which sense it often coincides with the notion of 'writing', preferred by *The Field Day Anthology of Irish Writing* (vols. 1–3, 1991; vols. 4–5, 2002), or 'the textual form of art'. On the whole, the more inclusive meaning (which also covers popular or oral literature and genres such as history-writing or religious disquisition) is current when we address older periods (medieval or classical), whereas literature for the more recent periods tends to focus on poetry, theatre, and fictional narrative (relegating non-fictional prose such as travel-writing, autobiography, history-writing or criticism to the margins). The term 'literature' is, then, a historical variable rather than a historical category. What the

Men browsing at a bookstall, Eden Quay. Dublin, 1952/53. Photograph: Nevill Johnson. Copyright © RTÉ Stills Library.

term includes or excludes tends to shift over time, and by rights those shifts themselves ought to be historically described and accounted for by anyone claiming to write a History of Literature.

Another problem lies in the fact that, properly speaking, literature has no history. It just *is*, like rain. If on a winter evening I stand in front of my bookcase, wondering what to read, I can pick up Calvin, Calvino or *Calvin and Hobbes*; this Christmas holiday I plan to sit down with Montaigne's *Essais* and Thomas Pynchon's *Against the Day*. Literature is a canon — that is to say, a selected, available corpus; and while the constitution of that corpus may be the result of historical processes of production and selection, its presence and availability are situated in a here and now, where authors from many countries and epochs meet on a single bookshelf. As Jorge Luis Borges put it, *para el concepto clásico, la pluralidad de los hombres y de los tiempos es accesoria, la literatura es siempre una sola* [according to the classical view, the plurality of people and periods is incidental, literature is always in the singular].

So what 'history' does literature have? How can we align it along an axis of temporal development? At least three modes are possible. To begin with, there is the history of one's own literacy. It is a personal, private one, the biography of textual encounters, the progress from fairy-tales via television shows to comic books, juvenile reading and onwards. It is not easy to describe this history of the acquisition of literary competence in other than individual, private terms; yet in the explanation why literary conventions are resistant to innovation, the persistence of stereotypes, the cognitive play of narrative 'frames' that programme our understanding of the world (as in Ronald Reagan's use of the term 'Evil Empire'), it is becoming increasingly clear that our deepest-seated prejudices and beliefs are the result of stories encountered and assimilated early

on in our childhood. For that reason alone, the neglect of juvenile, folk-oral and biblical narratives in literary histories is in itself a huge blind spot. All the more so since in this sphere, texts (and in particular the most famous, canonical texts) are assimilated by hearsay and reputation as much as through actual reading. Everyone is familiar with the general plot line that 'Romeo and Juliet', 'Don Quixote' and 'Gulliver' stand for, without necessarily having read the texts by Shakespeare, Cervantes and Swift. *Treasure Island* is now probably more widely known through the Muppets' spoof version than from Stevenson's original.

All this indicates that literary texts circulate, ramify, are recycled, propagate themselves. Their life is not just the result of an author's productive inspiration, but consists of the entire subsequent trajectory of readings, rereadings, adaptations, and instances of how they are read, received, reactivated. To no small extent, literary history is the history of books being taken from shelves, opened, working their way into minds, into other books, opera libretti or film scripts. Books exude a galvanizing radiance, operative across generations, and that too constitutes a literary history.

Indeed, in the case of older texts this is almost the only type of historicity we can assign to them: a *functional* one. The actual genesis of the *Iliad*, of the *Táin*, or of the Old Testament must be largely a matter of antiquarian–anthropological conjecture; such texts enter literary history through their being copied, recopied, debated, experienced. Significantly, there is no obvious genetic moment that we can assign to such texts (unlike, say, 'The Lake Isle of Innisfree'). We do not have a publisher's contract or a date of first publication, we do not even have the name of a single identifiable author, and their initial presence in the literary system is signalled by an imperfectly preserved manuscript tradition.

1 See the comments in Bernard Cerquiglini, *Éloge de la variante: Histoire critique de la philologie* (Paris, 1989), and in Lionel Gossman, *Between History and Literature* (Cambridge, MA, 1990). On authorship, see Seán Burke, ed., *Authorship from Plato to the Postmodern: A Reader* (Edinburgh, 1995), and his *The Death and Return of the Author: Criticism and Subjectivity in Barthes, Foucault and Derrida* (Edinburgh, 1998 [1992]).

2 More specifically in my 'Literary History, Cultural Identity, and Tradition', in Steven Tötösy de Zepetnek, Milan V. Dimic and Irene Sywenky, eds., *Comparative Literature Now: Theories and Practice / La Littérature comparée à l'heure actuelle: Théories et réalisations* (Paris, 1999), 389–97, and 'Identiteit in de literatuurgeschiedenis', in D. Perie, S. Leibovici and M. Engelberts, eds., *Identiteit: Filosofie, literatuur, maatschappij* (Delft, 2002), 77–84.

We should realize that this is the condition of a very large portion of the world's literary heritage. Only in a commercial, well-administered print culture, where authors take up a salient position in a society's public sphere, can we tether texts firmly to a genetic moment and authorship. Somewhere in the centuries following Chaucer, Villon and Dante the idea of the modern 'author' emerges (or, to be precise, the notion of 'authorship' crosses over from the field of theology and religion into the field of secular *belles-lettres*) and it becomes possible to speak of a literary history as a concatenation of authors and their productive moments.[1]

And that brings us, finally, to literary history as we generally understand it: as the historical survey of a succession of authors who in succeeding generations wrote different things according to shifting programmes and poetical standards. In other words, our default understanding of literary history is a very specific one (let's call it genetic-productive history), which is particular to Western post-medieval print culture. It hinges on the genetic power of an author's creativity as its motivating force, and as a result is often narrated in the mode of innovation versus inherited convention. Literary history, in other words, narrates the literary dimension of Western modernity.[2]

CHIL follows this genetic mode of literary history-writing. The earliest chapters deal with the earliest periods. The Latin and Gaelic writings of Medieval Ireland are surveyed (by Tomás Ó Cathasaigh and Máire Ní Mhaonaigh), in contributions that are particularly welcome in that they summarize information which until now was restricted largely to specialist publications. The chapters interweave literary (mythical, legendary) motifs, materials, genres and conventions, often of unspecific historical provenance and date, with the known and datable activities of historical actors and figures. In the subsequent chapters, the reader is taken along a chronological

progress to the contemporary period, ending with a chapter on Irish cinema and literary historiography, and afterwards on 'the new millennium'. There is, on the whole, a narrative arc in all this that combines the national mode of history-writing (Ireland never ceased to express and assert its own, proper identity) with a postmodern-Whig sense of progress (Irish literature is becoming ever more inclusive, vibrant and reflective of diversity). Overall, the tone is one of axiomatic celebration; this is a showcase, not a history of failure or decline.

While each of the chapters gives a good (and in some cases, a very good) survey of its period, their succession is in fact specious. As I pointed out, the genetic-progressive arrangement, where each generation of authors stands on (and kicks against) the shoulders of their elders, only works for modern print literature. In this case, modern print literature means English-language Irish literature from Swift onwards, and (*pace* Gearóid Denvir's stout assertions to the contrary) Gaelic-language Irish literature from Douglas Hyde onwards. In those filiations we can trace a diachronic dynamics, some form of consciously experienced progress. But most manuscript poetry in Irish circulated, not in collections-by-author, but as part of *duanaire* poem-books or as part of manuscript collections reflecting the taste and interests of the collector/scribe rather than the individual personality of the author.

One of the first secular authors in Europe who received an *opera omnia* edition of his complete works (reflecting the idea that the author's personality was the premier focus that gave all his texts their collective interest) was Giovanni Pontano, in 1518. Tadhg Dall Ó hUiginn (1550–91), by contrast, was less fortunate. His poems remained dispersed over many different poem-books, organized, not under the heading of their author (who in any case was often confused with his much older namesake Tadhg Óg),

Couple browsing books, Merchant's Arch, Temple Bar, Dublin, 1969. Photograph: National Library of Ireland.

but according to the addressee. It was only in 1820 that his name figured in a poets' list compiled by the antiquary Edward O'Reilly, and not until 1922 that Eleanor Knott gave an edition of Tadhg Dall's collected poems under that poet's own name, for the Irish Texts Society, belatedly reflecting a modern, print-culture interest in the author as the premier organizing focus of literature.

The anthology (whether it be a *duanaire* or a *romancero*, or indeed the Greek prototype) is in fact the oldest persisting mode of literary organization; older, in any case, than the authorial one. The Bible itself is a

collection not unlike *Leabhar na hUidhre*. In most European countries we see that the thematic poem-book collection leads a tenacious life long after the 'invention of the author', much as manuscript circulation remains important long after the introduction of print.[3] *A fortiori* in Ireland, where Gaelic literature was thwarted for a long time from gaining access to the printing press (and where that other mode of literary broadcast, the theatre, was absent, certainly for Gaelic letters), the circulation of texts did not necessarily reflect the career of an author 'rising to fame'. Most of the things we know about bardic poetry or about the *aisling-*

3 For the Low Countries, see Nelleke Moser, '"Poezijlust en Vriendenliefd": Literaire Sociabiliteit in Handschrift en Druk na 1600', *Spiegel der letteren* (special issue on W. van Anrooij and J. Reynaert, eds., 'Handschrift en Druk'), forthcoming.

4   See also Richard Terry,
    *Poetry and the Making of
    the English Literary Past,
    1660–1781* (London,
    2001).
5   Niklas Luhmann, *Soziale
    Systeme: Grundriss einer
    allgemeinen Theorie*
    (Frankfurt, 1984);
    Siegfried J. Schmidt, *Die
    Selbstorganisation des
    Sozialsystems: Literatur
    im 18. Jahrhundert*
    (Frankfurt, 1989)

poets of the eighteenth century had to be dug up, in an almost archaeological process, by philologists from dispersed manuscripts. The relation between later periods and earlier ones is more often than not one of recuperation rather than filiation. Thomas Kinsella testifies to this condition in his essay 'The Irish Writer'. When looking for 'the past in himself', and regressing beyond the nineteenth century, Kinsella encounters 'a great cultural blur': 'I must exchange one language for another, my native English for eighteenth-century Irish'. It is a sense of discontinuity that Kinsella describes as 'coming, so to speak, from a broken and uprooted family, of being drawn to those who share my origins and finding that we cannot share our lives'. This condition is quite different from the position of someone like Proust, who, across Sainte-Beuve, Balzac and Racine, stands in an unbroken filiation of authors, each of whom was cognizant of their own historical place and generational position *vis-à-vis* their predecessors.

The Western 'invention of authorship', in other words, created historical consciousness both about and within the author. It allowed the Accademia della Crusca to edit Dante, prompted the publication of Shakespeare's First Folio, and allowed Dr. Johnson to write his *Lives of the Poets* (usually seen as one of the mainsprings of modern literary history-writing) — but it is also operative in the author's own self-image and self-historicization, at least from the moment that at Edmund Spenser's funeral (or so Camden has it) his fellow-poets threw elegies into his tomb.[4] The sense of history that T. S. Eliot invokes in *Tradition and the Individual Talent* is operative within literature itself, and it is easily amenable to being replicated and discussed by literary historians. But, once again, that only holds for literary historians dealing with an author-centred, historically self-aware literary system (which is precisely that, a *system*, with its own organization and describable dynamics, as per Niklas Luhmann and Siegfried

Schmidt).[5] Things are not so simple when dealing with medieval literature, or with pre-modern or non-European literature, or with much of Irish literature.

Whenever literary histories deal with these uncongenial periods or fields, they will impose a chronology and teleology that is all too often misleading. Literary histories of England will tend to begin with *Beowulf*; those of France with the *Chanson de Roland*; those of Germany with the *Nibelungenlied*; those of Ireland with the Ulster cycle. In each case, a national Big Bang, the nation's own *Iliad*, stands at the beginning of the narrative (not so, I am happy to say, with Ó Cathasaigh's opening chapter in *CHIL*, which leads with St. Patrick). But in all of those cases, the epic in question dropped out of circulation around the time of Gutenberg, only to be retrieved, many centuries later, by modern philologists in the Edward O'Reilly/Eleanor Knott mode. The first edition of the *Nibelungenlied* is from 1807; *Beowulf*, 1815; *Chanson de Roland*, 1836; *Táin Bó Cuailgne* was, from 1600 onwards, known only as an echo and a reputation until almost the end of the nineteenth century. Leibniz did not know the *Nibelungen*, Voltaire was ignorant of the *Chanson de Roland*, Addison of *Beowulf*, Swift and Ó Rathaile had no knowledge of the *Táin* — though all of them would have been familiar with Virgil or the Psalms. Vernacular epic did not show up in these author's rear-view mirrors, although the linear-progressive presentation of literary history would suggest otherwise.

Such processes of oblivion and recuperation are hidden from view in that type of literary history that is concerned only with the production line, with linear progress and innovation, and which merely wishes to chart how things at certain periods came to be done differently. Production-line literary history charts innovatory moments: the arrival of new schools, new paradigms, new types of poetics, for example the onset

A man at a bookstall, Bachelor's Walk, Dublin, 1973. Photograph: Richard Tillbrook, National Library of Ireland.

of the Enlightenment, of Romanticism, of modernism. This stands to reason. We like our artists to be original, creative, rebellious, experimental, non-complacent, so those are the terms in which we herald their achievement and signal their historical importance. But that bright spotlight leaves much in the shadows. What was the literary frame of reference of each succeeding generation? What was forgotten or obsolescent? What older patterns were still prevalent, albeit no longer glamorous or attention grabbing? What was, from generation to generation, the *arrière-garde*? What did people actually *read*? Who were the Agatha Christies, Ian Flemings, Robert Ludlums and Maeve Binchys of the eighteenth and nineteenth centuries, the

Georges Simenons and the Patrick O'Brians? Such questions are all the more pressing when we deal with literatures of scarcity and literatures that are inherently less strongly fixated on innovation, originality and nonconformism.

In any case, the genetic, innovation-oriented approach to literary history can no longer stand complacently on its own, and will need to be complemented by a reception-oriented one: a history of recycling, of reading, of reprints, copies and anthologies. Book histories like the recent *Guide to Irish Fiction, 1650–1900* (2006) by Rolf and Magda Loeber may give us a greater insight into a society's reading culture and provide a much-needed backdrop for a properly contextualized history of literary innovation.

In his essay '*Qu'est-ce qu'un auteur?*', Michel Foucault reminds us that 'First of all, texts are objects of appropriation.' Many of the *CHIL* essays take a contrary view and treat literature primarily as an expression. It is at this point that the question of Irishness comes in. *Irish* literature seems implicitly to mean: such literature as in some way or other expresses an Irish condition or experience (hence, no Thomas Mayne Reid, no Eriugena, no Ernest Dowden in *CHIL*). Irishness can be expressed through the medium of Latin, Gaelic, English or cinema; it can be by tonsured clerics or tattooed lesbians; what unites them between the covers of *CHIL* is the shared Irishness. The category of nationality trumps all others.

I do not want to labour the obvious, and rather cheap, point that the notion of Irishness begs questions almost as badly as a 'literary history of authors whose names contain the letter Q'; the intriguing thing is, rather, that this Irishness, whatever one wishes to make of it, is treated as the quality that is being *expressed* or reflected in what we call 'Irish literature'. Would it not make more sense to see Irishness as the factor that gives a given corpus of texts the potential of being *appropriated* as Irish? Texts belong to

Irish literature to the extent that they can be appropriated as such. Not only is canonicity a function of a text's reception trajectory; its very nationality is likewise located in its appropriating audience, its readership, at least as much as in the author's background or outlook. What is more, this act of appropriation can be contested between various competitors, for culture is always in short supply: both Duns Scotus and Ossian/Oisín have been hotly claimed by Ireland and Scotland. Authors such as Shaw and Wilde and, outstandingly, Edmund Burke, who until a few decades ago were usually seen as plain-vanilla English (when that term was still used to refer to a language rather than a nationality), have become progressively more Irish over the past few decades. In this respect, *CHIL* presents a paradox. Certainly in the earlier chapters, the Gaelic and English traditions are like oil and vinegar, largely heedless of each other, and the common appellation 'Irish' is (as Metternich said about Italy) merely a geographical expression until well after Swift. Nonetheless, the various traditions are set forth as jointly embodying a shared Irish identity — an identity which, one may suspect, was retroactively created for them by readers' categorizations and subsequent appropriations, and now consolidated by this survey.

Irish literature is, indeed, as the editors point out in their Introduction, a canon rather than a corpus. A challenging task for future literary historians might be to trace, not the chronologically arranged texts and authors forming part of that canon but the history of how that canon came to be formed as it did. *CHIL* is a rock-solid History of Irish Literature, but in all too many instances it tends to idealize the Irishness of its subject matter into an admiringly invoked motivating force, some sort of national *élan vital*. Take one step back and what we might achieve is a metahistory of Irish literature: the history of how a certain canon came to be configured as 'Irish', was contested, formed and variously appropriated until it reached the shape and substance it now has. ■

THE SALMON FISHER TO THE SALMON

The ridged lip set upstream, you flail
Inland again; your exile in the sea
Unconditionally cancelled by the pull
Of your home water's gravity.

And I stand in the centre, casting.
The river, cramming under me, reflects
Slung gaff and net, and a white wrist flicking,
Setting you up the well-dressed specks.
Flies well dressed with tint and flech
Walton thought garden-worms, perfumed
By oil crushed from dark ivy berries
The lure that took you best. But here you're doomed
By senseless hunger in your eyes.

Ripples arrowing beyond me,
The current strumming rhythms up my leg:
Involved in water's choreography
I go like you by gleam and drag

And will strike when you strike, to kill.
We're both annihilated with the fly.
You can't resist a gullet full of steel.
I will turn home fish-smelling, scaly.

Seamus Heaney.

How to Remember?

Ciaran Carson

The Ulster Renaissance: Poetry in Belfast, 1962–1972
Heather Clark
Oxford: Oxford University Press, 2006. 256 pages. ISBN 978-0-19-928731-4

Memory plays tricks. Any time a shard of memory comes to light, whether dug up or stumbled upon, it is altered by the act of remembering. The facts of any case are open to negotiation. Our memory is a story constantly revised each time we enter it for confirmation of what we think we are or were in thought and word and deed. The little that we do remember is a retrospective construct, a self-ingratiating fable, perhaps.

Of course there may be material back-up: documents, letters, drafts, typescripts, certificates, poems fully or partially achieved, receipts, photographs. Ephemera. Carbon copies. Flimsies. These too are open to interpretation. One can doubt their authenticity, or raise questions as to their selectivity. A researcher is not to know how much material a poet has consigned to the public domain of a university archive, and how much he might have retained, or burned, or lost. The poet himself might not even know. One fills in or makes up the gaps in the record. Or one might not perceive a gap in the record. The writing of history depends on such circumstances, and we must make of them what we can: as the football pundits say, you can only play the team that's put in front of you. So it is with Heather Clark's painstaking study, which, in focusing on the work of Seamus Heaney, Derek Mahon, Michael Longley, James Simmons and Paul Muldoon in the decade 1962–72, makes considerable use of the correspondence of those poets, their recorded recollections, and their archival holdings in Emory University in Atlanta, Georgia, an institution that seems to have cornered much of the market for the papers of contemporary Irish poets. Without access to these materials, Clark's book would be a very different one; it might well not have been written at all. And it is quite possible that no such access would exist were it not for Coca-Cola, a point to which I will return in due course. History is full of unexpected contingencies.

Clark's narrative begins with an arrival and ends with a departure. In 1962 Philip Hobsbaum came to lecture in Queen's University Belfast and for four years conducted a series of weekly writing workshops. The workshops then continued under the aegis of Seamus Heaney; and when he left Belfast for County Wicklow in 1972, the workshops ceased, though a loose clique of sorts continued to operate in various drinking establishments in the university area, where writers like Longley, Muldoon, Frank Ormsby, John Morrow, Robert Johnstone, Douglas Marshall and myself would gather to indulge in gossip and the wicked but friendly banter known in Belfast as 'slagging'. In any event, the poets

Seamus Heaney, 'The Salmon Fisher to the Salmon', Groupsheet, Longley Papers, Manuscript Archives and Rare Book Library, Emory University.

Seamus Heaney, May 1970. Photograph: (John) Edward McKenzie Lucie-Smith, bromide print, National Portrait Gallery, London.

associated with the comparatively decorous Hobsbaum and Heaney workshops became known as the Belfast Group. Would these poets be the poets they turned out to be had there been no such thing as the Group? Was it a Group, or a group? A coterie? A mutual admiration society? Did its product constitute an Ulster Renaissance? Was there ever a Naissance? Do such definitions matter? Clark lays her cards more or less squarely on the table:

> While acknowledging that both history and literature will always shift and subvert any perimeters we place around them, I want to challenge the notion that the terms 'Belfast Group' and 'Ulster Renaissance' are a kind of reductive shorthand made up by critics and journalists to fabricate a common goal or voice. On the contrary, this notion is the myth that needs revising. Studying these poets' (and their poems') relationships with one another complicates rather than limits our understanding of their individual achievements, and raises provocative questions about the social nature of literary production. As Longley put it, 'Moving forward with coevals and potential rivals has a key role and it's very seldom that someone flowers on their own.' Longley hints at precisely the claim that I make in this study: that during the sixties and early seventies, these poets honed their craft both in accordance with and opposition to each other — a poetic practice which Bloom, referring to the relationship between dead and living writers, calls 'creative correction' or 'willful revisionism'. It was in part such revisionism that drove the Ulster Renaissance, inspiring a long-running poetic dialogue which has produced some of the finest poetry of the twentieth century, and making Belfast, says Edna Longley, 'Irish poetry's strangest port of call'. To learn from this dialogue, we must explore the intimate, interpersonal relationships that propelled these poets'

work, along with the events which helped Belfast — once characterized by Louis MacNeice as a city of 'hard cold fire' — to become, in Ciaran Carson's words, the 'mouth of the poem'.

I should say at this point that though I was involved in the last few sessions of the Group, I am quite rightly more or less excluded from Clark's study, along with John Montague, Medbh McGuckian and Tom Paulin, since like them I was not 'as closely involved in the local renaissance as those who met under Hobsbaum's roof'. But I should point out that my gloss on 'Belfast' as 'the mouth of the poem' (in my essay 'Farset' in *Belfast Confetti*) was intended to be taken playfully, as a spurious and ironic etymology for the Irish *Béal Feirste*, from which 'Belfast' derives. *Béal* can indeed mean 'a mouth', or 'an opening', or 'an approach'; *fearsad*, of which *feirste* is the genitive, can mean, according to Dinneen's wonderful *Irish–English Dictionary*, many things, including: a shaft; a spindle; the ulna of the arm; the fibula of the leg; a club; an axle; a bar or bank of sand as at low water, a deep narrow channel on a strand at low tide; a pit or a pool of water; a verse; a poem. In other words, I wanted to loosen up the possible definitions of 'Belfast'. I wanted to make it multivalent and polysemic. I wanted it to resist easy interpretation. I wanted it to imply whatever its beholder saw in it. Noting that Dwelly's *Gaelic–English Dictionary* gives 'wallet' as another possible meaning for *fearsad*, I could say that 'Belfast' means 'the opening of the wallet'. Which brings us back to the archive, since none of the Irish poets in it, to my knowledge, gave their papers to Emory for free. And, as a way of trying to make sense of the recollections of the poets cited by Clark, their contributions to the archive, and their subsequent place in her literary history, I want to indulge myself in some memories of my own, flimsy and unreliable as they are.

Lyric Theatre, Belfast, *c.* 1976. Back row, left to right: Paul Muldoon, John Hewitt, Patrick Galvin, Frank Ormsby, Ciaran Carson. Front row: Seamus Deane, John Boyd, Michael Longley. Photograph: private collection, Belfast.

When, in 1993 (I only know the year because I've just looked it up on the online archive catalogue), I was approached by one of the Kennys of the eponymous bookshop in Galway to sell my 'papers' to Emory University, I was surprised and gratified that anyone should be prepared to pay good money for the contents of a few cardboard boxes gathering dust under my bed. And the money was very welcome just then, so I had little hesitation in entering into what seemed to me a good deal, first with Kennys and subsequently with Steve Enniss of Emory. It is an arrangement that continues to this day, as I consign periodic batches of written, scrawled or printed material to the Special Collections Department of the Robert W. Woodruff Library, named for the president of the Coca-Cola company who in 1979 endowed Emory University with a gift of $105 million. The Coke connection only came to my notice some years after the initial sale of my papers, when before reading my poems there I attended a reception in the impressive penthouse gallery of the Woodruff Library tower

block and found it given over to a display of Coca-Cola memorabilia — vintage bottles, trays, urns, mirrors, calendars, posters and other advertising materials, bills, receipts, correspondences. I learned then that Coca-Cola was invented in Atlanta by the pharmacist and morphine addict John Pemberton, who in 1886 brewed the first batch of Coca-Cola in a three-legged brass kettle in his back yard. The economy of Atlanta, and thus of its educational establishments, has been Coke-dependent for over a century.

Emory began as a small liberal arts college in the small town of Oxford, some forty miles east of Atlanta. In 1914 Asa Candler, the founder of the Coca-Cola company and the brother of a former president of the college, gifted Emory $1 million dollars and 72 acres of land in Atlanta. It became a university that maintains its Coca-Cola links to this day. To give one example, its Coca-Cola Artists in Residence Program currently provides 'an opportunity to meet mutual educational goals through the

Michael Longley, Seamus Heaney and Derek Mahon, 1977. Photograph: Heaney Papers, Manuscript Archives and Rare Book Library, Emory University.

unique creativity of the arts, to improve the outlook for arts education in Atlanta, and to improve the quality of life in the community'. I wonder if they give out free Coke at the events held under the auspices of that programme. *I'd like to buy the world a Coke.* At any rate, besides the Ciaran Carson Archive in the Special Collections of the Robert W. Woodruff Library, there is a Coca-Cola Archive. I was tempted, when I first heard of this serendipitously alliterative coincidence, to write, and sell to Coca-Cola for what I thought might be considerable profit, an 'Ode to Coke' — or maybe it would be called 'My First Coke' — a poem which, in Proustian fashion, would extol the virtues of the said beverage, and would be

filled with words like 'gush', 'buzz', 'fizz', 'smack', 'glug', 'lip' and 'rush'. I never got round to it, but I still entertain the notion, while acknowledging that the Irish poets in Emory's Special Collections have been to some extent bought by Coca-Cola gold. Posterity comes at a price, though I should say that some of us who gave our papers to Emory — Longley, Muldoon and myself — once entertained the idea of doing some mischief to posterity by inventing a literary feud between ourselves, complete with vituperative or apologetic letters that would then be consigned to the archive. But we were too lazy, if not too moral, to engage in such a conspiracy.

Anyway, maybe we are only getting back our dues. Back in Belfast in the 1970s, or maybe it was the 1980s, some of us drank a great deal of Coke, not for itself — they had taken out the cocaine in 1905 — but as a mixer for the notorious DRAC, Dark Rum and Coke, 'in a tall glass, with plenty of ice, please'. You needed the ice to cut the syrupy sweetness of both dark rum and Coke. In venues like the Welly or the Bot or the Eg (aka the Wellington Park Hotel, the Botanic Inn and the Eglantine Inn) we would gather in twos or threes or fours or fives to drink DRACs and Guinness and Bushmills and Powers and talk. Heaney and Mahon had left Belfast by then. So 'we' would have included Longley, Muldoon, Ormsby, Johnstone, Morrow, the critic Michael Allen, among others. We talked a great deal about a great many things, and poetry was not necessarily at the top of the agenda, which was fluid. There was lots of smoke in the air: 'in those days', as Michael Longley says, 'they hadn't put the cancer in cigarettes'. As a matter of fact, the first words Michael ever spoke to me were occasioned by a cigarette. We were at a Group meeting, standing side by side at the back of the small, packed back room of the English Department at 4 University Square. 'Oh, a Parkie,' he said, 'I'd love a Parkie, haven't had one for years.' He seemed to me to be putting on a proletarian Belfast accent. I was smoking Park Drive untipped at the time, a powerful working-class cigarette. I proffered him the open packet — how often do you see that once familiar gesture nowadays? — and he took one, I gave him a light, and, as I remember it, for he does not remember it, he said, 'The name's Longley. Michael Longley.' Of course I knew who he was, as I think he must have known I must have known. I was delighted to meet this luminary of the poetry scene. Was it 1970 that we first met? 1971? Who was the featured poet? I can't remember, though I think it might have been Heaney. As I tell it, the encounter is banal, but not inconsequential. Over the years Michael and I shared many cigarettes, and

thus many conversations, the vast bulk of which we cannot now remember. There are so many things we can't remember.

Wondering if my memory of those times might be improved by consulting the catalogue of my papers in the Robert J. Woodruff Library, I enter its virtual Irish Literary Portal and go to 'The Ciaran Carson Papers'. I've looked at the catalogue in a cursory manner before, but only now do I realize its full extent, and the full extent of my memory loss, for when I click on 'Subseries 2.2b: Uncollected Poems', and scroll down the page, I realize that there is much here that I have no recollection whatsoever of having written. Many of the titles are a mystery to me: 'At the Poetry Reading'; 'At the Zoo'; 'For Reasons of Security'; 'Firing Range'; 'To the German Language'; 'Wrong Side of the Fence'; and, ironically, 'How to Remember'. Now what that was about? There is a poem called 'Paul', which I guess has nothing to do with Paul Muldoon, for when I note that it precedes another called 'Philomena', I now do remember that at some time or other I embarked on what I thought might be a series of poems named for Christian martyrs. It came to nothing; or rather, it came to these two entries in the archive.

But I am inadvertently reminded of Paul Muldoon, and some of the uncountable, and sometimes unaccountable, times we spent together drinking DRACs, back in whatever years they were. Back then, we drank and smoked as if there were no tomorrow. Paul was working in the BBC, I in the Arts Council, and we would often meet 'after work', which usually meant about 4 p.m., in the Bot or the Welly. After one such meeting, when the bars had closed, we ended up in Paul's flat in Notting Hill off the Malone Road, where Paul thought there might be further drink; or maybe we bought a carry-out. I don't know what time it was when we found we had run out of cigarettes. So we decided that the best place to purchase

Paul Muldoon, 'The Indians on Alcatraz', Groupsheet, Longley Papers, Manuscript Archives and Rare Book Library, Emory University.

THE INDIANS ON ALCATRAZ

Through time their sharp features have softened and blurred
As if they still inhabited the middle distance,

As if these people have never stopped riding hard
In an opposite direction, the people of the broken lances

Who have seemed forever going back. Now they have willed this reservation,
It is as if they accept that they are islanders at heart,

As if this island running away to sea and seed, bartered
For with bright trinkets, has forever been the faroff destination

Of the bands of little figures on horseback returning, returning.
After the newspaper and television reports I remark

On how people can still be themselves, but each morning
Leaves me more grateful for the fact that they never attack after dark.

                                                        Paul Muldoon.

more cigarettes was the BBC Club, which maintained a late licence, so we could get a drink there as well; and we decided that the best way of getting there was to drive there in Paul's dilapidated Hillman Imp convertible.[1] We got into the car to find that Paul was incapable of driving, so I undertook the task instead, I who had failed my driving test about ten years before and hadn't done anything about it since. Somehow we got there. We entered the club, bought cigarettes and drink and stayed and talked some more until we were asked to leave. When we emerged, we'd forgotten where I'd parked the car, and the memory ends with us staggering through the streets of Belfast, searching for the means to get home. I am reminded now that this Notting Hill is one of the Muldoon abodes — *Chez Moy*, a phrase I believe I coined — that figures in his poem 'History'. It is a poem, among other things, about the unreliability of memory and history. I thought it might be cited in Clark's book, but it is not.

Where and when exactly did we first have sex?
Do you remember? Was it Fitzroy Avenue,
Or Cromwell Road, or Notting Hill?
Your place or mine? Marseilles or Aix?
Or as long ago as that Thursday evening
When you and I climbed through the bay window
On the ground floor of Aquinas Hall
And into the room where MacNeice wrote 'Snow',
Or the room where they say he wrote 'Snow'.

1 After writing this, I met Paul Muldoon in London. According to him, the vehicle in question was a Triumph Herald.

Table of drink in Wellington Park Hotel, Belfast, April 1978. Left to right: John Morrow, Ciaran Carson, Frank Ormsby, Jimmy Simmons, Michael Longley. Photograph: BBCNI (Wilfred Green).

What exactly did we talk about, at his place or mine? It's all a blur now, but it seems we had good times, and we never fell out, unless it was falling out of pubs. I was deeply impressed by Paul ever since I first set eyes on him, then a pale, thin wisp of a boy from the Moy delivering his poems in a whisper at an undergraduate reading in a dim-lit room in Queen's University. I could catch barely half of the words, but what I heard seemed startlingly brilliant. Some weeks later I went up and introduced myself to him in the Snack Bar of the Students' Union, and we became increasingly close friends. I was daunted by him from the beginning, and when I look back now at the contents of the single worksheet I presented to the Group in about 1971 — I've just found it online at Emory — I see that half of the poems are near enough Muldoon pastiches. I learned the necessary anxiety of that influence, while remaining grateful for the ongoing presence and development of his poems throughout the years. I could not help but be influenced.

I mention all this as some kind of parallel to the kind of thing that might have gone on between Heaney, Longley, Simmons, Mahon, and indeed Muldoon, in the period covered by Clark's survey. Though relationships between the former three particularly, according to Clark, were somewhat more volatile from time to time. Words were uttered unadvisedly over drink, words that were difficult to retract when they could not be remembered the morning after. By 1976, says Clark, the relationship between Heaney and Longley had grown tense:

> Things came to a head one night during a drunken row at the Hammonds' home when Longley belligerently claimed that Mahon was a better poet than Heaney. The next morning, after calling David Hammond to find out exactly what he had said, he wrote an achingly sincere six-page letter of apology to Marie Heaney in which he castigated himself for his stormy, offensive behaviour. He was envious of Heaney's fame, he admitted, but knew he also enjoyed it 'by proxy'. He was annoyed people assumed his admiration of Mahon equalled a criticism of Heaney, though he also felt Heaney did not deserve more attention. He said his resentment had been building for years …

The letter to Marie Heaney can be read in the Michael Longley Papers in Emory University. But Marie Heaney never read it: it was never sent. Is the archive a kind of public confessional? Are some poets more indiscreet than others at what they allow into the public domain? Certainly, some appear to have little compunction in showing themselves as driven by vanity and envy. In June 1968 James Simmons writes to Tony Harrison, 'The Irish papers still won't publish my poems. Derek Mahon is Poetry Book Society Choice for Autumn. Grrr. Heaney is Somerset Maugham Award.' A few months earlier he had written to Harrison:

> The Ulster Arts Council played a rather dirty trick on Jimmy — They rejected, when approached by him to back a tour of poetry and singing — no cash, etc. Yet 3 months later sent Heaney, Longley and a singer called David Hammond all around the province — I could spit — I supposed their material is safe with just enough SEX thrown in to make an audience feel mature and sophisticated.

This was after Simmons, his wife and a friend, sponsored by the Arts Council, had performed bawdy songs and poetry before an audience of 'shocked senior citizens' in Bangor, most of whom left the hall before the night was over. Nor did Simmons's predilection to kiss and tell go down well with the Longleys on occasions:

> Simmons had also become involved in a more personal feud with Michael Longley. In July 1970, the Longleys spent a weekend in Portrush with the Simmonses, where they enjoyed some sailing and a day out in Ballycastle. However, after a long Saturday night spent drinking, an alcohol-fuelled row erupted between the two poets. Longley had apparently implied that Simmons's poetry was clumsy, and his morals — particularly his laissez-faire attitude to marital fidelity — shoddy. Simmons argued there was nothing wrong with publishing a confessional poem about an affair, but Longley, Edna, and Simmons's wife Laura disagreed. Furious, he stormed off to bed.

> Edna and Michael left Portrush the next morning, wondering if they would ever be invited back. Longley was deeply troubled by the argument, and wrote Simmons a humble letter of apology …

Unlike the letter to Marie Heaney, this one was sent: it is in the James Simmons Papers in Emory. More strained relations were to follow, particularly the big Field Day Row, involving, on one side, Heaney, Seamus Deane, Brian Friel, Hammond and Paulin, with the Longleys on the other. It's a subject that could take up several books by itself, and I don't propose to rehearse the pros and cons of that debate in this review. In any event, whatever grievances existed between Heaney and the Longleys have now largely been put aside. Perhaps some memories of those grievances have been expunged, or revised, and the participants can see the past in a kindlier light than they did at the time.

Heather Clark's conclusions are much the same, though she is more convinced than I am of the value of expressions like 'Renaissance' or 'Group'. Belfast is a small place. It is indisputable that from 1962 to 1972 a number of poets lived in Belfast. They gathered in pubs, back rooms and flats. They talked and drank together. Sometimes they read each other's work, and took it in. The looked over their shoulders at each other, and were influenced by each other. They gossiped about each other. Sometimes they fell out. Sometimes they forgot why they had fallen out. They wrote letters that were never sent, and poems that were never published. Only they know what they destroyed, or perhaps they have forgotten what they destroyed. Sometimes they wrote about the same thing, since the same things were present all around them: islands, for one thing, were much written about. We all live on an island. I'm reminded of Leopold Bloom's definition in *Ulysses* of a nation as 'the same people living in the same place'. One need not offer the tag of 'Renaissance' to describe an accident of history and place. In any event, whatever was happening did not end in 1972. The conversations and the poetry kept going.

In November 2006, as director of the Seamus Heaney Centre for Poetry at Queen's University, I was privileged to organize, with Frank Ormsby, a Gala Poetry Evening in the Whitla Hall to celebrate the publication of *The Blackbird's Nest*, an anthology, edited by Frank, of the work of poets associated with Queen's. It had been my aim, when accepting the Heaney Centre post, to re-create some of the atmosphere I felt at those Group readings and pub conversations in small back rooms in the early seventies. I also wanted to extend that room into the world at large on occasions. Longley, McGuckian, Alan Gillis, Jean Bleakney,

Chris Agee, Gearóid Mac Lochlainn, Sinead Morrissey, Leontia Flynn, Ormsby and myself read that night to a packed hall of some eleven hundred people — surely among the biggest audiences ever for poetry in these islands. It was visible and audible evidence that poetry in Belfast, some thirty-odd years after the demise of the original Belfast Group, is alive and well. Seamus Heaney had intended also to read, but was unable to be present due to illness. The evening was ended by Longley, who paid tribute to his 'old friend', wished him a speedy recovery, and, besides reading his own contribution to the anthology, read Seamus's. He read the work beautifully, with evident love. The evening was recorded by Paul Maddern, a young poet studying at the Heaney Centre, as part of a thesis that will explore the dynamics of poetry readings. Perhaps some day a copy of that recording might find its way to the Special Collections Archive in Emory. And it need not be bought by Coca-Cola money; it can be a gift outright. ■

Pied Beauty

Bríona Nic Dhiarmada

Trén bhFearann Breac: An Díláithriú Cultúir agus Nualitríocht na Gaeilge
Máirín Nic Eoin
Baile Átha Cliath: Cois Life, 2005. 580 pages. ISBN 1-901176-51-7

Hugo Hamilton's recent best-selling memoir was entitled *The Speckled People* (2003). Hamilton, the child of a German/Gaeilgeoir family who grew up in Dublin in the 1950s and 1960s, explains its title's provenance thus: 'We are the new Irish. Partly from Ireland and partly from somewhere else, half-Irish and half-German. We're the speckled people, he says, the "brack" people, which is a word that comes from the Irish language …'[1]

1   Hugo Hamilton, *The Speckled People* (London and New York, 2003), 7
2   See Lillis Ó Laoire, 'Níl sé Doiligh é a Iompar!/ No Load to Carry: A Personal Response to the Current Situation of Irish', in Ciarán Mac Murchaidh, ed., *Who Needs Irish?* (Dublin, 2004), 61, quoted in Nic Eoin, *Trén bhFearann Breac*, 245.
3   Nic Eoin, *Trén bhFearann Breac*, 18

Fionnuala Ní Chiosáin
Infant View
2001
acrylic, oil, gouache & sumi ink on aluminium
56.5 x 76.5 cm
courtesy of the artist and the Kerlin Gallery

Hamilton's use of 'brack' (Irish *breac*, 'speckled') has an echo in a recent essay on identity and the Irish language by scholar and *sean-nós* singer Lillis Ó Laoire, who commented that 'the world we live in today is a speckled world and we must realize that we are all *breacdhaoine* "speckled people"'.[2] And likewise, Máirín Nic Eoin employs the word in a similar sense in her enormously significant new work, *Trén bhFearann Breac*, the title translating as 'Through the Speckled Land'. The title comes from a poem of the same name, 'Trén bhFearann Breac', by contemporary poet Colm Breathnach, which, according to Nic Eoin, clarified for her the central theme of the book.

In all of the above cases the word *breac* operates as a gloss on hybridity, a concept popularized in cultural and literary discourse by post-colonial theory. Indeed, the stated aim of Nic Eoin's work is to examine modern and contemporary literature in Irish using analytical methods that recognize the socio-linguistic reality in which those who write in the language operate. Nic Eoin's subtitle, *An Díláithriú Cultúir agus Nualitríocht na Gaeilge* (Cultural Dislocation and Modern Literature in Irish), makes overt a concern for another preoccupation of post-colonial criticism — dislocation. Tellingly, while post-colonial perspectives have been at the centre of the most lively debates in Irish Studies in recent years, this is the first full-length book in Irish to enter those debates. This is perhaps surprising given the historical circumstances of the language and literature. Nic Eoin herself draws attention to the apparent resistance of Irish-language scholars to position themselves within this debate:

> *Is beag scoláire nó criticeoir Gaeilge atá tar éis páirt a ghlacadh sa phlé agus peirspictíocht na Gaeilge a thabhairt ar ghné ar bith de na hábhair imris is argóna a chothaigh an tionscnamh. Is beag criticeoir Gaeilge atá tar éis seasamh poiblí a ghlacadh faoin mbunargóint maidir le bailíocht choincheap na hiarchoilíneachta mar bhunchoincheap léirmhínithe agus stair chultúrtha na hÉireann, nó stair chultúrtha agus liteartha na Gaeilge, faoi chaibidil.*[3]

Few Irish-language scholars or critics have participated in the debate or brought the Irish-language perspective to the points of argument and disagreement that underpin the enterprise. Few Irish-language scholars have taken a public position on the basic argument about the validity of the post-colonial as a basic interpretative concept when discussing the cultural history of Ireland or the cultural and literary history of the Irish language.

The reasons why this might be so, although addressed, are not fully answered here, but Nic Eoin's book opens the door for further enquiry. Questions might include the following: Was it the case that, in the contemporary period, some Irish-language critics and writers were eager or anxious to distance themselves from the tenets of what could be seen as an outmoded and narrow version of cultural nationalism and the old binary opposition of Gael and Gall and preferred to ignore the political nature of Irish-language literature, which then became somehow naturalized or unproblematized? Or, on the other hand, did Irish-language scholars take it as read that Irish-language literature belonged *de facto* to the pre-colonial, the (anti)colonial and the post-colonial and that therefore in a sense it was a non-debate?

It is also certainly the case, as Nic Eoin mentions, that Irish-language scholars whose work deals quite overtly with the impact of colonialism and conquest on literary production, but who did not necessarily cloak their work in the theoretical attire and discourse of post-colonialism, have been left outside the debate, however relevant their work might be. Nic Eoin herself states that her own approach is based on the premise that the term or classification 'post-colonial' is of little importance within the Irish-language critical context. She acknowledges at the same time that the post-colonial project is one that has much to offer to Irish-language critics, who might, she

suggests, creatively ally themselves with its practitioners. She quotes Martine Pelletier's 1999 essay on Field Day, where Pelletier, speaking of 'Ireland's literature generally, and the Field Day plays in particular', noted that they clearly evince several of the characteristics most often perceived as central to post-colonial literature: an obsession with identity which often translates into an anxiety about origins, a questioning of authenticity, an interest in hybridity, a form of in-between-ness or *entre-deux*, which is indeed inseparable from the experience of colonial occupation. Concurrently there exists a fascination for language in many guises, where the post-colonial can meet the post-modern.[4]

Nic Eoin takes these same themes to be central in both modern Irish-language literature and criticism but goes on to assert that this literature offers another perspective, a different insight from that of Irish literature in English — the perspective of 'a language community who have suffered minoritization in their own country'.[5]

One might validly make the point that, almost a decade on from Pelletier's remarks, there have been enormous changes in Irish life: the peace process in the North, the continued economic boom in the South, and the new populations of immigrants and migrant workers. These changes are beginning to have consequences for the post-colonial debate — with questions of hybridity and multiculturalism becoming, if anything, more critical than ever before.

Nic Eoin most importantly does put forward the idea that the type of textual criticism that came to the fore in the 1960s in Irish was an attempt to escape from the cultural prescriptions of the Corkery school and of the Revivalists. She is not here concerned with questions of ideology as with supplying a new paradigm for the 'state of the language of literature in Irish'.[6] What Nic Eoin seeks to do is not simply to redress

4 Martine Pelletier, 'Field Day and "The Irish-English Collision"', *European Journal of English Studies*, 3, 3 (1999), 332, quoted in Nic Eoin, *Trén bhFearann Breac*, 45

5 Nic Eoin, *Trén bhFearann Breac*, 45

6 Nic Eoin, *Trén bhFearann Breac*, 13

7   See Gearóid Denvir, 'Ó
    Shíolteagasc go Critic:
    Litríocht Dhioscúrsúil
    na Gaeilge san Aois
    Seo', *Léachtaí Cholm
    Cille*, 26 [Léann na
    Gaeilge] (Maigh Nuad,
    1996), 178–218.

8   Cathal Ó Searcaigh,
    'The View from the
    Glen', *Irish Pages*, 2, 2
    (2004), 229–35

9   Chinua Achebe, 'The
    African Writer and the
    English Language', in
    Patrick Williams and
    Laura Chisman, eds.,
    *Colonial Discourse and
    Post-Colonial Theory:
    A Reader* (Hemel
    Hempstead, 1993),
    quoted in Nic Eoin,
    Trén bhFearann Breac,
    23

10 Ngugi wa Thiong'o,
    *Decolonising the
    Mind* (London, 1986);
    Michael Hartnett, *A
    Farewell to English*
    (Loughcrew, 1975)

the balance but to change the very nature of the debate and the whole thrust of literary criticism in the language from the old binary opposition between 'traditionalists and modernists', as Gearóid Denvir has called them, or 'nativists and progressives' to use Philip O'Leary's terms.[7] Nic Eoin seeks, however, to correct what she sees as the overcompensatory nature of modern and contemporary criticism in the Irish language with its insistence on the primacy of the text as the site of analysis — itself a necessary response to the fetishization of language/ linguistic purity both as ideology and aesthetic — to a critical stance that would concern itself with the linguistic *context*, that of minority/minoritized discourse not simply as sociological or historical backdrop but as a signifier itself inscribed, according to Nic Eoin, in every aspect of textuality. In the hands of more literal and less theoretically adept critics than Nic Eoin this might become seriously reductive, a return to the old days of the 'language and cultural police', the 'linguistic McCarthyites who inspected your grammar and your syntax', as Cathal Ó Searcaigh put it in a recent essay.[8]

Nic Eoin gives due mention to the work of Declan Kiberd, one of the few critics, post-colonial or otherwise, to work in both languages and literatures. Her own thesis, while forthright in its political/cultural engagement, avoids narrow reductionism. Still, there are blind spots where a comparative approach — a reading across linguistic boundaries as well as within one's own language tradition might best elucidate the specificity of particular texts. Would it not help us to read Gearóid Mac Lochlainn's poetry in light of Ciaran Carson's for example, or in light of Eoin McNamee's prose, and vice versa; to read Micheál Ó Conghaile in light of Jamie O'Neill or Colm Tóibín, and vice versa: to read Nuala Ní Dhomhnaill in light of Medbh McGuckian and Eiléan Ní Chuilleanáin as has been done by Ríóna Ní Fhrighill, with her comparative reading of Ní Dhomhnaill and Eavan

Boland), as well as, of course, Máire Mhac an tSaoi and Caitlín Maude?

In her first chapter, Nic Eoin surveys and critiques the rise of post-colonial theory internationally within literary and cultural studies, noting their anglophone tendencies and origins and drawing attention in particular to the marginalization of literary and cultural texts and production in native/ indigenous/pre-colonial languages by the very same theoretical practices that sought to chart or unveil the processes of assimilation and acculturation that were themselves a central part of the colonial enterprise.

Nic Eoin argues strongly, however, for a two-way dynamic — if Irish-language critics have something to learn from post-colonial theory, then post-colonial critics and criticism has much to learn from Irish-language literature and criticism. As an example of what an Irish-language perspective could bring to the post-colonial discourse internationally, Nic Eoin cites the debate concerning the use of indigenous languages in African literature, contrasting the very different approach of two writers, Nigerian novelist Chinua Achebe and Kenyan writer Ngugi wa Thiong'o. Achebe writes in English, but a 'new English', as he puts it, a world language 'able to carry the weight of my African experience'.[9] Ngugi, having initially made his name also writing in English, chose in 1977 to write only in Gikuyu and Kiswahili, two of Kenya's indigenous languages. In his later book *Decolonising the Mind* (1986) he formally bade 'farewell to English as a vehicle for any of my writings', which, although it is not mentioned here by Nic Eoin, is an uncanny echo of a phrase used by Michael Hartnett in his collection *Farewell to English* (1975), where he too bade 'farewell to English verse / to those I caught in English nets'.[10]

Ngugi's decision to write in Gikuyu has been criticized, however, on the basis of its supposed essentialism by, among others,

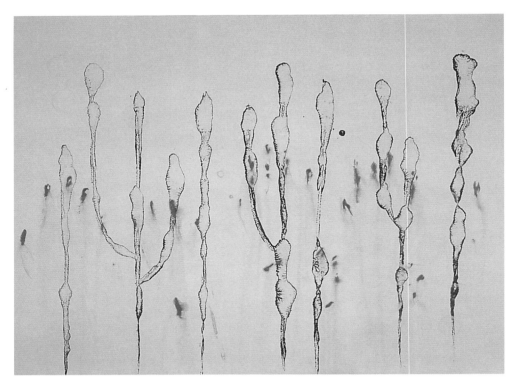

Fionnuala Ní Chiosáin
On the Grass
2001
acrylic, emulsion and
gouache on aluminium
62.5 x 83.5 cm
courtesy of the artist and the
Kerlin Gallery

Bill Ashcroft, Gareth Griffiths and Helen Tiffin of *The Empire Writes Back* (1989) fame, one of the founding texts of post-colonial literary theory, which of course was concerned with uncovering the subversive strategies by which English was being reshaped or appropriated by Asian and African writers from the imperial 'standard' language to a 'neutral' vehicle capable of transmitting the post-colonial experience. Nic Eoin strongly contests their equation, and indeed conflation, of a return to the native language as a return to some 'essential cultural identity' that does not exist, as outlined both in their Introduction and in their selective choices from Ngugi's work in *The Post-Colonial Studies Reader* (1996).[11]

Nic Eoin, on the other hand, sees both validity and points of comparison with the Irish situation in Ngugi's claim for the recognition of what Nic Eoin terms 'current living cultures' and Ngugi's insistence that (post-colonial) literature should not further the process of devaluation instigated by the colonial project itself. She draws explicit parallels between Ngugi's stance — which, she claims, has more to do with issues of educational rights and communication rights for [native] language communities than any essentialism — and the stance of certain Gaeltacht writers in Ireland in the 1930s, when similar issues were sources of both worry and anger to them.[12] Nic Eoin makes the point that the Irish experience, in particular the fact that a modern literature exists in Irish, with some Irish-language writers having achieved international recognition, has much to say in relation to debates around language in general and the role of indigenous languages in the post-colonial setting in particular. She notes specifically the deafening silence surrounding these issues from established Irish post-colonial critics working in an international context. Nic Eoin does acknowledge that major theoretical figures within post-colonialism such as Gayatri Spivak, for example, have what she terms 'an accurate understanding in the abstract'

11 Bill Ashcroft, Gareth Griffiths and Helen Tiffin, eds., *The Empire Writes Back* (London and New York, 1989) and Bill Ashcroft, Gareth Griffiths and Helen Tiffin, comps., *The Post-Colonial Studies Reader* (London and New York, 1995)

12 Nic Eoin, *Trén bhFearann Breac*, 25

Fionnuala Ní Chiosáin
Window
2001
acrylic and sumi ink on
aluminium
62.5 x 83.5 cm
courtesy of the artist and the
Kerlin Gallery

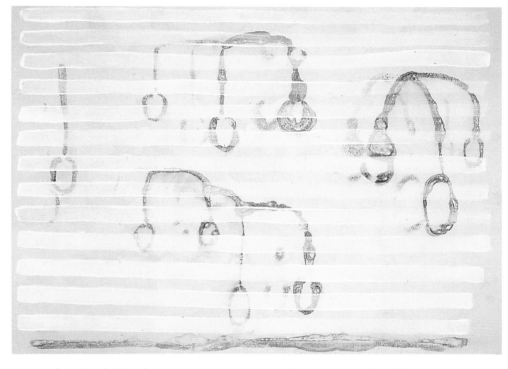

13 Nic Eoin, *Trén
bhFearann Breac*, 22

(*cruinnthuiscint theibí*) of issues of power and language and of the 'new colonialism' of globalized communications, not to mention the dangers inherent in the world dominance and hegemony of English. However, according to Nic Eoin, the location of such critics within Western anglophone academe and their exclusionist linguistic practice of writing theoretically in English and dealing only or primarily with texts in English have contributed further to the marginalization of indigenous/minority literatures and cultural discourse. Discussing Spivak in particular, she draws interesting parallels to what is essentially Nic Eoin's own situation, and indeed dilemma, as an Irish-language critic:

Ach, ar ndóigh, dá scríobhfadh Gayatri Spivak in aon cheann de theangacha dúchasacha na hIndia, is cinnte nach mbeadh trácht cloiste againne inniu ar a saothar. Ní bheadh ann don saothar taobh amuigh dá phobal áitiúil féin: bheadh sé díreach ar aon chéim le critic na Gaeilge — gan a bheith luaite sna hinnéacsanna idirnáisiúnta tagartha, gan a bheith léite ag scoláirí atá ag obair i réimsí gaolmhara trí mheán an Bhéarla. Seans maith nach mbeadh mórán trácht cloiste uirthi fiú amháin san India féin.[13]

Of course, if Gayatri Spivak were to write in any of the indigenous languages of India, it is certain that we would not have heard of her work. The work would not exist outside its own local community: it would be exactly like Irish-language criticism — not mentioned in the international reference indices, not read by scholars working in English in related fields. There is a good chance that even in India she would be pretty much unknown.

And indeed this very book is evidence of Nic Eoin's own stance concerning the power relations of language in critical discourse and highlights a dilemma for critics working in the Irish-language tradition: should they themselves write in English or Irish?

Nic Eoin has chosen to write here in Irish (although she is not a strict separatist) even though that guarantees her arguments will remain unread or marginalized outside an Irish-language audience. To write in English would risk a further marginalization and impoverishment of critical discourse in the Irish language and might well elicit the charge of pandering to the hegemony of English. Indeed, Nic Eoin's book highlights the whole question of audience. As well as asking ourselves, Who is listening?, we might also pose the question, To whom are we speaking? Nic Eoin here is clearly addressing an Irish-speaking audience when making her critique of post-colonial theory and its marginalization of minority discourse, before going on to give a hugely invigorating reading of much modern and contemporary Irish-language literature. Nic Eoin is particularly scathing when she comes to English-language post-colonial critics within Irish Studies who have made international reputations and who, she claims, marginalize and palimpsestize (a term borrowed here from Gearóid Denvir, as she acknowledges) the Irish language, its culture and criticism. But surely it is these very critics themselves, not to mention those younger scholars and students who read them, who are most in need of hearing, if not necessarily agreeing with, Nic Eoin's arguments. She utilizes David Lloyd's term 'ideological encirclement' to characterize the exclusion of Irish-language concerns from a critical enterprise that claims to uncode minority discourse and to theorize questions of 'minoritization' and marginalization. Until, however, those working in the field of Irish Studies become fully bilingual, or at the very least fully aware of its necessity, this important and compelling work will remain a closed book to monolingual critics.

If I have a caveat to enter about the underlying thesis in this book, it would be that cultural dislocation as a condition is not confined to Irish speakers alone, nor is linguistic identity monocultural or monolithic: Irish-language writers write from a constellation of identities. The bilingual road signs Kildare/*Cill Dara*; Portarlington/ *Cúil an tSúdaire* etcetera, which are a source of cultural unease in Colm Breathnach's poem as he makes his journey from Cork to Dublin, are also there to be seen by monolingual English speakers, as well as the myriads of new Irish whose native language is Polish or Lithuanian or Latvian or indeed the indigenous languages of Nigeria and other parts of Africa. If anything, the (bilingual) Irish speaker is at an advantage, being able to uncode and decipher both. And here I would come down on the side of the debate that celebrates, or at the very least ungrudgingly accepts, the hybrid, the view of Homi Bhabha that 'the borderline work of culture' — in contemporary Irish terms, the encounter between Irish and English and other linguistic and cultural forces — creates 'a sense of the new as an insurgent act of cultural translation'.[14] Pied Beauty is always in the eye of the beholder. This book does much to nourish it. ∎

14 Homi Bhabha, *The Location of Culture* (London and New York, 1994), 7, quoted in Nic Eoin, *Trén bhFearann Breac*, 261.

Reviews

Ireland and the Fiction of Improvement
Helen O'Connell
Oxford: Oxford University Press, 2006
x + 228 pages. ISBN 978-0-19-928646-1

Anyone worried that contemporary Irish Studies is too keen on self-congratulation and 'ethnic uplift' will be greatly reassured by Helen O'Connell's ambitious new study of the discourse of 'improvement' in relation to nineteenth-century Irish literature. Indeed, it would be hard to imagine a critic less enthusiastic about the literary traditions that she surveys than O'Connell, who begins her book with an investigation of some of the improving pamphlets, tracts and stories disseminated in Ireland during the decades of intense agrarian unrest that followed the Rebellion of 1798, the Act of Union and the ending of the Napoleonic Wars.

Initially, improvement was a key theme in seventeenth- and eighteenth-century English works concerned mainly with explaining new agricultural methods. In England, improvement discourse was designed to help farmers adjust to the new demands of an expanding commercial economy. But in an associated pamphlet literature, the nostrums of improvement — hard work, sobriety, frugality — were also extended into the realms of the moral and the domestic. Improvement writers depended heavily on the production of didactic fables, which contrasted the fortunes of the blissfully 'improved' with those of their miserably 'unimproved' neighbours. This enabled improvers to give lots of advice in a readily digestible form — although it also involved them in relating lurid and often unintentionally hilarious tales about starvation, drunkenness and unsupervised children being devoured by pigs. In fact, as O'Connell points out, such cautionary stories about debased lifestyles often flew in the face of these writers' supposed commitment to an aesthetic of dreary realism and 'plainness'.

In Ireland, improvement discourse aimed to focus sadly unsettled minds on the practical business of managing crops, animals and households, in order to wean the rural poor away from a hand-to-mouth existence, which supposedly fostered 'backwardness' and religious or political delusion. Reforming members of the élite class were particularly disturbed by the improvidence, illiteracy and violence of Irish peasants, and fretful about the vulnerability of the rural masses to Jacobinism and anti-Protestant millenarian fantasy. Improvers were also keen to displace an already existing printed popular literature, which was circulated in the form of cheap, mass-produced chapbooks. Indeed, they attempted to imitate the distribution network of this rival form of fiction, often delivering improving pamphlets directly to both landlords and 'peasant' readers. However, as Niall Ó Cíosáin, an authority on the print culture of the period, has noted, improvement literature was never as widely read as its well-meaning authors hoped. Ó Cíosáin's judgement is recorded in *Ireland and the Fiction of Improvement*, but without any reflection on its implications for O'Connell's thesis about the long-term influence of this literary mode. In this regard, more comparative analysis of the fates of improvement discourse in England and Ireland might have been helpful. O'Connell does not sufficiently discuss how fiction that was so imitative of English models was inevitably more politically freighted in an Irish setting.

O'Connell argues that literary historians assume that Irish fiction is predominantly romantic or modernist in form, and that Ireland lacks a realist tradition of stories of 'thriving, stable communities united by a shared rhetoric and frame of reference'. Side-stepping the question of whether or not any such writing could be called 'realistic' in Irish conditions, she proposes that improvement literature represents just such a overlooked Irish realism; O'Connell goes so far as to suggest that it is the most significant of *all* Irish literary discourses in both the nineteenth and twentieth centuries. But although she advances a large claim about this neglected genre of fiction, it is clear that O'Connell is profoundly unimpressed by the productions of such writers as Mary Leadbetter or Martin Doyle. Although she analyses improving narratives of 'cottage life' with an admirable deadpan seriousness, the absurdity of such tales as 'solutions' to intense agrarian

1 Such a view is perhaps echoed by those who claim that the amount of time spent on learning Irish in schools in independent Ireland made a more 'practical' education impossible and delayed the economic take-off of the Irish Republic for decades.

and political conflict is clear enough. Moreover, O'Connell is not at all interested in considering any positive interpretations of the ebullience, energy and 'unruliness' of the subordinate culture, which feature in improvement discourse as merely evidence of degeneracy or sedition. There is no attention here to the possibility of autonomous political consciousness or agency on the part of the underclass. That is to say, O'Connell is totally unconcerned with investigating 'history from below' or 'alternative modernities', in the style of current post-colonial criticism in Ireland and elsewhere. In addition, she sees the characteristic attitudes and deficiencies of improvement discourses as permeating virtually all the 'high' or canonical genres of nineteenth-century Irish writing as well. Sternly warning against the 'romanticization' of this literary period, O'Connell claims that neither Anglo-Irish nor Catholic nationalist writers had any real interest in popular culture or in the remnants of Gaelic culture such as the Irish language. Like improvement writers, all the major Irish novelists evidently wished only to create an orderly public sphere, 'governed by the rationality of markets and profits and unburdened by the claims of memory or difference'.

Such an unfashionably negative account of Irish literary history certainly has its appeal. Although many improvement writers were women — Maria Edgeworth foremost among them — any feminist presumption that women's writing is likely to have 'subversive' tendencies is not for O'Connell. She places both Edgeworth and Lady Morgan firmly within a tradition of counter-revolutionary liberalism, and has a rather scathing footnote about Marilyn Butler's recent attempt to bolster Edgeworth's radical credentials in particular (Butler is herself reacting against readings of Edgeworth's colonial politics by Seamus Deane and others). Indeed, O'Connell accuses élite Irish women writers generally of bad faith, in laying claim to 'freedoms' that they sought to deny to the masses. Although she allows William Carleton a certain 'nostalgia' for his hedge-school education, she has no time for any sentimental notion of Carleton as Ireland's first 'authentic' peasant writer. O'Connell

underlines the fact that Carleton's depictions of Irish 'superstition' and of agrarian secret societies such as the Ribbonmen are primarily based, not on first-hand experience, but on prior textual representations of the peasantry in improvement literature and evangelical writing. Important theorists of the English novel, such as Nancy Armstrong, have examined the influence of putatively minor genres, such as the conduct book, on domestic fiction. Here, O'Connell asserts that in Carleton we can see not just the influence of such instructive or didactic writing on fiction, but also the effect of his tales and novels on Irish improvement writers in turn, as they adopt some of his themes and plots in their own work.

The most fascinating and original passages of *Ireland and the Fiction of Improvement* deal with Carleton's representation of the Irish language and of hedge-school education, noting how his stories tend to suppress any evidence of Irish-language literacy and instead treat both Irish and Latin as forms of 'dead' language. Hence, improvers did not share the pride of many nineteenth-century nationalists in the relatively high levels of popular literacy and the widespread familiarity with classical languages and literature in Ireland. These reformers advocated technical and practical instruction alone, in order to keep Irish children on the straight and narrow path to prosperity and salvation.[1] The improvement writers in effect imply that, in certain circumstances, the printed literature disseminated by the hedge schools seemed actually to reinforce an ignorant 'Catholic' orality, rather than displace it.

O'Connell is also acute on how Carleton's Catholic origins (for he was surely the most prominent Irish convert to Protestantism in the entire century) appeared to license a return to an explicitly anti-Catholic polemic in improving fiction, and especially in the early stories that Carleton wrote for the evangelical journal the *Christian Examiner*. Due to the unpopularity of the strident evangelicalism of Hannah More in particular, most later Irish improvement writers were ostensibly non-sectarian or secular in tone.

But Protestant authors of improvement literature were in general unsure of how critical they could be of Irish religious practices such as 'merry wakes', pilgrimages or 'stations', without putting off Catholic readers. Caesar Otway, Carleton's patron and the editor of the *Christian Examiner*, explained that sometimes gentle satire was more effective in weaning the peasantry away from such time-wasting activities. O'Connell records Otway's satisfaction that Carleton's 'quiet and not ill-natured exposure' of stations in one of his later, less sectarian stories had contributed to the rapid passing away of 'some of the follies that are associated with the religion of the people'.

Carleton is central to *Ireland and the Fiction of Improvement* because he arguably represents a 'crossover' of improvement discourse from the Protestant élite to the broader Catholic population (although of course Carleton is not necessarily at all typical of Catholic novelists in this regard). For O'Connell ultimately wants to construct improvement fiction not merely as an episode in the short history of Anglo-Irish reform, but as a key part of the longer historical narrative of the emergence of Irish nationalism and, eventually, of an Irish nation state. To do this, she must assert that improvement discourse was imported almost wholesale by nationalist modernizers. Hence, the cottage idyll of Leadbetter is presented as *identical* to Eamon de Valera's pastoral vision of independent Ireland, although O'Connell states that improvement was even more 'reactionary' in the case of a Catholic nationalist like the Young Irelander Charles Gavan Duffy. This involves her in a number of tendentious arguments. First of all, she implies that all forms of investment in 'improving' the appalling conditions of the Irish poor involved staking one's faith on a homogenizing, culturally empty version of capitalist modernization. This is to foreclose any speculation on the relationship between culture and different versions of modernization — whether, for example, as a whole line of nationalists from Michael Davitt and James Connolly to W. B. Yeats and de Valera believed (or hoped), the 'spiritual' Irish had an different attitude towards material possessions than the 'materialistic' English.

To accept the argument of this important and provocative book in its entirety would mean discounting cultural nationalism, in both its Ascendancy and popular nationalist guises, as ultimately irrelevant to nineteenth-century Ireland. In O'Connell's account, when J. M. Synge declared his wonder at hearing an 'illiterate native of a wet rock in the Atlantic telling a story that is so full of European associations', he strikes an entirely new note. The Revivalism of artists such as Synge or Yeats, she suggests, is the first real challenge to improvement discourse. This seems implausible; Synge's views on the importance of the Irish language, for example, were anticipated by Thomas Davis and many others. In short, O'Connell overlooks the central irony of anti-colonial nationalism: that it is 'traditional' and 'modernizing' at the same time. The latter may win out, but the former cannot simply be ignored. Finally, O'Connell's lucid, mordant accounts of the authors she reads omit much mention of what Brendan Bradshaw refers to as the 'catastrophic dimension' of nineteenth-century Irish history. Most of the works she investigates in detail pre-date the Famine, and she neglects to investigate the kinds of discourse born of that catastrophe — from, for example, John Mitchel's fiery denunciations of British government policy, to the strange Gothic sentimentalism of the novelist Charles Kickham.

The book has almost nothing to say about the Land War, which saw the final transfer of the land — improved or otherwise — away from the landlord class. But above all, O'Connell's book is curiously unsympathetic to almost all the actors in this history. As O'Connell establishes, rather than the Irish being 'improved' out of any remotely enviable 'pre-modern' condition, they urgently needed to be rescued from a particularly harsh form of colonial exploitation. If either the reformers or the nationalists of the nineteenth century had been able to work out how to reap some of the benefits of 'modernization' without subjecting people to the depredations of capitalism (and some did indeed at least try to do this), then they would have been far wiser than the politicians and writers of 'Celtic Tiger' Ireland.

Emer Nolan

Connemara:
Listening to the Wind
Tim Robinson
Dublin: Penguin Ireland, 2006
439 pages. ISBN 978-1-844-88065-2

This large, expansive book opens with an extraordinary journey (surely an amalgam of many different expeditions) into Roundstone Bog, a twenty or thirty square mile blanket bog behind the Connemara coastal town that gives it its name. It ends, hundreds of pages later, on Mám Éan, a saddle pass 1,200 feet up in the Mám Tuirc mountain range, the traditional boundary line between Connemara and the Joyce Country. There, by dint of further scrambling, the author finds a vantage point where he can look back over the expanse of land towards his own home in the distance. This Viconian structure allows him to embrace 'the little bit of the world I am only now, after so many years, beginning to know as home'. What is remarkable is the density of the exploration over such a relatively limited territory. And there are two other books to follow as part of a projected trilogy.

This is a walker's book. It is one of the wonders of Tim Robinson's prose style that he incarnates in words the act of walking itself, the physical movements across often difficult, dangerous terrain, the stumbles and splashes, the muscularity of the effort, the breathing spaces when at rest and then the onward rush once again. For the most part, this movement is conducted in isolation, although he is clearly a man who delights in human encounters and there are many delightful ones in the book. His one concession to prudence is possession of a mobile phone.

Robinson's mind brims with knowledge, which he applies to the landscape as an expert reader might con the mysteries of an ancient text. He obviously has a deep knowledge of the earth sciences, but he combines that with a mastery of language and a richly displayed knowledge of folklore and history, philosophy and literature. The physical landscape, ostensibly empty and desolate, comes alive in the 'biotic dance' of vegetation, and in the accounts of the tragicomic contributions of humans to the habitat over the centuries. Rare heaths, lichens, heathers and gorse jostle with local characters in this splendid and unexpected narrative.

'A bog is its own diary; its mode of being is preservation of its past.' With its hundred lakes and its black blanket, 'the detritus of thirty or forty centuries of plant life compressed', Roundstone Bog is unusual because of its extent of relatively untouched ground. At first Robinson feels that he should approach the subject 'sensibly', drawing upon the reference libraries devoted to the area's topography, hydrography, archaeology, ecology and history. He doesn't do this. Instead he walks it. But there is a sense in which he adopts that first choice as well, because he carries those libraries around in his head and puts them to immediate use out in the open air, with quotation after vivid quotation.

The book is also an account of the education of the author. This includes a session learning how to cut turf manually with the *sleán*, surely one of the most back-breaking activities in human husbandry. But the education, typically, works two ways. Robinson gives a whimsical account of a tutorial that he conducts with his fellow turf-cutters. This leads to the notion that if the depth of a bank of bog is three thousand years old, 'then one end of a sod of turf is five hundred years older than the other'. In turn, this prompts a reflection on magic, the way in which the imagination of the people converts the wonders of scientific fact into a different kind of miracle.

In the tenth chapter, about a third of the way through, the tone of the book changes. There we have its central section, alighting upon 'the historic kernel of Connemara'. The new tone comes from the intimately personal introduction of the home in Roundstone shared by Robinson and his partner (referred to, throughout, as M) for the past twenty years. It is like entering a populated space after a journey though a remote fastness.

Through the islands and the habitations, Robinson enters the recorded history of the area. The centrepiece is a brilliantly concise account of the Martin family of Ballynahinch Castle, including 'Humanity' Dick Martin, the founder of the Society for the Prevention of Cruelty to Animals. The story has all the decayed vitality of an Edgeworth novel, and Maria, indeed, makes her appearance with her account of a journey into this wilderness in 1833 in a highly inappropriate four-horse carriage.

It is characteristic of Robinson that the Martins of Ballynahinch allow him to explore backwards and forwards to other tribes. In this way we get not only the wild O'Flahertys but the more dimly seen Conmaicne people who give the area its name and who reach back into myth. Then it is forward again to 1924 and the arrival of yet another exotic. Ranji, the Indian prince, fitted in without the slightest difficulty as master of the castle, giving the place the kind of colour relished by this writer.

But there are many other individual characters as well, some of them directly engaged by Robinson, some brought to life from his reading. Alexander Nimmo, the whirlwind technocrat and bridge-builder who came on a blitz to the area in the 1820s and is clearly something of a hero to Robinson. The family of Robinsons (no relation) who stand in for all the land agents of the West of Ireland. The Dutch geobotanist Victor Westhoff, with his abnormal sense of smell. Beartla, the Connemara pony breeder, an outlandish, tragic character like a figure out of a Jack B. Yeats painting whose current descendants can still be seen each year at the fair of Maam Cross. This kind of writing, brilliant pen-portraiture, is one of the main pleasures of the book.

Since Robinson's journey hasn't ended, merely reaching a temporary halting place on that sacred pass in the mountains, it would be foolish to seek out its conclusion. Besides, this expert guide and cartographer is a querist. He is filled with a spirit of resistance to all certainties and even to straight lines on a map: 'My favourite mode of walking being not a single-minded goal-bound linear advance but a cross-questioning of an area, or even a deliberate seeking out of the *fóidín mearaí*, the 'stray sod' that is said to put anyone

who treads on it wandering ...' This physical freedom from direction has its counterpoint in the favoured mental state of the writer, a condition of generous scepticism, an intellectual poise between competing versions of the truth: 'The boundary region between established truth and unstable imaginings that is my preferred territory ...'

Robinson takes his place, then, in the current debate between atheists and the religious creeds, between Darwinism and Creationism, but there is no dogmatism in his text. He frequently reminds us of his declared atheism and his detestation of 'Irish Catholic miserabilism'. When he reaches that mountain pass, however, he does so in the company of pilgrims to a place that is considered sacred. He stands aside and observes but there is no dismissal of the people and their faith. Instead, what he offers in this book, in several astonishing passages of vision, is the present landscape set against the millions of years of the earth's existence and the huge forces over time that have created this rock or that continent.

While it offers its readers an encyclopaedic array of information on this beautiful area of the West, the book is also a personal testament. It is filled with reflections and asides with a warm self-mockery. This genial man is capable of grouchiness, particularly on the subject of despoliation of the countryside and what passes for development, from wind-farms to summer homes. The book, then, does have a conclusion, but at a deeply personal level, a kind of Zen effacement of the self before the laid-out display of nature: 'Sometimes I come back from such a walk with my head so empty it seems not a single thought or observation has passed through it all day and I feel I have truly seen things as they are when I'm not there to see them.'

Tim Robinson makes a nonsense of nationality. An Englishman who came to the Aran Islands in 1972 and moved to Roundstone in 1984, he has given himself and his great talents to this country in a way that can only leave the native awe-stricken. Perhaps, after all, there is something

1 For examples, see Craig Calhoun, *Habermas and the Public Sphere* (Cambridge, Mass., 1992); Joan B. Landes, *Women and the Public Sphere in the Age of the French Revolution* (Ithaca, 1988); Harold Mah, 'Phantasies of the Public Sphere: Rethinking the Habermas of Historians', *Journal of Modern History*, 72 (2000), 153–82; Hannah Barker and Simon Burrows, eds., *Press, Politics and the Public Sphere in Europe and North America 1760–1820* (Cambridge, 2002); T. C. W. Blanning, *The Culture of Power and the Power of Culture: Old Régime Europe 1660–1789* (Oxford, 2002).

2 Vincent Morley, *Irish Opinion and the American Revolution, 1760–1783* (Cambridge, 2002), 1

3 See especially J. G. Simms, *Colonial Nationalism 1698–1776* (Cork, 1976); J. C. Beckett, *The Making of Modern Ireland 1603–1923* (London, 1981); T. W. Moody and W. E. Vaughan, eds., *New History of Ireland Volume 4: Eighteenth-Century Ireland 1691–1800* (Oxford, 1986).

4 For example, see Thomas Bartlett, '"A People Made for Copies Rather than Originals": The Anglo-Irish 1760–1800', *International History Review* (1990), 11–25; Jacqueline Hill, *From Patriots to Unionists: Dublin Civic Politics and Irish Protestant Patriotism, 1660–1840* (Oxford, 1997); Joep Leerssen, 'Anglo-Irish Patriotism and Its European Context: Notes towards a Reassessment', *Eighteenth-Century Ireland: Iris an Dá Chultúr*, 3 (1988), 7–24.

of the outsider's freshness in the very detail of his observations. The local, claiming to know everywhere, is often incapable of seeing what is in front of him. Certainly, Robinson is part of the tradition of visiting earth scientists to this country. There is an amusing account towards the beginning of the book of a sodden seminar on the bog in 1935. It is drawn from Robert Lloyd Praeger's *The Way that I Went* (1937). English, Swedish, Danish and Irish scientists engage in heated discussion as they, literally, sink to their knees in the soft surface of the bog. Robinson is of this group, with one important distinction — he has made his home here and is now one of Ireland's finest writers.

Thomas Kilroy

Irish Opinion and the American Revolution, 1760–1783
Vincent Morley
Cambridge: Cambridge University Press, 2002
x + 366 pages. ISBN 0-521-81386-7

Washington i gCeannas a Ríochta: Cogadh Mheiriceá i Litríocht na Gaeilge
Vincent Morley
Baile Átha Cliath: Coiscéim, 2005
xliii + 124 pages. ISBN: none assigned by publisher

The publication in 1989 of an English translation of Jürgen Habermas's *The Structural Transformation of the Public Sphere* (1962) provoked considerable scholarly interest in 'public opinion' in the eighteenth-century anglophone world. Habermas's argument about the emergence of a space for reasoned debate in the bourgeois public sphere was accepted, nuanced and challenged in a slew of publications on the press and print culture, associational culture and sociability in venues ranging from the theatre to the tavern.[1] In that context, it is surprising that Vincent Morley's *Irish Opinion and the American Revolution, 1760–1783* is the first major study of Irish public opinion in the eighteenth century since R. B. McDowell's *Irish Public Opinion, 1750–1800* appeared in 1944. It is no less surprising

that he does not engage with either Habermas's provocative thesis or indeed probe many of the questions that the resulting work has raised.

Nevertheless, *Irish Opinion and the American Revolution* is an invigorating read. In a polemical Introduction, Morley takes aim at the dominant representations of Irish opinion in the latter half of the eighteenth century. Most especially, he argues, that the notion that society was divided between a politically apathetic Catholic majority, a 'colonial nationalist' Anglican political élite, and a republican Presbyterian community distorts 'the true state of opinion in eighteenth-century Ireland'.[2] His own starting point is that Irish society in the latter half of the century — and indeed at all times throughout the century — remained divided along religious lines; political attitudes largely mirrored ethnic origins. He claims that the Anglican élite remained locked in the mindset of the colonist, that Presbyterians mostly wished to benefit fully from the political system and not to overturn it, and that Catholic opinion was extremely politically engaged, rejecting the legitimacy of the state.

Earlier generations of historians conceived late eighteenth-century Irish demands for increased control over government spending, free trade and greater legislative independence as colonial nationalism, an opinion that can be traced beyond W. E. H. Lecky to Sir Jonah Barrington's *Rise and Fall of the Irish Nation* (1833).[3] As Morley points out, that orthodoxy has been subject to sustained criticism on the grounds that Anglican attitudes did not constitute nationalism at all.[4] His vision of Anglican opinion acknowledges a striving for greater independence while asserting the continuing grasp of old mentalities on the political élite. Similarly, Morley believes that an obsession with finding antecedents for the democratic republicanism of the United Irishmen has distorted the study of eighteenth-century Presbyterian opinion, resulting in a rather deadening teleology — all roads lead to Cave Hill. Morley denies the existence of any strong body of republican opinion in Irish Presbyterianism before the American Revolution; the majority of Presbyterians, he contends,

A parliamentary reformer represented as a republican. An accompanying verse reads 'Your Petitioner Sheweth / That he Humbly wishes to / Reduce the Church to Gospel Order / By Rapine, Sacrilege and Murther / To Make Presbytery supream / And Kings themselves submit to him / And not content all this to do / He must have Wealth & honor too / Or else with Blood & Desolation / He'll tear out of [*sic*] th' Heart o' th' Nation'. See *Drawcansir: or, The Mock Reform. An Heroic Poem* (Dublin, 1784). Courtesy of the National Library of Ireland.

sought not to overturn the constitutional status quo but to be fully included within it. Historians who have related United Irish republicanism to the democratic organization of the Presbyterian Church or to the ideas of the Scottish Enlightenment have simply misread the tea leaves. And apparently, so too did contemporary Anglicans who, remembering the 1640s, were quick to dismiss Dissenters as republicans.

However, Morley's harshest criticism of the historiography concerns its understanding of Catholic opinion. The crux of his argument is that the 'failure of historians to comprehend the political culture of the majority of the Irish population … is a predictable consequence

of their inability either to utilise the vernacular sources or to assimilate the findings of scholars who publish in Irish'.[5] Historians, he argues, have ignored the best source for analysing Catholic attitudes — literature in the Irish language. Far from revealing a politically apathetic population, prose and verse in Irish demonstrate the persistence of ideals of loyalty to the rightful crown, Church and country: the hope that military support from abroad — France — would result in a Jacobite and Gaelic restoration was not the delusion of a defeated people but a realistic reflection of Ireland's potential strategic importance in a century defined by warfare. This argument for the importance of Irish-language literature as a source, which received

5   Morley, *Irish Opinion*, 3

6   Morley, *Irish Opinion*, 12–13
7   Morley, *Irish Opinion*, 2

its first major scholarly formulation as far back as Daniel Corkery's *Hidden Ireland* (1925), has implications for a recent debate about the question of the relationship of state and society in eighteenth-century Ireland. Sean Connolly's challenging *Religion, Law and Power: The Making of Protestant Ireland 1660–1760* (1992) argued that eighteenth-century Ireland was characterized not by a confrontation between a brutal colonial class and an oppressed colonized majority, but was rather fundamentally an *ancien régime* European society, with the different classes bound together by patterns of deference and customs. Morley argues that Connolly has mistaken appearance for reality — Ireland looked like an *ancien régime* state but 'this superficially imposing edifice was a hollow façade which lacked an essential feature of normal *ancien régime* states … a sense of legitimacy grounded on immemorial usage and sanctified by a church commanding the allegiance of the people'.[6]

Morley argues that 'a middle stratum of comfortable tenant farmers, craftsmen, schoolteachers, publicans, shopkeepers and priests' maintained a 'vigorous' oral and manuscript literary tradition in Irish.[7] He claims that this literature reflected the opinion of the rural masses and revealed that they never accepted the legitimacy of the constitution in church and state. He corroborates this evidence with the comments of often paranoid élite observers on the disloyalty of the masses. On the other hand, Morley notes, by mid-century the Catholic landed gentry, Church hierarchy and some merchants accepted that the state could only be reformed rather than overthrown, and sought to win relief from the Penal Laws through loyalty to the Hanoverian state. This gap in the attitude of Catholics of different classes was vividly illustrated by the killing of three Whiteboys by an association to preserve law and order founded by a Catholic priest and defended by his bishop in Ballyragget, County Kilkenny, in February 1775. Morley's reassertion of the case that Ireland was exceptional in European terms, a colonial society in Western Europe, is an important historiographical contribution in itself.

The arguments sketched above frame Morley's analysis of Irish opinion on the American Revolution. Drawing on parliamentary speeches, newspapers, pamphlets and sermons, as well as Irish-language literature almost exclusively in manuscript, he presents a chronological account of the development of opinion to the war. Actions matter as well as words: he discusses recruitment to the British army, attacks on soldiers by civilians and the activities of Irish privateers who served Britain's enemies. Before 1776, he argues, the American crisis was very much secondary to domestic concerns for all sections of Irish society: pro-American sentiment was confined to an extreme Patriot minority in a loyal political nation; popular Catholic consciousness was unaffected until the outbreak of war. Morley argues that once the war broke out, Protestant opinion divided. Most Protestants feared that a British victory in America would see a jubilant and arrogant London government infringe on Irish rights. However, they feared that an American victory would result in the break-up of the Empire. The Patriot opposition expressed strong support for the rebel American colonists, but this support ebbed as British defeats threatened the Empire. Irish Protestants, including the Patriots initially at least, remained suspicious of Catholics, a suspicion heightened as war with France became inevitable. The Volunteer units that sprang up from 1778 aimed to defend against French invasion and Catholic rebellion. As such, Morley says, they began as expressions of support for the war effort, though not necessarily for the administration in London.

How then does he account for the fact that by 1779 a placard inscribed 'Free Trade or This' appeared mounted on a Volunteer cannon at a parade outside parliament? Rather than taking inspiration from American ideas, he says the campaign for free trade and the disastrous economic effects of the war politicized the Volunteers, and wider opinion. English difficulties encouraged Protestants to seek support from their Catholic brethren, a significant breach in traditional politics. One radical pamphlet, *Moderation Unmasked* (1780), anticipated Wolfe Tone by more than a decade: 'Why should we recollect that we have different appellations — Protestants, Roman Catholics, Dissenters? Let them be forgotten, and they are forgotten — We remember only that we have the common one of Irishmen.'[8] Simultaneously, the free trade campaign encouraged the growth of separatist sentiment among Ulster Presbyterians, exemplified by Joseph Pollock's *Letters of Owen Roe O'Nial*, which in 1779 called for an independent Ireland under French protection. Morley contends that such sentiments were clearly influenced by America, but were shared by only a small radical minority of Presbyterians; most Protestant opinion continued to support the British connection, albeit on altered terms, and despite some Catholic relief measures, it continued to reject Catholic participation in politics. What then of the Catholic majority? Morley continues to differentiate Catholics on class lines. The élite remained loyal to the government, even seeking to raise troops; the middle and lower classes remained alienated from the state, though attitudes towards Protestant Patriots began to soften as the campaigns for free trade and legislative independence gathered steam.

⁂

Morley develops his analysis of the politics of literature in Irish — one of the most welcome aspects of his *Irish Opinion and the American Revolution* — in his *Washington i gCeannas a Ríochta: Cogadh Mheiriceá i Litríocht na Gaeilge*, an annotated anthology of poems and songs on the American war by various Irish-language poets, most notably Eoghan Rua Ó Súilleabháin of County Kerry, Séamus Ó Dálaigh of County Limerick, and Tomás Ó Míocháin of County Clare. The verse proved an adaptable medium, expressing not only the political but also the social and economic discontents of the people. Again, Morley argues that the poetry reflects not the voice of the very poor but rather that of the lower middle classes and clergy, later

the backbone of nineteenth-century Catholic nationalism. The items reproduced in the anthology show that, while happy to see England in trouble, the poets initially viewed the conflict as a war between two sets of foreign Protestants; in other words, the earliest poems make little reference to the constitutional issues at stake. However, once France and then Spain became involved attitudes changed. Military intervention in Ireland seemed imminent. The poets now spoke of a French-backed Stuart restoration, but, in a development mirroring the Protestant Patriot appeal for Catholic support, they began to praise the Volunteers and Protestant Patriot political leaders such as Henry Grattan and Henry Flood, as well as Protestant American heroes like Washington. In Morley's opinion, then, the ideas of the American Revolution, and subsequent events in Ireland, began altering the views of the Irish-speaking lower orders on politics, meaning that when the Protestant republican United Irishman James Napper Tandy sought an alliance with the Defenders in the 1790s, 'the path had been cleared for him by George Washington'.[9]

⁂

Morley's books are important contributions to the study of eighteenth-century Ireland on several levels. They restore a necessary sense of chronology and nuance to the impact of the American Revolution, provocatively arguing that it did not redefine Irish politics but rather provided the stimulus for longer-term tensions to be released. As such, Morley's work — and that of Jimmy Kelly, Breandán Mac Suibhne and Danny Mansergh — provide a better perspective for the 1790s than assuming that the origins of the revolutionary decade can be found in 1789 or 1791.[10] Likewise, Morley's work — like that of Breandán Ó Buachalla, Éamonn Ó Ciardha, Cornelius Buttimer and Louis Cullen — has demonstrated that the rich seam of Irish-language material can be usefully mined by historians of society and culture and, consequently, students of popular politics and public opinion.[11] In particular, Morley, by making

8   Morley, *Irish Opinion*, 241

9   Vincent Morley, *Washington i gCeannas a Ríochta: Cogadh Mheiriceá i Litríocht na Gaeilge* (Baile Átha Cliath, 2005), xxxviii

10 See James Kelly, *Prelude to Union: Anglo-Irish Politics in the 1780s* (Cork, 1992), and 'Conservative Protestant Political Thought in Late Eighteenth-Century Ireland', in S. J. Connolly, ed., *Political Ideas in Eighteenth-Century Ireland* (Dublin, 2000), 185–220; Breandán Mac Suibhne, 'Politicization and Paramilitarism: North-west and South-west Ulster, c. 1772–98', in Thomas Bartlett, David Dickson, Dáire Keogh and Kevin Whelan, eds., *1798: A Bicentenary Perspective* (Dublin, 2003), 243–78; Danny Mansergh, *Grattan's Failure: Parliamentary Opposition and the People in Ireland 1779–1800* (Dublin, 2005).

11 Breandán Ó Buachalla, *Aisling Ghéar: Na Stiobhartaigh agus an tAos Léinn, 1603–1788* (Baile Átha Cliath, 1996); Éamonn Ó Ciardha, *Ireland and the Jacobite Cause, 1685–1776: A Fatal Attachment* (Dublin, 2002); C. G. Buttimer, 'Cogagh Sagsana Nuadh Sonn: Reporting the American Revolution', *Studia Hibernica*, 28 (1994), 63–101; L. M. Cullen, *The Hidden Ireland: Reassessment of a Concept* (Gigginstown, 1988)

12 See, *inter alia*, the discussion of sociability threaded through Martyn J. Powell, *The Politics of Consumption in Eighteenth-Century Ireland* (Houndmills, 2005).

texts available in an accessible form, has done a great service to his fellow-historians.

But many of Morley's key arguments are open to challenge. His division of public opinion along denominational lines is problematic. Political divisions cut across denominational lines, and were further complicated by other factors such as class and geography; indeed, Morley's own abandonment of rigid denominational categories at key points in his argument — for example, in his accounts of the free trade campaigns and constitutional demands where he describes the opinions of loyalists, that is, of a political rather than a denominational section of opinion — underline the danger of the rigid categorization he at times appears to promote. The model presupposes divisions within public opinion not always evident at the time. His emphasis on inherited divisions in society can obscure developments that were drawing many people closer together. For example, although he discusses the influence of John Locke and Scottish philosophy, there is little discussion of the impact of Enlightened ideas of toleration on Irish political culture nor is there much sense of the growth in sociability that saw people of different classes and religious backgrounds come together on both informal and formal occasions, in theatres, coffee houses, learned societies, or even in attending charity sermons.[12]

The use Morley makes of Irish-language sources is also problematic. He makes a convincing case that the poems and songs express popular social and economic discontent, even if they represent the middling classes primarily. However, the extent to which they represent genuine political opinion remains a vexed question. For instance, Morley insists that the Jacobite sentiment in much Irish-language literature was a realistic political programme in the context of international relations, yet even before the middle of the century the Stuarts were a beaten docket and, from 1766, the papacy and the French had decided not to back them in another race: were the poets, who Morley demonstrates to be well aware of international developments, ignorant on this point or were they following a

script in their poems, delivering to their audience expected themes not necessarily reflective of real-life politics? Discontent with the status quo does not automatically translate into believing its destruction imminent or achievable. It is highly unlikely that all those singing or listening to Jacobite songs intended to act on their sentiments — certainly in more recent times the singing of a rebel song signified little about practical political opinions and intentions, and certainly not among the delegates at a recent Fianna Fáil Ard Fheis drunkenly singing 'Seán South of Garryowen'. The extent to which Irish-language poems and songs were performance pieces within traditional literary tropes, and the question of how that may have affected the political language within them has not been adequately addressed.

Morley's work represents a major contribution to the historiography of eighteenth-century Ireland. His polemics, his nuanced account of the impact of the American Revolution, and his scholarship on underused and Irish-language sources demand serious consideration. However, contemporaries, as he himself shows, felt themselves to be an integral part of Europe. An analysis less focused on traditional divisions in a rapidly changing society and more responsive to the implications of the increasing interaction between people of different denominations within Ireland's flourishing public sphere would have allowed a greater insight into how far Ireland partook of shared European political, social, intellectual and cultural developments on the cusp of the modern era.

Ultán Gillen

War, State and Society in Mid-Eighteenth-Century Britain and Ireland
Stephen Conway
Oxford: Oxford University Press, 2006
x + 346 pages. ISBN 978-0-19-925375-3

The history of war has changed in the last two decades. The subject was once the preserve of historians of strategy and diplomacy, but now social and cultural historians probe the experience of war (and military service) for combatants and civilians, while political historians produce increasingly sophisticated analyses of the impact of war and the threat of war on the relationship of state and society. Stephen Conway is the author of the well-received study *The British Isles and the American War of Independence*, published in 2000, in which he presented the most comprehensive assessment to date of the impact of that conflict on Britain and Ireland. In that volume he argued that the experience of conflict served to hasten administrative and organizational changes that reinforced what John Brewer has termed the 'fiscal-military state' and intensified the sense of national identity that Linda Colley influentially described in *Britons: Forging the Nation, 1707–1837* (1992). In *War, State and Society in Mid-Eighteenth-Century Britain and Ireland*, Conway is concerned with the same general issue but the focus is the sequence of wars fought in the middle decades of the eighteenth century; that is, from the quirkily named War of Jenkins's Ear, which began in 1739, through to the conclusion, in 1763, of the (by comparison) unimaginatively titled Seven Years War.

Ireland features less prominently here than in his earlier book; this is not surprising since the wars of the mid-eighteenth century had less impact upon the course of domestic and Anglo-Irish politics and on the Irish economy and society. Still, Conway has trawled more deeply than most non-Irish specialists in the Irish archival record. His account of the impact of war on Cork city — one of his three regional case studies — captures the ambivalent sentiments of that city's population as they sought to reconcile their irritation at the augmented military presence, their joy at the successes of the king's army, and their determination to ensure that nothing interrupted the business of making money or threatened the city's place as one of Europe's major trading centres. The involvement of some of the city's major families and office-holders in smuggling seems to confirm that the people of Cork were at heart more interested in profit than supporting the war effort. Yet the

declarations of loyalty and support for the crown were as warm and enthusiastic there as they were in Berkshire. They were, perhaps, less effusive than those emanating from Edinburgh, but then Cork had less to prove than the Scottish capital in the wake of the '45.

Conway also offers a useful analysis of Irish service in the military in these years. Many thousands of men from all parts of Ireland and from the main religious groups served in what were becoming ethnically and religiously more diverse armed forces. The attempt made in 1762 by Lords Kenmare and Kingsland to establish a 'Roman Legion' of seven regiments of Irish Catholics foundered on the rock of Irish Protestant intransigence and the intensified anti-Catholicism generated by the Seven Years War. In practice, however, Irish Catholics served in the army in large numbers, particularly in North America. Irishmen constituted 27.5 per cent of the military rank and file in the American colonies, as against a modest 4.1 per cent (overwhelmingly Ulster Protestants) of those serving in Britain. Identity, Conway's analysis suggests, was more flexible and layered in the mid-eighteenth century than it was to become with the emergence of modern nationalism. In this context, his brief assessments of the impact of the threat of invasion on public consciousness, of the inspiration provided by heroes, and of the fear of external enemies, are both engaging and insightful. It is telling from an Irish perspective to note the praise lavished on General William Blakeney of County Galway for his role in defending Minorca in 1756, and the rapturous celebration of Admiral Edward Vernon's capture of Porto Bello from the Spanish in 1739, but while Conway refers, frequently, to these events, he understates their import for Irish Protestants and their genuine pleasure at British military success. As a result, he underestimates the strength of pan-British Protestantism, and the significance of the Irish and, to a lesser extent, of the American colonial contribution to Britain's emergence out of the Seven Years War with the largest global empire.

1 Stephen Conway, *War, State and Society in Mid-Eighteenth-Century Britain and Ireland* (Oxford, 2006), 306

2 Conway, *War, State and Society*, 54

This notwithstanding, Conway qualifies Colley's influential conclusion as to the centrality of war (particular war with France) as a factor in promoting the growth of British identity in the eighteenth century. In so doing, he demonstrates his commitment not only to employ but also to modify, when appropriate, the interpretative paradigms of Brewer, Colley and others. At its most general, his thesis is that 'everywhere war acted as a dynamic force', and to this end he assesses the impact of a generation of war on the state, armed forces, economy, society, politics, religion, 'the nation' and the regions in a sequence of thematic chapters.[1] Saliently, he endorses Brewer's argument that Britain prevailed in this prolonged struggle with France because its fiscal-military state gave it an advantage over its rivals that facilitated its emergence in the course of the long eighteenth century as the dominant global power. Having argued previously that the American War of Independence hastened important advances in that direction, it is notable that the evidence he adduces in respect of the conflicts of the 1740s and 1750s elicits a more cautious conclusion.

In contrast to Conway's earlier book, this volume includes a highly informative analysis of the circumstances of Britain's continental rivals, illustrating how war also caused them to embrace organizational and administrative reform and reminding the reader of the obvious — that the outcome of the prolonged power struggle between Britain and France was never a foregone conclusion. In explaining Britain's ultimate success, he places great emphasis on 'a highly productive partnership between government and private effort' that enabled London to marshal the men and materials required for war.[2] Private interests were not only involved in supplying provisions but also ordnance, shipping, sailors and military recruits. For Conway, this demonstrates that, despite the enduring attachment to clan and region, the Protestant population was united behind the war effort. The British state may have been able to raise more revenue than its opponents, but the energy of Protestantism was no less important in overcoming internal dissent (Jacobitism, most notably) and estrangement (in the shape of the Catholic population of Ireland) and, ultimately, winning wars.

Like its predecessor, this book is a fine example of a 'Three Kingdoms' or 'Four Nations' approach to history, the starting point of which is that since histories of Britain and Ireland are inextricably intertwined, it makes sense to consider them together. That approach is useful to a point. And yet it is apparent from this, and Conway's previous study, that while the ill-named 'New British History' can do much to illuminate the shared history of Britain and Ireland, not least geopolitical aspects of Anglo-Irish relations, it can also elide regional difference. This study makes a significant contribution to the understanding of the importance of war in the mid-eighteenth century to the evolution of the British fiscal-military state. Conway's account of that evolution also lends strength to his contention that demands of fighting the Seven Years War represented a significant break with the past and a step forward to the more all-consuming conflicts that became the norm of the late eighteenth and early nineteenth century. It is an important book and one that historians of Ireland will find informative and rewarding.

James Kelly

Religion and Reformation in the Tudor Diocese of Meath
Brendan Scott
Dublin: Four Courts Press, 2006
174 pages. ISBN 1-85182-995-4

The Earldom of Desmond, 1463–1583:
The Decline and Crisis of a Feudal Lordship
Anthony McCormack
Dublin: Four Courts Press, 2005
224 pages. ISBN 1-85182-882-6

The student of English history faces a bewilderingly large literature. Exploration of any large-scale thematic topic requires delving into a massive bibliography of local studies — county, parish, family, and so on. And that bibliography just keeps getting bigger. But the Irish case is different; there is no analogous profusion of local histories. Even the great earldoms and bishoprics have only recently, if at all, attracted serious study.

This imbalance is partly the result of historiographical trends. Debate over the origins and character of the English Civil War and its role, or lack thereof, in various teleological accounts of England's past, Whiggish, Marxist or modernization, was largely responsible for the profusion of English local studies since the 1970s. In this environment such histories were not antiquarian exercises but rather model-testing case studies. Irish historiography lacked similar controversy, its primary concern being not an internal struggle for self-definition but rather a series of hegemonic moves by a colonizing neighbour. As such, its issues were chiefly 'national' or 'confessional' in focus and often considered in express comparison with British and English constitutional and ecclesiastical developments. Within the small, but growing, cohort of professional Irish historians there was limited push toward the local.

A curious effect of this can be seen in some of the major works of the last thirty years or so. Studies such as Nicholas Canny's *Elizabethan Conquest* (1976), Brendan Bradshaw's *Irish Constitutional Revolution* (1979), Ciaran Brady's *Chief Governors* (1994), and even Steven Ellis's survey, *Tudor Ireland* (1985), all tackled major questions and/or covered large swaths of time. Yet none of them had a substantial secondary literature to engage. As a result, they read as much as exercises in method and source use as they do historiographical interventions; there just simply was not a sufficient body of local studies to which these authors could appeal when constructing their narratives.

This is beginning to change. Early modern Irish history is going through its own localist moment: in the last few years important books have appeared on such diverse topics as Gaelic lordship in Leinster, the life and career of the 'Wizard' earl of Kildare, Tyrone's rebellion, and society and politics in Sligo.[1] In part this is due

to dynamics internal to Irish historical studies itself, not least a deeper engagement with theory, increased attention to Irish-language sources, and a sense of the limits of both nationalist and revisionist narratives. External influences have played a role too. The emergence of the so-called 'New British History' had the perhaps curious effect of increasing the attention paid to Irish localities. For if the magisterial matters of early modern Britain were indeed to have had genealogical branches arising from the 'Celtic fringe', then it became incumbent upon researchers to dig up more of what was really going on in Irish (and Welsh and Scottish) soil. In short, Irish local studies came to have a new importance.

Irish historians' 'provincial turn' is not, however, a mirror image of that undertaken by their English counterparts. A significant distinguishing feature is the greater attention paid by Irish historians to larger European contexts. The New British History may have prodded English historians to take more seriously events in the Stuarts' other kingdoms, but in doing so, as many of its critics pointed out, it left the archipelago oddly disconnected from the Continent. By contrast, the best recent work on Ireland has been attentive to wider contexts. We seem to be witnessing, therefore, the simultaneous making of Irish history, British *and* European.

Brendan Scott's *Religion and Reformation in the Tudor Diocese of Meath* and Anthony McCormack's *The Earldom of Desmond, 1463–1583: The Decline and Crisis of a Feudal Lordship* take their place in this growing body of tightly defined local studies capable of shedding new light on broad historiographical issues. Scott's exploration of one diocese in the 'long' Tudor period (a sizeable portion of the discussion addresses conditions after the death of the last Tudor monarch, Elizabeth I, in 1603) charts the opportunities for reform, and the impediments to the same, in Ireland in the wake of Henry VIII's break with Rome in 1534. The fate of reform in this diocese would serve as bellwether for efforts beyond the Pale. Understanding in detail what happened here — an area in which

1 Chris Maginn, *Civilizing Gaelic Leinster: The Extension of Tudor Rule in the O'Byrne and O'Toole Lordships* (Dublin, 2005); Vincent Carey, *Surviving the Tudors: The 'Wizard' Earl of Kildare and English Rule in Ireland* (Dublin, 2002); Hiram Morgan, *Tyrone's Rebellion: The Outbreak of the Nine Years War in Tudor Ireland* (Dublin, 1993); Mary O'Dowd, *Power, Politics and Land: Early Modern Sligo, 1568–1688* (Dublin, 1991)

the crown might have had some realistic hope of reforming success — contributes much to our understanding of the politics of religion in sixteenth-century Ireland. In spite of the title, there is not much religion in this book. Rather, this is a structural account, a study of institutions, of material and educational constraints, and of the élite politics that were so much a part of the fortunes of reform and resistance.

Scott organizes the book into five thematic chapters covering the pre-Reformation Church, the early attempts at reform, matters of finance and state of the clergy, religious houses and dissolution, and the emergence of recusancy. Richly detailed and well-researched, this account of the mechanics of reform draws out carefully the very real possibilities that existed for an Irish (Gaelic and Hiberno-Norman) break with Rome and the circumstances that led to its rejection and resistance. It also raises points of comparison and contrast with contemporary English trends: his picture of the strength of the late medieval Church suggests similarities with the Catholic Church in England; his discussion of the heavy secular duties, to the detriment of religious duties, occasioned by Meath's 'frontier' characteristics suggests the very real differences in the roles of Irish and English bishops.

If Scott tackles the great ecclesiastical issue in early modern Anglo-Irish relations, McCormack addresses the great secular one: the eclipse of the native élite in the wake of Tudor reform. Organized chronologically, it traces the rise and fall of Fitzgerald authority in the Munster earldom of Desmond from the eighth earl's appointment as lord deputy in 1463, through the troubles that followed Henry's split with Rome, and ending with the rebellions of 1569–73 and 1579–83. McCormack's account of the earldom's sophisticated administrative structure in the early 1500s is a significant contribution to a growing body of work that challenges the notion that Irish élite politics was merely might-makes-right warlordism.

The bulk of the text, however, concerns the period post-1534. Of particular significance

is McCormack's provocative rereading of contemporary power relations in this era of direct rule from London. The primary conflict determining Fitzgerald authority, it is argued, was not with an aggrandizing, centralizing crown but rather with an age-old, local rival — the Butler earls of Ormond. Violence is thus attributed not to Gaelic barbarism or English colonial excess but to local instability bequeathed by the unfinished nature of the Norman invasion; foreign intrigues are driven, not by competing claims to sovereignty — Hiberno-Norman aristocratic versus Anglo monarchic — but by the exigencies of the running conflict with the Butlers.

Both of these books are empirical works of a very high order. Their close contact with the sources, however, is not matched by a similarly intimate engagement with the historiography. Beneath these seemingly straightforward empirical accounts are certain historiographical assumptions worth greater interrogation. Most conspicuously, both authors are influenced by the current zeitgeist of cultural negotiation. There is no place in either for conflictual models of cultural contact, and ideology has largely been replaced by considerations of power politics amongst competing élites in a developing multiple monarchy. Scott's main thesis is that religious reform was not doomed to failure and might very well have worked had sufficient financial means and administrative attention been devoted to it. Recusancy, thus, emerges as an unintended consequence of the estrangement of Meath's gentry and nobility from the corridors of power in Dublin. He pits this argument against what he says is a 'Catholic nationalist line', but it is unclear who currently totes it. Nor must one subscribe to such a confessionally charged position to feel there may have been more than administrative causes behind Protestantism's still birth in Ireland and that perhaps there were those with an interest in seeing the Church of Ireland constructed as the preserve of a persecuted minority.

Likewise, McCormack paints a compelling picture in which co-operation between crown and native élites may have been possible. Here interpersonal rivalries and factional politics spanning both kingdoms conspire to doom Fitzgerald authority in Desmond. The rule-proving exception is Fitzmaurice's performance of rebellion as Counter-Reformation freedom-fight. In McCormack's account, Fitzmaurice stands alone in his religious fervour and Desmond was a reluctant participant in his own rebellion, preferring instead to negotiate a settlement with a crown that Fitzmaurice would have deemed heretical. Various Fitzgerald earls, thus, may have test-driven the revolutionary rhetoric of faith and fatherland but they did so without conviction; this would be the preserve of the Baltinglasses and Tyrones of the world.

Conspicuously missing from both of these pictures, then, is a role for ideology. Indeed, events are taken to drive ideas and not the other way around. This may have been the case — and it is a position compellingly argued — but it is not an opinion universally shared. McCormack's dismissal in a footnote of the view that the dark side of Renaissance thought had an influential part to play in the distancing of native and newcomer, crown and nobility, is not sufficient. A greater engagement with the richness of debate on early modern Anglo-Irish relations would have made these excellent studies richer still.

One of the great questions raised by Scott's and McCormack's studies is what to do with the classic chronology of English ascendancy and Hiberno-Norman (to use McCormack's preferred term) and Gaelic decline. They both tell tales of contingency and negotiation, but they do little to disturb the place of dates like 1534 and 1583 in a seemingly deterministic logic of English domination and Irish resistance. Was there really no chance for Protestant reform in Meath by the 1580s? Does 'why the Reformation failed in Ireland' thus stand, after all, as *une question bien posée*? For that matter, was the final 'decline' of the Desmond earldom really settled in 1583 with the fifteenth earl's beheading? In his conclusion McCormack writes off both the crown's efforts to install a compliant Fitzgerald earl as a means to calm Munster during the Nine Years War and its concerns over local support of the *súgán* earl,

James fitz Thomas Fitzgerald. But this was a major subplot of the conflict. Moreover, the collapse of Fitzgerald authority in the earldom did not equal that of the earldom itself. It remained quite important, as James I's installation of Richard Preston — Scottish courtier and husband of Elizabeth Butler, daughter of Thomas, tenth earl of Ormond — to the title in 1619 makes clear. Thus while these may not be nationalist tales of English treachery and Irish defiance, their choice of chronological framing nevertheless leaves a similar impression of ideological hardening and political distancing occurring by the middle of Elizabeth's reign.

Is this really the extent of the revision offered by Irish historiography's provincial turn? I suspect it is not. But we will not know until we see considerably more local studies of the empirical rigour and careful contextualization of McCormack's and Scott's. Only then may we start to look for lines of continuity across dates and events still taken as signposts of tectonic change in the Irish historical landscape.

Brendan Kane

The Irish in the San Francisco Bay Area: Essays on Good Fortune
Edited by Donald Jordan and Timothy J. O'Keefe
San Francisco: Irish Literary and Historical Society, 2005
x + 310 pages. ISBN 0-931180-00-7

Oro en Paz, Fierro en Guerra (Gold in Peace, Iron in War) is the motto of San Francisco. In the early gold-rush days the Irish came with thousands of others to this remote port. Those who came from within North America travelled by three routes: they trekked across country usually via Missouri, departing once the grass had grown enough to feed the teams of oxen; or they came by sea, around Cape Horn or else to Panama, crossing the isthmus by riverboat and mule before waiting in Panama City for another steamer up the coast. By the isthmus was fastest. Initially this way took at least six weeks, then

1   J. S. Holliday, *Rush for Riches: Gold Fever and the Making of California,* (Berkeley, Los Angeles and London, 1999), 94

three with the advent of faster transportation and improved roads. It was also the most expensive and disease-ridden journey. The 14,000 mile trip round the hazardous waters of Cape Horn took between five and eight months.[1] Most people travelled across country, but that too was onerous, dangerous and slow. It was primarily young, able people with some means, like the forty-niners, or Argonauts, as they were known, who made it to San Francisco.

Most of the Irish Argonauts were under thirty years of age, male and Catholic. But unlike the vast majority of the new arrivals, not all the Irish began their journey from elsewhere within the United States. In the early 1850s a significant number came from Australia and thus had already some experience in making their way in a foreign and sometimes unfriendly land. Significantly, there were many family groups in the Australian contingent. So while the white population of California was reportedly 90 per cent male in 1850, as were the Irish who travelled from the eastern states, because of the more mixed Australian-Irish component, the Irish element overall was just over two-thirds male.

Some of the Irish had experience and skills that could be immediately put to profitable use: running guest houses and restaurants, mining, teaching, construction and shopkeeping. They were often urbanized, English-speaking, and well aware of how the anarcho-capitalist system of the gold-rush period worked. However, many were unlettered and consequently assigned to a lower rung of the social ladder than their literate European competitors. There was a pronounced tendency towards endogamy amongst the first- and second-generation Irish, which seems to have been driven by religion as much as ethnicity. Despite this, they were not ghettoized, but spread geographically throughout the city, marbled through various economic strata. The nativism, hostility and exclusion experienced by the Irish in the eastern states were not replicated to anything like the same extent in San Francisco.

The boom in the city's population was astonishing: it rose from 459 in 1847 to over 30,000 by the end of 1849 and close to 60,000 by 1860. Lawlessness was widespread. In 1851 a Committee of Vigilance was formed after a series of arson attacks had destroyed swathes of the city, and again in 1856 to counter political corruption. Of 1,200 murders committed in San Francisco between 1850 and 1853, it is claimed that the official legal system managed to sentence and convict only one defendant. Justice, however, was brutal, with floggings, brandings, ear clippings, and the like, meted out for non-capital crimes and with the lynch mob ever ready to swing into action. Confidence in the police and politicians was thin and more than once prisoners were seized from jails and hanged to prevent their escaping or receiving an official pardon. This militia violence reached a zenith in 1856, when twenty-nine people were hanged, imprisoned or exiled by the Committee of Vigilance.

The Irish largely voted for the Democratic Party; Irish-born candidates were elected to city and state positions in San Francisco long before this became possible on the East Coast. Amongst these was David C. Broderick, a second-generation East Coast Irish-American who later became a US senator for California, serving in the Washington DC building his father had worked on as a stonemason. By 1856 Broderick's Democratic Party had been running elements of the San Francisco public sector for several years. Allegations of corruption were widespread; the Committee of Vigilance intervened in that year when one James P. Casey, a former Sing Sing inmate as well as a member of the Board of Supervisors, an inspector of elections and deputy county treasurer, shot the oddly named James King of William, an editor of a muckraking newspaper. When King died six days later, Casey and another man, Charles Cora, were hanged. All twenty-nine people targeted by this committee were Catholic; many were Irish or Irish-Australian and largely Democrats and supporters of Broderick, who himself died violently three years later in a duel at Lake Merced just outside San Francisco.

The mercantile class who formed the committee had widespread support, but generally not from the Irish establishment, although the Catholic clergy did not speak out against it. Yet several Irish men who were to experience spectacular political, economic and social success accepted the committee's justifications of its violent practices. Perhaps the display of quasi-military force was more persuasive than its arguments, but these Irish may also have truly believed that society was in peril. Or they may have believed that they themselves would not fall foul of the militia. But aside from these brief episodes of organized violence directed at them as political rather than as religious opponents, the Irish generally settled in quickly and remuneratively in the boom town.

Some Irish had already settled in California before it was ceded to the United States and prior to the discovery of gold. No other non-native ethnic groups, with the exception of the sparse Hispanic *Californios*, were present in this Spanish territory when the Irish arrived. As Timothy O'Keefe writes in his Introduction to *The Irish in the San Francisco Bay Area*:

> Unlike the immigrant experience in East
> Coast cities, there was no dominant and
> exclusive propertied elite … A social and
> economic hierarchy would soon be created
> through hard work, talent, thrift, cleverness,
> and good fortune, but it was not a birthright.
> The playing field was relatively level and,
> with one notorious exception, open to all
> comers.[2]

The notorious exception was the Chinese immigrant population, to whom there was widespread opposition among the Irish. This flared most fiercely when the economic boom weakened; once the initial spectacular and easier placed mining finds (gold from panning gravel deposits by hand or simply picked up from the ground) had tapered off, there was sudden underemployment and popular discontent. At first this had fixed upon Mexicans, Chileans and French, and these 'foreigners' were so punitively taxed for a brief period that many of them departed. Attention then turned to the Chinese, who had initially been welcomed for their

willingness to take menial and unrewarding work, but soon bore the brunt of the xenophobic white reaction to any economic downturn. All white California was predominantly anti-Asian in outlook, but the Irish, then the largest white ethnic immigrant group and therefore the chief competitors to the Chinese, were loudest in their hostility.

Foremost among the supporters of the job-anxious workingmen was Denis Kearney, a Cork-born drayman and demagogue, who began his career with tirades against super-rich capitalists, and who, it has been claimed, initially defended the rights of Chinese workers. The best known of the millionaire moguls targeted by Kearney were the railroad's Big Four: Leland Stanford, Mark Hopkins, Collis P. Huntingdon and Charles Crocker. Some years earlier, in the early 1860s, these four obscure Sacramento merchants had combined to build the Central Pacific Railroad and became fabulously wealthy in the process. They were also, not coincidentally, responsible for the flood of Chinese workers in San Francisco, as they had laid off thousands once the railroad reached the city and track-laying was complete. In the midst of a labour glut that depressed wages, three of these nabobs were simultaneously building sumptuous mansions atop Nob Hill.

Kearney combined virulent opposition to Chinese labour and immigration with pro-worker rhetoric. The Workingmen's Trade and Labor Union, which he helped to found, backed by the *San Francisco Chronicle*, literally and figuratively took up the cudgels against the Chinese. The upshot was a raft of anti-Asian legislation. Daniel Meissner, in his analysis of Irish and Chinese labour in mid-nineteenth century San Francisco argues that the Chinese were 'denied the right of naturalization, barred from specific fields of employment, physically and legally harassed in urban occupations, and refused access to open housing and public schools'.[3] The Irish were determined not to be consigned to the life of an underclass similar to the kind of existence many of them had endured in the east. They realized that the Chinese presence actually assisted Irish

2 Timothy J. O'Keefe,
   'Introduction', in Donald
   Jordan and Timothy J.
   O'Keefe, eds., *The Irish in
   the San Francisco Bay Area:
   Essays on Good Fortune* (San
   Francisco, 2005), 2

3 Daniel Meissner, 'California
   Clash: Irish and Chinese
   Labor in San Francisco,
   1850–1870', in Jordan and
   O'Keefe, *The Irish in the San
   Francisco Bay Area*, 76

4 Meissener, 'California Clash',
   76
5 Janet Nolan, 'Pioneers in the
   Classroom', in Jordan and
   O'Keefe, *The Irish in the San
   Francisco Bay Area*, 171
6 Holliday, *Rush for Riches*, 240

assimilation, because the difference between the Irish and the Anglo-Americans paled, if that is the word, against the much more vivid contrast between Chinese and white cultures. In any event, as Meissner concludes, 'competing for limited resources and opportunities in a dynamic but finite economic market, Irish and Chinese laborers in San Francisco were destined to clash. Inevitably, only one side would prevail.'[4]

Irish women were remarkably successful, with one in four holding down a skilled blue-collar or white-collar job by 1880. As Janet Nolan points out in her essay 'Pioneers in the Classroom' 'these women entered professional work in numbers unrivalled by any other second-generation immigrant women in San Francisco at the time'.[5] Nolan shows the obstacles overcome and achievements attained by Irish women teachers, which included equal pay and rights of advancement. These were fought for and won at a time when universal suffrage was not yet secured. But education was a highly politicized arena. In many American cities the question of public schools versus Catholic schools was a vexed one, especially in relation to the funding of private schools by public money. Initially, both public and private schools were publicly funded. This did not last. In the mid-1850s a brokered compromise emerged whereby a number of Catholic teachers were awarded posts in public schools and others passed school board examinations; these, whilst remaining in parochial schools, were paid from the public purse. This compromise left the majority of the Irish Catholics faced with a choice between the secular public elementary school, which was (and is) free, and the parochial school, which was (and remains) relatively expensive. By and large, they voted with their pockets, despite strong exhortations from the pulpits. Those who chose to travel the religious education route did so, not only because of their Catholic convictions but also because they could afford to. The classes were less crowded and, perhaps crucially, they accepted children at a younger age. O'Keefe begins the story of men's Catholic colleges the Bay Area by telling how Bishop Joseph Sadoc Alemany of Monterey diocese, whose flock

included the Catholics of Babylon by the Bay, visited Ireland and wrote to Cardinal Paul Cullen, Archbishop of Dublin, imploring him to send teachers. Alemany (who later visited James Casey before he was hanged) was satisfactorily answered.

While gold mining was obviously an early attraction, the most famous Irish mining millionaires were the Silver Kings: James G. Fair, James C. Flood, John W. Mackay and William S. O'Brien. Flood and O'Brien ran a public house that dispensed a famous free 'auction lunch'; its stew was especially toothsome. They also dispensed stockbroking advice. Mackay and Fair were mine superintendents. Reputedly, Mackay could almost smell silver. The four formed a partnership in 1867. Between them they surveyed and gradually bought up stock in certain unsuccessful mines on the fabled Comstock lode in Nevada. Then they began sinking shafts to find the silver they believed must be there. In 1874 their tunnels struck a concentration of gold and silver almost 400 feet wide. Their partnership had paid around $100,000 for the Bonanza mine that within a few years produced some $105,000,000 in gold and silver.[6]

Mining had, of course, other consequences. The relatively unintrusive hand panning had quickly been succeeded by damming and flume building and then by hydraulic mining, which directed streams of pressurized water at river banks and beds. This led to the massive and ongoing despoliation of the natural environment and was banned by the California Supreme Court in 1884. The disembowelling of the mountains continued, however. So much timber had been used in the mining that as early as 1876 the Comstock was known as the 'Tomb of the forests of the Sierras'. There were also ecological penalties to be paid for the provision of water to the city, which was often unclean and always expensive. In the mid-nineteenth century the Spring Valley Water Company began buying up farms in the San Andreas Valley to acquire the watershed. The company built dams, but by the 1860s engineers realized that the supply would have to come from the water-rich high

Sierras, more than a hundred miles from the city. William Bourn, who was of Irish ancestry, left New York in 1850 for gold-rush California and successfully mined the miners as a store-owner, banker and investor. But five years after gaining control of the fabulous Empire Mine (largest of the California gold mines) in 1869, he mysteriously shot himself to death in his San Francisco mansion. In 1879 his son and successor, also William Bourn, set about buying up and consolidating San Francisco utilities. He eventually became president of Pacific Gas and Electric and of the Spring Valley Water Company. (The younger Bourn bought Muckross Park Estate in Killarney for his daughter as a wedding present; it is now in the hands of the Irish state, bequeathed in 1931 by Arthur Vincent, Bourn's son-in-law.) The Spring Valley Water Company was highly unpopular and notoriously greedy. Even after, perhaps because of, elaborate litigation in 1880, there was an annual squabble between the company and the Board of Supervisors concerning the price of water. Civic leaders wanted municipal control of an assured water source.

James Duval Phelan was the son of an Irish-born forty-niner, who had come to San Francisco from New York, set up as a merchant and made a fortune in real estate. Born in the city in 1861, Phelan was thus financially secure. He became well travelled and well educated and made a career in politics. James P. Walsh comments that Phelan 'presided over California's conversion from a wealthy frontier outpost to a regional culture that he helped engrave on the popular imagination of America — indeed of the World'.[7] Walsh explains that Phelan's exemplary success sprang from the country's 'abundance, novelty and remoteness' and the fact that the Irish who came to California were 'better prepared to exploit the enhanced experiences' on offer.[8] Phelan's accomplishments were manifold; he became a successful mayor and later a US senator. He was ambitious for San Francisco and sought to win for the city a reputation for refinement in art, for culture and for striking public spaces, like the Civic Center. He knew that making San Francisco beautiful was in the city's long-term interest, as it would draw and hold a desirable population and attract visitors. On the debit side, his political platform was vehemently anti-Asian.

In 1901 Mayor Phelan, as a private citizen, filed for the water rights on the Tuolumne River and drew up the controversial Hetch Hetchy plan to build a publicly owned reservoir in Yosemite National Park. He signed these rights over to the city in 1903. He and his supporters were determined, especially in the aftermath of the 1906 earthquake, to secure a reliable water supply. So a city, seven miles square, sought to claim for itself 652 square miles of watershed over 160 miles away in a nationally protected park. Hetch Hetchy Valley very similar to the renowned Yosemite Valley and outraged environmentalist John Muir considered that damming it was a sacrilege: 'Dam Hetch Hetchy! As well dam for water-tanks the people's cathedrals and churches, for no holier temple has ever been consecrated by the heart of man.'[4] The conservationists were joined in opposition by farmers in Modesto and Turlock, concerned that their water and energy were being given away. Further opposition came from William Bourn's Spring Valley Water Company and from Pacific Gas and Electric. Like Phelan, Bourn was interested in the cultivation of the city and Bay Area; after the 1906 earthquake, he inaugurated a policy of public service by the famously rapacious Spring Valley company. Public works, including architect Willis Polk's exquisite Sunol Water Temple, were commissioned. Bourn was not, however, about to allow his Spring Valley business leak away from him and he fought the Hetch Hetchy plan strenuously. Several US Senate hearings held between 1909 and 1913 culminated in the Raker Act, passed with the support of the publishing empire of William Randolph Hearst, and San Francisco was granted the right to dam the Tuolumne River in Hetch Hetchy Valley. All but the conservationists, who wanted to exploit the valley for a form of eco-tourism, were placated by clauses protecting their interests.

Michael Maurice O'Shaughnessy, an Irish man educated at the old Royal University of Dublin who had come around the Horn to San

7   James P. Walsh, 'The Evolution of the Thesis', in Jordan and O'Keefe, *The Irish in the San Francisco Bay Area*, 273

8   Walsh, 'The Evolution of the Thesis', 274

Francisco in 1885, was appointed San Francisco city engineer in 1912. O'Shaughnessy built or completed important tunnels in the city — the Stockton Street tunnel, and the Twin Peaks and Sunset railway tunnels. But it is for his Hetch Hetchy dam, begun in 1914, that he is mostly remembered. It took ten years to complete the dam and twenty years before the water reached San Francisco. On 24 October 1934, the first Hetch Hetchy water flowed into the Bay Area. But the man who had done so much to make it happen did not get to taste a drop; M. M. O'Shaughnessy died twelve days earlier at the age of seventy-two. In the final stages of the project he had been shunted aside politically; indeed as the costs mounted, it was dismissively said that his initials stood for 'more money'.

Today the 167-mile-long system of pipes and tunnels brings to San Francisco water of such high quality that it does not require filtering, perhaps the best-tasting water of any city in the world. However, the system remains controversial, not only for the affront to nature of the dam and reservoir, but also because of the diversion of its hydro-electric profits to meet current municipal liabilities and for the failure to maintain it adequately. This failure, in particular, endangers the water supply not only to San Francisco but also to many of the municipalities and districts of the South Bay.

In 'Diplomatic Snapshots' Dermot Keogh reviews the correspondence from the Irish Consulate in San Francisco from 1933, when the consulate was established, until 1947, when the 'founding' consul, Matthew Murphy, departed. Keogh shows how Murphy attempted, with some difficulty, to explain Irish neutrality during the Second World War to an uncomprehending and often unsympathetic audience whose more immediate concern was the war against Japan. He was also somewhat hindered in his task by the nationality of his wife, who was German. Murphy was also hampered by a paucity of funds, but he had an entrée to San Simeon, William Randolph Hearst's famous mansion. Hearst was a capricious and complex character. Because of his parents' Irish ancestry and his childhood experiences travelling in Ireland with his mother, he was sympathetic to Ireland's political stance on neutrality. It complemented his own view that wars between European countries were counterproductive. Hearst had met and liked Eamon de Valera (not to mention Adolf Hitler) and had often been at loggerheads with the British establishment and press. When Ireland's refusal to allow its ports to be used by the Allies came under fire, Murphy was glad of the support of the *San Francisco Examiner*, a Hearst paper.

Born in the gold rush, almost destroyed by the earthquake of 1906, shaken by earlier quakes in the 1860s and by the recent convulsion of 1989, San Francisco has become one of the most stylish and self-consciously beautiful of American cities. In his address to the opening of the United Nations Conference in San Francisco in April 1945, US Secretary of State Edward R. Stettinius Jr. inevitably gave in to the spirit of the place. 'San Francisco', he said, 'is a symbol in our history. To us the West has always meant the future.' To the pioneers, it was 'the promised land'; since their arrival, he declared, San Francisco has been regarded 'as a place where all hopes came true, where all purposes could be accomplished'. No matter how blowsy the rhetoric, there is still, in the city and its history, that faint dusting of gold.

David Owens

Contributors

Alan Ahearne lectures in Economics at the National University of Ireland, Galway. A former senior economist at the Federal Reserve Board in Washington, DC, he publishes in leading academic journals and his research has featured in *The Economist*, *Financial Times*, *Wall Street Journal* and *New York Times*. He also holds an appointment as research fellow at Bruegel, a Brussels-based economics think tank.

Guy Beiner specializes in the historical study of forgetting and remembrance in modern Ireland. His most recent publication is *Remembering the Year of the French: Irish Folk History and Social Memory* (2006). He is currently a lecturer in Modern History at Ben-Gurion University.

Ciaran Carson is Professor of Poetry at Queen's University, Belfast. His translation of the Old Irish epic *Táin Bó Cuailnge* will be published by Penguin Classics in autumn 2007. In addition to many volumes of poetry, he has also published several prose works, including *Last Night's Fun* (1996), a memoir of the Irish traditional music scene, and a critically acclaimed translation of Dante's *Inferno*, published by Granta in 2002.

Mary P. Corcoran is a senior lecturer in Sociology at the National University of Ireland, Maynooth. Her research and teaching interests include Irish migratory processes, urban transformations and social change, and civic/public cultures. Her publications include *Irish Illegals: Transients between Two Societies* (1993), *Place and Non-Place* (2004) and *Uncertain Ireland* (2006).

Seamus Deane is Keough Professor of Irish Studies at the University of Notre Dame. He has published extensively on political and literary culture, including *Celtic Revivals: Essays in Modern Irish Literature, 1880–1980* (1985),

The French Revolution and Enlightenment in England, 1789–1832 (1988), and *Strange Country: Modernity and Nationhood in Irish Writing since 1790* (1999). His most recent book is *Foreign Affections: Essays on Edmund Burke* (2005). He edited the *Field Day Anthology of Irish Writing*, 3 vols. (1991) and he edits *Field Day Review*.

Brian Dillon is a writer and critic, and the United Kingdom editor of *Cabinet*, a cultural quarterly based in New York. His first book, *In the Dark Room*, an exploration of emotional and cultural memory, won the Irish Book Award for Non-Fiction, 2005. Penguin will publish his *Tormented Hope: Nine Hypochondriac Lives* in 2008.

Terry Eagleton is John Edward Taylor Professor of English Literature at Manchester University. His many books include *Literary Theory: An Introduction* (1983, 2nd edn. 1996), *Crazy John and the Bishop and Other Essays on Irish Culture* (1998) and *The Idea of Culture* (2000). His latest books are *How to Read a Poem* (2007) and *The Meaning of Life* (2007).

Catherine Gallagher is the Eggers Professor of English Literature at the University of California at Berkeley. Her books include *The Industrial Reformation of English Fiction: Social Discourse and Narrative Form, 1832–67* (1985), *Nobody's Story: The Vanishing Acts of Women Writers in the Literary Marketplace* (1994), *The Body Economic: Life, Death, and Sensation in Political Economy and the Victorian Novel* (2006) and (with Stephen Greenblatt) *Practicing New Historicism* (2000).

Conor Gearty is Professor of Human Rights Law and Rausing Director of the Centre for the Study of Human Rights at the London School of Economics. His publications include *Terror* (1990), (with K. D. Ewing) *The Struggle for*

Civil Liberties (2000), and *Can Human Rights Survive?* (2006). Oxford University Press will publish his *Civil Liberties* in autumn 2007.

Ultán Gillen teaches History at Merton College, University of Oxford. His research interests include the Enlightenment, revolution and counter-revolution in late eighteenth-century Ireland. He is working on a book on Irish reactions to the French Revolution.

Timothy W. Guinnane is the Philip Golden Bartlett Professor of Economic History at Yale University. He is the author of *The Vanishing Irish: Households, Migration, and the Rural Economy in Ireland* (1997) and editor (with William A. Sundstrom and Warren C. Whatley) of *History Matters: Essays on Economic Growth, Technology and Demographic Change* (2003). He is currently at work on several projects related to the demographic and financial history of Western Europe, including Ireland.

Deana Heath lectures in History at Trinity College, Dublin. A historian of South Asian and global history, she has published numerous articles on colonialism and culture, post-colonialism, and Indian cinema and is currently working on a book, *Creating the Modern Colonial Subject: Obscenity, Censorship and Modernity*, to be published in 2008.

Brendan Kane is assistant professor of History at the University of Connecticut. He is currently completing a study of the politics of honour in early modern Ireland and England, based on his PhD thesis, '"The Beauty of Virtue": Honor in Early Modern Ireland and England, 1541–1641' (Princeton University, 2004).

James Kelly is Head of the History Department at St. Patrick's College, Drumcondra. He is the author of several books on late early modern Irish history, including biographies of Grattan and Flood and a study of the duel in eighteenth-century Ireland. His study of Irish legislation from the mid-seventeenth

century to the Act of Union, *Poynings' Law and the Making of Law in Ireland 1660–1800*, will be published in 2007.

Matthew Kelly teaches History at Southampton University. His first book, *The Fenian Ideal and Irish Nationalism, 1882–1916*, was published in 2006. He is currently working on a study of the Young Ireland tradition and, in particular, the *Nation* newspaper.

Thomas Kilroy is a playwright and novelist. He has received numerous literary awards, including the Guardian Fiction Prize for his novel *The Big Chapel* (1972). In 2004 he was honoured with a Lifetime Achievement Award in the Irish Times/ESB Theatre Awards. He is a member of Aosdána.

Richard Kirkland is a reader in Irish Literature at King's College London. He is the author of numerous books and articles on Irish culture. His most recent publication is *Cathal O'Byrne and the Northern Revival in Ireland, 1890–1960* (2006).

Joep Leerssen holds the Chair of Modern European Literature at the University of Amsterdam. He has served as director of the Huizinga-Instituut (National Research Institute for Cultural History) from 1996 to 2006, and as Erasmus Lecturer at Harvard University in 2003. Among his Ireland-related publications are *Mere Irish and Fíor-Ghael* (1986, 2nd edn. 1996) and *Remembrance and Imagination* (1996). His most recent books are *De Bronnen van het Vaderland* ('The Sources of the Fatherland', 2006) and *National Thought in Europe: A Cultural History* (2006).

Ian McBride is a senior lecturer in History at King's College London. He is the author of *Scripture Politics: Ulster Presbyterians and Irish Radicals in Late Eighteenth-Century Ireland* (1998) and (as editor) *History and Memory in Modern Ireland* (2001). He is currently finishing volume four of the New Gill History of Ireland, to be entitled *Eighteenth-Century Ireland: The Isle of Slaves*.

David W. Miller is Professor of History at Carnegie Mellon University. His publications include *Church, State and Nation in Ireland, 1898–1921* (1973) and *Queen's Rebels: Ulster Loyalism in Historical Perspective* (1978), which will shortly be reissued in the UCD Press series 'Classics of Irish History'. His current project is a book under the working title 'Ulster Presbyterians and Irish Catholics in the Famine Era, 1829–69'.

Bríona Nic Dhiarmada teaches in the Department of Languages and Cultural Studies, University of Limerick. Her most recent book on the poetry of Nuala Ní Dhomhnaill, *Téacs Baineann: Téacs Mná*, was Cumann Merriman's Book of the Year, 2006.

Emer Nolan is author of *Joyce and Nationalism* (1995) and *Catholic Emancipations: Irish Fiction from Thomas Moore to James Joyce* (2007). Her edition of Thomas Moore's *Memoirs of Captain Rock* will be the first volume in a new Field Day series of classic texts in Irish History and Literature. She lectures in English at the National University of Ireland, Maynooth.

Brendan O'Leary is Lauder Professor of Political Science at the University of Pennsylvania and a constitutional advisor to the Kurdistan Government. Recent co-authored and co-edited books include *The Northern Ireland Conflict* (2004), *The Future of Kurdistan in Iraq* (2005) and *Terror, Insurgency and the State* (2007). *Understanding Northern Ireland: Colonialism, Control and Consociation*, co-authored with John McGarry will be published by Routledge in late 2007.

David Owens is a civil servant in the Irish Department of Finance. He is currently on special leave at the University of California Berkeley Extension, where he is completing a project on detectives in 1920s Ireland.

Stephen Rea is an actor. His many credits include lead roles in the original stage-productions of Brian Friel's *Translations* (1980), Thomas Kilroy's *Double Cross* (1986), Harold Pinter's *Ashes to Ashes* (1996), and (on film) *The Crying Game* (1993), *The Butcher Boy* (1997), and *The Good Shepherd* (2004). Most recently, he appeared in the première of Sam Shepard's *Kicking a Dead Horse* in the Abbey Theatre, Dublin. He is a director of Field Day, which he founded in 1980 with Brian Friel.

Michael Rubenstein is assistant professor of English at the University of California, Berkeley. He teaches courses in twentieth-century Irish Literature, the twentieth-century novel, and post-colonial anglophone literature. He is currently finishing a book, *Electrifictions: The Engineering Cultures of Modern Irish Literature*.

Tim Robinson is the author of *Stones of Aran* (1986), a close personal study of one of the Aran Islands, where he lived for many years. He has also published collections of essays and short fictions, and maps of the Aran Islands, the Burren and Connemara.

Jennifer Todd is Irish Research Council for the Humanities and Social Sciences (IRCHSS) Senior Research Fellow, 2006–07. She has recently published on ethnicity and identity in *Archives Européennes de Sociologie* (2004), *Theory and Society* (2005), *Ethnopolitics* (2006), *Political Studies* (2007) and *Nations and Nationalism* (2007). The author (with Joseph Ruane) of *The Dynamics of Conflict in Northern Ireland* (1996), she teaches in the School of Politics and International Relations, University College Dublin.

Field Day Files Editors: Seamus Deane and Breandán Mac Suibhne

Joe Cleary
Outrageous Fortune
Capital and Culture in Modern Ireland

Marjorie Howes
Colonial Crossings
Figures in Irish Literary History

Field Day Music Editors: Séamas de Barra and Patrick Zuk

Séamas de Barra
Aloys
Fleischmann

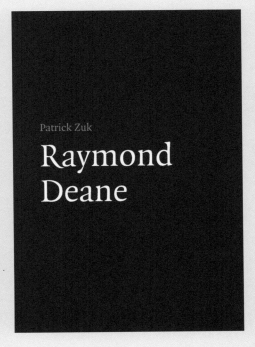

Patrick Zuk
Raymond
Deane